40,000 SELECTED WORDS

Organized by Letter Sound and Syllable

by Valeda D. Blockcolsky,
Joan M. Frazer and
Douglas H. Frazer

Communication Skill Builders

3830 E. Bellevue/P.O. Box 42050
Tucson, Arizona 85733
(602) 323-7500

Originally published as *30,000 Words*

Communication Skill Builders, Inc.®
3830 E. Bellevue/P.O. Box 42050
Tucson, Arizona 85733
(602) 323-7500

10 9 8 7 6 5
Printed in the United States of America

Catalog No. 2300 (Softbound) ISBN 0-88450-798-X
Catalog No. 2403 (Hardbound) ISBN 0-88450-799-8

Preface

40,000 Selected Words is a sourcebook of words sorted by consonant sounds in the English language. It has been prepared for Communication Disorder Specialists, teachers in Special Education and ESL, regular classroom teachers, students, parents, and professionals dedicated to the task of improving communication skills. The lists are comprehensive and varied enough to be used with children or adults.

Professionals who teach speech sounds to students use materials that facilitate teaching consonant sounds and blends. When professionals control each level of complexity, student success rate should be enhanced. The variables that control these levels may be the length of a word, the phonetic environment of the sound, the position of the sound in a word, and the combination of blends or clusters within a word. This book extends the range of materials available by offering a large selection of words organized according to these variables.

These alphabetical word lists are arranged with each consonant sound in initial, medial, and final positions. The blends or sound clusters for each consonant follow in family groupings (for example, /br/ initial, /br/ medial, /rb/ medial, /rb/ final). Consonant blends are listed under each consonant in the blend (the /br/ blend will be found in the /b/ section as well as in the /r/ section).

The first letters of each heading represent the sounds of words in the list. They do not always match the spellings of the words in the list. Phonetic symbols of the International Phonetic Alphabet (IPA) are shown between slashes / / after the letter representation.

Each group of words representing a consonant blend, in a specific position, is organized by number of syllables. Words of 1 to 6 syllables may be listed.

Contents

B

Pronounced: /b/
Spelled: b, bb

B /b/ Initial—one syllable

baa
babe
Babs
back
bad
bade
badge
bag
bail
bailed
bait
bake
baked
bald
bale
ball
balm
ban
band
bang
banged
bank
banned
bar
barb
Barb
bare
bared
bark
barked
barn
barred
base
bask
basked
bass
baste
bat
bath
bathe
bathed
bawl
bawled
bay
be
Bea
beach
beached
bead
beak
beam
beamed
bean
bear
beard
beast
beat
beau
bed
bee
beech
beef
been
beet
beg
begged
bell
belle
Belle
belt
bench
benched
bend
bent
Bert
berth
best
bet
Beth
bib
bid
bide
bier
bike
biked
bile
bilge
bilk
bilked
bill

Bill
billed
bills
bin
bind
Bip
birch
bird
birth
bit
bite
boar
board
boast
boat
bob
Bob
bobbed
bog
bogged
boil
boiled
bold
bolt
bond
bone
boo
book
booked
boom
boomed
boon
boot
booth
bore
bored
born
borne
boss
botch
both
bought
bounce
bound
bout
bow
bowed
bowl
bowled
box
boxed
boy
Boyd
Bub
buck
Bucks
bud
Bud
budge
buff
bug
build
built
bulb
bulge
bulk
bump
bun
bunch
bunk
bunt
burl
Burl
burn
Burns
burnt
burr
Burr
burst
bus
bush
bussed
but
Butch
buy
buzz
by
bye
Byrd
byte
____
____
____

B /b/ Initial—two syllables

baba
babble
babbled
babies
baboon
baby
backache
backfire
backfired
background
backhand
backhouse
backing
backlash
backlog
backstop
backup
backwoods

bacon
badger
badgered
baffle
baffled
baggage
bagpipe
balance
balanced
ballad
ballet
balloon
ballot
balsa
balsam
Bambi
bamboo
bandage
bandaged
bandit
bandstand
Bangor
banjo
banker
banking
banner
banter
bantered
barber
bareback
barely
bargain
bargained
barley
baron
barracks
barrage
barraged
barrel

barter
bartered
baseball
baseboard
basement
bashful
basic
basket
baton
batter
battle
battled
Bayley
Baylor
bayou
beach ball
beach boy
beachhead
beacon
beagle
beaker
bean-bag
beanie
bearing
beating
beaver
because
beckon
beckoned
Becky
becloud
become
bedbug
bedding
bedlam
bed rest
bedrock
bedroll
bedroom

bedside
bedspread
bedtime
beehive
beeline
beeswax
before
began
Bella
Belmont
bender
Berlin
Bernard
Bernice
berry
Berry
Bertha
Beryl
Bessie
Bethel
Bethune
betroth
betrothed
Betsy
Betty
bias
biased
Bible
biceps
bidder
Big Bird
bigot
big top
bike path
biking
billboard
billfold
billiards
billion

billow
billowed
Billy
binder
binding
biped
birdbath
birdhouse
birdseed
birthday
birthstone
biscuit
bishop
bison
bitter
bizarre
boa
boardwalk
boasted
boastful
Bobbi
bobbin
Bobby
bobcat
bobsled
bobtail
bodice
body
bogus
boiler
Boise
bolster
bombard
Bombay
bonbon
bonfire
bongo
Bonnie
bonus
boohoo
bookcase
bookend
bookmark
bookshelf
bookworm
booster
booting
border
bordered
boric
borrow
borrowed
bossy
Boston
bother
bothered
bottle
bottled
bottling
bottom
bouillon
boulder
Boulder
bounty
bouquet
bowstring
boxcar
boxer
boxing
boycott
boyish
Boy Scouts
bubble
bubbled
bucket
buckle
buckled
buckskin
Buddha
buddy
Buddy
budget
buffer
buffered
buffet
buffoon
buggy
builder
building
build-up
bulky
bulldog
bulldoze
bullfrog
bullied
bully
bumper
bumpy
bundle
bundled
bungle
bungled
bunk bed
bunny
Bunyan
buoy
burden
burdened
burgher
buried
burlap
Burma
Burmese
burned-out
burner
burrow
burrowed

Burton
bury
bushel
bushy
business
busy
butcher
butchered
butler
butter
buttered
button
buttoned
buzzard
buzzer
buzzing
bygone
bylaw
byline
byname
bypass
bypassed
byway
____
____
____
____

B /b/ Initial—three syllables

Babinski
babushka
baby doll
Babylon
babysat
babysit
bachelor
backgammon
backhanded
badminton
bakery
Balboa
balcony
ballistics
baloney
Baltimore
banana
bandana
bandmaster
bandwagon
banister
bankruptcy
baritone
barnacle
barricade
barrier
barrister
baseball park
basketball
bassinet
Baton Rouge
battalion
battery
battleship
bayberry
Bay City
bay window
beachcomber
beanshooter
Beatrice
becoming
bedridden
beforehand
befuddle
befuddled
beginner
beginning
begonia
behavior
beholden
belated
belittle
belittled
belongings
beloved
benefit
Benita
Benjamin
Bermuda
Bernadine
Bethlehem
betrothal
beverage
Beverly
bewilder
bewildered
bicuspid
bicycle
bifocal
big-hearted
bike safety
bilingual
billionaire
bimonthly
bird watcher
bittersweet
biweekly
boardinghouse
bobby socks
bobolink
bobsledding
bodily
bodyguard
boisterous

bologna
bonanza
bon voyage
bookkeeper
boomerang
bootery
borderline
botany
boulevard
bountiful
bowlegged
bubble bath
bubble gum
buccaneer
bucketful
Buckingham
buckle-up
buffalo
buffaloed
bulldozer
bulletin
bumblebee
bungalow
Bunker Hill
buoyancy
bushmaster
businesslike
businessman
bus safety
bus station
buttercup
butterfly
buttermilk
butternut
butterscotch
buttonhole
bypassing
by-product
____
____
____
____

B /b/ Initial—four syllables

baby buggy
baby carriage
bacteria
baking powder
baking soda
barometer
Bavarian
belligerent
benediction
benefactor
beneficial
Beverly Hills
bicarbonate
bilateral
biography
biologist
biology
biophysics
boating safety
Bohemian
boilermaker
bone conduction
boogie-woogie
Bostonian
botanical
Boulder Canyon
Boulder City
business woman
butterfly net
buying power
____
____
____

B /b/ Medial—two syllables

Abby
Abel
abide
aboard
abound
about
above
abyss
Babar
Babbitt
babies
baboon
baby
backbone
bareback
bedbug
bobber
Bobbi
bobbin
bobbing
Bobby
bobcat
booby
cabby
cabin
caboose
chubby
clobber
cobweb
cowbell

cowboy
Cuba
cubic
cupboard
debate
Debbie
debug
debut
dobbin
dubbing
Eben
fibber
fibbing
fiber
gabby
Gaby
Gibby
go-by
good-bye
grabbing
grubby
habit
Hibbing
high beam
high boy
Hobbit
hobble
hobby
hubbub
hubby
hubcap
jabber
jabbered
jabot
jay bird
keyboard
kickball
knobby
labor
labored
Libby
lobby
logbook
lubber
Lubbock
Mabel
Mabelle
mailbox
maybe
mobile
neighbor
obey
obeyed
oboe
Phoebe
rabbit
rabid
Rayburn
Reba
rebate
rebel
rebid
rebind
rebirth
reborn
rebound
rebuild
rebus
rebut
Reuben
ribbon
Robbie
Robbin
Robert
robin
robot
Robyn
rubber
rubbing
ruby
Ruby
scrubbing
Seabee
shabby
Sibyl
skyborne
slobber
sober
soybean
subject
subway
tabby
Tabby
taboo
tea bag
throbbing
Toby
toyboat
tubby
tuber
tubing
tugboat
two-bits
Wabash
webbing
whalebone
Yuba

B /b/ Medial—three syllables

abdomen
Abigail
abolish
abounding
about face
aboveboard
above ground
abutment
acrobat
adobe
aerobics
alphabet
Annabelle
Audobon
autobahn
babushka
babydoll
baby grand
Babylon
baby-sit
baby step
baby talk
baby tears
baby tooth
basketball
bayberry
blackberry
blueberry
Bobbielee
bobby pin
bobbysocks
bobolink
bugaboo
cabinet
candy bar
cheeseburger
chili beans
cowboy boots
cowboy hat
cubbyhole
data base
day labor
debated
debating
debonair
Deborah
dewberry
dubious
ebony
fabulous
fiberglass
foam rubber
gaberdine
gadabout
gazebo
gibberish
Gila Bend
good-neighbor
habitat
halibut
hawberry
hibernate
hobby-horse
honeybee
inhabit
jubilant
Labor Day
laborer
labor force
labyrinth
ladybug
liberal
liberate
liberty
lima beans
lobbying
log cabin
Nairobi
navy beans
neighborhood
nobody
obelisk
obeying
obsessive
October
peek-a-boo
phobia
pinto beans
Rebecca
rebounder
rebounding
rebozo
rebuilding
rebuttal
Rock-a-Bye
rubber band
rubber stamp
rubbery
sabotage
safety belt
shabbier
shabbiest
shrubbery
somebody
stabilize
storybook
strawberry
subsequent
tubercle
tuberous
vagabond
volleyball
wallaby

____

B /b/ Medial—four syllables

abalone
abolition
absolution
Alabama
anybody
baboonery
baby buggy
baby carriage
chinaberry
debility
deliberate
inhabited
neighborhood watch
nobility
obedient
observation
protuberant
tubercular
Winnebago
____
____

B /b/ Medial—five syllables

abomination
aborigine
Babylonian
disability
inability
obituary
observatory
submarine captain
subterranean
____
____
____

B /b/ Final—one syllable

Abe
babe
bib
blab
blob
bob
Bob
bribe
Bub
cab
chub
club
cob
Cobb
crab
crib
cub
cube
dab
daub
deb
Deb
dib
drab
drub
dub
ebb
fib
flab
flub
fob
gab
Gabe
gibe
glib
globe
gob
grab
grub
hob
hub
jab
jibe
job
Job
knob
lab
lob
lobe
lube
mob
nab
nub
probe
pub
rib
rob
Rob
robe
rub
Rube
SAAB
scab
scribe
scrub
shrub
Sib
slab
slob

snob
snub
sob
strobe
stub
sub
swab
tab
Tab
throb
tribe
tub
tube
web
____
____
____
____

B /b/ Final—two syllables

ad-lib
ascribe
backrub
ball club
bathrobe
bathtub
bike tube
book club
boys club
Calab
carob
Cherub
cobweb
confab
corncob
corn crib
Danube
Deneb
describe
doll crib
doorknob
ear lobe
fan club
flashcube
girls club
glass tube
glee club
golf club
health club
hobnob
hubbub
ice cube
imbibe
inscribe
Jacob
Joab
kabob
Kaibab
king crab
Moab
mole crab
nabob
prefab
prescribe
press club
Punjab
rehab
sand crab
sand dab
sea crab
ski club
Skylab
smack-dab
snow job
sparerib
subscribe
test tube
tire tube
transcribe
tree crab
wardrobe
wolf cub
yacht club
____
____
____

B /b/ Final—three syllables

astrolabe
beef kabob
Blue Danube
bouillon cube
Christmas club
cotton swab
country club
flying club
Four-H Club
garden club
giant crab
health spa club
inner tube
jockey club
kennel club
lion cub
Lion's Club
Mr. Webb
oyster crab
pedicab
photo lab

picture tube
Piper Cub
reading lab
rub-a-dub
running club
service club
shish kebab
soft-shell crab
spider web
tanning club
taxicab
ticket stub
women's club
writing lab
____

BL /bl/ Initial—one syllable

blab
blabbed
black
blade
Blaine
Blake
blame
blamed
blanch
Blanche
bland
blank
blare
blared
blast
blaze
blazed
bleach
bleached
bleak
blear
bleat
bled
bleed
blench
blend
bless
blessed
blest
blew
blight
blimp
blind
blink
blinked
blintz
blip
bliss
blithe
blitz
bloat
blob
bloc
block
blocked
blocks
blond
blood
bloom
bloomed
blot
blotch
blotched
blouse
blow
blown
blue
blues
bluff
bluffed
blunt
blur
blurb
blurred
blurt
blush
blushed
Blythe
____

BL /bl/ Initial—two syllables

blackball
blackballed
black bear
black belt
blackbird
blackboard
blacken
Blackett
black eye
black flag
Blackfoot
blackhead
blacking
blacklist
blackmail
blackmailed
blackout
Black Sea
black sheep
blacksmith
blackthorn

blacktop
black whale
blameless
blanket
blarney
blasé
blaspheme
blasphemed
blast off
blatant
blazer
blazon
blazoned
bleachers
bleary
blemish
blemished
blessed
blessing
blinder
blinders
blindfold
blinding
blinker
blinkers
blissful
blister

blistered
blithesome
blizzard
blockade
blocker
blockhead
blockhouse
bloodhound
bloodline
bloodstream
blood test
blossom
blossomed
blotchy
blotter
blower
blowgun
blowout
blowpipe
blowtorch
blubber
blubbered
bluebell
blue belt
bluebird
blue cheese
blue fish

bluegill
bluegrass
blue jay
blue jeans
blue moon
blueprint
bluer
Blue Ridge
blue shark
blue sky
bluest
bluets
blue whale
bluffer
bluffing
bluing
bluish
blunder
blundered
bluster
blustered
Blytheville
____
____
____
____
____

BL /bl/ Initial—three syllables

black and blue
blackberry
black market
black widow
blamelessly
blameworthy
blandishing
blandishment
blasphemy
bleeding heart

blindman's bluff
blockbuster
bloodmobile
blood pressure
Blue Angels
blueberry
bluebonnet
bluebottle
blue color
bluejacket

blue marlin
Blue Moutains
blue ribbon
blustery
____
____
____
____
____
____

BL /bl/ Medial—two syllables

ablaze
abloom
babbling
bubbling
bubbly
cobbler
dabbling
doublet
doubly
dribbling
emblaze
emblem
gambling
giblet
glibly
gobbler
gobbling
goblet
goblin
grabbler
hobbling
mumbling
nibbling
nimbly
nosebleed
oblate
oblige
oblique
oblong
problem
public
publish
pueblo
Pueblo
rambler
Red Bluff
sandblast
sand-blind
semblance
sibling
squabbling
sublease
sublet
sublime
tableau
tablet
trembling
troubling
tumbler
tumbling
warbler
warbling
wobbly
____

BL /bl/ Medial—three syllables

ablation
ablution
cable car
emblazing
emblazon
emblem book
emblements
establish
established
Navy blue
night blindness
notably
obligate
obliging
obligor
public school
publisher
publishing
red-blooded
republic
resemblance
San Pablo
shoulder blade
sublimate
unpublished
____
____
____
____
____

BL /bl/ Medial—four syllables

ablactating
ablepsia
army blanket
baby-blue eyes
disestablish
emblazonment
establishment
obligation
obligato
oblique angle
obliterate
publication
public domain
publicity
publishing house
reestablish
republican
subliminal

BL /bl/ Final—two syllables

Abel
able
amble
babble
Bible
brabble
bramble
bubble
bumble
cable
crumble
cymbal
dabble
double
drabble
dribble
fable
feeble
fumble
gable
gamble
global

gobble
grumble
hobble
humble
jumble
label
libel
marble
mumble
nibble
nimble
noble
pebble
quibble
ramble
rebel
rubble
ruble
rumble
sable
scramble
scribal

scribble
squabble
stable
stubble
stumble
Sybil
table
thimble
treble
tremble
tribal
trouble
tumble
verbal
wabble
waddle
warble
wobble

BL /bl/ Final—three syllables

affable
assemble
audible
cannibal
capable
constable
decibel
disable
durable
edible
flammable
flexible
gullible
horrible

legible
liable
livable
lovable
notable
portable
possible
preamble
probable
quotable
resemble
sellable
sensible
sociable

soluble
suitable
syllable
terrible
timetable
unable
usable

BL /bl/ Final—four syllables

acceptable
advisable
agreeable
answerable
available
comfortable
convertible
dependable
desirable
eligible
enjoyable
favorable
formidable
habitable
handleable
honorable
Honorable
hospitable
illegible
impossible
incredible
inedible
inflammable
invisible
miserable
perishable
practicable
preferable
presentable
profitable
questionable
reasonable
reassemble
receivable
reliable
remarkable
respectable
responsible
separable
tolerable
unchangeable
unmatchable
unprintable
unquenchable
unspeakable
unsuitable
unthinkable
valuable
variable
vegetable
veritable
vulnerable
____
____

BL /bl/ Final—five syllables

dishonorable
indivisible
inevitable
inhospitable
innumerable
inoperable
irresistible
recoverable
unalterable
unapproachable
unavoidable
unbelievable
undesirable
unmistakable
unprofitable
unquestionable
unreasonable
unreliable
unutterable
unwarrantable
____
____
____
____

LB /lb/ Medial—two syllables

Albert
album
ball bat
ball boy
bellbird
bell book
bell boy
billboard
callboard
call box
coalbin
Delbert
Elbe
Elbert
Elbie
elbow
file box
Galbraith
Gilbert
Holbrook
mailbag
mailbox
Melba
Melbourne

Milbank
millboard
Millburn
nail bag
Olbers
pillbox
roll bar
sailboat
school band
school board
schoolbooks
school bus
skull bone
spellbound
steel box
tool box
wallboard
whalebone
Wilbanks
Wilbur
____

LB /lb/ Medial—three syllables

Albany
albatross
Alberta
albino
ball bearings
bell-bottoms
bell buoy
doll buggy
Elberta
Elberton
elbow grease
elbowroom
Gilberta
melba toast
mulberry
Mulberry
nail-biting
wheelbarrow

LB /lb/ Final—one syllable

alb
bulb
Kalb
Kolb
____
____

LB /lb/ Final—two syllables

DeKalb
flashbulb
light bulb
wet bulb
____
____

BR /br/ Initial—one syllable

brace
braced
brad
Brad
brag
bragged
braid
braille
brain
braise
braised
brake
brakes
bran
branch
brand
Brant
brash
brass
brat
brave
brawl
brawn
bray
brayed
braze
breach
breached
bread
breadth
break
breath
breathe
bred
breech
breed
breeze
Brent
Bret
brew
brewed
bribe

bribed
Brice
brick
bricked
bride
bridge
brief
briefed
brig
bright
brim
brimmed
brine
bring
brink
brisk
broach
broached
broad
brogue
broil
broiled
broke
Bronx
bronze
bronzed
brooch
brood
brook
Brooks
broom
broth
brought
brow
brown
browse
browsed
Bruce
bruise
bruised
brunch
brunt
brush
brushed
brusque
brute
Bryce
____
____
____
____

BR /br/ Initial—two syllables

bracelet
bracer
braces
bracing
bracken
bracket
brackish
Bradford
Bradley
braggart
Brahma
brainless
brainstorm
brainwash
brain wave
brainy
brakeage
brake drum
brake dye
brakeman
brake shoe
bramble
brandish
brandished
brand-new
brass band
brassy
bravo
brazen
brazier
Brazil
breadfruit
breakage
breakdown
breaker
breakfast
breakneck
breakup
breastbone
breastplate
breaststroke
breathing
breathless
breeches
breeder
breeding
breezy
Brenda
brethren
brewer
Brian
briar
brickbat
brickwork
brickyard
bridal
bridegroom
bridesmaid
bridge house
bridge lamp

Bridgeport
bridge sign
Bridget
Bridgeton
Bridge View
Bridgeville
bridgework
bridging
bridle
bridled
bridling
briefcase
briefing
briefly
briefness
brier
brigade
Brigham
brighten
brightened
brilliance
brilliant
brimful
brimstone
brindle
briny
brisket
bristle
bristled
Britain
British
brittle
broadcast
broadcloth
broaden
broadened
broad jump
broadloom
broadside
Broadway
brocade
brochure
brogan
broiler
broken
broker
bromide
bromine
bronchi
bronco
Bronze Age
brooded
brooder
brooding
brooklet
Brooklyn
broomstick
brother
browbeat
brownie
Brownie
brownish
brown rice
bruin
Bruins
brunette
brush fire
brush work
Brussels
Brutus
Bryan
Bryant
____
____
____
____
____
____
____

BR /br/ Initial—three syllables

bravado
bravery
Brazil nut
breakable
breakwater
breathtaking
brevity
bribery
bric-a-brac
bricklayer
bridle path
brigadier
brilliancy
bringing-up
British Isles
Britisher
broadcaster
broadcasting
broad jumper
broad-minded
broccoli
broken down
brokerage
bronchial
bronchitis
Brooklyn Bridge
brotherhood
brotherly
brouhaha
Brussels sprouts
____
____
____

BR /br/ Medial—two syllables

abrade
Abram
abreast
abridge
abridged
abroad
abrupt
cambric
Cambridge
clothes brush
cobra
cornbread
daybreak
Debra
debrief
debris
drawbridge
embrace
eyebrow
fabric
fibrous
float bridge
Gambrel
hairbrush
Hebrew
hybrid
inbred
Libra
membrane
nail brush
outbreak
paint brush
purebred
rye bread
sagebrush
sea breeze
shoebrush
sweetbread
toll bridge
toothbrush
vibrant
vibrate
whisk broom
white bread
windbreak
zebra
____
____

BR /br/ Medial—three syllables

Abraham
abrasive
abridgment
algebra
Brooklyn Bridge
celebrate
embracement
embracer
embrasure
embroider
Gabriel
gingerbread
Labrador
library
London Bridge
lubricate
Nebraska
paint brushes
pawnbroker
Rainbow Bridge
rebroadcast
scatterbrain
sombrero
thoroughbred
umbrella
unabridged
unbroken
underbrush
upbringing
vertebra
vertebral
vertebrate
vibration
whole wheat bread
____
____

BR /br/ Medial—four syllables

abbreviate
abranchial
abreaction
candelabra
celebrated
celebration
celebrity
embraceable
embracery
embroidery
Golden Gate Bridge
invertebrate
librarian
lubrication
Natural Bridge
____
____
____

RB /rb/ Medial—two syllables

air base
airborne
air bus
arbor
barbed wire
barbells
barber
bareback
Burbank
carbon
choirboy
Corbet
Corbin
Corby
derby
disturbed
doorbell
Fairbanks
forbear
forbid
forborne
garbage
gerbil
harbor
Herbert
marble
morbid
nearby
orbit
sherbet
turban
turbid
turbine
turbot
urban
verbal
verbose
warble
warbler
yearbook
____
____

RB /rb/ Medial—three syllables

Ann Arbor
Barbara
barbaric
barbecue
barber chair
barber shop
fur bearer
harboring
orbital
overbear
tetherball
turbulence
turbulent
undisturbed
urbanite
urbanize
verbalize
verbally
verbatim
____
____

RB /rb/ Medial—four syllables

barbecue sauce
carbon paper
carburetor
orbicular
overbearing
roller derby
urbanity
verbosity
____

RB /rb/ Final—one syllable

barb
Barb
blurb
curb
garb
herb
Herb
verb
____

RB /rb/ Final—two syllables

absorb
adverb
disturb
exurb
potherb
proverb
rhubarb
suburb
superb

BER /bɚ/ Medial—three syllables

cheeseburger
fiberglass
gabardine
hamburger
harboring
hibernate
Kimberly
liberal
liberate
liberty
limburger
lumbering
lumberjack
lumberyard
membership
neighborhood
numbering
number line
rubber band
rubber stamp
shrubbery
slumberer
tubercle
tuberous
____
____
____

BER /bɚ/ Medial—four syllables

deliberate
remembering
tubercular
____
____
____

BER /bɚ/ Final—two syllables

barber
blubber
clobber
fiber
labor
neighbor
rubber
saber
slobber
sober
tuber
____

BER /bɚ/ Final—three syllables

belabor
foam rubber
October
____
____
____

MB /mb/ Medial—two syllables

amber
Amber
Bambi
bamboo
Bombay
chamber
chambers
combine
combined
combo
combust
comeback
Dumbo
embank
embark
embed
ember
emboss
gambit
game bag
game bird
gumbo
imbibe
imbibed
Lambert
Lemberg
limber
Limberg
limbo
Lombard
lumbar
lumber
mambo
member
nameboard
number
numbered
Romberg
rumba

samba
slumber
slumbered
somber
tambour
timber
trombone
umber
______
______
______
______

MB /mb/ Medial—three syllables

ambition
bambino
bamboo shoots
bamboozle
Columbus
combustion
cucumber
cumbersome
December
embankment
embargo
embarrass
embassy
gamboling
hamburger
Kimberly
Limburger
lumbering
lumberjack
lumbermill
lumberyard
membership
November
numbering
numberline
ombudsman
outnumber
rambunctious
reimburse
remember
remembered
September
sombrero
somebody
tambourine
unnumbered
Zambezi
Zambia
______

MB /mb/ Medial--four syllables

ambassador
ambiguous
Cambodia
Columbia
combination
combustible
mumbo jumbo
______
______

MBER /mbɚ/ Final—two syllables

amber
Amber
chamber
ember
limber
lumber
member
number
slumber
somber
timber
umber
______
______
______

MBER /mbɚ/ Final—three syllables

cucumber
December
November
outnumber
remember
September

BY /bj/ Medial—three syllables

ambulance
ambulate
tabulate
tubular
______
______

BY /bj/ Medial—four syllables

contributor
distributor
tabulated
tabulator
tribulation
tributary
____
____
____

BZ /bz/ Final—one syllable

babes
bibs
cabs
clubs
cobs
crabs
cribs
cubes
cubs
dabs
debs
dubs
fibs
fobs
gabs
garbs
gobs
grubs
hobs
hubs
jibes
jobs
knobs
labs
lobes
mobs
nabs
probes
ribs
robes
rubs
sobs
stubs
subs
swabs
tabs
throbs
tribes
tubes
tubs
webs
____
____
____
____

BZ /bz/ Final—two syllables

bathrobes
bathtubs
bear cubs
book clubs
boys' clubs
cobwebs
doorknobs
earlobes
flashcubes
girls' clubs
golf clubs
health clubs
ice cubes
sand crabs
sea crabs
spareribs
wolf cubs
____
____
____
____

CH

Pronounced: /tʃ/
Spelled: ch, tch, te, ti, tu

CH /tʃ/ Initial—one syllable

Chad
chafe
chaff
chain
chair
chalk
champ
chance
change
changed
chant
chap
chapped
chaps
char
chard
charge
charged
Charles
charm
charms
chart
chase
chaste
chat
chaw
cheap
cheat
check
cheek
cheep
cheer
cheered
cheers
cheese
chess
chest
Chet
chew
chick
chide
chief
child
chill
chime
chin
chink
chintz
chip
chipped
chips
chirp
chit
chive
choice
choke
choose
chop
chopped
chops
chore
chose
chow
chub
chuck
Chuck
chug
chum
chummed
chump
chunk
church
churl
churn

CH /tʃ/ Initial—two syllables

cello
Chadwick
chairman
chalice
challenge
challenged
chamber
Chandler
changing

channel
chapel
chaplain
chapter
charcoal
charge card
Charleston
Charlestown
Charlie
charming
charter
chartered
chastise
chattel
chatter
cheaper
checkbook
checker
checkers
check mark
checkmate
checkroom
checkup
cheekbone
cheerful
cheery
cheese cake
cheesecloth
cheetah
Cheney
cherish
cherry
cherub
chessboard
chessman
Chester
chestnut
chicken
chickweed
Chico
chilblain
childbirth
childhood
childish
childlike
children
Chile
chili
chilly
chimney
china
China
Chinese
chipper
chipmunk
chirrup
chisel
chitchat
Choctaw
choker
choosy
chopper
chopping
choppy
chopsticks
chortle
chosen
chow chow
chowder
chow mein
chubby
chuck full
chuckhole
chuckle
chumming
chummy
Churchill
churchyard
chutney
____
____

CH /tʃ/ Initial—three syllables

Challenger
challenges
challenging
champion
chancellor
changeable
chain letter
chariot
charity
charley horse
charwoman
chatterbox
checkerboard
cheddar cheese
cheerleaders
cheerily
Cherokee
cherry bomb
cherry pie
Cherryvale
Cherryville
Chesapeake
chewing gum
chickadee
Chickasaw
chicken coop
chicken pox
chicory
chief of staff
Chihuahua

chili sauce
Chilkoot Pass
chimpanzee
China Sea
Chinatown
chinchilla
Chippewa
chokecherry
chocolate
chop suey
chuck-a-luck
chuck wagon
chuckwalla
churchgoer
____
____
____
____

CH /tʃ/ Initial—four syllables

challengingly
chancellery
chancellorship
Chancellor's List
charioteer
charitable
Chattanooga
cherry pepper
chicken chow mein
chili pepper
chili powder
chinaberry
Chinese checkers
chocolate chip
____

CH /tʃ/ Medial—two syllables

achieve
armchair
beachball
beachcomb
beachhead
bechance
benches
bleacher
blotchy
blue cheese
branching
broaches
bunches
butcher
capture
catcher
catching
catch-up
chitchat
chow chow
cincture
clincher
coaches
coachman
corn chips
creature
crouching
crunchy
crutches
culture
denture
discharge
ditches
duchess
enchain
enchant
etching
exchange
feature
fetches
fetching
fire chief
fixture
flincher
fracture
franchise
future
gesture
godchild
grandchild
Gretchen
hat check
hatchet
hatching
henchman
high chair
hitchhike
hitching
hope chest
hunchback
ice chips
inches
itching
ketchup
key chain
kitchen
latches
launcher
launching
launch pad
lecture
lunch box

luncheon
lunches
lunchroom
lunchtime
matches
mischief
mixture
moisture
moocher
nachos
Natchez
nature
notches
notchy
Pancho
pasture
patches
patchwork
peaches
peach tree
peachy
picture
pinch-hit
pitch-black
pitcher
pitches
pitchfork
pitching
poacher
posture
preacher
punchball
punch bowl
punch card
puncher
punch line
puncture
question
Rachel
rancher
ranchman
rancho
rapture
reaching
recharge
Richard
richer
richest
Richie
righteous
roaches
rupture
satchel
scratch pad
scripture
sculpture
sea chest
sketchy
statue
stature
statute
stepchild
stitches
structure
switching
teacher
teaching
texture
Thatcher
tincture
touchdown
touches
touching
trenchant
venture
voucher
vulture
watchdog
watcher
watchful
watching
watchman
witchcraft
witchy
____
____
____

CH /tʃ/ Medial—three syllables

actual
adventure
amateur
anchovy
Apache
beachcomber
bedchamber
bewitching
bird watcher
chinchilla
chokecherry
combustion
congestion
conjecture
cow catcher
cowpuncher
cultural
curvature
detachment
digestion
disenchant
dispatcher
dog catcher
enchanted

encroachment
exchequer
factual
fistula
fluctuate
flycatcher
forfeiture
furniture
futureless
hatchery
hitchhiker
immature
impeachment
kitchenette
launching pad
ligature
matchable
matchmaker
mutual
natural
night watchman
overture
picturesque
police chief
premature
punching bag
punctuate
ritual
rupturing
sandwiches
scratchable
signature
situate
statuesque
structural
structuring
taco chips
tactual
teachable
titular
teacher's aide
treacherous
venturesome
venturous
watchtower
witchery
____
____

CH /tʃ/ Medial—four syllables

agriculture
approachable
barbecue chips
caricature
chocolate chips
contractual
detachable
effectual
estuary
eventual
habitual
hickory chips
Indian chief
legislature
literature
manufacture
maturation
miniature
Natural Bridge
natural gas
naturalist
naturalize
naturally
perpetual
perpetuate
potato chips
reproachable
sanctuary
situation
spiritual
temperature
tortilla chips
unnatural
____
____
____

CH /tʃ/ Medial—five syllables

ineffectual
infatuation
intellectual
obituary
unapproachable
____

CH /tʃ/ Final—one syllable

batch
beach
bench
blanch
Blanche
bleach
blotch
botch
branch

breach
breech
broach
brooch
brunch
bunch
Butch
catch
clench
clutch
cinch
coach
couch
crouch
crunch
crutch
ditch
drench
Dutch
each
etch
fetch
French
grouch
hatch
hitch
hunch
hutch
itch
latch
leach
leech
lunch
match
Mitch
much
munch
niche
notch
ouch
patch
peach
pitch
poach
pooch
pouch
preach
punch
quench
ranch
reach
retch
rich
Rich
roach
scotch
scratch
screech
scrunch
sketch
slouch
snatch
snitch
speech
splotch
stench
stitch
stretch
such
swatch
switch
teach
thatch
touch
trench
twitch
vetch
watch
which
witch
wrench
wretch
____
____

CH /tʃ/ Final—two syllables

approach
attach
beseech
bewitch
cockroach
crosspatch
cross stitch
detach
dispatch
door latch
dude ranch
enrich
hemstitch
homestretch
hopscotch
impeach
key punch
Long Beach
mismatch
night watch
nonesuch
nuthatch
ostrich
outmatch
outreach
outstretch
pipe wrench

rematch	ski coach	track coach
reproach	South Beach	unlatch
retouch	swim coach	wrist watch
sandwich	topnotch	________

CH /tʃ/ Final—three syllables

avalanche	honeybunch	P.E. coach
baseball coach	lettuce patch	pocket watch
butterscotch	Mission Beach	pony ranch
briar patch	mix and match	rabbit hutch
cattle ranch	monkey wrench	Union Beach
crescent wrench	Myrtle Beach	West Palm Beach
feather stitch	Newport Beach	wrestling coach
football coach	overreach	wrestling match
hockey coach	overstretch	________

CHER /tʃɚ/ Medial—three syllables

archery	futurism	________
cultural	futurist	________
futureless	rupturing	________

CHER /tʃɚ/ Medial—four syllables

naturalist	________	________
naturally	________	________

CHER /tʃɚ/ Final—two syllables

archer	future	posture
bleacher	gesture	preacher
butcher	launcher	puncture
capture	leacher	rancher
catcher	lecture	richer
clincher	luncher	rupture
creature	lurcher	rupture
culture	mixture	stature
facture	moisture	teacher
feature	nature	Thatcher
fixture	pasture	venture
flincher	picture	voucher
fracture	pitcher	watcher

CHER /tʃɚ/ Final—three syllables

adventure
back scratcher
bird watcher
departure
dogcatcher
flycatcher
furniture
indenture
ligature
overture
signature

CHER /tʃɚ/ Final—four syllables

agriculture
legislature
literature
manufacture
miniature
temperature

RCH /rtʃ/ Medial—two syllables

archduke
archer
Archie
arching
archway
birch bark
churches
Churchill
fortune
kerchief
lurcher
lurching
marches
marching
merchant
nurture
nurtured
orchard
parchment
perchance
perches
perching
porches
purchase
purchased
researched
scorching
searchlight
starchy
surcharge
torchlight
virtue

RCH /rtʃ/ Medial—three syllables

archbishop
archdeacon
archduchess
archduchy
archerfish
archery
Archibald
arch support
cheddar cheese
departure
fortunate
handkerchief
interchange
marching band
March of Dimes
merchandise
misfortune
neckerchief
nurturing
orange orchard
overcharge
pear orchard
purchaser
purchasing
sea urchin
starchiest
virtual

RCH /rtʃ/ Medial—four syllables

apple orchard
archery set
birch bark basket
fortunately
fortune cookie
fortune hunter
fortuneteller
fortunetelling
grapefruit orchard

merchant marine	purchase order	________________
mortuary	torchlight parade	________________
purchasable	unfortunate	________________

RCH /rtʃ/ Final—one syllable

arch	March	search
birch	parch	smirch
church	perch	starch
lurch	porch	torch
march	scorch	________________

RCH /rtʃ/ Final—two syllables

blowtorch	out march	white birch
cornstarch	research	________________

RCHT /rtʃt/ Final—one syllable

arched	perched	starched
marched	scorched	________________
parched	searched	________________

D

Pronounced: /d/
Spelled: d, dd, ed

D /d/ Initial—one syllable

dab
dad
Dale
dam
damp
Dan
dance
dare
dark
dart
dash
date
dawn
day
deaf
deal
Dean
dear
Deb
debt
deck
Dee
deed
deem
deep
deer
deft
dell
delve
den
dense
dent
depth
desk
deuce
dew
dice
Dick
did
dig
dike
dill
dim
dime
din
dine
dip
Dirk
dirt
dish
disk
ditch
dive
do
dock
dodge
Dodge
doe
does
dog
dole
doll
dome
Don
done
don't
door
dorm
dot
Dot
dots
doubt
Doug
dough
douse
dove
down
Doyle
dub
duck
duct
dud
dude
due
dues
dug
duke
Duke
dull
dump

dune
dunk
dusk
dust
Dutch
dye
dyed
____
____

D /d/ Initial—two syllables

dabble
Dagan
dagger
daily
dainty
dairy
daisy
Daisy
Dallas
damage
damask
dampen
damper
Dana
dancer
dandruff
dandy
danger
Daniel
Danish
Danny
Danube
Darlene
dartboard
data
daughter
David
Davy
Dawson
daydream
daylight
Dayton
deacon
dead end
deadline
dealer
Dean's List
Dearborn
debate
Debbie
debit
debris
decade
decal
decamp
decay
decayed
deceit
deceive
decent
decide
decode
decor
decoy
decrease
deep freeze
Deep South
default
defeat
defend
defense
deflate
defrost
degree
Deland
delay
Delbert
delete
Delhi
delight
Della
delta
Delta
deluxe
demand
demise
demure
Dena
denim
Denise
Denmark
Dennis
denounce
dentist
Denton
Denver
deny
depart
depend
depict
deplane
deploy
deport
depose
depot
depress
derby
derive
descend
desert
design
desire

Des Moines
dessert
detail
detour
Detroit
device
devil
devote
devour
devout
Dewey
DeWitt
Dexter
dial
diesel
diet
digit
dimple
Dina
Dinah
dinky
dinner
dipper
discount
discus
discuss
disdain
disease
disgrace
disguise
dish cloth
dish pan
diskette
dismiss
dismount
dispatch
display
dispute
distance
distinct
divan
diver
diverge
divide
divine
divorce
Dixie
Dixon
dizzy
doctor
doctrine
dodger
Dodgers
dogcart
doghouse
dog sled
dog tag
dogwood
doily
doing
doleful
dollar
doll house
dolly
Dolly
dolphin
Donald
donate
donkey
Donna
donor
doorbell
doorknob
doorman
doormat
door prize
doorstep
doorstop
doorway
Dora
Doran
Doreen
Doris
dory
dosage
Dottie
double
doubtful
doubtless
doughnut
Douglas
downbeat
downcast
down draft
downfall
downfield
downgrade
downhill
Downing
downpour
downstairs
downtime
downtown
downwind
dozen
dozer
dual
dubbing
Dublin
duchess
duckling
dude ranch
Dudley
duel
duet
dugout
dullish

Duluth
dumbbells
Dumbo
dumpling
dump truck
dumpy
dungeon
duplex
during
dusky
dust cloth
duster
dusting
dust mop
dustpan
dust proof
duststorm
dusty
Dutchman
Dutch treat
duty
dyeing
____
____

D /d/ Initial—three syllables

daffodil
dangerous
daredevil
data base
data disk
Deanna
Deborah
debutante
decanter
decibel
decided
decimal
decipher
decision
declaring
declining
decoder
decoding
decorate
dedicate
deduction
deep freezer
deep fryer
defiance
deficit
definite
Delaware
delegate
delicate
delinquent
Delores
demagogue
demanding
demeanor
demolish
demonstrate
Denali
denial
department
deposit
deprecate
deputy
derelict
derisive
description
designate
desperate
destitute
destroyer
detective
deterrent
detonate
devastate
deviled eggs
devotee
dewberry
diagram
dialect
dialing
dialogue
diamond
Diana
diary
dictator
difference
different
difficult
digestion
digression
dilated
dilemma
diligence
dimension
diminish
dinosaur
diploma
diplomat
disconnect
discretion
disfigure
dishtowel
dishwasher
disk jockey
dislocate
disorder
dissipate
distinguish

distribute
diversion
diving board
diving boat
diving suit
division
document
dogberry
dogcatcher
dog collar
dog paddle
dog sledding
doll buggy
domestic
dominate
domineer
Dominic
dominion
Dorothy
double take
double talk
double time
down-to-earth
duffel bag
dungaree
duplicate
duration
dust devil
Dutch Harbor
dynamic
dynamite
____
____

D /d/ Initial—four syllables

dandelion
debilitate
declaration
deferential
definition
degenerate
delegation
deliberate
delineate
delirious
democracy
democratic
demolition
designation
desirable
despotism
destination
dexterity
diabetic
diagnosis
diagonal
diameter
dictionary
difficulty
dignitary
directory
dirigible
disadvantage
disarmament
disconcerting
disconsolate
discontinue
discourteous
discovery
discriminate
disinfectant
disintegrate
dispensation
disposition
disseminate
Dominion Day
dormitory
double bassoon
double boiler
double-breasted
double-decker
Dutch East Indies
dyslexia

D /d/ Initial—five syllables

depository
deteriorate
dilapidated
disability
disagreeable
disciplinary
disintegration
dissatisfaction

D /d/ Initial—six syllables

decarbonization
democratically
desalinization
disorganization
disorientation
disqualification

D /d/ Medial—two syllables

Ada
Adam
Adams
adding
beading
bedding
bidder
biddy
birthday
bleeder
bleeding
body
broaden
buddy
Buddy
cadet
chowder
cider
Cody
daddy
deaden
dead end
deadline
disdain
Eddie
Eden
Edie
edit
Edith
feeding
Friday
glider
guiding
guide dog
headache
heading
hidden
hiding
hoodoo
hot dog
Ida
Judy
kiddie
ladder
laddie
lady
ladies
leader
leading
loading
louder
maiden
May Day
meadow
modem
muddy
needed
nodding
odor
plodder
powder
pudding
radar
radish
raider
reader
reading
ready
rider
riding
roadway
rudder
Rudolph
Rudy
sadden
shadow
shudder
siding
skydive
soda
speeder
speeding
spider
strident
sudden
Sweden
threader
Thursday
tidy
today
trident
Tuesday
vandal
voodoo
waded
wading
wedding
Wednesday
woody
Woody
____
____

D /d/ Medial—three syllables

abdomen
Adeline
adenoids
adequate
advocate
anecdote
baby doll
Bermuda
Bernadine
bobsledding
Canada
cheddar cheese
cheerleaders
chickadee
comedy
data disk
Edison
editing
face powder
Father's Day
federal
First Lady
floppy disk
Florida
gadabout
honeydew
Idaho
idea
Kennedy
Madison
medial
medicine
medieval
moderate
Mother's Day
nobody
odorous
powderhorn
powdery
radio
rodeo
shadowing
sky diver
soda pop
somebody
spider web
tedious
tidal wave
tostada
video
____

D /d/ Medial—four syllables

adding machine
adenoidal
adenoma
anybody
auditory
avocado
cadaverous
Cambodia
Colorado
deciduous
medicinal
misadventure
North Dakota
riding safety
scuba diver
scuba diving
South Dakota
video game
video tape
Yankee Doodle
____

D /d/ Medial—five syllables

cock-a-doodle-do
expediency
hydrodynamics
macadamia
rudimentary
____
____
____
____

D /d/ Final—one syllable

ad
add
aid
aide
bad
bead
bed
bid
bide
blade
bled
bleed
blood
bode
bowed

Boyd
brad
Brad
braid
bread
bred
bride
broad
brood
bud
Bud
cad
Chad
clad
Claude
clod
cloud
Clyde
cod
code
could
creed
cried
crude
dad
dead
deed
did
died
dread
dud
dude
dyed
Ed
fad
fade
fed
feed
fled
flood
food
Fred
fried
gad
glad
glade
glide
good
grad
grade
greed
grid
guide
had
head
heed
hid
hide
hood
I'd
jade
Judd
Jude
kid
knead
lad
laid
lead
led
lid
lied
load
loud
mad
made
maid
Maude
mead
mid
mod
mode
mood
mowed
mud
Ned
need
nod
odd
ode
pad
paid
plaid
played
plead
pled
plowed
pod
pride
quad
quid
raid
read
red
reed
rid
ride
road
rod
Rod
rode
rowed
sad
said
sand
sawed
seed
send

shade
shed
shied
should
shrewd
side
skid
shred
Sid
sled
slid
slide
sod
spade
squad
squid
spread

stayed
Swede
tad
Tad
Ted
Thad
thread
thud
tide
toad
Todd
trod
trade
tread
tweed
tried
used

void
vowed
wad
wade
Wade
wed
we'd
weed
wide
wood
would
you'd
____
____
____
____
____

D /d/ Final—two syllables

abide
abroad
acrid
added
afraid
ahead
aided
Alfred
amid
applaud
arcade
arid
aside
avid
avoid
batted
beachhead
beaded
bedside
bedspread

beside
biped
birch wood
birdseed
blockade
bobsled
broadside
brocade
brown bread
bunk bed
canned food
carload
cascade
cat food
charade
cited
co-ed
concede
crowded
crusade

David
decade
decide
decode
divide
dog food
dog sled
download
dried food
elude
embed
Enid
exceed
exclude
fireside
fireweed
firewood
first aid
fish food
flash flood

flood tide
gifted
hardhead
hardwood
hated
hayride
hayseed
headed
high tide
hillside
hot rod
hunted
impede
include
inlaid
inside
instead
invade
junk food
knotted
landslide
limeade
low tide
luge sled
mermaid
mislead
misread
Morse code

muted
needed
nodded
outside
padded
painted
parade
persuade
pine wood
plywood
pointed
postpaid
precede
prepaid
punted
railroad
rated
reside
rooted
rotted
rounded
routed
rye bread
salad
seafood
seaside
seaweed
seeded

sided
slotted
snow slide
spotted
spruce wood
stampede
succeed
suited
tight wad
toll road
tooted
tour guide
unpaid
upload
waded
wayside
welded
white bread
Whiz Kid
widespread
winded
woodshed
yuletide
zip code
____
____
____
____

D /d/ Final—three syllables

a la mode
accepted
alkaloid
appointed
attitude
barricade
brotherhood
Cable Guide
centigrade

centipede
certified
chicken feed
Chinese food
classified
copperhead
expected
fishing rod
foreign aid

gingerbread
hearing aid
heating pad
Hollywood
intercede
invalid
lemonade
limited
myriad

neighborhood
one-man sled
orangeade
overhead
overplayed
pony ride
pyramid
riverside
Riverside
Robin Hood
serenade
soft-hearted
sourdough bread
spirited
super slide
supersede
talented
teacher's aide
teaching aid
tossed salad
tourist guide
two-man sled
two-sided
united
visited
water bed
____
____
____
____

DER /dɚ/ Medial—three syllables

elderish
elderly
eldermost
orderly
powderhorn
powdering
powdery
spider web
tenderfoot
thunderbolt
thunderclap
thunderhead
thunderous
thunderstorm
thunderstruck
tinderbox
underbrush
underclothes
underdog
underfoot
underground
underling
undermine
underneath
underpass
undersea
undershirt
underside
understand
understood
undertake
undertook
underwear
underweight
underwent
wanderer
wandering
wanderlust
wanderoo
wilderness
wonderful
____

DER /dɚ/ Medial—four syllables

elderberry
elder statesman
kindergarten
misunderstand
misunderstood
orderliness
powdering tub
powder monkey
thundershower
undercover
undergarment
underlying
understanding
undertaker
undertaking
underwater
____
____

DER /dɚ/ Final—two syllables

alder
bidder
binder
bladder
bleeder
blender
blinder
blunder
border

boulder
chowder
cider
cinder
colder
condor
elder
Elder
fender
fielder
flounder
folder
gander
glider
grinder
grounder
herder
hinder
ladder
launder
leader
louder
odor
order
plodder
plunder
powder
raider
reader
render
rider
rudder
sander
sender
shudder
slander
slender
speeder
spider
splendor
spreader
tender
threader
thunder
tinder
udder
under
weeder
____
____
____

DER /dɚ/ Final—three syllables

asunder
bewilder
calendar
cheerleader
commander
consider
crusader
cylinder
disorder
embroider
faultfinder
free-loader
insider
islander
lavender
left-hander
outsider
remainder
reminder
ringleader
shareholder
stepladder
____
____

DER /dɚ/ Final—four syllables

Alexander
ambassador
ice cream vendor
winter splendor
____
____

DL /dl/ Medial—two syllables

badly
Bradley
deadline
deadlock
deadly
gladly
Hadley
headlight
headline
heedless
huddling
hurdler
idling
kindling
loudly
madly
meddling
medley

midland
needless
needling
oddly
paddling
padlock
red light
sadly
seedless
seedling
soundly
swindling
toddler
toddling
twiddling
wedlock
widely
windlass
____
____
____

DL /dl/ Medial—three syllables

bridal veil
candlestick
candlewick
handlebars
idleness
meddlesome
middle age
middle ear
Middle East
Middle West
____
____

DL /dl/ Final—two syllables

bridal
bridle
bundle
candle
caudal
cradle
dwindle
fiddle
griddle
handle
huddle
hurdle
idle
idol
kindle
ladle
medal
meddle
middle
model
muddle
needle
noodle
paddle
pedal
peddle
poodle
puddle
riddle
saddle
sandal
scandal
spindle
swindle
tidal
toddle
twiddle
vandal
wheedle
yodel
____
____

LD /ld/ Medial—two syllables

Alden
alder
Baldwin
boulder
Boulder
builder
building
build-up
childhood
childish
children
cold cuts
colder
coldest
cold front
cold pack
cold snap
cold wave
Elden
elder
Elder
eldest
fielded
fielder

field goal
field trip
file disk
folder
folding
gelding
golden
goldfinch
goldfish
gold mine
gold pan
gold rush
gold stream
holder
holding
hold-up
mildew
molding
olden
older
oldest
scalding
scolding
seldom
Sheldon
shielded
shoulder
smolder
Waldon
welded
Welden
welder
welding
wildcat
wildfire
wildlife
wild west
yielded
yielding
____
____
____

LD /ld/ Medial—three syllables

beholden
blindfolded
bulldozer
bulldozing
cul-de-sac
deviled eggs
elderly
Eldora
field glasses
field worker
folding chair
golden age
goldenrod
gold nugget
gold panner
grandchildren
left fielder
old-fashioned
right fielder
shareholder
shelled pecans
shelled walnuts
shipbuilder
shouldering
unfolding
unwieldy
unyielding
upholder
wilderness
wildflower
withholding
World Series
____

LD /ld/ Final—one syllable

bald
billed
bold
build
called
child
cold
field
filed
filled
fold
gild
gold
guild
held
hold
mild
mold
mulled
old
polled
pulled
rolled
scald
scold
shelled
shield
skilled
sold
spilled

told
veiled
weld
wield
wild
world
yield
____
____

LD /ld/ Final—two syllables

afield
age-old
ahold
airfield
appalled
appealed
Arnold
backfield
beheld
behold
billfold
blindfold
coal field
cornfield
corralled
Donald
downfield
enfold
foothold
foretold
Gerald
grandchild
Harold
household
infield
infold
left field
marbled
marveled
outfield
rebuild
retold
right field
Ronald
Sea World
stepchild
stronghold
threefold
threshold
twofold
unfold
unsold
untold
upheld
uphold
windshield
withheld
withhold
____
____
____

LD /ld/ Final—three syllables

battlefield
center field
centerfold
emerald
football field
initialed
interfold
landing field
MacDonald
manifold
marigold
soccer field
____
____
____

DR /dr/ Initial—one syllable

drab
draft
drag
drain
drake
Drake
dram
drank
drape
draped
draw
drawl
drawn
dread
dream
dreamed
dreams
dreamt
dredge
dredged
drench
dress
dressed
drew

dried	drone	drudge
drift	drool	drug
drill	droop	drum
drilled	drop	drummed
drink	dropped	drunk
drip	drought	drupe
dripped	drove	dry
drive	drown	________
droll	drowse	________

DR /dr/ Initial—two syllables

draftsman	dreamland	droopy
drafty	dreary	dropkick
dragging	dredger	droplet
dragnet	dredging	droplight
dragon	dresser	dropping
dragoon	dressing	druggist
drag race	dribble	drugstore
drag strip	drier	druid
drainage	driest	drummer
drainpipe	drifter	drumstick
drama	drifting	dry cell
drastic	driftwood	dry clean
drawback	drilling	drydock
drawbridge	drip-dry	dryer
drawer	drive-in	dry goods
drawing	driven	dry ice
drawstring	driver	dry milk
dreadful	drive-through	dryness
dreamer	driveway	________
dreaming	drizzle	________

DR /dr/ Initial—three syllables

Dracula	dramatize	dreadfully
draft dodger	drapery	dreamily
dragonfly	drawing board	dressing gown
Drakensburg	drawing card	dressing room
dramatic	drawing frame	dressing up
dramatist	drawing room	dressmaker

drillmaster
drinkable
drive-in bank
driver's seat
driving range
drollery
drop kicker
dropsical
drop table
drowsiness
drudgery
drum major
drummer boy
dry cleaner
dry cleaning
dry goods store
dry measure
____
____
____
____

DR /dr/ Initial—four syllables

draconian
dramatical
dramaturgy
drastically
Dravidian
drawing table
dromedary
drosophila
dry battery
____
____
____

DR /dr/ Medial—two syllables

address
adrift
Andrew
Audrey
bass drum
bed rest
bedroll
bedroom
Cedric
children
coughdrop
dandruff
daydream
dewdrop
drip-dry
eardrop
eardrops
eardrum
eye drops
fire drill
foundry
fruit drink
gumdrop
headdress
hindrance
hum-drum
hundred
hundredth
hydrant
hydrate
hydro
laundry
lime drink
line drive
Madrid
Mildred
nose drops
Pedro
quadrant
quadrille
raindrops
Sandra
scoundrel
snare drum
snowdrift
soft drink
sundress
sun-dried
sundries
sundrops
sundry
tawdry
tendril
tundra
undress
withdraw
withdrawn
withdraws
withdrew
wondrous
Woodrow
____
____
____
____
____
____
____
____
____
____
____

DR /dr/ Medial—three syllables

Adrian
Andrea
apple drink
bongo drums
cathedral
dehydrate
eye dropper
Fredericksburg
grapefruit drink
hair dresser
hair dryer
hydraulics

hydrogen
hydrophone
hydroplane
kettle drum
lemon drink
line drawing
orange drink
overdrawn
overdrive
quadrangle
quadruped
quadruple

quadruplet
race driver
San Pedro
screwdriver
snapdragon
truck driver
withdrawal
withdrawing
____
____
____
____

DR /dr/ Medial—four syllables

adrenalin
dehydrated
driving safety
hydroponics
lemon-lime drink
melodrama

overdrawing
Padre Island
philodendron
photodrama
pineapple drink
quadrennial

quadruplicate
rhododendron
salad dressing
taxi driver
____
____

DR /dr/ Medial—five syllables

ambulance driver
hydrodynamics
hydrophobia

hypochondriac
quadrilateral
____

____
____
____

RD /rd/ Medial—two syllables

Airedale
birdhouse
birdie
birdseed
border
burden
card tricks
cardboard
cording
cordless
cordwood

garden
guarded
guardhouse
guardrail
hair-do
hard-boiled
harden
hardhead
Harding
hardly
hardship

hardware
hardwood
hardy
herdsman
hors d'oeuvre
hurdle
hurdler
ordain
ordeal
order
ordered

pardon
sturdy
tardy
third base
third class
Third World
Verde
warden
warder
wardrobe
yardage
yard light
yardstick
Zardax
____

RD /rd/ Medial—three syllables

bird watcher
borderline
cardinal
card table
concordance
concordant
corduroy
disorder
disordered
gabardine
gardener
Garden Grove
gardening
Garden State
guardian
Hoover Dam
Labor Day
ordering
orderly
ordinal
ordinance
ordinate
overdo
overdone
overdue
preordain
recorder
recording
regarding
regardless
reorder
rewording
rose garden
Saturday
stamdardize
standard time
stewardess
stewardship
unguarded
wardenship
____
____
____
____
____

RD /rd/ Medial—four syllables

accordion
coordinate
disorderly
Garden City
gardenia
garden party
guard of honor
guardianship
inboard motor
ordinary
ordination
outboard motor
standardizing
Verde River
____

RD /rd/ Medial—five syllables

coordination
guardian angel
ordinal number
ordinarily
overburdensome
____

RD /rd/ Final—one syllable

bard
beard
bird
board
bored
Byrd
card
chard
chord
cleared
cord
ford

Ford
gird
gourd
guard
hard
heard
herd
hoard
horde
lard
lord
moored
poured
roared
scared
scarred
scored
shared
spared
sparred
stared
steered
stirred
stored
third
toward
ward
weird
word
yard
____
____
____

RD /rd/ Final—two syllables

aboard
accord
afford
appeared
award
awkward
backboard
backward
backyard
barnyard
Bedford
Bernard
Big Bird
billboard
blackbird
blackboard
blizzard
bluebird
bombard
Buford
buzzard
cardboard
charge card
chessboard
Clifford
clipboard
Coast Guard
colored
Concord
cornered
courtyard
coward
cupboard
custard
dashboard
discard
eastward
Edward
flashcard
front yard
game bird
gizzard
graveyard
Harvard
hazard
Howard
inboard
inward
keyboard
kickboard
landlord
leeward
Leonard
leopard
lifeguard
lizard
Lombard
mallard
Maynard
measured
mouth guard
mud guard
mustard
nameboard
night guard
numbered
onward
orchard
outboard
outward
Oxford
pampered
password
postcard
prepared
punch card
Radford
rear guard

record
regard
reward
Rexford
Richard
rip cord
Ruford
safeguard
scoreboard
scorecard
seaboard
shepherd
shipyard
skateboard
skyward
songbird
southward
Spaniard
splattered
springboard
standard
Stanford
starboard
steward
stockyard
surfboard
switchboard
tagboard
tattered
thundered
timecard
tutored
unheard
upward
vineyard
wallboard
washboard
watchword
watered
wayward
westward
Willard
wizard
____
____
____
____
____

RD /rd/ Final—three syllables

aboveboard
afterward
birthday card
bodyguard
boulevard
checkerboard
Christmas card
color guard
cribbage board
disregard
diving board
drawing board
early bird
harpsichord
horned lizard
hummingbird
leotard
lumberyard
mockingbird
outnumbered
overboard
remembered
report card
Rocky Ford
room and board
rose-colored
rust-colored
Rutherford
Scotland Yard
shuffleboard
smorgasboard
spinal cord
substandard
thank-you card
union card
unnumbered
unwatered
Weatherford
____
____
____
____

ND /nd/ Medial—two syllables

Andy
bandage
bandstand
branding
Brandon
Brenda
bundle
Candace
candle
candy
Candy
cinder
Cindy
condemn
condor

dandy
fender
flounder
foundry
gander
Gandhi
Glenda
Glendale
grinder
grounded
grounder
handbag
handball
handbook
handcuff
handful
handle
handsaw
handshake
handsome
handspring
handy
hinder
Hindi
Hindu
hundred
indeed
indent
indulge
jaundiced
kindly
kindness
landing
landlord
landscape
landslide
Landy
launder
laundry
Linda
London
mandate
Mandy
Monday
plunder
ponder
Randolph
random
Randy
reindeer
render
rounded
rounding
round trip
roundup
sandbox
sandbug
sandbur
sand crab
sander
Sandy
sender
send-off
slander
slender
splendor
Sunday
sunder
tandem
tender
thunder
tundra
undamped
under
undone
undress
vendor
Wendy
window
windup
windy
wonder

ND /nd/ Medial—three syllables

Amanda
amendment
appendage
appendix
bandaging
candy bar
condition
conducive
conduction
conductor
endurance
handicap
handicraft
handiwork
handwriting
handwritten
Honduras
India
Indian
inundate
landlady
Laplander
laundromat
left-handed

London Bridge
mandarin
meander
plundering
sandalwood
sandbagging
sand dollar
sandpaper
sandpiper
storm window
Sunday School
sundial
tendency
tenderfoot
thunderbolt
thunderclap
thunderhead
thunderous
thunderstorm
thunderstruck
tinderbox
underbrush
underclothes
underdog
underfoot
underground
underline
undermine
underneath
underpass
undersea
undershirt
underside
understand
understate
understood
undertake
undertook
undertow
underwear
underweight
underwent
underworld
unfounded
wanderer
wanderlust
wonderful
____
____
____
____

ND /nd/ Medial—four syllables

candelabra
Cinderella
condemnation
conditional
incandescent
indecently
indelible
indentation
independent
Indiana
indicative
indiscretion
Indonesia
kindergarten
mendaciously
mendacity
undulating
____

ND /nd/ Medial—five syllables

appendicitis
condominium
hypochondriac
incandescently
incendiary
indefensible
independency
indeterminate
indiscriminate
industrialist
Indy 500
serendipity
underachiever
underdeveloped
underestimate
underexposure
underprivileged
understandingly

ND /nd/ Final—one syllable

and
band
bend
bind
bland
blend
blind
blond
bond
bound
brand
canned

end
find
fined
fond
found
fund
gland
grand
grind
ground
hand
hind
hound
kind
land
lend
mend
mind
mound
pond
pound
rend
rind
round
sand
send
skinned
sound
spanned
spend
stand
strand
tend
trend
vend
wand
weaned
wind
wound
yawned
____
____

ND /nd/ Final—two syllables

abound
aground
airbound
almond
amend
ascend
astound
attend
backbend
background
backhand
bandstand
behind
beyond
bloodhound
Cleveland
combined
command
commend
compound
confound
contend
dachshund
dead end
defend
demand
depend
descend
diamond
England
errand
expand
extend
fairground
farmland
Finland
firebrand
foreground
grassland
greyhound
headband
highland
Holland
homeland
husband
inland
intend
Ireland
island
jocund
kickstand
left-hand
legend
longhand
mainland
mankind
Midland
misspend
offend
Portland
pretend
profound
quicksand
Raymond
rebound
refund
remand
remind
respond

right-hand
Roland
rotund
second
shorthand
side band
snowblind
snowbound
spellbound
stagehand
thousand
unbind
unwind
up-end
upland
waistband
woodland
wristband

ND /nd/ Final—three syllables

apprehend
beforehand
comprehend
condescend
contraband
correspond
countermand
dividend
fairyland
Gila Bend
integrand
intertwined
marching band
Maryland
New England
Newfoundland
New Zealand
overland
recommend
Rhode Island
rhythm band
rubber band
savings bond
secondhand
Sugar Land
Sutherland
Switzerland
Tamarind
underground
underhand
understand
upper hand
vagabond
wonderland
wraparound

ND /nd/ Final—four syllables

merry-go-round
misunderstand
superintend

DW /dw/ Initial—one syllable

Duane
dwarf
Dwayne
dwell
dwelled
dwelt
Dwight

DW /dw/ Initial—two syllables

dwarfish
dwelling
dwindle
dwindling

DZ /dz/ Final—one syllable

adds
aids
beads
bids
codes
creeds
crowds
dads
deeds

fades
fads
feeds
floods
gods
goods
grades
guides
heads
hides
kids
lads
leads
lids
loads
modes
needs
nodes
nods
odds
odes
pads
pleads
pods
raids
reads
reds
rides
rids
roads
seeds
shades
sheds
sides
sleds
slides
spades
speeds
suds
tides
toads
trades
wades
wads
weds
weeds
woods

ZD /zd/ Final—one syllable

braised
brazed
breezed
caused
closed
dazed
eased
gazed
grazed
hosed
paused
phased
phrased
pleased
posed
praised
raised
seized
sized
sneezed
teased
wheezed

LDZ /ldz/ Final—one syllable

builds
fields
folds
holds
molds
scalds
scolds
worlds
yields

NDZ /dzs/ Final—one syllable

bends
binds
ends
finds
glands
grinds
hands
kinds
lands
lends
mends
minds

ponds
rends
rinds
sands
sends
sounds
spends
stands
tends
winds
____
____

RDZ /rdz/ Final—one syllable

bards
beards
birds
boards
cards
chords
cords
gourds
guards
hoards
lords
towards
wards
words
yards
____
____
____

RDZ /rdz/ Final—two syllables

backyards
blackbirds
bluebirds
buzzards
clipboards
cupboards
discards
flashcards
kick boards
leewards
leopards
lifeguards
lizards
orchards
postcards
punch cards
rear guards
rewards
score cards
shepherds
skateboards
songbirds
Spaniards
surfboards
timecards
vineyards
wizards
____
____
____

DY /dj/ Medial—two syllables

woodyard
____
____

DY /dj/ Medial—three syllables

Scotland Yard
trade union
____

LVD /lvd/ Final—one syllable

delved
shelved
solved
____
____
____

LVD /lvd/ Final—two syllables

absolved
dissolved
evolved
involved
resolved
revolved
unsolved
____
____

RVD /rvd/ Final—one syllable

carved
curved
served
starved
swerved

RVD /rvd/ Final—two syllables

deserved
observed
preserved
reserved
unnerved

DTH /dθ/ Final—one syllable

breadth
width

DTH /dθ/ Final—two syllables

bandwidth
hairbreadth
hundredth
thousandth

DTH /dθ/ Final—three syllables

one hundredth
two thousandth

THD /ðd/ Final—one syllable

bathed
breathed
clothed
loathed
scathed
seethed
sheathed
smoothed
soothed
swathed
teethed
tithed
writhed

F

Pronounced: /f/
Spelled: f, ff, gh, ph

F /f/ Initial—one syllable

face
fact
facts
fad
fade
fail
faint
fair
faith
Faith
fake
fall
falls
false
fame
fan
fang
fanned
fans
far
farce
fare
farm
farmed
fast
fat
fault
fawn
Faye
fear
feast
feat
fed
fee
feed
feel
feet
feign
fell
felt
fence
fend
fern
fetch
fete
fib
fibbed
field
fiend
fierce
fifth
fig
fight
file
filed
fill
filled
film
filth
fin
find
fine
fined
fir
fire
firm
first
fish
fist
fit
five
fix
fizz
foal
foam
fob
foe
fog
foil
foist
fold
folk
fond
food
fool
foot
for
force
ford
Ford

fork
form
fort
forth
fought
foul
fouled
found
four
fourth
fowl
fudge
full
fun
fund
fur
fuss
fussed
fuzz
phase
Phil
phone
phoned
phones
____
____
____

F /f/ Initial—two syllables

fable
fabric
facet
facial
facing
factor
failing
failure
Fairbanks
fairground
Fairview
fairway
fairy
faithful
falcon
falter
famine
famish
famous
fan belt
fancy
Far East
farewell
farm belt
farmer
farmhouse
farming
farmland
farmyard
farther
fashion
fasten
fatal
father
fathom
fatigue
fatten
faucet
faulty
favor
fearful
feather
feature
feeble
feline
Felix
fellow
felon
female
fencing
ferment
ferry
fertile
fervid
fervor
fester
festive
festoon
fever
fiber
fickle
fiction
fiddle
fiddler
fidget
Fifi
figment
figure
Fiji
filbert
file disk
filing
filling
fillings
Fillmore
filter
final
finals
finesse
finger
finish
Finland
Finnish
firebrick

fire drill
firefly
fire hat
fireman
fireplace
fireproof
fire sale
fireside
fire thorn
firetrap
fire truck
fireweed
firewood
fireworks
first aid
first base
first class
first name
Fisher
fishing
fishy
fitness
fitting
fittings
fizzle
focal
focus
foible
follow
folly
foment
fondant
fondle
fondue
foolish
footage
football
foothill
footlights

footnote
footprint
footrest
footstep
footstool
forage
forbid
forebear
forecast
forego
forehead
foreign
foreman
foremost
foresee
foresight
forgave
forget
forgive
forgot
formal
format
former
For Rent
For Sale
Fort Knox
Fort Wayne
Fort Worth
forward
fossil
foster
Foster
founder
foundry
fourscore
fourteen
fuchsia
fullback
fuller

fumble
function
fungus
funnel
funny
furlough
furnace
furnish
furry
further
fusses
fussy
phalanx
phantom
pharoah
pharynx
pheasant
Phillip
Phoebe
Phoenix
phoneme
phonic
phonics
phony
phooey
phosphate
photo
Phyllis
physique
____
____
____
____
____
____
____
____
____
____

F /f/ Initial—three syllables

Fabian
factory
factual
faculty
fairy tale
fairyland
fallacy
familiar
family
fanatic
fanciful
fantastic
fantasy
fascinate
Father's Day
favorite
Fayetteville
feasible
featherstitch
featherweight
feathery
federal
federate
feminine
feminist
Ferdinand
ferocious
Ferris wheel
fertilize
festival
fiance′
fiasco
fiddlesticks
fiery
fiesta
filament
fingernail
fingerpaint
fingerprint
finicky
fire alarm
firecracker
fire engine
fire escape
fire fighter
fire marshal
fire safety
fire station
fire tower
first lady
foliage
follicle
follower
following
follow-through
follow-up
football field
forever
forgetful
forgetting
forgiven
forgiving
formation
formula
foundation
Four-H-Club
four-wheeler
furniture
pharmacist
pharmacy
Philippi
Philippines
Philistine
Phillipsburg
phlebitis
phobia
phonetics
phonograph
photocell
photoflash
photo lab
physical
physician
____
____
____
____

F /f/ Initial—four syllables

facilitate
facility
fashionable
fastidious
fatality
favorable
federation
felicity
Felicity
fidelity
Fiji Islands
formaldehyde
formidable
fundamental
pharyngeal
phenomena
phenomenal
phenomenon
philanthropy
philharmonic
philodendron

philology
philosopher
philosophy
phonetical
phonetician
phonography
phonology
photographer
photography

F /f/ Medial—two syllables

afar
affair
affect
affirm
affix
afford
afield
afire
afoot
afore
afoul
aphid
aphis
beefsteak
befall
befit
befog
before
blackfish
bluefish
boastful
boldface
boldfaced
bonfire
boxful
breakfast
brimful
buffer
buffet
buffing
buffoon
Buford
cafe
caffeine
campfire
camphor
catfish
chiff-chaff
chiffon
Clifford
clubfoot
codfish
coffee
coffer
coiffeur
comfort
confab
confer
confide
confine
confined
confirm
conform
confound
crawfish
crayfish
crow's-foot
cupful
daffy
deafen
deface
defame
default
defect
defend
defense
defer
defile
define
deform
defunct
defy
differ
differed
diffuse
dishful
dumbfound
efface
effect
effort
enfold
enforce
Fifi
gaffer
Gifford
goldfinch
goldfish
gopher
graphic
guffaw
half-hour
handful
hayfork
headfirst
headphone
heartfelt
heifer
hyphen
infant

infect
infer
infest
infirm
inform
jiffy
joyful
laughing
laughter
leafy
lifeboat
lifeguard
lifelike
lifeline
lifetime
loafer
loafers
loafing
lowfat
mouthful
muffin
muffle
offend
offense
offer
offhand
offing
offshoot
offshore
offspring
often
outfield
outfit

paleface
pan fish
platform
playful
prefer
prefix
profane
profess
profile
profit
profound
proofread
prophet
puffin
puffing
rainfall
refer
refine
reform
refund
roughage
roughen
roughhouse
roughshod
safeguard
safer
safety
sapphire
scaffold
seafood
Sioux Falls
snowfall
sofa

Sophie
sophist
spoon-fed
spoonful
state fair
stiffen
stuffer
suffer
suffice
suffix
syphon
taffy
talkfest
thankful
threefold
tiffin
tinfoil
toffee
toughen
traffic
trophy
two-fold
unfold
wafer
watchful
wayfare
whitefish
windfall
wishful
wistful
zephyr
____
____

F /f/ Medial—three syllables

about-faced
aerophone
affable
affection

afferent
affirmant
amorphous
amplify

artifact
atrophy
awfully
balefully

beautify
bedfellow
befuddle
benefit
bifocal
bike safety
bona fide
buffalo
bus safety
calcify
cellophane
centrifuge
certified
certify
Chief of Staff
chiffonier
chloroform
chlorophyll
clarify
classify
close-fisted
coffeehouse
comforter
conference
confidante
confidence
confident
confiscate
Confucius
confusion
crucifix
crucify
daffodil
decipher
de facto
defection
defiance
deficient
deficit
dictaphone
difference
difficult
diffidence
diffident
discomfort
disinfect
edifice
edify
effective
efficient
effigy
elephant
emphasis
emphasize
emphatic
euphony
fire safety
frankfurter
glorify
gratify
half-and-half
horrify
infamous
infancy
infantry
infarction
infection
infernal
infinite
interfere
Jefferson
Josephine
laughable
lymphocyte
magnify
megaphone
microfilm
microphone
modify
mortify
nonfiction
notify
nullify
offensive
offering
officer
official
officious
Pacific
pacifist
pacify
paraffin
petrify
phosphorus
preference
profession
professor
proficient
purify
qualify
ratify
referee
reference
refinement
Rocky Ford
safari
safety belt
safety pin
Santa Fe
satisfy
saxophone
seafarer
signify
Sophia
Sophocles
sophomore
soundproofing

sousaphone	terrific	verify
specify	terrify	vilify
suffocate	unfasten	______________
telephone	unfurnished	______________

F /f/ Medial—four syllables

affidavit	confederate	infirmity
affiliate	confidential	information
affinity	confirmation	inoffensive
affirmative	confiscation	insufficient
amphibian	conformation	intensify
anaphora	coniferous	manufacture
anaphoric	defamation	officiate
antiphonal	defensible	peripheral
antiphony	deferential	philosopher
artificial	deficiency	photographer
beautifying	definition	preferential
benefactor	defoliate	profitable
beneficial	differential	radiophone
biographer	diversify	referendum
biographic	driving safety	reformation
biography	emphysema	riding safety
biophysics	emulsify	safety glasses
boating safety	esophagus	safety helmet
cacography	flying safety	scientific
cacophony	geographer	seat belt safety
calligraphy	identify	South Pacific
catastrophe	indifference	topographic
certificate	ineffective	topography
circumference	infallible	typographic
climbing safety	inferior	walking safety
coefficient	infinitive	water safety
confectioner	infirmary	______________

F /f/ Medial—five syllables

affiliation	cafeteria	encephalitis
angiography	configuration	hemophilia
asphyxiation	diophoretic	hydrophobia
bibliography	edification	infatuated

informational
insufferable
modification
officiary
paraphernalia
sophisticated
unforgettable
____
____

F /f/ Final—one syllable

beef
biff
bluff
brief
buff
calf
chafe
chaff
chef
chief
clef
cliff
Cliff
cough
cuff
deaf
doff
fife
fluff
gaff
goof
graph
grief
gruff
guff
half
hoof
huff
if
Jeff
knife
laugh
leaf
life
loaf
miff
muff
off
pouf
prof
proof
puff
quaff
reef
roof
rough
ruff
safe
scoff
scuff
sheaf
skiff
spoof
staff
stiff
strife
stuff
thief
tiff
tough
trough
waif
whiff
wife
woof
____
____
____
____

F /f/ Final—two syllables

aloof
behalf
belief
blow-off
carafe
cast-off
checkoff
cutoff
dandruff
distaff
dust proof
enough
fire chief
fire proof
giraffe
housewife
jackknife
Joseph
kerchief
kickoff
layoff
midriff
penknife
plaintiff
play-off
pontiff
rainproof

relief	stop-off	take off
sheriff	sun proof	tariff
show-off	sun roof	________

F /f/ Final—three syllables

autograph	homograph	spirograph
barograph	monograph	tamper-proof
carving knife	neckerchief	telegraph
Chief of Staff	paragraph	tomograph
coral reef	phonograph	unbelief
dictograph	photograph	waterproof
epitaph	pocket knife	weatherproof
half-and-half	powder puff	________
handkerchief	spectrograph	________

F /f/ Final—four syllabes

angiograph	choreograph	oscillograph
cardiograph	Indian chief	________

FER /fɚ/ Medial—three syllables

afferent	inference	reference
conference	offering	referent
difference	phosphorus	suffering
different	preference	________

FER /fɚ/ Medial—four syllables

indifference	preferable	reoffering
indifferent	preferential	________
inferential	referable	________
long-suffering	referential	________

FER /fɚ/ Final—two syllables

buffer	gaffer	prefer
camphor	golfer	refer
chauffeur	gopher	roofer
confer	infer	rougher
deafer	loader	safer
defer	loafer	scoffer
differ	offer	suffer

sulphur
transfer
wafer
zephyr
____
____

FER /fɚ/ Final—three syllables

bus transfer
decipher
____
____
____
____

FL /fl/ Initial—one syllable

flab
flagged
flagged
flail
flair
flaired
flak
flake
flakes
flame
flamed
flank
flap
flapped
flare
flared
flash
flashed
flask
flat
flaunt
flaw
flax
flay
flea
fleck
fled
flee
fleece
fleet
flesh
flew
flex
flick
flies
flight
flinch
fling
flint
flip
flipped
flirt
flit
Flo
float
flock
flood
floor
flop
flopped
floss
flounce
flounced
flour
flout
flow
flown
Floyd
flu
flub
flue
fluff
fluffs
fluke
flume
flung
flunk
flush
flute
flux
fly
phlegm
phlox
____
____

FL /fl/ Initial—two syllables

flabby
flaccid
Flag Day
flagging
flagman
flagpole
flagrant
Flagstaff
flaky
flameproof
flaming
flanker

flannel
flapjack
flapper
flare-up
flashback
flashbulb
flash card
flashcube
flash flood
flashgun
flashing
flashlight
flashy
flatbed
flatboat
flatcar
flatfoot
flatter
flattop
flautist
flavor
flaxseed
flection
fledgling
fleecy
Flemish
fleshy
Fletcher
flexion
flicker
flier
flight path
flighty
flimsy
flip-flops
flipper
flippers
flipping
flitter
float bridge
floater
floating
float plane
flocking
floodlight
floorboard
floor lamp
floor show
floozy
floppy
Flora
floral
Florence
florid
florist
flossy
flounder
flourish
flow chart
flower
flowing
fluent
flue pipe
fluffy
fluid
flunky
flurry
fluster
flutist
flutter
flying
flywheel

FL /fl/ Initial—three syllables

flabbergast
flagrantly
flamboyant
flamenco
flamethrower
flamingo
flammable
flannelette
flashier
flatiron
flattery
flavoring
flea-bitten
flea market
flexible
flight control
floating dock
flood control
floodwater
floorwalker
floppy disk
Florentine
florescent
Florida
flotation
flotilla
flower girl
flowerpot
fluctuate
fluency
fluffier
fluid ounce
fluorine
flutter kick
flyable
fly-casting

flycatcher
flying fish
phlegmatic
____
____
____

FL /fl/ Initial—four syllables

floriculture
fluctuation
flying safety
flying saucer
____
____

FL /fl/ Medial—two syllables

afflict
aflame
afloat
blowfly
chiefly
conflict
cornflakes
deflate
deflect
firefly
flip-flops
horsefly
housefly
ice floe
inflame
inflate
inflict
leaflet
muffler
pamphlet
reflect
roughly
snowflake
soufflé
stiffly
top-flight
____

FL /fl/ Medial—three syllables

affliction
affluence
affluent
butterfly
camouflage
cornflower
deflation
deflection
deflower
disfluent
dragonfly
genuflect
ice flowers
inflation
inflection
influence
overflow
reflection
reflector
sunflower
wallflower
____
____
____

FL /fl/ Medial—four syllables

cauliflower
conflagration
genuflection
inflammable
inflammation
inflatable
inflexible
influential
influenza
superfluous
____
____

FL /fl/ Final—two syllables

armful
artful
awful
baffle
baleful
careful
changeful
cheerful
doleful
doubtful
dreadful
Eiffel

faithful
fateful
fitful
forceful
fretful
frightful
fruitful
gainful
gleeful
graceful
grateful
handful
harmful
healthful
heedful
helpful
hopeful
hurtful
joyful
mournful
mouthful
muffle
needful
pailful
painful
peaceful
playful
raffle
restful
rightful
rueful
ruffle
sackful
scoopful
scuffle
shuffle
skillful
sniffle
spiteful
spoonful
stifle
thankful
thoughtful
trifle
tuneful
useful
waffle
wakeful
wasteful
watchful
willful
wishful
woeful
wrathful
wrongful
youthful
____

FL /fl/ Final—three syllables

beautiful
bountiful
colorful
deceitful
disdainful
disgraceful
distasteful
distressful
distrustful
dutiful
eventful
fanciful
forgetful
masterful
meaningful
merciful
pitiful
plentiful
reproachful
resentful
resourceful
respectful
sorrowful
teaspoonful
unlawful
unthankful
untruthful
wonderful
____
____

FL /fl/ Final—four syllables

tablespoonful
uneventful
unmerciful

LF /lf/ Medial—two syllables

Alfred
baleful
bullfinch
bullfrog
elfin
elfish
elfkin
elflock
golfer

golfing
Gulf Stream
self-care
self-ease
self-fed
self-help
selfish
self-pride
self-serve
self-taught
shellfish
sulfa
sulfate
sulfine
sulfite
sulfur
welfare
willful
wolf cub
wolfhound
wolfish
wolf pack
____
____

LF /lf/ Medial—three syllables

alfalfa
alphabet
bellflower
Bellflower
bisulphate
bullfiddle
self-addressed
self-assured
self-aware
self-composed
self-concept
self-conscious
self-contained
self-control
self-defense
self-esteem
self-giving
self-glory
self-image
self-imposed
selfishly
self-pity
self-possessed
self-regard
self-reproach
self-respect
self-righteous
self-searching
self-serving
self-support
skillfully
skillfulness
sulfatic
sulfitic
sulfuric
unselfish
____
____
____

LF /lf/ Medial—four syllables

alphabetic
self-appointed
self-assurance
self-awareness
self-confidence
self-determined
self-directed
self-discipline
self-evident
self-reliance
self-sacrifice
self-sufficient

LF /lf/ Final—one syllable

elf
golf
gulf
Ralph
self
shelf
wolf
____
____

LF /lf/ Final—two syllables

Adolf
Adolphe
bookshelf
engulf
gray wolf
herself
himself
itself
myself

oneself
ourself
Randolph
Rudolph
thyself
werewolf
white wolf
yourself
____

FR /fr/ Initial—one syllable

frail
frame
Fran
franc
France
Frank
fraud
fray
freak
Fred
free
freeze
freight
French
fresh
fret
fried
friend
fright
frill
fringe
frisk
Fritz
frock
frog
from
frond
front
frost
froth
frown
froze
fruit
fry
phrase
____

FR /fr/ Initial—two syllables

fraction
fracture
fragile
fragment
fragrance
fragrant
framework
framing
Frances
franchise
Francis
Frankfurt
Franklin
frantic
Frazer
freakish
freckle
Freda
freedom
freefall
freehand
free-lance
free lunch
Freeport
freestyle
free throw
free time
freeway
free will
freezer
freighter
Fremont
French fries
French horn
Frenchman
French toast
frenum
frenzied
frenzy
frequent
freshen
freshman
fretful
friar
friction
Friday
Frieda
friendly
friendship
frigate
frighten
frigid
frisky
fritter
frizzy
frogman
frolic
frontage
frontal
fronted

frontier	frosty	fryer
front page	frozen	frying
front room	frugal	________________
frostbite	fruitcake	________________
frosted	fruit cup	________________
frosting	frustrate	________________

FR /fr/ Initial—three syllables

fractional	frictional	fruitfulness
fragmental	friction tape	fruit salad
frankfurter	friendliness	frustrating
fraternal	frivolous	frustration
Frederica	frizzier	frying pan
Frederick	frolicking	phrenetic
Fredricksburg	frolicsome	phrenitis
freewheeling	frontal lobe	________________
frequency	front runner	________________
fresh water	frostbitten	________________
fricative	frost warning	________________

FR /fr/ Initial—four syllables

fractionary	fraternity	phraseogram
fragility	fraternizing	phrenology
fragmentary	frighteningly	________________

FR /fr/ Medial—two syllables

affray	deep freeze	Jeffrey
affront	deepfry	leapfrog
afraid	defraud	refrain
A-frame	defray	refresh
Alfred	defrost	scot-free
befriend	fish fry	sea front
belfry	girl friend	Wilfred
boyfriend	grapefruit	Winfred
breadfruit	Hausfrau	________________
bullfrog	Humphrey	________________
carefree	infract	________________
cold front	infringe	________________
confront	Jack Frost	________________

FR /fr/ Medial—three syllables

affricate	infraction	unfriendly
Africa	infrared	unfrozen
antifreeze	infrequent	unfruitful
deep freezer	infringement	waterfront
defrosted	refreshing	Winifred
defroster	refreshments	______
defrosting	sassafras	______
Good Friday	unafraid	______

FR /fr/ Medial—four syllables

confrontation	refrigerate	unfrequented
infractible	San Francisco	unfriendliest
infrequently	South Africa	unfruitfulness
refreshingly	tutti frutti	______

FR /fr/ Medial—five syllables

infrangibleness	refractometer	refrigerative
refractivity	refrigeration	refrigerator

RF /rf/ Medial—two syllables

airfield	fearful	starfish
barefaced	forfeit	surface
barefoot	Garfield	surfboard
careful	orphan	surfer
cheerful	parfait	surfing
curfew	perfect	______
earful	perform	______
earphone	perfume	______

RF /rf/ Medial—three syllables

butterfat	interfere	performer
carefully	interfold	performing
carefulness	labor force	tenderfoot
colorful	orphanage	underfoot
counterfeit	perfection	waterfall
fire fighter	perfectly	______
forfeiture	perforate	______
interface	performance	______

RF /rf/ Medial—four syllables

butterfinger	morphology	________
imperfection	performing arts	________

FS /fs/ Medial—three syllables

cough syrup	lifesaving	________
life cycles	________	________

FS /fs/ Final—one syllable

beefs	fluffs	ruffs
bluffs	goofs	scoffs
briefs	huffs	scuffs
buffs	Jeff's	spoofs
chefs	muffs	staffs
chiefs	proofs	stuffs
cliffs	puffs	whiffs
coughs	reefs	________
cuffs	roofs	________

FS /fs/ Final—two syllables

beliefs	handcuffs	show-offs
cast offs	kerchiefs	takeoffs
cutoffs	layoffs	tariffs
giraffes	play-offs	________

FS /fs/ Final—three syllables

photographs	telegraphs	________
powder puffs	________	________

SF /sf/ Initial—one syllable

sphere	________	________
sphinx	________	________

SF /sf/ Initial—two syllables

spheric	________	________
spheroid	________	________

SF /sf/ Initial—three syllables

spherical	________	________

SF /sf/ Initial—four syllables

spherically

SF /sf/ Medial—two syllables

asphalt
blaspheme
cat's fur
forceful
graceful
henceforth
houseful
peaceful
thenceforth
transfer
transfix
transform
transfuse
useful

SF /sf/ Medial—three syllables

atmosphere
blasphemer
blasphemous
blasphemy
disfavor
disfigure
gas fixture
gas furnace
hemisphere
lithosphere
misfortune
phosphorus
satisfy
stratosphere
transference
transfigure
transformer
transfusion
usefulness

SF /sf/ Medial—four syllables

asphyxiate
dysphasia
satisfaction
transferable
transformation
transfusible

FT /ft/ Medial—two syllables

after
chieftain
Clifton
driftwood
fifteen
fifteenth
fifty
half time
left field
left hand
lifter
lift-off
lift truck
lofty
nifty
rafter
ruffed grouse
sifter
softball
soft drink
softness
software
softwood
thriftless
thrift store
thrifty

FT /ft/ Medial—three syllables

afterglow
afterlife
aftermath
aftermost
afternoon
aftertaste
afterthought
afterwards
afterworld
after-years
hereafter
leftovers

shoplifter
soft-hearted
soft-shell crab
thereafter
thriftier
thriftiest
thriftily
____
____

FT /ft/ Final—one syllable

aft
cleft
craft
croft
daft
deft
draft
drift
gift
goofed
graft
heft
huffed
laughed
left
lift
loft
oft
raft
rift
roofed
ruffed
shaft
shift
shrift
sift
soft
swift
Taft
theft
thrift
tuft
waft
weft
____
____

FT /ft/ Final—two syllables

adrift
aircraft
airlift
aloft
crankshaft
day shift
gearshift
handcraft
hayloft
ingraft
life raft
makeshift
night shift
ski lift
skin graft
snowdrift
spacecraft
spendthrift
uncuffed
uplift
witchcraft
woodcraft
____
____

FT /ft/ Final—three syllables

birthday gift
Christmas gift
handicraft
leather craft
leisure craft
overdraft
pleasure craft
rubber raft
water craft
____
____
____

G

Pronounced: /g/
Spelled: g, gg, gh, gu, gue

G /g/ Initial—one syllable

gab
gad
gag
gage
Gail
gain
gained
gait
gale
Gale
gall
game
games
gang
gap
garb
gas
gash
gasp
gate
gauche
gauge
gaunt
gauze
gave
Gayle
gaze
gear
geese
get
ghost
gift
gig
Gil
gild
gill
gilt
gird
girl
girth
give
go
goad
goal
goals
goat
gob
goes
gold
golf
gone
gong
good
goods
goof
goofed
goofs
goose
gorge
got
gouge
gout
gown
guard
guess
guessed
guest
guide
guild
guilt
guise
gulch
gulf
gull
gulls
gulp
gum
Gus
gush
gust
guy
Guy
____
____
____
____
____
____
____
____

G /g/ Initial—two syllables

gable
Gaby
gadget
gaily
gainful
gala
gallant
galley
gallon
gallop
gallstone
galore
galosh
gambit
gamble
game bag
game bird
gander
Gandhi
Ganges
gangway
garage
garden
Garfield
garish
garland
garlic
garment
garnet
garnish
garret
garter
Gary
gaseous
gasket
gaslight
gateway
gather
gaudy
gavel
Gavin
Gaylord
gazelle
gazette
Gertrude
getting
geyser
ghastly
ghostly
ghost town
Gibby
Gibson
giddy
gifted
Gilbert
Gilda
Gilford
gimmick
girdle
girlhood
girlish
given
giving
gizzard
goal post
goalie
goatee
gobble
goblet
goblin
go-cart
Godfrey
goggle
going
goiter
golden
goldfinch
goldfish
goldie
good-bye
goodness
gopher
Gordon
gorgeous
gosling
gossip
govern
guarded
Guernsey
guffaw
guidance
guidebook
guide dog
guidepost
guiding
guilty
guinea
gully
gumbo
gumdrop
guppy
gurgle
gusto
Guthrie
____
____
____
____
____
____
____
____
____
____

G /g/ Initial—three syllables

gadabout
gaiety
Galena
Galilee
gallery
galvanize
Galveston
game tokens
gardener
garden hose
gardenia
gardening
gasoline
gas station
gathering
Gaza Strip
gazebo
getaway
Gettysburg
Gideon
goal keeper
godfather
golden age
goldenrod
golden years
gooseberry
gorilla
government
governor
guarantee
guardian
Guiana
guinea fowl
guinea hen
guinea pig
gurgitate
____
____
____

G /g/ Medial—two syllables

again
against
agape
agate
agaze
aghast
Agnes
auger
August
bagful
baggage
bagman
bagpipe
began
beget
beggar
begging
begin
begone
begot
beguile
begun
bigger
biggest
bighead
bighorn
bigot
bogus
braggart
bragging
brigade
buggy
bygone
chigger
chugging
cognate
cognize
cougar
Dagan
dagger
digger
digging
disgorge
disguise
disgust
dogcart
dogear
dogfight
dogfish
dogged
doggy
dogie
dogma
dog sled
dog tag
dragging
dragnet
dragon
dragoon
drugstore
dugout
eager
Edgar
eggnog
eggplant
eggshell
ego
engage
engulf

figure
flagman
flagship
flagstone
foggy
foghorn
fragment
frigate
headgear
hogshead
Hugo
ignite
ignore
ingot
jagged
jigger
jiggle
jigsaw
jogging
juggle
lagger
lagging
lagoon
leaguer
legal
leghorn
Logan
logger
logging

logo
log on
luggage
lugger
magnet
magpie
meager
misguide
muggy
nagging
nosegay
nugget
pagan
piggy
pigment
pignut
pigpen
pigskin
pigtail
quagmire
ragman
ragtime
Reagan
regain
regale
regard
regards
rigor
roguish

rugger
saga
sea gull
segment
shaggy
signal
soggy
stagger
stagnant
sugar
swagger
swaggered
tiger
toga
tollgate
trigger
triggered
tugboat
vagus
vigor
wagging
wagon
Yoga
yogi
Yogi
zygote
____
____
____

G /g/ Medial—three syllables

Abigail
Agatha
agonize
agony
arrogance
beginning
begonia
billy goat

bowlegged
bugaboo
Carnegie
castigate
category
chuck wagon
clogginess
cognizance

conjugate
corrugate
demigod
diagnose
dignify
dignity
disgusted
disregard

dogmatic
doll buggy
eagerly
egotist
elegance
fatiguing
four-legged
gigantic
hexagon
hobgoblin
ignorance
ignorant
illegal
instigate
legacy
legally
legation
ligament
lumbago
magazines
magnify
magnolia
marigold
megaphone
misgiving
misgivings
misgovern
Mother Goose
navigate
negative
New Guinea
Niagara
Oregon
outgoing
outrigger
pagoda
pentagon
pigheaded
pogo stick
Portugal
prodigal
prognosis
recognize
regalia
regardless
regatta
regular
regulate
renegade
rigorous
seagoing
self-regard
signature
signify
spaghetti
Sugar Land
synagogue
Thanksgiving
tiger-eye
tiger moth
toboggan
together
two-legged
unguarded
unguided
untangled
vagabond
vigorous
vinegar
whirligig
woolgather
____
____
____
____

G /g/ Medial—four syllables

allegation
alligator
altogether
antagonist
antagonize
baby buggy
beginner's luck
coagulate
Copenhagen
delegation
derogative
egotism
enigmatic
esophagus
Gulf of Guinea
illegally
investigate
legality
magnificent
mahogany
merry-go-round
monogamous
navigation
navigator
negotiate
obligation
polygamous
prolongation
propaganda
protagonist
regality
significance
significant
tiger beetle
tiger lily
togetherness

unregarded
video game
vinegary

G /g/ Medial—five syllables

egomania
egotistical
ingurgitation

G /g/ Final—one syllable

bag
beg
big
bog
brag
brig
brogue
bug
clog
cog
crag
Craig
dig
dog
Doug
drag
dug
egg
fig
flag
flog
fog
frog
fugue
gag
gig
Greg
hag
hog
hug
jag
jig
jog
jug
keg
lag
league
leg
log
lug
Mag
Meg
mug
nag
peg
Peg
pig
plague
plug
prig
rag
rig
rogue
rug
sag
shag
shrug
slug
smog
smug
snag
snug
sprig
stag
swag
swig
tag
thug
trig
tug
twig
vague
vogue
wag
Whig
wig
yegg

G /g/ Final—two syllables

agog
bean-bag
bear hug
bedbug
bigwig
bird dog
bowleg
brown bag
bulldog

clothes bag
colleague
dog tag
eggnog
fatigue
game bag
ground fog
groundhog
guide dog
hand bag
hedgehog
hot dog
humbug
ice bag
ice fog
intrigue
jet lag
June bug
lunch bag
nutmeg
prologue
ragtag
renege
sand bag
sand bug
shag rug
shindig
shoe bag
sled dog
spark plug
tea bag
The Hague
time-lag
trash bag
unclog
washrag
wigwag
zigzag

G /g/ Final—three syllables

analog
bunny hug
carpetbag
catalog
chili dog
deviled egg
dialogue
ditty bag
doodlebug
duffel bag
garbage bag
guinea pig
jitterbug
ladybug
laundry bag
lightning bug
litter bag
litterbug
moneybag
monologue
paper bag
Persian rug
plastic bag
polliwog
prairie dog
punching bag
sandwich bag
shopping bag
shoulder bag
sleeping bag
synagogue
travelogue
underdog
vacuum bag
water bag
water bug
water dog
waterlog
whirligig
Winnipeg

G /g/ Final—four syllables

card catalog
carry-on bag
desk catalog
gift catalog
potato bug
prescription drug
seeing-eye dog
traveling bag

GER /gɚ/ Medial—three syllables

rigorous
vigorous

GER /gɚ/ Final—two syllables

beggar	jigger	rigor
bigger	lager	stagger
chigger	leaguer	tiger
cougar	logger	vigor
dagger	lugger	________
eager	meager	________

GER /gɚ/ Final—three syllables

cheeseburger	Limburger	vinegar
hamburger	outrigger	________

NGER /ŋɚ/ Medial—three syllables

fingerling	fingerprint	lingering
fingernail	fingerspell	________

NGER /ŋɚ/ Final—two syllables

finger	longer	wringer
hanger	ringer	younger
hunger	singer	________
linger	swinger	________

GL /gl/ Initial—one syllable

glad	glean	gloss
glade	gleaned	glove
glance	glee	gloves
glanced	glen	glow
gland	Glenn	glue
glare	glib	glued
glared	glide	glum
glass	glimpse	glume
glaze	gloat	________
glazed	globe	________
gleam	gloom	________

GL /gl/ Initial—two syllables

glacier	glad rags	glancing
gladden	Gladys	glaring
gladness	glamor	glary

glasses
glasshouse
glassine
glassware
glasswork
glassy
glazement
glazier
glazing
gleaning
glee club
gleeful
Glenda
Glendale
glided
glide plane
glider
gliding
glimmer
glisten
glitter
gloaming
global
globate
gloomy
glory
glossy
glottis
Glover
glowing
glowworm
glucose
gluing
gluten
glutton
____

GL /gl/ Initial—three syllables

glamorize
glamorous
glandular
glass blower
glass blowing
glass cutter
glaucoma
gleefully
glimmering
glistening
glitter ice
glittery
globe-trotter
glomerate
gloomier
Gloria
glorify
glorious
glossary
glossier
glycerin
glyptodont
____
____

GL /gl/ Initial—four syllables

gladiator
gladiola
glamorously
Gloriana
glorifier
gloriously
glossology
____
____

GL /gl/ Medial—two syllables

aglow
boggling
bugler
Douglas
dress gloves
eaglet
eagling
eyeglass
giggler
giggling
giggly
haggling
hourglass
igloo
joggling
juggler
juggling
lymph gland
neglect
piglet
scrub gloves
spyglass
straggling
sunglow
unglue
unglued
wineglass
work gloves
wriggler
wriggly

GL /gl/ Medial—three syllables

aglimmer
aglitter
baseball glove
boondoggler
boxing glove
dark glasses
everglade
Everglades
eyeglasses
fiberglass
field glasses
leather gloves
looking glass
neglectful
negligence
negligent
plastic glass
rubber gloves
semi-glaze
semi-glazed
semi-gloss
sunglasses
water glass
window glass
______
______
______.

GL /gl/ Final—two syllables

beagle
bugle
eagle
gargle
giggle
gurgle
haggle
jiggle
joggle
juggle
legal
regal
smuggle
snuggle
straggle
struggle
waggle
wiggle
wriggle
______
______

GL /gl/ Final—three syllables

bedraggle
boondoggle
illegal
Portugal
prodigal
salt bagel

NGL /ŋl/ Medial—two syllables

angler
angling
Anglo
England
English
jingler
jingling
jungly
mingling
wrangler
wrangling
______

NGL /ŋl/ Medial—three syllables

Anglican
anglicize
anglify
drinking glass
Englander
Englisher
English horn
Englishman
New England

NGL /ŋl/ Final—two syllables

angle
dangle
dingle
jangle
jingle
jungle
mingle
shingle
single

spangle
tangle
tingle
wrangle

NGL /ŋl/ Final—three syllables

commingle
entangle
Kris Kringle
left angle
quadrangle
rectangle
right angle
triangle
untangle

NGTH /ŋθ/ Medial—two syllables

lengthen
lengthways
lengthwise
lengthy
strengthen

NGTH /ŋθ/ Final—one syllable

length
strength

NGTH /ŋθ/ Final—two syllables

full-length
half-length
wave-length
whole-length

GR /gr/ Initial—one syllable

grab
grace
Grace
grade
grades
graft
grain
gram
grand
grange
grant
Grant
grape
grapes
graph
grasp
grass
grate
grave
gray
graze
grease
great
Greece
green
greet
Greg
grew
grey
grid
grief
grieve
grill
grilled
grim
grime
grin
grind
grip
gripe
grit
groan
groom
groomed
groove
grooved
grope
gross

grouch
ground
grounds
group
grouse
grove
grow
growl
grown
growth
grub
grudge
gruff
grump
grunt
____
____
____

GR /gr/ Initial—two syllables

grabbing
graceful
gracious
grackle
grader
grade school
grading
grafting
Graham
grammar
grandad
grandeur
grandma
grandniece
grandpa
Grand Prix
grand slam
grandson
grandstand
grand tour
granite
grantee
grantor
granule
grapefruit
grapevine
graphic
graphite
grasping
grassland
grass snake
grassy
grateful
grating
gravel
graveyard
gravy
grazing
greasing
greasy
Great Dane
greater
greatest
Great Falls
Great Lakes
greatly
greedy
greenbacks
greenhouse
greeting
greetings
gremlin
Greta
Gretchen
greyhound
griddle
Griffin
Griffith
grillwork
grimace
grimy
grinder
grinding
grindstone
grinning
griping
gripping
gristle
gritty
grizzle
grizzled
grizzly
grocer
groggy
grooming
groomsman
grooving
groovy
groping
grotesque
grotto
grouchy
ground crew
grounder
ground floor
ground fog
groundhog
ground rules
ground wave
groundwire
groundwork
Grover
growing

grown-up
grubby
gruesome
grumble
grumpy
Grundy
grunion
____
____

GR /gr/ Initial—three syllables

gracias
graciously
gradual
graduate
granary
Grandberry
Grand Canyon
grandchildren
granddaughter
grandfather
grandiose
grand jury
grandmother
grandnephew
grandparents
granny knot
granulate
grasshopper
gratify
gratitude
gravity
Great Britain
Great Divide
Gregory
gridiron
Griselda
grizzly bear
groceries
grocery
ground cover
Ground Hog Day
grounds keeper
ground squirrel
ground zero
grueling
____
____
____
____

GR /gr/ Initial—four syllables

gradually
graduation
graduator
grammarian
grammatical
grandfather clock
Grand Old Party
grand piano
Granite City
graphology
gratifying
gratuitous
gravitation
great-grandparent
gregarious
grotesquerie
group therapy
____

GR /gr/ Medial—two syllables

aggrieve
aggrieved
agree
agreed
aground
angry
background
begrudge
bluegrass
blue-green
bridegroom
congress
degrade
degree
digress
disgrace
downgrade
egress
egret
engrave
engross
fairground
flagrant
foreground
fragrance
fragrant
hungry
ingrain
Ingram
ingrate
Ingrid
ingroup
land grant

migrate
mongrel
outgrow
outgrowth
Pilgrim
program
progress
regrade
regress
regret
regroup
school ground
tigress
upgrade
vagrant
____
____
____

GR /gr/ Medial—three syllables

aggregate
aggression
aggressive
agreement
allegro
anagram
au gratin
autograph
cablegram
centigrade
centigram
citrus grove
concord grapes
congregate
congressman
congruent
congruous
diagram
dictograph
disagree
disgraceful
disgruntle
emigrant
evergreen
Evergreen
filigree
homograph
immigrant
immigrate
ingrowing
integrate
kilogram
lettergram
Mardi Gras
migration
milligram
monogram
overgrown
overgrowth
paragraph
pedigree
phonograph
photograph
regression
Rio Grande
segregate
seismograph
study group
telegram
telegraph
underground
undergrown
undergrowth
ungraceful
ungracious
ungrateful
upgrading
vagrancy
wintergreen
____
____
____
____

GR /gr/ Medial—four syllables

aggravation
agriculture
allegretto
audiogram
biographer
biographic
biography
calligrapher
coffee grinder
conflagration
congratulate
congregation
congressional
congruity
disagreement
disintegrate
federal grant
geography
incongruent
incongruous
ingratiate
ingratitude
ingredient
integration

integrative
integrity
mimeograph
organ grinder
photographer
photography
regretfully
regrettable
retrogression
segregated
segregation
stenographer
subaggregate
subgranular
technography
telegrammic
telegrapher
telegraphic
telegraphy
tympanogram
typographer
typography
undergrading
ungraciously
ungrantable
ungraspable
____

GR /gr/ Medial—five syllables

agricultural
bibliography
biographical
diagrammatic
disagreeable
disintegrated
disintegration
geographical
incongruity
ingratiating
ingratiation
oceanographer
oceanographic
oceanography
topographical
undergraduate
ungrammatical
____

RG /rg/ Medial—two syllables

argue
bargain
Bergen
cargo
ergo
forget
forgive
forgot
gargle
gurgle
jargon
Largo
Morgan
mortgage
organ
sorghum
stargaze
target
tour guide
Virgo
____

RG /rg/ Medial—three syllables

argument
burgundy
cheeseburger
embargo
forgetful
forgetting
forgiven
forgiveness
forgotten
hamburger
Limburger
Margaret
organdy
organic
organize
pipe organ
undergo
____

RG /rg/ Medial—four syllables

burgomaster
disorganize
forget-me-not
forgettable
forgivable
kindergarten
organ grinder
organism
organizer

undergarment	________	________
unforgiven	________	________

RG /rg/ Medial—five syllables

organization	________	________
unforgettable	________	________

RG /rg/ Final—one syllable

berg	erg	________
burg	morgue	________

RG /rg/ Final—two syllables

Clarksburg	Lordsburg	Salzburg
Goldberg	Newberg	Strasbourg
Hamburg	Oldsberg	Strindberg
iceberg	Pittsburgh	Tilburg
Lemberg	Romberg	Youngberg
Lindberg	Roseburg	________

RG /rg/ Final—three syllables

Brandenburg	Hindenburg	Regensburg
Cederberg	Luxembourg	Reichenberg
Edinburg	Oldenburg	Rosenburg
Gettysburg	Petersburg	Swedenborg
Heidelberg	Phillipsburg	Williamsburg

RG /rg/ Final—four syllables

East Harrisburg	________	________
Johannesburg	________	________

GW /gw/ Initial—one syllable

Guam	Guelph	Gwin
guan	Guinn	Gwyn
guar	Gwen	________

GW /gw/ Initial—two syllables

guaco	guanine	Gwenda
guana	guano	________
guanay	guava	________

GW /gw/ Initial—three syllables

guacharo	Guayama	Guinevere
guanaco	guayule	Gwendolyn
Guarani	Guenevere	________

GW /gw/ Initial—four syllables

guacamole	Guadalupe	________
Guadalcanal	Guantanamo	________
Guadalquivir	Guatemala	________

GW /gw/ Initial—five syllables

guacamole dip	Guadalupe Palm	________
Guadalajara	Guantanamo Bay	________

GW /gw/ Medial—two syllables

agua	languet	sanguine
aguar	languid	ungual
anguine	languish	unguent
anguish	lingua	unguis
anguished	lingual	wigwag
dogwood	linguist	wigwam
hogwash	penguin	________
jaguar	pinguid	________
language	ragweed	________

GW /gw/ Medial—three syllables

alguazil	language arts	tagua nut
alguien	language cards	teguexin
bilingual	languages	unguical
distinguish	languishing	________
extinguish	languishment	________
iguana	linguiform	________
inguinal	linguistics	________
La Guaira	sign language	________

GW /gw/ Medial—four syllables

Aguadilla	La Guardia	sanguineous
Agua Fria	language patterns	unguentary
extinguisher	language workbook	________

GY /gj/ Medial—two syllables

egg yolk	figured	________
figure	figures	________

GY /gj/ Medial—three syllables

figure eight	figure out	regular
figure-ground	figure skate	regulate
figurehead	figuring	transfigured

GY /gj/ Medial—four syllables

father figure	regulated	triangular
figure skating	regulating	________
regularly	regulation	________

GZ /gz/ Medial—two syllables

exact	exert	exist
exalt	exhaust	exult
exam	exhort	zigzag
exempt	exile	________

GZ /gz/ Medial—three syllables

eczema	exemption	exhibit
exacting	exertion	existence
exaction	exertive	existent
exactly	exhaustion	exotic
examine	exhaustive	exultant
example	exhaustless	________

GZ /gz/ Medial—four syllables

exactitude	exemplify	exorbitance
exaggerate	exemptible	exorbitant
examinant	exhaustible	exordium
examinate	exhibitive	exuberance
examinee	exhibitor	exuberant
exasperate	exhilarant	exuberate
executant	exhilarate	exultancy
executive	exhortation	exultation
executrix	existential	________
exemplary	exonerate	________

GZ /gz/ Medial—five syllables

exaggeration
exaggerative
exaggerator
examinable
examination
exasperation
executory
exercitation
exhibitory
exhilaration
exhilarative
exoneration
exonerator
exorbitancy
exotically
exuberancy
____
____

GZ /gz/ Final—one syllable

bags
begs
bogs
bugs
cogs
digs
dogs
eggs
gags
hogs
hugs
jigs
jogs
kegs
lags
legs
logs
lugs
mugs
nags
pegs
pigs
rags
rigs
rogues
rugs
sags
tags
togs
tugs
wags
wigs
____
____
____
____

H

Pronounced: /h/
Spelled: h, wh, g, j

H /h/ Initial—one syllable

hack
Hack
had
hail
hair
Hal
half
hall
halt
ham
hand
hang
Hank
Hans
hard
hare
harp
harsh
has
hash
haste
hat
hatch
haul
haunt
have
hawk
hay
Hayes
haze
he
head
health
heap
hear
hearse
heart
heat
heath
heave
heel
heels
height
heist
helm
help
hem
hemp
hen
hence
her
Herb
herd
here
hers
hi
hid
hide
high
hike
hill
him
hind
hinge
hint
hip
his
hiss
hit
hitch
hive
ho
hoard
hoarse
hoax
hob
hock
hoe
hog
hoist
hold
hole
home
hone
honk
hood
hoof
hook
hoop
hoot

hop
hope
horn
horse
hose
host
hot
hound
house
how
Hoyle
hub
huff
hug
hulk
Hulk
hull
hum
hump
hunch
hung
hunt
hurl
hurt
hush
husk
hut
hutch
hymn
who
whole
who'll
whom
whose
____
____

H /h/ Initial—two syllables

habit
hacksaw
haddock
hailstone
hailstorm
hair-do
Haiti
halfback
half-hour
half time
halfway
hallway
halter
hammer
hammock
hamper
hamster
handbag
handball
handknit
handlace
handle
handsaw
handset
handshake
hanger
hanker
Hannah
hapless
happy
harangue
hardback
hard hats
hardhead
Harding
hardwood
Harlem
Harlen
Harley
harmful
harness
Harold
harpoon
harried
Harris
Harry
Harvard
Harvey
hassock
hatbox
hatchet
Hattie
haughty
hausfrau
havoc
hayrack
hayride
haystack
hazard
Hazel
headache
headboard
headlight
headset
health farm
health food
healthy
hearing
heartburn
heartsick
heat rash
heathen
heather
Heather
heatstroke

heatwave
Hebrew
heckle
hedge hog
hedgehop
Hedy
heedful
Heidi
heifer
heighten
heinous
Helen
Helga
hello
Helma
helmet
helping
hemlock
henna
Henry
Herbert
Herman
hermit
heron
herself
Hester
Hibbing
hidden
hiding
hi-fi
high jump
high rise
high school
high tide
high time
highway
hiker
Hilda
hillside
hilltop
hilly
Hilton
himself
Hindu
hippo
Hiram
hitchhike
hoary
hobby
hockey
hodgepodge
hoeing
hogan
Holland
hollow
holly
Holly
holster
holy
homeland
homely
homemade
homer
Homer
homeroom
home run
homespun
homework
honey
Hong Kong
hoodwink
hoofer
hookup
Hopi
hopping
hopscotch
Horace
hornet
horrid
horseback
horseshoe
hot bath
hot dog
hotel
hot rod
Hot Springs
housetop
housewife
housing
Houston
hovel
hover
Howard
howling
humble
hummock
Humphrey
hundred
hungry
Huntsville
hurdle
hurrah
hurry
hydrant
hygiene
hymnal
hymnbook
hyper
hyphen
hypo
Jai Alai
Jose
whole wheat
wholesale
wholesome
who's who

____

H /h/ Initial—three syllables

Gila Bend
habitat
hair dryer
hairdresser
half-and-half
half brother
half-dollars
halibut
Hall of Fame
Halloween
hamburger
handicap
handicraft
handiwork
handkerchief
handlebar
handwriting
Hanukkah
haphazard
happiness
harbinger
hardscrabble
Harlingen
harmonize
harmony
harpsichord
Harriet
Harrison
Hawaii
Hawaiian
hearing aid
heating pad
heavyweight
helium
hemisphere
herbicide
hermitage
heroic
Hidalgo
high jumper
high water
Hilary
Hildegard
hippogriff
history
hitch hiker
hobby horse
hockey skate
hockey stick
holiday
holiness
hollyhock
Hollywood
homecoming
homemaker
Honduras
honeybee
honeycomb
honeydew
Hoover Dam
horizon
horned lizard
horseradish
hospital
housemother
Hovercraft
however
Hudson Bay
hula-hoop
hula skirt
humdinger
hummingbird
hurricane
hyacinth
hydrogen
hydroplane
hyena
hypnosis
hypnotic
hypnotize
hypocrite
Julio
whodunit
whoever
wholehearted
____
____
____
____
____

H /h/ Initial—four syllables

gila monster
habberdasher
hallelujah
harmonica
hearing-impaired
helicopter
hepatitis
heredity
historian
historical
histrionic
Honolulu
horticulture
hot-air balloon
hydrometer
hyperfunction
hypergolic
hypocrisy

hypodermic	hypothermal	________________
hypolithic	hypothesis	________________
hypotenuse	hypothesize	________________

H /h/ Initial—five syllables

hemophilia	hippopotamus	hydrotherapy
hermetically	hooliganism	hypochondriac
herpetology	hydrodynamics	________________

H /h/ Medial—two syllables

aha	fire hat	porthole
ahead	fishhook	pothole
ahem	Fordham	redhead
ahoy	forehand	rehash
Amherst	forehead	rehear
Baja	greenhouse	rehearse
beehive	groundhog	reheat
behave	hedgehop	roundhouse
behind	heigh-ho	sandhog
behold	high heels	Sandhurst
behoove	hitchhike	sea horse
bellhop	inhale	treehouse
birdhouse	keyhole	unhook
blackhead	lighthouse	uphill
blockhouse	manhole	wahoo
boohoo	manhunt	White House
chuckhole	mayhem	yahoo
cohort	mishap	yoo-hoo
cowhide	mohair	________________
doghouse	O'Hare	________________
doll house	one-half	________________
downhill	packhorse	________________
eyehole	playhouse	________________

H /h/ Medial—three syllables

abhorrent	beholden	clothes hanger
Abraham	buttonhole	cohesion
anyhow	Captain Hook	cubbyhole
behavior	city hall	dehydrate

Elihu	Ohio	rocking horse
grasshopper	overhaul	sand hopper
hobby horse	Pearl Harbor	study hall
hula hoop	pigeonhole	tomahawk
inhaler	porterhouse	unhappy
inherent	potholder	unholy
inherit	rehearsal	unwholesome
inhibit	rehearsing	____________
O'Hara	Robin Hood	____________

H /h/ Medial—four syllables

aircraft hangar	inhibition	safety helmet
Beverly Hills	inhibitor	____________
exhalation	Irish wolfhound	____________
inhalation	mahogany	____________
inharmonic	Red Riding Hood	____________

J

Pronounced: /dʒ/
Spelled: ch, d, dg, dge, di, g, gg, j

J /dʒ/ Initial—one syllable

gee
gel
gem
gene
Gene
gent
George
germ
gibe
gin
gist
gym
gyp
jab
jabbed
jack
Jack
jacks
jade
jag
Jake
jam
jamb
James
jammed
Jan
Jane
jar
jarred
jaunt
jaw
jaws
jay
Jay
Jayne
jazz
Jean
Jeanne
jeans
jeep
jeer
jeers
Jeff
jell
jerk
jerked
Jess
jest
jet
Jew
jib
jibe
jibed
jig
jigged
Jill
jilt
Jim
jinx
Jo
Joan
job
Job
jock
Jock
Joe
jog
jogged
John
join
joist
joke
jolt
Jon
Josh
jot
jounce
jounced
joust
Jove
jowl
joy
Joy
Joyce
Judd
Jude
judge
judged
jug
juice

jump	junked	____________
jumped	just	____________
June	jut	____________
junk	jute	____________

J /dʒ/ Initial—two syllables

gender	jackstraw	Jerri
genie	Jacob	Jerry
genius	jagged	Jersey
gentle	jaguar	Jesse
genus	jailbird	Jessie
Georgette	Jamestown	jester
Georgia	Jamie	Jesus
Gerald	Janet	Jethro
gerbil	jangle	jetsam
German	jangled	jet set
Germane	Janice	jetty
gerund	Japan	jewel
gesture	jargon	jiffy
giant	Jarvis	jigger
giblet	jasmine	jiggle
Gina	Jason	jigsaw
ginger	jasper	jimmied
Ginger	Jasper	jimmy
ginseng	jaundice	Jimmy
giraffe	jaundiced	jitney
gymnast	javelin	jittered
gypsum	jawbone	jitters
gypsy	Jaycees	Joanne
gyrate	jayhawk	jockey
jabber	jaywalk	Joel
jackal	jealous	joggle
jacket	Jeanine	joggled
Jack Frost	Jeffrey	Johnson
Jackie	jellied	Joline
jackknife	jelly	jolly
jackknifed	Jenny	Joseph
jackpot	Jensen	jostle
Jackson	Jerome	jostled

journal
journey
joyful
joyous
joyride
Judah
judgment
Judith
Judson
Judy
juggle
juggled
juggler
juicy
Julia
Julian
Julie
Julius
jumble
jumbled
jumbo
jumper
junction
juncture
Juneau
June bug
jungle
junior
junket
junk food
Juno
jurist
juror
jury
justice
Justin

J /dʒ/ Initial—three syllables

gelatin
Gemini
general
generate
generous
genetic
Geneva
Genevieve
genial
gentleman
genuine
Geraldine
Germany
germicide
germinate
giant crab
gigantic
gingerbread
gymnastics
jackrabbit
Jacksonville
Jacqueline
jalopy
jamboree
janitor
Japanese
Jasper Park
jawbreaker
jazzercise
jealousy
Jefferson
jellybeans
jellyfish
Jennifer
Jeopardy
Jessica
jettison
jitterbug
Johanna
Johnny Reb
Jonathan
Josephine
Joshua
journalist
jovial
jubilance
jubilee
judicial
jugular
jujitsu
julienne
Juliet
juniper
jury room
justified
justify
juvenile
juxtapose

J /dʒ/ Initial—four syllables

generalize
generally
generation
geography
geologist
geology
geometry
gesticulate
giant slalom
gigantism
gingerbread man
gymnasium
jack-in-the-box
jack-o'-lantern
javelin throw
Jerusalem
joshua tree
journalism
jubilation
junior college
junior high school
jurisdiction
jurisprudence
jurisprudent
jury duty
justifying
juvenescence
juvenescent
juxtaposing
____
____
____
____

J /dʒ/ Medial—two syllables

adjoin
adjoined
adjourn
adjunct
adjust
ageless
agent
age-old
agile
aging
ajar
badger
badgered
blue jay
Bridget
bridgework
budget
bulges
bulging
cages
codger
cogent
cudgel
deject
digest
digit
disjoin
disjoined
disjoint
dodge ball
dodger
Dodgers
dodging
dredger
edges
edgewise
Edgewood
Egypt
eject
Eugene
fidget
fledgling
fragile
frigid
fudging
gadget
hedgehog
hedgehop
hedges
high jump
hodgepodge
judges
judging
judgment
ledger
legend
legion
lodger
lodging
logic
magic
major
midget
misjudge
object
pageant
page boy
pages
pigeon
pledger
pledging
prejudge
prejudged
project
pudgy

rajah
regent
region
reject
rejoice
rejoiced
rejoin
rejudge
ridgepole
rigid
Roger
snow job
sojourn
soldier
squeegee
stagecoach
staging
stodgy
subject
suggest
tragic
urgent
vigil
wage scale
wager
wages
____

J /dʒ/ Medial—three syllables

adages
adjutant
agency
agitate
algebra
allegiance
arranges
astringent
bandaging
bluejacket
cabbages
cogitate
collegian
collegiate
cottage cheese
cotton gin
courageous
credulous
deluges
digestion
diligence
divulgence
divulges
Dodge City
dowager
drudgery
drum major
educate
effigy
ejection
elegy
engagement
eugenic
eulogize
eulogized
eulogy
fugitive
G.I. Joe
high jumper
high jumping
hydrogen
imagine
imagined
imaging
indigence
indigent
indulgence
indulgent
jumping-jack
legible
logical
longitude
magenta
magical
magician
magistrate
majestic
majesty
majorette
management
manager
meninges
nitrogen
Norwegian
objected
objection
objective
origin
outrageous
oxygen
passageway
pigeonhole
pigeon-toed
plagiarize
plagiarized
procedure
prodigious
prodigy
progeny
projectile
pugilist
refugee
regency
Regency

regiment
regional
register
registered
registrar
rejection
religion
sledge hammer
strategic
strategy
suggestion
teenager
tragedy
vegetate
vigilant
villager
voyager
Voyager
windjammer

J /dʒ/ Medial—four syllables

adjacency
adjudicate
advantageous
Age of Reason
agility
agitation
agitator
algebraic
Algeria
apologize
apologized
astrologer
belligerent
biology
cajolery
cogitation
corrigible
degenerate
digestible
dirigible
education
educator
eligible
encouragement
exaggerate
geology
homogenize
hygienic
illegible
incogitant
incredulous
intelligence
intelligent
legislation
maharaja
majority
maladjusted
Middle Ages
mythology
neurology
original
originate
otology
pathology
pedagogy
photogenic
prejudicial
psychology
pugilistic
refrigerate
regenerate
regimental
registration
rejuvenate
vegetables
vegetation
vigilante
yellow jacket
yellow jasmine
zoology

J /dʒ/ Medial—five syllables

anthropology
apologetic
criminology
etiology
etymology
exaggeration
genealogy
ideology
imagination
incorrigible
indigestible
ineligible
physiology
Sagittarius
sociology
subjectivity

J /dʒ/ Final—one syllable

age
badge
bilge
bridge
budge
bulge
cage
dodge
Dodge
dredge
drudge
edge
fledge
fudge
gauge
grudge
hedge
huge
judge
ledge
lodge
Madge
midge
Midge
nudge
page
pledge
rage
ridge
sage
siege
sledge
sludge
smudge
stage
stooge
trudge
wage
wedge
____
____
____

J /dʒ/ Final—two syllables

abridge
adage
allege
avenge
backstage
baggage
bandage
begrudge
besiege
breakage
Bronze Age
cabbage
Cambridge
carriage
Carthage
cartridge
cleavage
college
Coolidge
cottage
courage
cribbage
damage
deluge
divulge
dosage
drainage
drawbridge
encage
engage
enrage
float bridge
footage
forage
frontage
garbage
herbage
hodgepodge
homage
hostage
Ice Age
image
indulge
knowledge
language
leakage
linkage
luggage
manage
marriage
message
mileage
misjudge
mortgage
oblige
old age
outage
outrage
package
partridge
passage
pillage
plumage
porridge
portage
postage

prejudge
rampage
ravage
refuge
roughage
rummage
salvage
sausage
savage
scrimmage
selvage
silage
South Bridge
spillage
spoilage
steerage
Stone Age
stoppage
storage
stowage
suffrage
teenage
toll bridge
tonnage
trackage
truckage
upstage
usage
vestige
village
vintage
voyage
wastage
wattage
wreckage
yardage
____
____
____

J /dʒ/ Final—three syllables

acknowledge
acreage
advantage
Anchorage
appendage
average
beverage
brokerage
Brooklyn Bridge
cartilage
Copper Age
coverage
discourage
disengage
disoblige
disparage
encourage
envisage
flowerage
foliage
golden age
hemorrhage
heritage
hermitage
horse carriage
Iron Age
leverage
lineage
London Bridge
middle age
mismanage
overage
parsonage
patronage
percentage
personage
pilgrimage
privilege
Rainbow Bridge
self-image
verbiage
____
____
____
____

JER /dʒɚ/ Medial—three syllables

dangerous
ginger ale
gingerbread
gingerly
gingersnap
injury
majorette
____
____

JER /dʒɚ/ Medial—four syllables

belligerent
exaggerate
gingerliness
major-domo
____
____

JER /dʒɚ/ Final—two syllables

badger
danger
dodger
dredger
ginger
Ginger
injure
larger
ledger
lodger
lounger
major
manger
merger
pledger
ranger
Roger
soldier
stranger
wager

JER /dʒɚ/Final—three syllables

avenger
drum major
endanger
Lone Ranger
manager
messenger
passenger
procedure
scavenger
teenager
villager
voyager
Voyager

JER /dʒɚ/Final—four syllables

astrologer
supercharger
train passenger

NJ /ndʒ/ Medial—two syllables

angel
banjo
congeal
congealed
congest
conjure
conjured
danger
dingy
dungeon
engine
enjoin
enjoy
enjoyed
ginger
ingest
inject
injure
injured
lounger
manger
Ninja
pongee
pungent
ranger
rangy
sponges
stranger
tangent
unjust
vengeance
vengeful

NJ /ndʒ/ Medial—three syllables

Angela
angelfish
angelic
Angelus
angina
avenger
Blue Angels
Challenger
challenges
challenging
changeable
congested
congestion
conjecture
conjugal

conjunction
dangerous
endanger
endangered
engendered
engineer
engineered
fire engine
ginger ale
gingerbread
gingerly
gingersnap
ingenious
injected
injection
injunction
injury
injustice
Lone Ranger
messenger
passenger
scavenger
tangerine
tangible
____
____
____

NJ /ndʒ/ Medial—four syllables

conjectural
conjugation
evangelic
evangelist
evangelize
injurious
intangible
meningitis
____

NJ /ndʒ/ Medial—five syllables

evangelical
ingenuity
laryngectomy
____
____
____

NJ /ndʒ/ Final—one syllable

change
flange
fringe
grange
hinge
lounge
lunge
mange
plunge
range
scrounge
singe
sponge
strange
tinge
twinge
____
____

NJ /ndʒ/ Final—two syllables

arrange
astringe
avenge
challenge
derange
downrange
estrange
exchange
expunge
impinge
lozenge
orange
revenge
scavenge
unhinge
____
____
____

NJ /ndʒ/ Final—three syllables

counter change
disarrange
interchange
prearrange
rearrange
____
____
____
____

RJ /rdʒ/ Medial—two syllables

bargeman	Georgia	perjured
barges	gorgeous	sergeant
charge card	largely	splurging
charger	larger	sturgeon
Chargers	largest	surgeon
charging	Margie	turgid
clergy	margin	urgent
cordial	Margy	Virgil
forger	merger	__________
forging	merging	__________
Georgetown	perjure	__________

RJ /rdʒ/ Medial—three syllables

allergic	energy	overjoy
allergy	enlargement	overjoyed
chargeable	enlarger	perjury
clergyman	forgery	recharger
convergence	insurgent	recharging
converges	lethargic	surgery
crackerjacks	lethargy	surgical
detergent	lumberjack	urgency
discharges	margarine	Virginia
divergent	Margery	__________
emergent	marginal	__________
energize	Marjorie	__________

RJ /rdʒ/ Medial—four syllables

Argentina	reenlargement	Virgin Islands
emergency	supercharger	Virgin Mary
energetic	superjacent	West Virginia

RJ /rdʒ/ Final—one syllable

barge	gurge	serge
charge	large	splurge
dirge	Marge	surge
forge	merge	urge
George	purge	verge
gorge	scourge	__________

RJ /rdʒ/ Final—two syllables

converge
discharge
diverge
emerge
engorge
enlarge
recharge
submerge
surcharge
upsurge
____
____

K

Pronounced: /k/
Spelled: c, cc, cch, ch, ck, cq, cque, cu, k, qu

K /k/ Initial—one syllable

cab
cache
cached
cad
cage
caged
Cain
cake
Cal
calf
call
called
calm
calmed
calves
cam
came
camp
camped
can
can't
cane
canned
cans
cap
cape
capped
car
card
care
cared
cart
carve
carved
case
cased
cash
cashed
cask
cast
cat
catch
caught
caulk
cause
caused
cave
caved
caw
cawed
cay
chord
coach
coached
coal
coarse
coast
coat
coax
coaxed
cob
cod
code
cog
coil
coin
coined
cold
colt
comb
combed
come
con
cone
coo
cooed
cook
cooked
cool
cooled
coop
coot
cop
cope
cord
cords
core
cored
cork
corn

corps
cost
cot
cote
couch
cough
coughed
could
count
coup
course
coursed
court
couth
cove
cow
cowl
Cox
coy
Coy
cub
cud
cuff
cuffed
cull
culm
cult
cup
cupped
cur
curb
curbed
curd
curl
curled
curt
Curt
curve
curved
cusp
cut
kale
Kay
keel
keeled
keen
keep
keg
kelp
kempt
Ken
Kent
kept
ketch
key
kick
kicked
kid
kids
kiln
kilt
Kim
kin
kind
king
King
kiss
kissed
kit
kite
Kurt
Kyle
____
____
____

K /k/ Initial—two syllables

cabbage
cabby
cabin
cable
cabled
caboose
cackle
cackled
cactus
caddie
caddied
cadet
cafe
caffeine
Caleb
calla
calling
callous
Calvin
cambric
Cambridge
camel
camp-out
camp stove
campaign
campaigned
camper
campfire
campground
camphor
campsite
campus
canal
cancel
canceled
cancer

Cancer
Candace
candid
Candide
candle
candy
Candy
canine
caning
canker
cankered
canning
cannot
canny
canoe
canon
canteen
canter
cantle
Canton
cantor
canvas
canvassed
canyon
Cape Cod
caper
capon
caprice
capsize
capsized
capsule
capsuled
captain
captive
capture
captured
carat
carbide
carbon
cardboard
careen
careened
career
carefree
careful
careless
Carey
carfare
cargo
caring
Carla
carload
Carmel
Carmen
carob
Carol
carpet
carriage
Carrie
carried
carrot
carry
Carter
carton
cartoon
cartridge
cascade
Casey
cashew
cashier
cashiered
cashmere
Casper
cassette
Cassie
caster
castle
castoff
catcher
catch-up
cater
catered
Cathy
cattle
catwalk
caucus
caudle
cauldron
caution
cautioned
cavern
cavort
cayenne
chaos
chorus
Coast Guard
cobalt
cobble
cobbled
cobbler
cobra
cobweb
cockpit
cockroach
cocksure
cocktail
cocky
cocoa
coddle
coddled
codfish
Cody
coed
coerce
coerced
coffee
cohort

coinage
coin box
cola
cold cuts
colder
cold front
cold pack
cold snap
cold wave
colic
collage
collar
collared
collate
collect
Colleen
college
Collette
collide
collie
cologne
Cologne
colon
colonel
color
colored
column
coma
combine
combined
combo
combust
comeback
comet
comfort
comic
coming
comma
command
commence
commenced
commend
comment
commerce
commit
common
compact
compare
compared
compass
compel
compelled
compete
compile
compiled
complain
complained
complete
complex
complied
comply
compose
composed
compound
comrade
concave
conceal
concealed
conceit
conceive
conceived
concept
concern
concerned
concert
concise
Concord
concrete
concur
concurred
condemn
condemned
condense
condensed
condole
condone
condor
conduce
conduct
condyle
cone shell
coney
confab
confect
confer
conferred
confess
confessed
confide
confine
confined
confirm
confirmed
conflict
conform
confound
confront
confuse
confused
congeal
congealed
Congo
Congress
Connie
conquer
Conrad
consent

conserve
conserved
consign
consist
console
consoled
conspire
conspired
Constance
consul
consult
consume
consumed
contact
contacts
contain
contained
contempt
contend
content
contest
contour
contract
contrast
control
controlled
converge
converged
converse
conversed
convert
convex
convey
conveyed
convict
convince
convinced
convoy
convoyed

cookbook
cooker
cookie
cooking
Coolidge
co-op
copied
copper
copy
Cora
coral
cordial
cording
cordless
Corey
Cornell
corner
cornered
cornet
cornfed
cornfield
corn grits
cornhusks
cornmeal
corn oil
corn shock
cornstarch
Cornwall
corny
corral
corralled
correct
corrupt
Cortez
cosmos
costume
costumed
cottage
cotton

cougar
cough drop
council
counseled
counter
countess
country
county
couple
coupled
courage
courthouse
courtly
courtroom
courtyard
cousin
cover
covered
coward
cowbell
cowboy
cower
cowgirl
cowhand
cowhide
cowlick
cowskin
cozy
cuddle
cuddled
culprit
culture
cultured
cumquat
cunning
cupboard
cupful
curfew
curling

currant
current
curried
curry
cursive
cursor
curtail
curtailed
curtain
Curtis
curtsy
cushion
cushioned
cuspid
custard
custom
customs
cutlass
cutlet
cutoff
cutoffs
cutout
cutting
cutup
cutworm
Kaiser
Kansas
Karen
Karl
Karla
Kashmir
kayak
keener
keeping
Kelly
Kenneth
Kenny
Kermit
ketchup
kettle
keyboard
key chain
keyhole
keynote
key punch
key ring
Key West
khaki
kibosh
kickball
kickboard
kicker
kickoff
kickstand
kiddie
kidding
kidskin
killjoy
kinder
kindle
kindled
kindling
kindly
kindness
king crab
kingdom
kismet
kissing
kitchen
kitten
____
____
____
____
____

K /k/ Initial—three syllables

cabinet
cablegram
calendar
caliber
caliche
calico
caloric
calorie
Camelia
cameo
camera
camporee
Canada
canary
candy bar
canister
canopied
canopy
cantaloupe
cantata
capable
capital
capitol
capricious
Capricorn
Captain Hook
caramel
caravan
carbonate
cardiac
cardinal
caretaker
carnation
Carnegie
carnival
carnivore

Caroline
Carolyn
carousel
carpenter
cartilage
casserole
castaway
casual
catalog
catalogued
cataract
cauterize
cauterized
caviar
cavity
chameleon
chaotic
character
chemistry
coconut
collision
collusion
colony
color blind
colorful
color guard
coloring
color wheel
colossal
columbine
Columbus
comedy
commentate
commission
commissioned
committee
companion
company
complexion
complicate
component
composure
computer
concentrate
condition
confession
confessor
confetti
congressman
consensus
consider
considered
consumer
continent
continue
continued
contradict
contrary
contribute
convenient
convention
conveyor
convulsion
convulsive
Copper Age
copperhead
copyright
coral reef
Coral Sea
corduroy
Cornelia
coronet
correction
correspond
corridor
cosmetic
cotton gin
cottonmouth
cottontail
cottonwood
councillor
counselor
counteract
counterfeit
country club
courier
courteous
courtesy
coverage
covering
coyote
cubbyhole
cul-de-sac
culminate
cultivate
cumbersome
curlicue
currency
currently
curvature
custody
customer
cutaway
kangaroo
katydid
kayaking
Kennedy
kennel club
Kentucky
kerosene
kibitzer
kilowatt
kimono
kindhearted
kingfisher
____
____

K /k/ Initial—four syllables

Cambodia
Capistrano
carcinoma
carnivorous
Carolina
catastrophe
category
caterpillar
cauliflower
coagulate
coalition
coincidence
Colorado
Columbia
combination
comedian
commendation
commentator
commiserate
commissioner
community
comparison
confirmation
congratulate
congresswoman
Connecticut
contemptuous
continental
conversation
cooperate
Copenhagen
Costa Rica
customary
kindergarten

K /k/ Initial—five syllables

Caledonia
California
coeducation
coincidental
commiserating
congratulations
conversational
cooperation

K /k/ Medial—two syllables

accord
accost
account
acne
acorn
akin
background
backhand
backslide
backstage
backstroke
backup
bacon
bake-off
baker
baking
beachcomb
beacon
beaker
becalm
becalmed
became
because
Becky
become
bedclothes
bicker
bickered
biking
blackbird
blackboard
blackcap
blacken
blackened
blackhead
blockade
blocker
blockhouse
blocking
bobcat
bookcase
bookmark
bookshelf
boycott
bracket
brackish
brakeman
breakage
breakdown
breaker
breakfast
breaking
breakneck
breakup
briquet
broadcast
brocade

broken
broker
buckboard
bucket
buckeye
Buckeye
buckteeth
buckwheat
bumpkin
checker
checkers
checkup
chicken
Chico
chock-full
cockpit
cocksure
cocoa
cooker
cookie
cooking
cracker
cracking
deacon
decade
decal
decay
decayed
decking
decode
decoy
dicker
dickered
docket
echo
echoed
encage
encaged
encamp
encamped
encase
encased
encore
flicker
flickered
flicking
focus
focused
fruitcake
glucose
go-cart
handcar
handcart
Hawkeye
hawkeyed
hiccup
hiccupped
hockey
hookup
hooky
income
jackal
jacket
jackknife
jackknifed
jockey
kicker
kickoff
knickers
knocker
knocking
knockout
lackey
lacquer
lacquered
lichen
likeness
liking
locate
locket
locking
lockjaw
locust
looker
looking
lookout
low-cost
lucky
lukewarm
maker
makeshift
making
mucous
mukluk
napkin
nickname
nicknamed
Nicky
Nicole
occur
occurred
outcast
package
packaged
packet
packhorse
packing
packsack
peacock
pecan
picket
picking
pickup
placket
pocket
pockmark
pockmarked

poker
poking
poky
procure
procured
pucker
puckered
pumpkin
Quaker
raccoon
racket
racquet
raincoat
raking
recall
recalled
record
recount
recourse
recur
recurred
rickshaw
Ricky
rocker
rocket
rocking
rocky
Rocky
rookie
sackful
seacoast
second
seconds
seeker
seeking
shaker
shaking
shaky
shortcake
sicken
sicker
sidecar
slicker
sneaker
snicker
snickered
soccer
socket
speaker
speaking
stockade
stock car
stocker
Stockholm
stocking
stricken
stucco
sucker
sucking
taco
taken
takeoff
taking
tokens
trucker
trucking
tucker
tuckered
tycoon
unkempt
unkind
vacant
vacate
Viking
vocal
waken
wakened
weaken
weakened
weekend
wicked
wicker
wicket
wildcat
wrecker
____
____

K /k/ Medial—three syllables

abacus
abdicate
acacia
accident
accomplice
accomplish
acknowledge
acknowledged
acolyte
acoustic
acreage
Africa
allocate
applicant
appliqué
appliquéd
apricot
awaken
awakened
backgammon
bakery
barricade
beachcomber
bed cover

bicuspid
bicycle
bookbinder
bookkeeper
breakable
broccoli
brokerage
bronchial
bronchitis
buccaneer
Buchanan
buckaroo
calico
caretaker
checkerboard
Cherokee
chickadee
Chickasaw
chicken coop
chicken feed
chocolate
chokecherry
coconut
complicate
cowcatcher
cucumber
Dakota
decanter
decorate
delicate
difficult
dislocate
Dracula
dressmaker
duplicate
educate
encounter
encountered
encourage
encouraged
encumber
encumbered
epicure
fabricate
factory
fiasco
firecracker
folk dancing
folk music
four-cycle
game tokens
hackamore
handicap
handicapped
handkerchief
Hanukkah
hickory
hockey stick
holocaust
homemaker
honeycomb
housekeeper
hurricane
Jackelyn
Kentucky
licorice
likeable
likelihood
linebacker
location
loudspeaker
lubricate
macaroon
mackerel
mannequin
McKenzie
McKinley
mechanic
medicate
moccasins
mockingbird
neckerchief
nutcracker
occasion
oncoming
pacemaker
pawnbroker
pelican
piccolo
pillowcase
pocket watch
precaution
psychosis
Rebecca
recommend
recover
recovered
ricochet
ricocheted
rookery
salt shaker
secondly
seersucker
shoemaker
silica
snickering
soccer ball
staccato
stomachache
succotash
talkative
teakettle
trachea
tricycle
unlikely
unlucky
vacation

vindicate
vocalize
vocalized
vocation
walking stick
walk over
watchmaker
wickerwork
womankind
woodpecker
Zachary
____

K /k/ Medial—four syllables

a cappella
academy
accommodate
accompany
accordion
accountable
agriculture
America
American
amicable
application
area code
authenticate
baby carriage
basilica
bicarbonate
decalcify
despicable
dictionary
difficulty
domesticate
duplication
economize
economized
economy
education
educator
eradicate
helicopter
hocus-pocus
impeccable
incandescent
incapable
incoherent
incorporate
jack-o'-lantern
locality
locomotive
lubrication
macaroni
mechanism
medicated
medication
melancholy
occasional
parochial
persecution
predicament
psychiatry
recuperate
secondary
semicolon
sukiyaki
terra cotta
ukulele
walking safety
____

K /k/ Medial—five syllables

accommodation
amplification
biochemistry
coeducation
discoloration
disconformity
edification
incalculable
inconsiderate
justification
mechanization
recuperation
____
____
____

K /k/ Final—one syllable

ache
auk
back
bake
balk
beak
beck
bike
black
Blake
bleak
bloc
block
book
brake

break
brick
broke
brook
buck
Buck
cake
caulk
chalk
check
cheek
chick
chock
choke
chuck
Chuck
click
cloak
cluck
cock
cook
creak
creek
croak
crock
deck
Dick
dike
dock
drake
Drake
duck
duke
Duke
eke
fake
flack
flake
fleck
flick
floc
flock
fluke
folk
freak
frock
Greek
hack
Hack
hawk
hike
hock
hook
jack
Jack
Jake
joke
kick
knack
knock
lack
lake
leak
leek
lick
like
lock
look
luck
Luke
Mack
make
meek
Mick
mike
Mike
mock
muck
neck
nick
Nick
nook
oak
pack
peak
peck
peek
pick
pike
pique
plaque
pluck
pock
poke
Polk
puck
quack
quake
quick
rack
rake
reek
Rick
rock
rook
sac
sack
sake
seek
shake
sheik
shock
shook
shriek
shuck
sick
slack

sleek
slick
smack
smock
smoke
snack
snake
sneak
soak
sock
speak
speck
spike
spoke
spook
squawk
squeak
stack
stake
stalk
steak
stick
stock
stoke
streak
strike
stroke
stuck
suck
tack
take
talk
teak
thick
tic
tick
tike
took
track
trek
trick
truck
tuck
tweak
Vic
wake
walk
weak
week
whack
wick
woke
wrack
wreak
wreck
yak
yoke
yolk
Zach
Zeke
____
____
____

K /k/ Final—two syllables

alack
alike
amuck
antic
antique
attack
attic
awake
awoke
backache
backpack
backstroke
backtrack
Bangkok
bareback
basic
bed check
bedeck
bedrock
beefsteak
bike rack
blackjack
black snake
blank check
boardwalk
bookrack
boric
broomstick
cakewalk
cambric
car rack
catwalk
cheese cake
chopstick
clambake
clinic
club steak
cold pack
comeback
cookbook
critic
crosswalk
cubic
cupcake
daybreak
deadlock
derrick
Derrick

dislike
drastic
drumstick
earache
earthquake
egg yolk
epoch
Eric
evoke
fabric
fire truck
fish hook
flapjack
flashback
flour sack
forsake
frantic
frolic
fullback
garlic
graphic
haddock
halfback
hammock
handbook
hand brake
handshake
hardtack
hassock
hayrack
haystack
headache
heartache
hectic
hemlock
hitchhike
homelike
homesick
horseback

humpback
hunchback
ice pack
ice pick
intake
invoke
jaywalk
jet black
joke book
kayak
king snake
kinsfolk
knickknack
lame duck
lampblack
lilac
lipstick
livestock
lunch break
lyric
magic
mandrake
mastic
medic
metric
mistake
Mohawk
mukluk
music
mystique
namesake
nitric
Norfolk
notebook
oblique
o'clock
opaque
outbreak
outlook

outtalk
padlock
panic
passbook
peacock
pet rock
physique
Pikes Peak
plastic
potluck
provoke
public
racetrack
rain check
ransack
rebuke
remake
repack
revoke
round steak
rustic
scrapbook
scrub oak
seasick
shamrock
shellac
shipwreck
sidewalk
slowpoke
small talk
smokestack
snowflake
spring chick
static
stomach
sun deck
sunstroke
sweepstake
technique

thumbtack
ticktock
tie rack
tie tack
toothache
toothpick
topic
townsfolk
traffic
tunic
unhook
unique
unlock
unpack
windbreak
wisecrack
wolf pack
woodchuck
yardstick
zwieback
____
____
____
____

K /k/ Final—three syllables

almanac
artichoke
artistic
athletic
atomic
baby chick
bionic
birthday cake
bivouac
buttonhook
candlestick
candlewick
Captain Hook
cardiac
Catholic
chaotic
chuck-a-luck
coffee break
comic book
cul-de-sac
domestic
fantastic
flutter kick
funny book
galactic
garter snake
gigantic
gunny sack
historic
hockey stick
hognose snake
hollyhock
ladylike
Little Rock
lumberjack
maverick
motorbike
overtake
overtook
Pacific
paperback
piggyback
pogo stick
politic
Pontiac
poppycock
quarterback
railroad track
rattlesnake
republic
sparrow hawk
specific
stomachache
storybook
T-bone steak
terrific
undertake
volcanic
weather cock
wedding cake
womenfolk
____
____
____
____
____

K /k/ Final—four syllables

arithmetic
certified check
chocolate cake
economic
epidemic
hydrologic
hypertonic
hypotonic
magazine rack
mathematic
optimistic
patriotic
South Pacific
supersonic
____

KER /kɚ/ Medial—three syllables

acreage
Anchorage
bakery
brokerage
checkerboard
discourage
handkerchief
licorice
mackerel
neckerchief
rookery
snickering
soccer ball
wickerwork
____

KER /kɚ/ Final—two syllables

acre
anchor
baker
banker
bicker
blocker
breaker
broker
canker
choker
clinker
conquer
cracker
flanker
flicker
hiker
kicker
knocker
locker
looker
poker
Quaker
rocker
seeker
shaker
slicker
sneaker
snicker
soccer
speaker
stocker
sucker
tanker
tucker
wicker
wrecker
____
____
____

KER /kɚ/ Final—three syllables

backpacker
dressmaker
hitch-hiker
homemaker
linebacker
loudspeaker
nutcracker
pact maker
pawnbroker
saltshaker
shoemaker
watchmaker
windbreaker
woodpecker
____

KL /kl/ Initial—one syllable

clack
claim
claimed
Claire
clam
clamp
clan
clang
clap
clapped
Clark
clash
clashed
clasp
clasped
class
Claude
clause
claw
clawed
clay
Clay
clean
cleaned
cleanse
clear
cleared

cleats
clef
cleft
clench
clerk
click
cliff
Cliff
climb
climbed
clinch
cling
Clint
clip
clipped
clique
cloak
cloaked
clock
clocked
clod
clog
clogs
clone
clop
close
closed
clot
cloth
clothe
clothes
cloud
clout
clove
clown
clowned
cloy
cloyed
club
cluck
clue
clued
clump
clumped
clung
clutch
clutched
Clyde
Kline
klutz
____
____
____
____

KL /kl/ Initial—two syllables

chloric
chlorine
clackers
claimant
clambake
clammy
clamor
clamshell
clapping
Clara
Clarence
clarice
classic
classmate
classroom
classy
clatter
clattered
cleanly
cleanup
clearance
clearing
cleaver
clement
Cleo
clergy
Cleveland
clever
cliché
client
Clifford
Clifton
climate
climax
climber
climbing
clincher
clinic
clinker
Clinton
clipboard
clipper
clippers
clipping
clippings
clobber
clockwise
clockwork
closet
close-up
closing
closure
clothespin
clothier
clothing
cloudburst
cloudy

clover
Clovis
clubhouse
club steak
clumsy
cluster
clutter
cluttered
____

KL /kl/ Initial—three syllables

chlorinate
chloroform
clairvoyance
clam chowder
clam digging
clandestine
Clarendon
clarify
clarinet
classical
classified
classify
Claudia
clavichord
clavicle
claviform
cleanliness
cleft palate
clemency
clergyman
clerical
clientele
cliff dweller
climactic
clinical
clinician
clodhopper
cloverleaf
club sandwich
Klamath Falls
____
____
____

KL /kl/ Medial—two syllables

acclaim
acclaimed
anklet
Auckland
backlash
backlog
ball club
Barclay
becloud
blacklist
book club
booklet
Boys' Club
bridge club
broadcloth
brooklet
buckling
cackling
cheesecloth
chuckler
chuckling
conclude
cycling
cyclone
declare
decline
disclose
dishcloth
dry clean
dry cleaned
duckling
dustcloth
eclipse
eclipsed
enclose
exclaim
exclude
fan club
first class
foreclose
foreclosed
Franklin
freckly
Girls' Club
glee club
health club
heckler
incline
inclined
include
knuckler
knuckling
land claim
likely
loin cloth
mukluks
necklace
Oakland
occlude
o'clock
outclass
pickling
preclude

press club
prickling
prickly
proclaim
proclaimed
quick lime
quickly
reclaim
recline
reclined
seclude
sparkler
sparkling
speckling
sprinkler
sprinkling
tackler
ticklish
time clock
trickling
twinkling
weakling
weakly
wreckless
yacht club
____
____
____
____
____

KL /kl/ Medial—three syllables

acclimate
alarm clock
biweekly
bricklayer
Christmas club
country club
dry cleaning
eclectic
ecliptic
enclosure
exclusion
exclusive
foreclosure
Four-H Club
Franklin stove
garden club
health spa club
inclement
inclined plane
inclusion
inclusive
jockey club
junior class
kennel club
Lion's Club
middle class
nuclear
nuclei
nucleus
obliquely
paper clip
prickly heat
prickly pear
proclaimer
proclaiming
Santa Claus
secluded
seclusion
second class
senior class
service club
tablecloth
thunderclap
unbuckling
underclothes
uniquely
unlikely
Women's Club
____
____
____
____
____
____

KL /kl/ Medial—four syllables

acclamation
athletic club
declaration
digital clock
electric clock
enclosable
exclamation
exclusively
grandfather clock
inclinable
inclination
includible
non-classified
Oklahoma
proclamation
proclivity
reclamation
reclining chair
vacuum cleaner
____
____

KL /kl/ Final—two syllables

ankle
buckle
cackle
chuckle
circle
crackle
cycle
fickle
fiscal
focal
freckle
grackle
heckle
jackal
knuckle
local
nickel
pickle
prickle
rankle
rascal
sickle
snorkel
spackle
speckle
sprinkle
stickle
tackle
tickle
trickle
twinkle
uncle
vocal
wrinkle
____
____

KL /kl/ Final—three syllables

article
bicycle
chemical
classical
clinical
cortical
critical
cubicle
cuticle
encircle
icicle
lexical
logical
lyrical
magical
medical
metrical
miracle
monocle
musical
mystical
mythical
nautical
obstacle
optical
oracle
particle
physical
pinnacle
pinochle
practical
radical
ramshackle
recycle
rhythmical
skeptical
spectacle
spherical
technical
tentacle
topical
tricycle
two-cycle
typical
vehicle
vesicle
____
____

KL /kl/ Final—four syllables

angelical
botanical
historical
honeysuckle
identical
illogical
ironical
kilocycle
mechanical
motorcycle
nonsensical
numerical
patriarchal
political
receptacle
reciprocal
sabbatical
semicircle

statistical
unicycle

KL /kl/ Final—five syllables

academical
alphabetical
analytical
anatomical
astrological
astronomical
biographical
categorical
chronological
economical
geographical
mathematical
mythological
pathological
unequivocal
unmechanical
unmethodical

LK /lk/ Medial—two syllables

Alcan
alcove
bulkhead
bulk mail
bulky
Elkhart
Elkhorn
elk rack
hulking
mail car
milkman
milkmen
milkshake
milk truck
milkweed
polka
railcar
silken
silk hat
silkworm
silky
sulking
sulky
talcum
welcome
welcomed

LK /lk/ Medial—three syllables

alcohol
alkali
alkaline
alkalize
alkalized
balcony
calculate
Chilkoot Pass
Elk City
Milky Way
silkiness
silk-screen print
silk stockings
unwelcome
volcanic
volcano
vulcanize

LK /lk/ Medial—four syllables

Alcan Highway
calculator
recalculate
talcum powder

LK /lk/ Final—one syllable

bilk
bulk
elk
hulk
Hulk
ilk
milk
silk
sulk
talc
whelk
yelk

LK /lk/ Final—two syllables

canned milk
dry milk
goat's milk
ice milk
real silk
skim milk
sour milk
spun silk
sweet milk

LK /lk/ Final—three syllables

buttermilk
lowfat milk
malted milk
powdered milk

KR /kr/ Initial—one syllable

Chris
Christ
chrome
crab
craft
crag
Craig
cram
crammed
cramp
cramped
crane
crank
crash
crate
crave
craw
crawl
crawled
creak
cream
crease
creased
creed
creek
creep
crepe
crept
crest
Crete
crew
crib
cribbed
crick
cried
crime
crisp
crisped
croak
crock
crop
cross
crossed
crouch
croup
crow
crowd
crowed
crown
crowned
crude
cruise
cruised
crumb
crumbed
crumbs
crunch
crush
crust
crutch
cry
kraut

KR /kr/ Initial—two syllables

Christa
Christian
Christine
Christmas
Christy
chroma
Chrysler
Chrystal
crabby
cracker
cracking
crackling
cradle
cradled
craftsman
crafty
craggy
cramming
cramping
crater
crayfish
crayon
crazy
cream cheese
create
creature
credit
creeper
creeping
creepy
crescent
crevasse
crewel
crewman
crewmen
cribbage
cricket
crimson
cripple
crippled
crisis
crispy
crisscross
crochet
crock pot
crocus
crooked
crop dust
cropper
cropping
croquet
crossbow
crossing
crossroad
crosswalk
croutons
crowbar
crowded
crowdy
crowning
crow's nest
crucial
crude oil
cruel
cruise car
cruiser
cruise ship
cruising
crumble
crumbled
crumbly
crummy
crumple
crunchy
crusade
crushing
crystal
Kristi
____
____
____
____
____
____
____
____
____
____
____
____

KR /kr/ Initial—three syllables

Christina
Christmas card
Christmas Day
Christmas Eve
Christmas tree
Christopher
chromosome
chrysolite
crackerjack
craftsmanship
cranberry
crash helmet
Crater Lake
creation
creative
creator
credible
cremation

crepe paper
cribbage board
criminal
critical
criticize
crocheting
crockery
crocodile
Cro-Magnon
crop duster
cross-country
crossover
cross section
crucify
cruelty
crusader
crustacean
crystallize
____
____
____

KR /kr/ Initial—four syllables

chronology
chrysanthemum
cracker barrel
cranberry tree
creativeness
creditable
credit rating
credit union
criterion
critical mass
cross-country skis
cross reference
crossword puzzle
____
____

KR /kr/ Medial—two syllables

accrete
accrue
accrued
acrid
across
aircraft
aircrew
Akron
bankrupt
book rack
cockroach
concrete
corn crib
decrease
decreased
decree
discrete
ecru
fulcrum
handcraft
increase
increased
king crab
macron
microbe
okra
packrat
pie crust
recruit
Red Cross
sacred
sand crab
scarecrow
sea crab
secret
secrete
spacecraft
stock room
tree crab
witchcraft
woodcraft
____
____
____
____

KR /kr/ Medial—three syllables

accredit
achromic
acrobat
acrylic
aircraftman
aircrewman
autocrat
bike crossing
deer crossing
democrat
doublecross
endocrine
giant crab
handcrafted
handicraft
hot cross buns
Hovercraft
hypocrite

increasing
increment
leather craft
microfilm
microphone
microscope
microwave
moose crossing
nutcracker
oyster crab
pancreas
pleasure craft
plutocrat
sacrifice
Santa Cruz
sauerkraut
secrecy
soft-shell crab
sour cream
synchronize
Veracruz
water craft
____
____

KR /kr/ Medial—four syllables

acrobatics
aristocrat
democracy
hypocrisy
increasingly
incredible
incredulous
incriminate
microscopic
plutocracy
railroad crossing
recreation
secretary
____
____

KR /kr/ Medial—five syllables

aircraft carrier
aristocratic
incriminating
microdetector
____
____

RK /rk/ Medial—two syllables

air-cool
arcade
archive
Arctic
barking
bearcat
Berkeley
carcass
charcoal
circle
circuit
circus
clerking
corkscrew
Corky
darken
darker
darkness
Dorcas
forecast
haircut
harken
jerkin
jerking
jerky
Larkin
larkspur
lurking
marker
market
marking
marquee
murky
orchid
parka
Parker
parking
parkway
perky
shirking
smirking
snorkle
spark plug
sparkle
sparkled
sparklers
sparkling
turkey
Turkey
Turkish
turquoise
workbench
workbook
working

workman
workmen
workroom
workshop
______
______

RK /rk/ Medial—three syllables

anarchist
anarchy
Antarctic
archaic
archangel
beef jerky
circular
circulate
darkener
embarking
encircle
marketing
Market Street
mazurka
mercury
Mercury
monarchist
monarchy
motorcade
motorcar
orchestra
overcame
overcast
overcoat
overcome
parking lights
parking lot
parking place
patchwork quilt
percolate
percussion
porcupine
remarking
sarcasm
sarcastic
Turkish bath
woodworking
workable
workmanship
work station
worktable
______

RK /rk/ Medial—four syllables

air-condition
altercation
Antarctica
Arcadia
Arctic Circle
Arctic Ocean
charcoal lighter
circuit breaker
disembarking
felt-tip marker
hierarchy
money market
orchestration
Park Avenue
parking meter
percolator
remarkable
semicircle
sheltered workshop
social worker
summer workshop
supermarket
turkey buzzard
______

RK /rk/ Final—one syllable

arc
ark
bark
Burke
Clark
clerk
cork
dark
Dirk
fork
hark
irk
jerk
Kirk
lark
lurk
marc
Marc
mark
Mark
park
perk
Perk
pork
quirk
shark
shirk

smirk	stork	work
spark	torque	York
stark	Turk	________

RK /rk/ Final—two syllables

birch bark	hallmark	postmark
birthmark	handwork	remark
bookmark	hayfork	salesclerk
bridgework	homework	skylark
check mark	housework	stonework
debark	landmark	town clerk
Denmark	loan shark	trademark
earmark	monarch	uncork
embark	network	woodwork
footmark	Newark	________
footwork	New York	________
framework	patchwork	________
frostwork	pitchfork	________
guesswork	pockmark	________

RK /rk/ Final—three syllables

baseball park	meadowlark	social work
Central Park	needlework	Sunset Park
city park	Noah's Ark	tuning fork
disembark	overpark	watermark
fancywork	overwork	waterwork
handiwork	patriarch	________
hierarchy	pencil mark	________
Jasper Park	question mark	________

RK /rk/ Final—four syllables

Denali Park	________	________
national park	________	________
quotation mark	________	________

RKT /rkt/ Final—one syllable

arcked	jerked	sparked
barked	marked	worked
irked	parked	________

RKT /rkt/ Final—two syllables

embarked
postmarked
remarked
uncorked
unmarked
unworked
____
____
____

KS /ks/ Medial—two syllables

accent
accept
access
axis
axle
bake sale
boxcar
boxer
boxful
boxing
boxwood
dachshund
Dexter
dextrose
Dixie
Dixon
exceed
excel
except
excerpt
excess
exchange
exchanged
excise
excite
excuse
excused
exhale
exhaled
expand
expanse
expect
expel
expelled
expend
expense
expert
expire
Expo
export
expose
exposed
expound
extant
extend
extern
extinct
extol
extort
fixate
fixing
fixture
foxhole
foxhound
Jackson
Knoxville
Maxine
mixer
mixing
mixture
mix-up
Nixon
oxcart
oxen
Oxford
oxide
perplexed
pixy
proxy
quicksand
Roxanne
sextet
sexton
sixpence
sixteen
sixteenth
sixth sense
sixty
succeed
success
taxi
Texas
toxic
toxin
vaccine
waxy
____
____
____
____
____
____
____
____
____
____
____
____
____

KS /ks/ Medial—three syllables

axiom
complexion
dexterous
dioxide
excavate
exceeding
excellence
excellent
excepting
exception
exceptive
excerption
excessive
exchequer
excision
excitant
excited
excitement
exciter
exciting
excursion
excursive
execute
exercise
exercised
exhalant
exlibris
exodus
exogen
exorcise
expanded
expansion
expansive
expectant
expedite
expensive
exponent
exporter
exposure
expulsion
extended
extension
extensive
extensor
external
extinction
extinctive
extinguish
extortion
exudate
flexible
galaxy
hexagon
Jacksonville
Lexington
luxury
maximum
Mexican
Mexico
oxidize
oxygen
quicksilver
saxophone
successful
succession
successive
successor
taxable
taxation
taxicab
taxpayer
vaccinate
vexation
____
____

KS /ks/ Medial—four syllables

accelerate
Alexander
approximate
complexity
excavation
excavator
exceedingly
excellency
excelsior
exceptional
excessively
exchangeable
excisable
excitable
excitation
excusable
execution
executor
exerciser
exfoliate
exhalation
exhibition
exotoxin
expectancy
expectation
expectorant
expedience
expedient
expendable
expenditure
experience
experiment
expiration

exportation
exposition
expositor
extendible
exterior
exterminate
externalize
extinguisher
fox terrier
index finger
luxuriant
luxurious
Mexican food
New Mexico
Old Mexico
proximity
relaxation
Route 66
St. Patrick's Day
success story
Texas Rangers
unexpected
vaccination
____

KS /ks/ Medial—five syllables

exceptionable
exceptionably
excitableness
excitatory
excommunicate
executable
exfoliation
exhibitioner
exhibitionist
ex officio
expediency
experimental
expiratory
extemporary
extenuation
extermination
Mexican Hat Dance
Mexico City
____
____
____

KS /ks/ Final—one syllable

aches
ax
backs
bakes
beaks
bikes
blacks
blocks
books
box
brakes
breaks
bricks
Bronx
brooks
Brooks
bucks
Bucks
cakes
checks
cheeks
chicks
chokes
chucks
clicks
cloaks
clocks
coax
cokes
cooks
Cox
cracks
creaks
creeks
croaks
crocks
crooks
decks
dikes
docks
drakes
ducks
dukes
fakes
fix
flakes
flax
flecks
flex
flicks
flocks
flukes
folks
fox
francs
freaks
frocks
Greeks
hawks
hex

hikes
hoax
hocks
hooks
irks
Jack's
jacks
Jake's
jinx
jokes
kicks
knacks
knocks
lacks
lakes
lax
likes
locks
looks
lox
lux
lynx
makes
minx
mix
necks
ox
picks
pox
racks
ranks
rex
Rex
rocks
sacks
seeks
shakes
shocks
six
slacks
smocks
smokes
snacks
snakes
socks
sphinx
spikes
spooks
squeaks
stacks
steaks
sticks
tacks
tax
Tex
ticks
tracks
tricks
trucks
tucks
vex
wakes
wax
weeks
whacks
wrecks
yaks
____
____

KS /ks/ Final—two syllables

affix
Alex
annex
antiques
apex
attacks
attics
Aztecs
bandbox
barracks
basics
beefsteaks
beeswax
black snakes
borax
classics
clinics
coin box
comics
complex
convex
cornflakes
critics
daybreaks
deluxe
Derrick's
derricks
duplex
epics
epochs
ethics
fabrics
Felix
garlics
hat box
icebox
index
influx
invokes
kayaks
larynx
latex

lyrics
mailbox
mistakes
musk ox
notebooks
padlocks
peacocks
perplex
Phoenix
physics
pillbox
prefix
race tracks
relax
sandbox
scrapbooks
shamrocks
silex
smallpox
snowflakes
sound box
suffix
surtax
sweepstakes
syntax
thorax
thumbtacks
toothpicks
triplex
woodchucks
wordbooks
workbooks
yardsticks
____
____
____

KS /ks/ Final—three syllables

aerobics
almanacs
appendix
artichokes
candlesticks
ceramics
chicken pox
comic books
elastics
equinox
garter snakes
income tax
lumberjacks
motorbikes
orthodox
paperbacks
pogo sticks
politics
railroad tracks
storybooks
____

KS + Adjoining Clusters, Medial—two clusters

exclaim
exclaimed
exclude
excrete
explain
explode
exploit
explore
express
expressed
extra
extract
extreme
extrude
foxglove
foxtrot
____
____

KS + Adjoining Clusters, Medial—three clusters

ecstasy
ecstatic
exclusion
exclusive
expletive
explicit
explorer
explosion
explosive
expressage
expression
expressive
expressly
expressman
express train
expressway
exquisite
extra bold
extraction
extractor
extradite
extravert
extremely
extremist

extricate	extrovert	________
extrinsic	extrusion	________

KS + Adjoining Clusters, Medial—four clusters

exclamation	expropriate	extravagant
exclusively	extractable	extraversion
excruciate	extradition	extremity
explanation	extraneous	extroversion
exploitation	extrapolate	________
explorative	extravagance	________

KS + Adjoining Clusters, Medial—five clusters

exclamation mark	exploratory	extrasensory
exclamatory	expropriation	extravascular
explanatory	extrajudicial	________

SK /sk/ Initial—one syllable

scab	scoot	skid
scald	scope	skiff
scale	scorch	skill
scaled	scorched	skilled
scamp	score	skim
scan	scored	skimmed
scanned	scorn	skimp
scant	scorned	skimped
scar	Scotch	skin
scarce	Scott	skinned
scare	scour	skip
scared	scoured	skipped
scarf	scout	skirt
scarred	scouts	skit
scat	scowl	skulk
scheme	scowled	skull
schemed	scuff	skunk
school	scum	skunked
scoff	skate	sky
scold	skeet	________
scoop	sketch	________
scooped	ski	________

SK /sk/ Initial—two syllables

scabbard
scabby
scaffold
scallion
scallop
scalloped
scallops
scalpel
scamper
scandal
scanty
scapegoat
scarcely
scarecrow
scarlet
scary
scatter
scattered
schedule
scheduled
scholar
schoolboy
school bus
schoolgirl
schoolhouse
schooling
schoolmarm
schoolmate
schoolroom
schooner
scolding
scooter
scorcher
scoreboard
scorecard
scornful
scot-free
Scotland
Scotsman
Scottie
Scottish
Scottsdale
Scottsville
Scotty
scoundrel
scouting
scuba
scuffle
scuffled
sculptor
sculpture
sculptured
scurried
scurry
scurvy
scuttle
Skagway
skateboard
skated
skater
skating
skeptic
sketchbook
sketchy
skidding
skier
skiing
ski jump
ski lift
skillet
skillful
skinny
skunkweed
sky blue
skyborn
skydive
Skylab
skylark
skyline
skyward
skyway
skywrite
____
____

SK /sk/ Initial—three syllables

scandalize
scapula
scatterbrain
scattering
scatter rug
scavenger
schematic
scholarship
scholastic
scorekeeper
Scorpio
scorpion
Scotland Yard
Scott City
scoutmaster
scuttlebutt
skate-a-thon
skatemobile
skeleton
ski-a-thon
skin diving
ski patrol
sky cover
sky diving

sky rocket
skyscraper
skywriter
skywriting
____
____

SK /sk/ Medial—two syllables

asking
basket
basking
biscuit
Boy Scouts
brisket
buckskin
calfskin
cascade
casket
cub Scout
day school
discard
discount
discourse
discuss
diskette
dusky
escape
escort
frisky
gasket
Girl Scouts
grade school
grass skirt
Haskell
high school
hopscotch
husking
husky
Husky
ice skate
kidskin
landscape
mascot
miscount
muskegs
musk ox
muskrat
musky
night school
oilskin
Oscar
outskirts
pesky
pigskin
plaid skirt
preschool
Redskins
rescue
risky
sealskin
sheepskin
threescore
tuskless
whiskbroom
whisker
whiskers
____
____

SK /sk/ Medial—three syllables

Alaska
basketball
basketful
basket weave
basketwork
breadbasket
butterscotch
confiscate
discolor
discomfort
disconcert
disconnect
discontent
discordance
discourage
discouraged
discover
discovered
discussion
escapade
escapement
escarpment
Eskimo
fire escape
gyroscope
hibiscus
hockey skate
horoscope
hula skirt
huskiness
ice skating
mascara
masculine
masquerade
May basket
microscope
misconstrue
mosquito
muscular

musketeer
muskmelon
musk oxen
Nebraska
onionskin
periscope
public school
roller skates
spectroscope
stethoscope
Stravinsky
summer school
Sunday School
telescope
wastebasket
whiskerless
whiskery
Wisconsin
____
____
____

SK /sk/ Medial—four syllables

baleen basket
birch bark basket
disconsolate
discontented
discontinue
discovery
Easter basket
Episcopal
escalator
figure skater
figure skating
kaleidoscope
microscopic
picnic basket
private schooling
roller skating
San Francisco
____

SK /sk/ Final—one syllable

ask
bask
bisque
brisk
brusque
cask
desk
disk
dusk
flask
frisk
husk
mask
mosque
musk
risk
rusk
task
tusk
whisk
____

SK /sk/ Final—two syllables

corn husk
face mask
file disk
gas mask
grotesque
mollusk
school desk
swim mask
unmask

SK /sk/ Final—three syllables

asterisk
data disk
floppy disk
mammoth tusk
office desk
picturesque
reading desk
____
____

KT /kt/ Medial—two syllables

active
cactus
Choctaw
doctor
doctrine
factor
Hector
lecturn
necktie

octane	spectant	victor
octave	tractor	Victor
pectin	vector	________
practice	victim	________

KT /kt/ Medial—three syllables

activate	director	nocturnal
actively	doctoral	objected
affected	effective	objective
affective	elective	obstructing
attracted	elector	octagon
attractive	electron	October
bisected	erector	octopus
character	exacting	pact-maker
conducting	exactly	perspective
conductor	factitious	practical
connecting	factory	prospective
connector	hectagon	prospector
deducted	impacted	reactor
destructive	inactive	selective
detective	infected	spectator
dictaphone	inflicting	transacting
dictation	instructor	________
dictator	neglected	________

KT /kt/ Medial—four syllables

activity	destructible	respectable
bacteria	directory	retractable
benefactor	objectable	Victoria
deductible	predictable	________

KT /kt/ Final—one syllable

act	cracked	joked
backed	docked	kicked
biked	ducked	knocked
blocked	duct	leaked
booked	fact	liked
checked	faked	locked
cooked	hiked	looked

packed
pact
peaked
picked
poked
raked
reeked
rocked
sacked
sect
shocked
sneaked
soaked
spooked
squeaked
stacked
staked
stocked
strict
tacked
tact
talked
ticked
tracked
tract
tricked
trucked
tucked
walked
wrecked
____
____
____

KT /kt/ Final—two syllables

abduct
abstract
affect
afflict
aspect
attacked
attract
barebacked
bisect
collect
compact
conduct
conflict
connect
constrict
construct
contact
contract
convict
correct
deduct
defect
deflect
deject
depict
detect
detract
direct
dissect
distract
district
effect
eject
elect
enact
erect
evict
evoked
exact
expect
extract
impact
induct
infect
inflict
inject
insect
inspect
instruct
intact
neglect
object
obstruct
perfect
predict
prefect
product
project
prospect
protect
protract
react
reflect
reject
respect
restrict
retract
select
subject
subtract
suspect
transact
____
____
____
____
____
____

KT /kt/ Final—three syllables

architect
cataract
derelict
dialect
disconnect
disinfect
incorrect
indirect
intellect
interject
intersect
misdirect
overact
recollect
reelect
self-respect
subcontract
viaduct

KW /kw/ Initial—one syllable

choir
quack
quacked
quad
quaff
quaffed
quag
quail
quaint
quake
quaked
qualm
quark
quart
quartz
quash
quashed
quay
queen
quell
quelled
quench
quenched
quest
quick
quid
quill
quilt
quince
quints
quip
quipped
quirk
quirt
quit
quite
quiz

KW /kw/ Initial—two syllables

quadrant
quadrate
quadrille
quadroon
quagga
quagmire
quaintly
Quaker
quaking
qualmish
quantize
quantum
quarrel
quarreled
quarry
quartan
quarter
quartet
quartile
quarto
quartzite
quasi
quatrain
quaver
queasy
Quebec
Queen Anne
quencher
queried
query
quester
question
questioned
quibble
quickbread
quicken
quickened
quickie
quickly
quicksand
quickstep
quiet

quilted
quilting
Quincy
quinine
quinsy
quintain
quintet
quisling
quitclaim
quitter
quiver
quizzer
quonset
quorum
quota
quotient
____
____

KW /kw/ Initial—three syllables

quadrangle
quadratic
quadriceps
quadrifid
quadrillion
quadruped
quadruple
quadruplet
Quakertown
qualified
qualify
qualities
quality
quandary
quantity
quarantine
quarrelsome
quarterback
quarterdeck
quarterhorse
quartering
quarter note
quavering
question mark
questionnaire
quicksilver
quick-tempered
quick-witted
quiescent
quietly
quintessence
quintuple
quintuplet
quixotic
quizzical
quotable
quotation
____
____

KW /kw/ Initial—four syllables

quadrangular
quadrennial
quadriplegic
quadruplicate
qualifier
qualitative
quantifier
quantitative
quartermaster
questionable
quinine water
quinquennial
quotation mark
____
____

KW /kw/ Initial—five syllables

quadrilateral
qualification
quantitatively
____
____
____

KW /kw/ Medial—two syllables

acquaint
acquire
acquired
acquit
aqua
awkward
backward
backwash
backwoods
banquet
bequeath
bequeathed
bequest
bookworm
brick wall

cakewalk
catwalk
chickweed
equal
equalled
equate
equip
equipped
frequence
frequent
inquest
inquire
inquired
knockwurst
likewise
liquid
loquat
lukewarm
milkweed
misquote
request
require
required
sequel
sequence
sequenced
sequin
shock wave
tranquil
unquote
walkway
____
____

KW /kw/ Medial—three syllables

acquaintance
acquainted
acquiesce
acquiesced
acquiring
acquittal
acquittance
acquitted
antiquate
aqualung
aquanaut
aquaplane
aquatic
aquatint
aqueduct
aqueous
aquiline
chuck wagon
chuckwalla
consequence
consequent
disquiet
equaling
equalize
equalized
equated
equating
equation
equator
equerry
equinox
equipage
equipment
equipping
equity
frequency
headquarters
hindquarter
inequal
infrequent
inquirer
inquiring
inquiry
liquefy
liquidate
liquified
loquacious
misquoted
misquoting
requirement
requiring
requisite
requital
requiter
sequential
sequoia
subsequent
tranquilize
tranquilly
unequal
unequaled
unquestioned
____

KW /kw/ Medial—four syllables

acquiescence
acquiescent
acquisition
acquisitive
antiquary
antiquated
antiquation
antiquity
aquamarine

aquarium
Aquarius
consequential
disqualified
disqualify
disquietude
disquisition
equality
equalizer
equalizing
equidistant
equitable
equitation
equivalence
equivalent
equivocal
equivocate
infrequented
inquisition
inquisitive
inquisitor
liquefaction
liquefying
liquidating
liquidation
liquidity
loquacity
post headquarters
requisition
tranquility
tranquilizer
unfrequented
unqualified
unquenchable
ventriloquist
____
____
____
____

KW /kw/ Medial—five syllables

antiquarian
disqualifying
equanimity
equatorial
equiangular
equilateral
equilibrium
equivalency
equivocation
unequivocal
unquestionable
____
____
____
____

KY /kj/ Medial—two syllables

backyard
brickyard
dockyard
stockyard
____
____

KY /kj/ Medial—three syllables

calculate
calculus
Hercules
molecule
ocular
oculist
porcupine
secular
speculate
succulent
Tokyo
____
____
____
____

KY /kj/ Medial—four syllables

accusation
articulate
calculated
calculator
curriculum
executor
gesticulate
lenticular
molecular
particular
ridiculous
security
spectacular
speculation
vermicular
vermiculate
____
____

SKR /skr/ Initial—one syllable

scram
scrap
scrape
scratch
scrawl
scream
screech
screen
screw
scribe
scrimp
script
scroll
Scrooge
scrub
scrunch

SKR /skr/ Initial—two syllables

scraggly
scramble
scrambled
scrapbook
scraper
scrapper
scratchy
scrawny
screening
screenplay
screentest
screwball
scribble
scribbled
scrimmage
scripture
scrub nurse
scrumptious
scruple

SKR /skr/ Initial—three syllables

screen writer
screwdriver
scrupulous
scrutinize
scrutiny

SKR /skr/ Medial—two syllables

ascribe
ascribed
corkscrew
describe
described
discreet
escrow
ice cream
inscribe
muskrat
postscript
prescribe
prescribed
silkscreen
subscribe
subscribed
subscript
transcribe
transcribed

SKR /skr/ Medial—three syllables

description
descriptive
ice-cream man
ice-cream truck
inscription
manuscript
prescription
skyscraper
subscription

SKS /sks/ Final—one syllable

asks
basks
casks
desks
disks
flasks
husks
masks
risks
tasks
tusks

SKW /skw/ Initial—one syllable

squab
squad
squall
square
squash
squat
squaw
squawk
squeak
squeal
squeeze
squelch
squib
squid
squint
squire
squirm
squirt
squish

SKW /skw/ Initial—two syllables

squabble
squabbling
squad car
squadron
squalid
squally
squalor
squander
square dance
square deal
square feet
square foot
square inch
squarely
square knot
square meal
square mile
square off
square root
squarest
square yard
squashy
squatted
squatter
squatting
squatty
squeaky
squeamish
squeegee
squeezer
squeezing
squelcher
squiggle
squirmy
squirrel
squirt gun
squishy

SKW /skw/ Initial—three syllables

square away
square inches
square meters
square rigger
square shooter
squashiest
squeezable

L

Pronounced: /l/
Spelled: l, ll

L /l/ Initial—one syllable

lace
lack
lad
lade
lag
lagged
laid
lain
lair
Laird
lake
lamb
lame
lamed
lamp
lance
land
lane
Lane
lank
lap
laps
lapse
lard
large
lark
lash
lass
last
latch
late
lathe
laud
laugh
laughed
launch
law
lawn
lay
lea
leach
lead
leaf
league
leak
lean
leap
leaped
learn
learned
lease
leased
leash
least
leave
leaves
led
ledge
lee
Lee
leech
leer
left
leg
lei
Len
lend
length
lens
lent
Lent
Les
less
let
Lew
lice
lick
licked
lid
lie
lied
lien
lieu
life
lift
light
lights
like
liked
limb

limbs
lime
limes
limp
limped
line
link
links
lint
lip
lisp
list
lit
live
lived
lives
Lloyd
load
loaf
loan
loath
loathe
loaves
lob
lobe
lock
lodge
lodged
loft
log
loge
logged
loin
long
look
looked
loom
loon
loop
loose
loot
lop
lopped
lord
lore
Lorne
lose
loss
lost
lot
Lou
loud
lounge
louse
love
loved
low
lox
lube
luck
lug
luge
lugged
Luke
lump
lunch
lung
lunge
lurch
lure
lured
lures
lurk
lush
lute
Lux
lye
lymph
Lynn
lynx
lyre
____
____
____

L /l/ Initial—two syllables

labor
labored
lacework
lacing
lacquer
lactose
ladder
laden
ladies
lady
lagging
lagoon
Lambert
lame duck
lancer
landed
land grant
landing
landmark
landscape
language
lantern
lanyard
larger
largest
larkspur
Larry

larva
laser
lasher
lashing
Lassie
lasso
lasting
last name
later
latest
latex
lather
lathwork
Latin
latter
lattice
laughing
laughter
launcher
launder
laundry
Laura
Laurie
lava
lavish
lawman
Lawrence
lawsuit
lawyer
layer
layered
layette
laying
layman
layoff
layout
lay up
lazy
leacher

leachy
leader
lead-in
leading
lead-off
leafage
leafy
Leah
leakage
leaning
lean-to
leap year
leapfrog
learning
leasing
leather
leaven
leaving
lector
lecture
ledger
leery
lee tide
leeward
leeway
left-hand
legate
legend
legion
legume
leisure
Lemberg
lemming
lemon
Lena
Leo
Leon
Leonard
lesion

lessee
lessen
lesson
letdown
letter
lettered
Lettie
lettuce
letup
leucite
levee
lever
levy
Lewis
liar
Libby
Libra
license
lichen
licking
lifeboat
life buoy
lifeguard
life raft
lifetime
life vest
lifter
lift-off
ligate
lighten
lighter
lighthouse
lighting
lightning
lightweight
light-year
likeness
likewise
liking

Lima
limber
Limberg
limbo
limeade
limestone
limit
Lina
Lincoln
Linda
lineage
line drive
line graph
lineman
linen
liner
lineup
linger
lingo
lining
linkage
linseed
lion
lipstick
liquid
listen
listing
liter
litter
liven
liver
livestock
live wire
livid
living
lizard
Lizzie
llama
loaded
loading
loafer
loaning
loathful
loathing
loathsome
lobby
lobster
locate
locker
locket
locking
lockjaw
locksmith
locus
locust
lodger
lodging
logbook
logger
logging
logic
log jam
logo
log on
Lois
loiter
London
lonesome
longhand
longhorn
longing
longish
long johns
long jump
long-range
long shot
longwise
looker
looking
lookout
looming
loony
looper
loopy
loper
Lopez
loppy
loquats
Lordsburg
lordship
Lorin
Lorraine
Lory
loser
losing
lost cause
lotion
Lottie
lotto
louder
loudmouthed
Louis
Louise
lounger
lousy
louver
lovebirds
lover
loving
lowboy
low-cost
lower
lowest
low fat
low tide
lozenge
Lubbock

lucid
lucky
Lucy
luggage
lugger
lumber
lumbered
lummox
lumpish
lumpy
lunar
luncheon
lunchroom
lunchtime
luring
luscious
luster
lustrous
lusty
Luther
luxate
lying
Lyndon
Lyndsay
lyric
____
____

L /l/ Initial—three syllables

Labor Day
labor force
Labrador
lacerate
ladybug
lambasted
landing gear
landing strip
landowner
Laramie
Las Vegas
latency
latitude
latticework
laughing gas
laughingstock
launching pad
laundromat
lavender
lawbreaker
lawn mower
lawn tennis
layer cake
layering
layover
lazy bones
lazy tongs
leadership
leather work
leftovers
legacy
legalize
legation
legato
legible
lomonade
lemon juice
lempira
lenient
Leningrad
Lenora
leprosy
Lethargic
Leticia
lettergram
letterhead
lettering
leverage
lexicon
Lexington
liaison
liberate
liberty
library
licensee
licorice
lieutenant
life jacket
lifesaver
lifesaving
ligament
ligature
light-footed
lightheaded
light meter
lightning bug
lightning rod
lima beans
limerick
lime water
limited
limiting
limousine
lineage
linebacker
line drawing
liniment
lip reading
liquidate
Lithia
lithograph
lithoprint
litterbug
Little Rock

livable
liverwurst
living room
load factor
location
locator
lodging house
log cabin
logistics
logogram
logograph
London Bridge
Lone Star State
long distance
longitude
longshoreman
longsighted
long-winded
lopsided
loquacious
Lorinda
lottery
loudspeaker
Louisa
lousiest
lowering
lowermost
Lowery
low pressure
low water
lubricant
luckier
luckiest
lucrative
lucubrate
lumbago
lumbering
lumberjack
lumber mill
lumberyard
luminous
luncheonette
Luxembourg
luxury
lyceum
Lydia
____
____
____
____
____
____
____
____

L /l/ Initial—four syllables

labialize
laborious
laceration
laminated
laryngeal
laryngitis
laryngoscope
lateral pass
lathing hatchet
lavatory
law abiding
lazy Susan
legality
legislation
legislative
legislator
legislature
legitimate
lenticular
Liberty Bell
librarian
lickety-split
lifeguard station
life preserver
limitation
Lincoln's Birthday
lineament
linoleum
literacy
literature
lithology
Little Dipper
liturgical
locality
locomotion
locomotive
loganberry
logarithmic
Londonderry
longevity
long-suffering
lopsidedness
Los Angeles
loving kindness
lower classman
low spirited
lunitidal
luxuriance
luxurious
____
____
____
____
____
____
____
____

L /l/ Initial—five syllables

laboratory
lackadaisical
liability
libertarian
Lithuania
longitudinal
Louisiana
____
____

L /l/ Medial—two syllables

Aileen
ailing
Alan
alarm
Alex
Alice
alike
alive
alley
allied
allot
allow
alloy
allure
ally
alone
along
aloud
Bailey
balance
balanced
baler
ballad
ballet
balloon
ballot
bay leaf
Bayley
Baylor
believe
bellows
belly
belong
below
billow
Billy
boiler
boiling
bowler
bowling
brilliant
broiler
bully
caller
Cally
ceiling
cellar
cello
Ceylon
chalet
challenge
Chile
chili
chilly
cola
collage
collapse
collar
colleague
collect
Colleen
college
Collette
collide
collie
cologne
Cologne
colon
color
colors
column
coolant
cooler
Coolidge
crawler
daily
Dallas
daylight
dealer
delete
Delhi
delight
deluxe
dialing
dilute
doily
dollar
Dolly
driller
drilling
drooler
duller
dweller
dwelling
Elaine
elapse
elate
elect
elite

ellipse
elope
elude
eyelash
eyelet
eyelid
failing
fallen
fallout
feelers
feeling
Felix
fellow
filings
fillet
filling
filly
follow
folly
foolish
freelance
freeload
free lunch
fully
gaily
gala
gallant
galley
gallon
gallop
galore
galosh
goalie
hallow
halo
healer
heeler
Helen
hello

highly
hilly
Holland
hollow
holly
Holly
holy
howler
Ireland
island
Jai Alai
jailer
jealous
jelly
Joline
jolly
Julie
July
Kelly
kilo
kneeling
knowledge
mailer
mailing
malice
mallard
mallet
mellow
melon
mileage
miler
miller
millet
molar
mollusk
Molly
Nellie
newly
nylon

oily
olive
Olive
palace
pallet
Pauline
peeling
pellet
Phillip
Phyllis
pilar
pilings
pillar
pillow
pilot
Poland
polar
poler
police
polish
Polish
polite
pollen
pollute
Polly
polo
polyp
pullet
pulley
pulling
railing
rally
really
relapse
relate
relax
relay
release
relic

relief
relieve
relieved
relish
rely
roller
ruler
ruling
sailing
sailor
salaam
salad
Sally
salon
salute
scaler
scholar
sealant
sealer
select
seller
shallow
shellac
Shelley
shilling
shoelace
shriller
shrillest
silence
silent
silly
silo
ski lift
skillet
Skylab
skylark
skyline
smaller
smallish

smeller
smelling
smiling
solar
solemn
solid
solo
speller
spelling
spilling
sprawler
squealer
stealer
stealing
stolen
stroller
strolling
stylish
stylist
stylus
swallow
swelling
swollen
tailing
tailor
talent
taller
tallish
tallow
tally
talon
Taylor
teller
telling
thriller
tiling
tiller
toilet
towline

trailer
trawler
troller
tulip
Tyler
valance
valid
valley
value
velour
villa
village
villain
volley
volume
Wallace
wallet
wallop
wallow
Wally
whaler
whaling
Willie
willing
willow
Willy
woolen
woolly
yelling
yellow
zealous
Zulu
____
____
____
____
____
____
____

L /l/ Medial—three syllables

a la carte
abolish
absolute
acknowledge
Adaline
Adela
Alamo
Alaska
Aletta
Alison
Alissa
allergic
allergy
alliance
allowance
aloha
ambulance
Amelia
analyze
angelic
angular
antelope
Apollo
avalanche
bachelor
balancing
ballistics
balloonist
ballyhoo
belated
beloved
billy goat
bobolink
bolero
bologna
bowlegged
broccoli
buffalo
bulletin
bungalow
calendar
calico
calorie
calypso
candlelight
cantaloupe
catalog
cavalier
celebrate
celery
cellophane
Challenger
challenges
challenging
chili sauce
chuck-a-luck
chuckwalla
circulate
civilize
colander
collarbone
collection
collector
collision
colony
colorful
color guard
coloring
Columbus
consoler
controller
counselor
dandelion
Delaware
delicate
delicious
deliver
demolish
Denali
desolate
develop
dialect
dialing
dialogue
diligent
discolor
Disneyland
easily
elastic
election
elective
electric
electrode
elegant
element
elephant
elevate
eleven
entailing
envelope
Evelyn
exhaling
fabulous
fairyland
family
fellowship
filament
finale
finalize
foliage
folio
follower
following
follow-through

follow-up
formula
four-wheeler
freeloader
galaxy
Galena
Galilee
gallery
galoshes
gasoline
gelatin
Gila Bend
gondola
gorilla
guerrilla
gullible
Gwendolyn
halibut
Halloween
happily
helium
holiday
Hollywood
hula hoop
hula skirt
Illinois
illusion
illustrate
impala
inhaling
insulate
intellect
invalid
isolate
Israeli
italic
Italy
Jackelyn
Jacqueline

jalopy
jealousy
jelly beans
jet pilot
jeweler
journalist
kilogram
kilowatt
make-believe
malamute
Malinda
mandolin
marmalade
marshmallow
marvelous
masculine
melody
metallic
militia
molasses
muscular
muskmelon
New Zealand
obsolete
ocular
oleo
Oliver
Olympics
omelet
Pamela
paralyze
pelican
penalize
pendulum
Philippines
Phillipsburg
photo lab
piccolo
polar bear

polar ice
polarize
polar lights
policeman
policy
polio
polishing
politics
polliwog
polygon
popular
populous
porcelain
propeller
qualified
quality
realize
really
rebelling
regular
regulate
related
relation
relative
relay race
relevant
relieving
religion
religious
reluctant
retailer
roller skates
rolling pin
salad bar
salami
salary
sand dollar
satellite
scholarship

sea lion
secular
silhouette
similar
simulate
singular
skeleton
socialize
solar heat
solar house
solarize
soloist
solution
spatula
specialist
specialize
specially
speculate
speedily
spelling bee
sterilize
stimulate
stimulus
succulent
Sun Valley
surveillance
swallowing
swallowtail
syllabus
symbolize
talented
talent show
tamale
telegram
telegraph
telephone
telescope
telethon
televise
three-wheeler
tolerance
tolerant
totally
tricolor
tubular
two-wheeler
umbrella
unbalanced
unduly
unruly
unwilling
utilize
Valeda
valentine
Valerie
vanilla
ventilate
verbally
vigilant
villager
viola
violate
violet
Violet
violin
vitalize
vocalist
vocally
volition
volleyball
volunteer
wallaby
xylophone
Yellowstone
zeppelin
____
____
____
____
____
____
____
____
____
____
____
____

L /l/ Medial—four syllables

a capella
abalone
ability
accelerate
accumulate
actually
affiliate
agility
Alabama
alimony
allegation
alleluia
alligator
aluminum
Amarillo
Amaryllis
Annapolis
armadillo
articulate
ballerina
belligerent
binoculars
biologist
California

capillary
caterpillar
celebration
celebrity
chameleon
chocolate chip
Cinderella
coliseum
colonial
Colorado
coloring book
Columbia
consolidate
constellation
curriculum
deliberate
development
ecology
electrician
elevation
elevator
escalator
evaluate
finality
fortuneteller
geology
helicopter
hilarious
Honolulu
hot-air balloon
humiliate
ideally
illuminate
illustration
incredulous
initialize
inoculate
intelligence
intelligent
intolerant
irregular
jack-o'-lantern
Jerusalem
Jolly Roger
jubilation
kaleidoscope
kilometer
lenticular
linoleum
literally
locality
malaria
Marco Polo
melancholy
metropolis
military
monopoly
multicolor
mythology
Napoleon
naturally
nevertheless
nobility
Olivia
palomino
parallel bars
paralysis
particular
penicillin
peninsula
personally
philodendron
philosopher
philosophy
polar axis
polar region
police station
political
politician
population
practically
prematurely
pussy willow
qualitative
realism
reality
regulation
relationship
resolution
revolution
ridiculous
roller coaster
roller skating
salad dressing
semicolon
semitrailer
spectacular
tarantula
technicolor
technology
telepathy
television
theologian
theology
tolerable
tolerably
twin propeller
typically
ukulele
unparalleled
unpopular
unqualified
usually
utility
utilizing
Valentine's Day
valuable

velocity	vitality	________
Venezuela	voluminous	________
ventilation	voluntary	________
violation	water colors	________
violinist	yellow jackets	________

L /l/ Medial—five syllables

acceleration	nationalism	specifically
accidentally	nationality	unbelievable
articulation	necessarily	underdeveloped
delicatessen	occasionally	universally
dilapidated	originally	unreliable
electricity	personality	unusually
immediately	polarization	utilization
incidentally	popularity	versatility
inequality	possibility	visibility
intellectual	preliminary	vocabulary
involuntary	principality	voluntarily
metabolism	qualification	________
Metropolitan	roller skating rink	________
miscellaneous	similarity	________

L /l/ Medial—six syllables

individually	totalitarian	________
revolutionary	utilitarian	________
theoretically	variability	________

L /l/ Final—one syllable

ail	bowl	deal
aisle	braille	dell
all	broil	Dell
bail	bull	dill
bale	call	dole
ball	cell	doll
bell	coal	Doyle
Belle	coil	drawl
bill	cool	drill
Bill	crawl	drool
boil	Dale	dull

dwell
eel
fail
fall
feel
fell
file
fill
foal
foil
fool
foul
fowl
frill
full
Gail
gale
gall
Gil
gill
goal
gull
hail
Hal
hall
haul
heal
heel
hill
howl
Hoyle
hull
ill
isle
jail
jell
kale
keel
kneel

Kyle
mail
male
mall
meal
Mel
mile
mill
mole
mule
nail
Neal
Nell
null
oil
owl
pail
pal
pale
Paul
peal
peel
Phil
pile
pill
pole
poll
pool
pull
quail
quell
quill
rail
real
reel
role
roll
rule
sail

sale
Saul
scale
school
scowl
scroll
seal
sell
shall
shawl
she'll
shell
shoal
shrill
sill
skill
skull
small
smell
smile
snail
soil
sole
soul
spell
spill
spoil
spool
sprawl
squall
squeal
stale
stall
steel
still
stole
stool
stroll
style

swell
tail
tale
tall
teal
tell
thrill
tile
till
toil
toll
tool
trail
twill
Vail
veal
veil
voile
wail
wall
well
whale
wheel
while
whole
who'll
will
Will
wool
Yale
yawl
yell
yule
zeal
____
____

L /l/ Final—two syllables

Adele
Airedale
airmail
anthill
appeal
April
avail
awhile
baseball
beach ball
bedroll
Beryl
Bethel
bluebell
Brazil
canal
cancel
capsule
Carol
cartwheel
cattail
Cheryl
chisel
Churchill
compel
compile
conceal
control
cordial
Cornell
corral
cowbell
cruel
Crystal
cue ball
cupful
curtail
Cyril
Daniel
decal
detail
dial
diesel
distill
dowel
downfall
downhill
dual
eggshell
enroll
entail
Estelle
exhale
exile
expel
eyeball
faithful
female
fire drill
fire sale
football
footstool
fragile
fuel
gazelle
handball
handbill
handrail
hangnail
Hazel
high school
hotel
inkwell
install
jackal

jewel
Joel
joyful
jump ball
keyhole
kickball
manhole
Maypole
meanwhile
meatball
misspell
module
molehill
morale
mortal
motel
mothball
muscle
Nashville
newsreel
Nicole
nightfall
nodule
Noel
North Pole
nutshell
oatmeal
oil well
ordeal
pailful
parole
pastel
payroll
pencil
pen pal
pigtail
pinball
pinwheel
porthole
rainfall
real
recall
recoil
refill
repeal
repel
reptile
retail
reveal
Rochelle
royal
Russell
sackful
sandpile
sawmill
schedule
scoopful
sea gull
seashell
sea wall
Sibyl
ski trail
sleigh bell
snowball
snowfall
standstill
steel wool
subsoil
symbol
tadpole
tinfoil
toadstool
toenail
topsoil
towel
town hall
turmoil
unroll
until
unveil
unwell
vial
viol
vowel
Wendell
windfall
windmill
____
____
____
____
____
____

L /l/ Final—three syllables

Abigail
aerial
alcohol
Annabelle
annual
aureole
axial
baby doll
basketball
bass viol
betrayal
bookmobile
bronchial
Bunker Hill
burial
buttonhole
carryall
casserole

casual
cathedral
Cherryvale
Cherryville
cottontail
denial
disloyal
factual
fairy tale
Fayetteville
Ferris wheel
fingernail
gradual
honor roll
hospital
ideal
infantile
initial
Israel
Jacksonville
jovial
juvenile
manual
Montreal
musical
mutual
nightingale
oriel
overall
overhaul
overrule
parasol
punctual
racquet ball
radial
renewal
ridicule
ritual
rock-n-roll
rummage sale
Samuel
serial
shrimp cocktail
ski patrol
snowmobile
soccerball
spinning wheel
summer school
Sunday school
sundial
Sunnyvale
swimming pool
tetherball
unequal
unreal
usual
versatile
vestibule
viceroyal
virtual
visual
wading pool
withdrawal
____
____
____
____
____
____
____
____
____

L /l̩/ Final—four syllables

arterial
certified mail
Liberty Bell
nursery school
parochial
perpetual
tutorial
unusual
vice-principal
____
____
____

L /l̩/ Final—five syllables

ceremonial
editorial
individual
intellectual
Roman numeral
testimonial
____
____
____

L /l/ Recurring—one syllable

Lil
Lille
loll
Lyle
____
____

L /l/ Recurring—two syllables

fulfill
ill will
label
ladle
lamplight
landlord
lapel
lapful
Lapland
largely
lastly
lately
lawful
lawless
legal
lentil
lethal
level
libel
lifeless
lifelike
lifeline
lifelong
lightly
likely
Lila
lilac
Lilly
lily
limelight
lingual
lintel
listless
little
lively
local
locale
Lola
lonely
long-lived
loophole
loose-leaf
lovelock
lovelorn
lovely
Lowell
lowlands
lowly
loyal
Lucille
lunch pail
Lulu
Lyell
pell-mell
roll call
solely
steel wool
telltale
toll call
wholesale
____
____
____

L /l/ Recurring—three syllables

April fool
colorful
color wheel
illegal
jelly roll
labeller
labial
ladylike
lamplighter
landlady
Laplander
laryngal
lastingly
latently
lateral
legislate
leveler
levelling
lexical
liable
liberal
likelihood
Lillian
lily pad
lily-white
limitless
lineal
linseed oil
literal
Little League
littler
littlest
livelier
liveliest
livelihood
Llewellyn
localize
locally
logical
logrolling
lollipop
Long Island
long leaf pine
long liner
Longfellow

lovable
loyalist
loyalty
Loyola
luckily
luculent
lullaby
lunular
molecule
olive oil
paddlewheel
parallel
salad oil
sea level
skillfully
wholesaler
willfully
____

LB /lb/ Medial—two syllables

Albert
album
ball bat
ball boy
bellbird
bell book
bell boy
billboard
callboard
call box
coalbin
Delbert
Elbe
Elbert
Elbie
elbow
file box
Galbraith
Gilbert
Holbrook
mailbag
mailbox
Melba
Melbourne
Milbank
millboard
Millburn
nail bag
Olbers
pillbox
roll bar
sailboat
school band
school board
schoolbooks
school bus
skull bone
spellbound
steel box
tool box
wallboard
whalebone
Wilbanks
Wilbur
____

LB /lb/ Medial—three syllables

Albany
albatross
Alberta
albino
ball bearings
bell-bottoms
bell buoy
doll buggy
Elberta
Elberton
elbow grease
elbowroom
Gilberta
melba toast
mulberry
Mulberry
nail-biting
wheelbarrow

LB /lb/ Final—one syllable

alb
bulb
Kalb
Kolb
____
____

LB /lb/ Final—two syllables

DeKalb
flashbulb
light bulb
wet bulb
____
____

BL /bl/ Initial—one syllable

blab
blabbed
black
blade
Blaine
Blake
blame
blamed
blanch
Blanche
bland
blank
blare
blared
blast
blaze
blazed
bleach
bleached
bleak
blear
bleat
bled
bleed
blench
blend
bless
blessed
blest
blew
blight
blimp
blind
blink
blinked
blintz
blip
bliss
blithe
blitz
bloat
blob
bloc
block
blocked
blocks
blond
blood
bloom
bloomed
blot
blotch
blotched
blouse
blow
blown
blue
blues
bluff
bluffed
blunt
blur
blurb
blurred
blurt
blush
blushed
Blythe

BL /bl/ Initial—two syllables

blackball
blackballed
black bear
black belt
blackbird
blackboard
blacken
Blackett
black eye
black flag
Blackfoot
blackhead
blacking
blacklist
blackmail
blackmailed
blackout
Black Sea
black sheep
blacksmith
blackthorn
blacktop
black whale
blameless
blanket
blarney
blasé
blaspheme
blasphemed
blast off
blatant
blazer
blazon
blazoned
bleachers
bleary
blemish
blemished
blessed

blessing
blinder
blinders
blindfold
blinding
blinker
blinkers
blissful
blister
blistered
blithesome
blizzard
blockade
blocker
blockhead
blockhouse
bloodhound
bloodline
bloodstream
blood test
blossom
blossomed
blotchy
blotter
blower
blowgun
blowout
blowpipe
blowtorch
blubber
blubbered
bluebell
blue belt
bluebird
blue cheese
blue fish
bluegill
bluegrass
blue jay
blue jeans
blue moon
blueprint
bluer
Blue Ridge
blue shark
blue sky
bluest
bluets
blue whale
bluffer
bluffing
bluing
bluish
blunder
blundered
bluster
blustered
Blytheville
____
____

BL /bl/ Initial—three syllables

black and blue
blackberry
black market
black widow
blamelessly
blameworthy
blandishing
blandishment
blasphemy
bleeding heart
blindman's bluff
blockbuster
bloodmobile
blood pressure
Blue Angels
blueberry
bluebonnet
bluebottle
blue color
bluejacket
blue marlin
Blue Mountains
blue ribbon
blustery
____
____
____

BL /bl/ Medial—two syllables

ablaze
abloom
babbling
bubbling
bubbly
cobbler
dabbling
doublet
doubly
dribbling
emblaze
emblem
gambling
giblet
glibly
gobbler
gobbling
goblet

goblin
grabbler
hobbling
mumbling
nibbling
nimbly
nosebleed
oblate
oblige
oblique
oblong
problem
public
publish
pueblo
Pueblo
rambler
Red Bluff
sandblast
sand-blind
semblance
sibling
squabbling
sublease
sublet
sublime
tableau
tablet
trembling
troubling
tumbler
tumbling
warbler
warbling
wobbly

BL /bl/ Medial—three syllables

ablation
ablution
cable car
emblazing
emblazon
emblem book
emblements
establish
established
Navy blue
night blindness
notably
obligate
obliging
obligor
public school
publisher
publishing
red-blooded
republic
resemblance
San Pablo
shoulder blade
sublimate
unpublished

BL /bl/ Medial—four syllables

ablactating
ablepsia
army blanket
baby-blue eyes
disestablish
emblazonment
establishment
obligation
obligato
oblique angle
obliterate
publication
public domain
publicity
publishing house
reestablish
republican
subliminal

BL /bl/ Final—two syllables

Abel
able
amble
babble
Bible
brabble
bramble
bubble
bumble
cable
crumble
cymbal
dabble
double
drabble

dribble
fable
feeble
fumble
gable
gamble
global
gobble
grumble
hobble
humble
jumble
label
libel
marble
mumble
nibble
nimble
noble
pebble
quibble
ramble
rebel
rubble
ruble
rumble
sable
scramble
scribal
scribble
squabble
stable
stubble
stumble
Sybil
table
thimble
treble
tremble
tribal
trouble
tumble
verbal
wabble
waddle
warble
wobble
____
____
____
____

BL /bl/ Final—three syllables

affable
assemble
audible
cannibal
capable
constable
decibel
disable
durable
edible
flammable
flexible
gullible
horrible
legible
liable
livable
lovable
notable
portable
possible
preamble
probable
quotable
resemble
sellable
sensible
sociable
soluble
suitable
syllable
terrible
timetable
unable
useable
____

BL /bl/ Final—four syllables

acceptable
advisable
agreeable
answerable
available
comfortable
convertible
dependable
desirable
eligible
enjoyable
favorable
formidable
habitable
handleable
honorable
Honorable
hospitable

illegible
impossible
incredible
inedible
inflammable
invisible
miserable
perishable
practicable
preferable
presentable
profitable
questionable
reasonable
reassemble
receivable
reliable
remarkable
respectable
responsible
separable
tolerable
unchangeable
unmatchable
unprintable
unquenchable
unspeakable
unsuitable
unthinkable
valuable
variable
vegetable
veritable
vulnerable
____
____

BL /bl/ Final—five syllables

dishonorable
indivisible
inevitable
inhospitable
innumerable
inoperable
irresistible
recoverable
unalterable
unapproachable
unavoidable
unbelievable
undesirable
unmistakable
unprofitable
unquestionable
unreasonable
unreliable
unutterable
unwarrantable
____

LD /ld/ Medial—two syllables

Alden
alder
Baldwin
boulder
Boulder
builder
building
build-up
childhood
childish
children
cold cuts
colder
coldest
cold front
cold pack
cold snap
cold wave
Elden
elder
Elder
eldest
fielded
fielder
field goal
field trip
file disk
folder
folding
gelding
golden
goldfinch
goldfish
gold mine
gold pan
gold rush
gold stream
holder
holding
hold-up
mildew
molding
olden
older
oldest
scalding
scolding
seldom

Sheldon	Welden	wild west
shielded	welder	yielded
shoulder	welding	yielding
smolder	wildcat	________________
Waldon	wildfire	________________
welded	wildlife	________________

LD /ld/ Medial—three syllables

beholden	golden age	shipbuilder
blindfolded	goldenrod	shouldering
bulldozer	gold nugget	unfolding
bulldozing	gold panner	unwieldy
cul-de-sac	grandchildren	unyielding
deviled eggs	left fielder	upholder
elderly	old-fashioned	wilderness
Eldora	right fielder	wildflower
field glasses	shareholder	withholding
field worker	shelled pecans	World Series
folding chair	shelled walnuts	________________

LD /ld/ Final—one syllable

bald	guild	shield
billed	held	skilled
bold	hold	sold
build	mild	spilled
called	mold	told
child	mulled	veiled
cold	old	weld
field	polled	wield
filed	pulled	wild
filled	rolled	world
fold	scald	yield
gild	scold	________________
gold	shelled	________________

LD /ld/ Final—two syllables

afield	airfield	Arnold
age-old	appalled	backfield
ahold	appealed	beheld

behold
billfold
blindfold
coal field
cornfield
corralled
Donald
downfield
enfold
foothold
foretold
Gerald
grandchild
Harold
household
infield
infold
left field
marbled
marveled
outfield
rebuild
retold
right field
Ronald
Sea World
stepchild
stronghold
threefold
threshold
twofold
unfold
unsold
untold
upheld
uphold
windshield
withheld
withhold
____
____
____
____
____
____

LD /ld/ Final—three syllables

battlefield
center field
centerfold
emerald
football field
initialed
interfold
landing field
MacDonald
manifold
marigold
soccer field
____
____
____

DL /dl/ Medial—two syllables

badly
Bradley
deadline
deadlock
deadly
gladly
Hadley
headlight
headline
heedless
huddling
hurdler
idling
kindling
loudly
madly
meddling
medley
midland
needless
needling
oddly
paddling
padlock
red light
sadly
seedless
seedling
soundly
swindling
toddler
toddling
twiddling
wedlock
widely
windlass
____
____
____
____
____
____
____
____
____

DL /dl/ Medial—three syllables

bridal veil
candlestick
candlewick
handlebars
idleness
meddlesome
middle age
middle ear
Middle East
Middle West
____
____

DL /dl/ Final—two syllables

bridal
bridle
bundle
candle
caudal
cradle
dwindle
fiddle
griddle
handle
huddle
hurdle
idle
idol
kindle
ladle
medal
meddle
middle
model
muddle
needle
noodle
paddle
pedal
peddle
poodle
puddle
riddle
saddle
sandal
scandal
spindle
swindle
tidal
toddle
twiddle
vandal
wheedle
yodel
____
____

LDZ /ldz/ Final—one syllable

builds
fields
folds
holds
molds
scalds
scolds
worlds
yields

LF /lf/ Medial—two syllables

Alfred
baleful
bullfinch
bullfrog
elfin
elfish
elfkin
elflock
golfer
golfing
Gulf Stream
self-care
self-ease
self-fed
self-help
selfish
self-pride
self-serve
self-taught
shellfish
sulfa
sulfate
sulfine
sulfite
sulfur
welfare
willful
wolf cub
wolfhound
wolfish
wolf pack
____
____

LF /lf/ Medial—three syllables

alfalfa
alphabet
bellflower
Bellflower
bisulphate
bullfiddle
self-addressed
self-assured
self-aware
self-composed
self-concept
self-conscious
self-contained
self-control
self-defense
self-esteem
self-giving
self-glory
self-image
self-imposed
selfishly
self-pity
self-possessed
self-regard
self-reproach
self-respect
self-righteous
self-searching
self-serving
self-support
skillfully
skillfulness
sulfatic
sulfitic
sulfuric
unselfish
____
____
____

LF /lf/ Medial—four syllables

alphabetic
self-appointed
self-assurance
self-awareness
self-confidence
self-determined
self-directed
self-discipline
self-evident
self-reliance
self-sacrifice
self-sufficient

LF /lf/ Final—one syllable

elf
golf
gulf
Ralph
self
shelf
wolf
____
____

LF /lf/ Final—two syllables

Adolf
Adolphe
bookshelf
engulf
gray wolf
herself
himself
itself
myself
oneself
ourself
Randolph
Rudolph
thyself
werewolf
white wolf
yourself
____

FL /fl/ Initial—one syllable

flab
flagged
flagged
flail
flair
flaired
flak
flake
flakes
flame
flamed
flank

flap
flapped
flare
flared
flash
flashed
flask
flat
flaunt
flaw
flax
flay
flea
fleck
fled
flee
fleece
fleet
flesh
flew
flex
flick
flies
flight
flinch
fling
flint
flip
flipped
flirt
flit
Flo
float
flock
flood
floor
flop
flopped
floss
flounce
flounced
flour
flout
flow
flown
Floyd
flu
flub
flue
fluff
fluffs
fluke
flume
flung
flunk
flush
flute
flux
fly
phlegm
phlox
____
____

FL /fl/ Initial—two syllables

flabby
flaccid
Flag Day
flagging
flagman
flagpole
flagrant
Flagstaff
flaky
flameproof
flaming
flanker
flannel
flapjack
flapper
flare-up
flashback
flashbulb
flash card
flashcube
flash flood
flashgun
flashing
flashlight
flashy
flatbed
flatboat
flatcar
flatfoot
flatter
flattop
flautist
flavor
flaxseed
flection
fledgling
fleecy
Flemish
fleshy
Fletcher
flexion
flicker
flier
flight path
flighty
flimsy
flip-flops
flipper

flippers	floppy	flue pipe
flipping	Flora	fluffy
flitter	floral	fluid
float bridge	Florence	flunky
floater	florid	flurry
floating	florist	fluster
float plane	flossy	flutist
flocking	flounder	flutter
floodlight	flourish	flying
floorboard	flow chart	flywheel
floor lamp	flower	__________
floor show	flowing	__________
floozy	fluent	__________

FL /fl/ Initial—three syllables

flabbergast	flexible	fluctuate
flagrantly	flight control	fluency
flamboyant	floating dock	fluffier
flamenco	flood control	fluid ounce
flamethrower	floodwater	fluorine
flamingo	floorwalker	flutter kick
flammable	floppy disk	flyable
flannelette	Florentine	fly-casting
flashier	florescent	flycatcher
flatiron	Florida	flying fish
flattery	flotation	phlegmatic
flavoring	flotilla	__________
flea-bitten	flower girl	__________
flea market	flowerpot	__________

FL /fl/ Initial—four syllables

floriculture	flying safety	__________
fluctuation	flying saucer	__________

FL /fl/ Medial—two syllables

afflict	chiefly	deflect
aflame	conflict	firefly
afloat	cornflakes	flip-flops
blowfly	deflate	horsefly

housefly
ice floe
inflame
inflate
inflict
leaflet
muffler
pamphlet
reflect
roughly
snowflake
souffle′
stiffly
top-flight

FL /fl/ Medial—three syllables

affliction
affluence
affluent
butterfly
camouflage
cornflower
deflation
deflection
deflower
disfluent
dragonfly
genuflect
ice flowers
inflation
inflection
influence
overflow
reflection
reflector
sunflower
wallflower

FL /fl/ Medial—four syllables

cauliflower
conflagration
genuflection
inflammable
inflammation
inflatable
inflexible
influential
influenza
superfluous

FL /fl/ Final—two syllables

armful
artful
awful
baffle
baleful
careful
changeful
cheerful
doleful
doubtful
dreadful
Eiffel
faithful
fateful
fitful
forceful
fretful
frightful
fruitful
gainful
gleeful
graceful
grateful
handful
harmful
healthful
heedful
helpful
hopeful
hurtful
joyful
mournful
mouthful
muffle
needful
pailful
painful
peaceful
playful
raffle
restful
rightful
rueful
ruffle
sackful

scoopful
scuffle
shuffle
skillful
sniffle
spiteful
spoonful
stifle
thankful
thoughtful
trifle
tuneful
useful
waffle
wakeful
wasteful
watchful
willful
wishful
woeful
wrathful
wrongful
youthful

FL /fl/ Final—three syllables

beautiful
bountiful
colorful
deceitful
disdainful
disgraceful
distasteful
distressful
distrustful
dutiful
eventful
fanciful
forgetful
masterful
meaningful
merciful
pitiful
plentiful
reproachful
resentful
resourceful
respectful
sorrowful
teaspoonful
unlawful
unthankful
untruthful
wonderful

FL /fl/ Final—four syllables

tablespoonful
uneventful
unmerciful

GL /gl/ Initial—one syllable

glad
glade
glance
glanced
gland
glare
glared
glass
glaze
glazed
gleam
glean
gleaned
glee
glen
Glenn
glib
glide
glimpse
gloat
globe
gloom
gloss
glove
gloves
glow
glue
glued
glum
glume

GL /gl/ Initial—two syllables

glacier
gladden
gladness
glad rags
Gladys
glamor
glancing
glaring
glary
glasses
glasshouse
glassine
glassware
glasswork
glassy
glazement
glazier
glazing
gleaning
glee club
gleeful
Glenda
Glendale
glided
glide plane
glider
gliding
glimmer
glisten
glitter
gloaming
global
globate
gloomy
glory
glossy
glottis
Glover
glowing
glowworm
glucose
gluing
gluten
glutton
____

GL /gl/ Initial—three syllables

glamorize
glamorous
glandular
glass blower
glass blowing
glass cutter
glaucoma
gleefully
glimmering
glistening
glitter ice
glittery
globe-trotter
glomerate
gloomier
Gloria
glorify
glorious
glossary
glossier
glycerin
glyptodont
____
____

GL /gl/ Initial—four syllables

gladiator
gladiola
glamorously
Gloriana
glorifier
gloriously
glossology
____
____

GL /gl/ Medial—two syllables

aglow
boggling
bugler
Douglas
dress gloves
eaglet
eagling
eyeglass
giggler
giggling
giggly
haggling
hourglass
igloo
joggling
juggler
juggling
lymph gland

neglect
piglet
scrub gloves
spyglass
straggling
sunglow
unglue
unglued
wineglass
work gloves
wriggler
wriggly

GL /gl/ Medial—three syllables

aglimmer
aglitter
baseball glove
boondoggler
boxing glove
dark glasses
everglade
Everglades
eyeglasses
fiberglass
field glasses
leather gloves
looking glass
neglectful
negligence
negligent
plastic glass
rubber gloves
semi-glaze
semi-glazed
semi-gloss
sunglasses
water glass
window glass

GL /gl/ Final—two syllables

beagle
bugle
eagle
gargle
giggle
gurgle
haggle
jiggle
joggle
juggle
legal
regal
smuggle
snuggle
straggle
struggle
waggle
wiggle
wriggle
____
____

GL /gl/ Final—three syllables

bedraggle
boondoggle
illegal
Portugal
prodigal
salt bagel

NGL /ŋl/ Medial—two syllables

angler
angling
Anglo
England
English
jingler
jingling
jungly
mingling
wrangler
wrangling
____

NGL /ŋl/ Medial—three syllables

Anglican
anglicize
anglify
drinking glass
Englander
Englisher
English horn
Englishman
New England
____
____
____

NGL /ŋl/ Final—two syllables

angle	mingle	wrangle
dangle	shingle	
dingle	single	
jangle	spangle	
jingle	tangle	
jungle	tingle	

NGL /ŋl/ Final—three syllables

commingle	quadrangle	untangle
entangle	rectangle	
Kris Kringle	right angle	
left angle	triangle	

LK /lk/ Medial—two syllables

Alcan	milkman	silky
alcove	milkmen	sulking
bulkhead	milkshake	sulky
bulk mail	milk truck	talcum
bulky	milkweed	welcome
Elkhart	polka	welcomed
Elkhorn	railcar	
elk rack	silken	
hulking	silk hat	
mail car	silkworm	

LK /lk/ Medial—three syllables

alcohol	Chilkoot Pass	volcanic
alkali	Elk City	volcano
alkaline	Milky Way	vulcanize
alkalize	silkiness	
alkalized	silk-screen print	
balcony	silk stockings	
calculate	unwelcome	

LK /lk/ Medial—four syllables

Alcan Highway	talcum powder	
calculator		
recalculate		

LK /lk/ Final—one syllable

bilk	ilk	whelk
bulk	milk	yelk
elk	silk	________
hulk	sulk	________
Hulk	talc	________

LK /lk/ Final—two syllables

canned milk	real silk	sweet milk
dry milk	skim milk	________
goat's milk	sour milk	________
ice milk	spun silk	________

LK /lk/ Final—three syllables

buttermilk	malted milk	________
lowfat milk	powdered milk	________

KL /kl/ Initial—one syllable

clack	Clay	clique
claim	clean	cloak
claimed	cleaned	cloaked
Claire	cleanse	clock
clam	clear	clocked
clamp	cleared	clod
clan	cleats	clog
clang	clef	clogs
clap	cleft	clone
clapped	clench	clop
Clark	clerk	close
clash	click	closed
clashed	cliff	clot
clasp	Cliff	cloth
clasped	climb	clothe
class	climbed	clothes
Claude	clinch	cloud
clause	cling	clout
claw	Clint	clove
clawed	clip	clown
clay	clipped	clowned

cloy
cloyed
club
cluck
clue
clued
clump
clumped
clung
clutch
clutched
Clyde
Kline
klutz
____
____
____
____

KL /kl/ Initial—two syllables

chloric
chlorine
clackers
claimant
clambake
clammy
clamor
clamshell
clapping
Clara
Clarence
clarice
classic
classmate
classroom
classy
clatter
clattered
cleanly
cleanup
clearance
clearing
cleaver
clement
Cleo
clergy
Cleveland
clever
cliché
client
Clifford
Clifton
climate
climax
climber
climbing
clincher
clinic
clinker
Clinton
clipboard
clipper
clippers
clipping
clippings
clobber
clockwise
clockwork
closet
close-up
closing
closure
clothespin
clothier
clothing
cloudburst
cloudy
clover
Clovis
clubhouse
club steak
clumsy
cluster
clutter
cluttered
____

KL /kl/ Initial—three syllables

chlorinate
chloroform
clairvoyance
clam chowder
clam digging
clandestine
Clarendon
clarify
clarinet
classical
classified
classify
Claudia
clavichord
clavicle
claviform
cleanliness
cleft palate
clemency
clergyman
clerical

clientele
cliff dweller
climactic
clinical
clinician
clodhopper
cloverleaf
club sandwich
Klamath Falls
____
____
____

KL /kl/ Medial—two syllables

acclaim
acclaimed
anklet
Auckland
backlash
backlog
ball club
Barclay
becloud
blacklist
book club
booklet
Boys' Club
bridge club
broadcloth
brooklet
buckling
cackling
cheesecloth
chuckler
chuckling
conclude
cycling
cyclone
declare
decline
disclose
dishcloth
dry clean
dry cleaned
duckling
dustcloth
eclipse
eclipsed
enclose
exclaim
exclude
fan club
first class
foreclose
foreclosed
Franklin
freckly
Girls' Club
glee club
health club
heckler
incline
inclined
include
knuckler
knuckling
land claim
likely
loin cloth
mukluks
necklace
Oakland
occlude
o'clock
outclass
pickling
preclude
press club
prickling
prickly
proclaim
proclaimed
quick lime
quickly
reclaim
recline
reclined
seclude
sparkler
sparkling
speckling
sprinkler
sprinkling
tackler
ticklish
time clock
trickling
twinkling
weakling
weakly
wreckless
yacht club
____
____
____
____
____
____
____
____
____
____
____

KL /kl/ Medial—three syllables

acclimate
alarm clock
biweekly
bricklayer
Christmas club
country club
dry cleaning
eclectic
ecliptic
enclosure
exclusion
exclusive
foreclosure
Four-H Club
Franklin stove
garden club
health spa club
inclement
inclined plane
inclusion
inclusive
jockey club
junior class
kennel club
Lion's Club
middle class
nuclear
nuclei
nucleus
obliquely
paper clip
prickly heat
prickly pear
proclaimer
proclaiming
Santa Claus
secluded
seclusion
second class
senior class
service club
tablecloth
thunderclap
unbuckling
underclothes
uniquely
unlikely
Women's Club
____
____
____

KL /kl/ Medial—four syllables

acclamation
athletic club
declaration
digital clock
electric clock
enclosable
exclamation
exclusively
grandfather clock
inclinable
inclination
includible
non-classified
Oklahoma
proclamation
proclivity
reclamation
reclining chair
vacuum cleaner
____
____
____
____
____

KL /kl/ Final—two syllables

ankle
buckle
cackle
chuckle
circle
crackle
cycle
fickle
fiscal
focal
freckle
grackle
heckle
jackal
knuckle
local
nickel
pickle
prickle
rankle
rascal
sickle
snorkel
spackle
speckle
sprinkle
stickle

tackle
tickle
trickle
twinkle
uncle
vocal
wrinkle

KL /kl/ Final—three syllables

article
bicycle
chemical
classical
clinical
cortical
critical
cubicle
cuticle
encircle
icicle
lexical
logical
lyrical
magical
medical
metrical
miracle
monocle
musical
mystical
mythical
nautical
obstacle
optical
oracle
particle
physical
pinnacle
pinochle
practical
radical
ramshackle
recycle
rhythmical
skeptical
spectacle
spherical
technical
tentacle
topical
tricycle
two-cycle
typical
vehicle
vesicle

KL /kl/ Final—four syllables

angelical
botanical
historical
honeysuckle
identical
illogical
ironical
kilocycle
mechanical
motorcycle
nonsensical
numerical
patriarchal
political
receptacle
reciprocal
sabbatical
semicircle
statistical
unicycle

KL /kl/ Final—five syllables

academical
alphabetical
analytical
anatomical
astrological
astronomical
biographical
categorical
chronological
economical
geographical
mathematical
mythological
pathological
unequivocal
unmechanical
unmethodical

LER /lɚ/ Medial—three syllables

allergic	gallery	scholarship
allergy	polar bear	tolerance
celery	polarize	tolerant
collarbone	polar lights	________
colorful	roller skates	________
coloring	salary	________

LER /lɚ/ Medial—four syllables

artillery	polar axis	tolerable
capillary	polar region	tolerably
intolerant	roller skating	________

LER /lɚ/ Medial—five syllables

intolerable	roller skating rink	________
polarization	similarity	________
popularity	________	________

LER /lɚ/ Final—two syllables

antler	jailer	smaller
baler	mailer	smeller
Baylor	miller	solar
bowler	Miller	speller
broiler	molar	sprawler
caller	parlor	squealer
cellar	peddler	stroller
collar	piler	tailor
color	pillar	taller
cooler	polar	Taylor
crawler	poler	teller
dealer	poplar	thriller
dollar	roller	tiller
driller	ruler	trailer
drooler	sailor	trawler
duller	scaler	troller
dweller	scholar	Tyler
feeler	sealer	whaler
healer	seller	________
heeler	shriller	________

LER /lɚ/ Final—three syllables

angular
bachelor
consoler
controller
counselor
discolor
four-wheeler
jeweler
littler
modular
muscular
ocular
patroller
popular
propeller
regular
retailer
sand dollar
secular
similar
singular
three-wheeler
tricolor
tubular
two-wheeler
wholesaler
____

LER /lɚ/ Final—four syllables

caterpillar
fortuneteller
irregular
lenticular
multicolor
particular
semitrailer
spectacular
storm cellar
technicolor
twin propeller
unpopular
watercolor
____
____

LM /lm/ Medial—two syllables

ailment
Alma
almond
Belmont
Delmar
Elma
Elmer
filmstrip
hallmark
helmet
Palmer
schoolmarm
schoolmate
Selma
stalemate
Talmud
Thelma
trailman
Wilma
____
____

LM /lm/ Medial—three syllables

almanac
almighty
almond paste
concealment
congealment
curtailment
derailment
enrollment
entailment
fulfillment
installment
instillment
palmetto
repealment
revealment
____
____
____

LM /lm/ Final—one syllable

elm
film
helm
realm
whelm
____
____
____
____

ML /ml/ Final—two syllables

camel	mammal	________________
dismal	normal	________________
formal	thermal	________________

ML /ml/ Final—three syllables

abnormal	decimal	subnormal
animal	enamel	________________
caramel	informal	________________

NL /nl/ Final—two syllables

channel	hymnal	shrapnel
colonel	journal	signal
final	kennel	spinal
flannel	kernel	tunnel
funnel	panel	________________

NL /nl/ Final—three syllables

arsenal	infernal	paternal
cardinal	internal	personal
criminal	marginal	rational
doctrinal	maternal	seasonal
eternal	national	sectional
external	nocturnal	sentinel
fictional	nominal	terminal
fractional	optional	________________
functional	ordinal	________________

NL /nl/ Final—four syllables

additional	irrational	provisional
congressional	nutritional	sensational
diagonal	occasional	________________
emotional	octagonal	________________
exceptional	original	________________

LP /lp/ Medial—two syllables

alpine	helpful	kelp crab
gulping	helping	kelpfish
helper	helpless	palpate

pulpit
scalpel
sculptor
sculpture
yelping

LP /lp/ Final—one syllable

alp
gulp
help
kelp
palp
pulp
scalp
whelp
yelp

PL /pl/ Initial—one syllable

place
placed
plaid
plain
plaint
plait
plan
plane
planed
plank
planned
plant
plants
plaque
plat
plate
play
played
plea
plead
please
pleased
pleat
pledge
pledged
plied
plight
plink
plinth
plod
plop
plopped
plot
plow
plowed
pluck
plug
plugged
plum
plumb
plume
plumed
plump
plunge
plunged
plunk
plus
plush
ply

PL /pl/ Initial—two syllables

placard
place kick
place mat
place name
placer
placid
placing
placket
plaintiff
plaintive
Plainview
Plainville
planar
planer
planet
plangent
planing
planking
plankton
planner
planning
plantar
planter
plant food
plasma
plaster
plastic

plateau
plated
plateful
plate glass
platelet
plate mark
plater
platform
plating
Plato
platoon
platter
playback
player
playful
playground
playhouse
playmate
playoff
playpen
playroom
playsuit
playthings
playtime
playwear
playwright
plaza
pleaded
pleading
pleasant
pleasing
pleasure
pledger
plenty
pleural
plexus
pliant
pliers
plodded
plodder
plodding
plopping
plotted
plotter
plotting
plover
plower
plowshare
plugging
plug in
plumage
plumber
plumbing
plummet
plumpness
plunder
plunger
plunging
plural
plushy
plus sign
Pluto
plying
Plymouth
plywood
____
____
____
____

PL /pl/ Initial—three syllables

placebo
place hitter
place holder
place-kicker
placement test
placer gold
Placerville
plagiarize
plainclothesman
plainspoken
plaintively
planetoid
plantable
plantation
plasterboard
platinous
platinum
platonic
platypus
plausible
play-by-play
playacting
playfully
playing card
playing field
pleasantry
plenteous
plentiful
pleurisy
plexiglass
pliable
pliancy
plowable
plundering
pluralize
plutocrat
Plutonic
Plymouth Rock
____
____
____
____

PL /pl/ Initial—four syllables

plagiarism
planarian
planetary
planimeter
plasticity
platform rocker
Pleasant Island
pleasurable
plenipotent
plentifully
pleximeter
plotting paper
plurality
plutonium
______

PL /pl/ Initial—five syllables

planetarium
player piano
pledge of allegiance
plutonically
______
______

PL /pl/ Medial—two syllables

airplane
air plant
air plot
amply
aplite
aplomb
applaud
applause
applied
apply
birthplace
complain
complaint
complete
complex
comply
deplane
deplete
deplore
deploy
deplume
displace
display
displease
eggplant
employ
explain
explode
exploit
explore
fireplace
float plane
gangplank
grappling
home plate
hopeless
houseplant
ice plant
imply
jet plane
perplex
pipeline
poplar
replace
replant
replay
replete
reply
sapling
seaplane
simply
ski plane
sleepless
someplace
stapler
stoplight
supplant
supply
surplus
top line
upline
upload
______

PL /pl/ Medial—three syllables

accomplish
amplify
anyplace
appliance
applicant
appliqué
applying
complacent
complement
completion
complexion
complicate

compliment
contemplate
diploma
diplomat
discipline
double play
duplicate
employee
employment
explicit
explosion
explosive
heating plant
implement
incomplete
multiply
octuplet
quintuplet
replenish
resplendent
simplify
supplement
supplicant
triplicate
unemployed
unpleasant
water plant
____
____
____

PL /pl/ Medial—four syllables

amplifier
application
cassette player
complexity
explanation
exploration
multiplier
simplicity
unemployment
____
____
____

PL /pl/ Final—two syllables

ample
apple
chapel
couple
cripple
crumple
dimple
gospel
grapple
maple
opal
Opal
people
pimple
purple
ripple
rumple
sample
scalpel
scruple
simple
staple
steeple
temple
topple
triple
Whipple
____
____
____

PL /pl/ Final—three syllables

deep purple
disciple
example
free sample
multiple
pineapple
principal
principle
quadruple
quintuple
rose apple
____

PL /pl/ Final—four syllables

acne pimple
bottle nipple
candied apple
cornmeal scrapple
Episcopal
keep it simple
lovely dimple
mini-sample
more than ample

municipal
participle
rotten apple
spotted dapple
vice-principal
____

LR /lr/ Medial—two syllables

all right
ballroom
railroad
schoolroom
seal ring
toll road
walrus
____
____

LR /lr/ Medial—three syllables

already
cavalry
civil rights
coral reef
cradle roll
gravel road
jewelry
middle ring
rivalry

RL /rl/ Medial—two syllables

airlift
airline
Arlene
Arlon
barely
barley
Berlin
burlap
burly
careless
Carla
carload
Charlene
Charlie
Charline
Charlotte
clearly
curling
curly
Darlene
darling
Earlene
early
fairly
fearless
furlong
furlough
garland
garlic
Girl Scouts
Harlan
Harlem
Harley
heirloom
hourly
marlin
merely
Merlin
moorland
nearly
oarlock
parlor
pearly
poorly
scarlet
Shirley
squarely
starlight
starling
starlit
sterling
surely
swirly
Verlene
whirlpool
whirlwind
yearling
yearly
____
____

RL /rl/ Medial—three syllables

Arlington
barleycorn
Barley Green
blue marlin
brotherly
charlatan
charley horse
Charlottesville
Charlottetown

cheerleaders
curlicue
eagerly
early bird
entirely
fatherly
garlic bread
garlic salt
gingerly
Harlingen
hourly wage
Kimberly
mannerly
masterly
maturely
miserly
motherly
neighborly
northerly
obscurely
orderly
overland
overlap
overlay
overlie
overload
overlook
overly
Parliament
Pearl Harbor
power line
powerless
properly
quarterly
scholarly
securely
severely
sisterly
Sutherland
tenderly
utterly
whirlabout
whirligig
whirlpool bath
whirlybird
wonderland
____
____

RL /rl/ Medial—four syllables

curling iron
everlasting
New Orleans
northwesterly
sitting parlor
southeasterly
sterling silver
____
____

RL /ɚl/ Final—one syllable

Beryl
burl
Burl
Carl
curl
Earl
furl
girl
gnarl
hurl
Karl
Merle
pearl
Pearl
purl
skirl
snarl
swirl
twirl
whirl
whorl
____
____
____

RL /ɚl/ Final—two syllables

blue pearl
unfurl
untwirl
white pearl
young girl
____

RL /ɚl/ Final—three syllables

baby girl
baton twirl
Campfire Girl
knit and purl
Minnie Pearl
yellow pearl

RLZ /ɚlz/ Final—one syllable

- Charles
- curls
- Earl's
- girls
- gnarls
- hurls
- pearls
- purls
- snarls
- swirls
- twirls
- whirls
- whorls
- ____________
- ____________

REL /rl̩/ Final—two syllables

- barrel
- choral
- coral
- floral
- moral
- mural
- oral
- peril
- quarrel
- rural
- spiral
- squirrel
- sterile
- ____________
- ____________

REL /rl̩/ Final—three syllables

- admiral
- apparel
- corporal
- cultural
- funeral
- general
- immoral
- imperil
- lateral
- liberal
- mackerel
- mineral
- natural
- numeral
- pastoral
- sculptural
- several
- ____________

REL /rl̩/ Final—four syllables

- bilateral
- collateral
- conjectural
- inaugural
- intramural
- rear admiral
- unnatural
- vice-admiral
- ____________

SL /sl/ Initial—one syllable

- slab
- slack
- slacks
- slam
- slang
- slant
- slap
- slash
- slat
- slate
- slave
- slaw
- sled
- sleek
- sleep
- sleet
- sleeve
- sleigh
- sleight
- slept
- slew
- slick
- slid
- slide
- slides
- slight
- slim
- slime
- sling
- slip
- slit
- sloop
- slope

slot	sluice	slush
sloth	slum	sly
slouch	slump	________________
slow	slung	________________
sludge	slunk	________________
slug	slur	________________
slugs	slurp	________________

SL /sl/ Initial—two syllables

slacken	slicing	sloth bear
slacker	slicker	slothful
slalom	slide rule	slouchy
slapstick	sliding	Slovak
slashing	slighting	slowdown
sledder	slightly	slowpoke
sledding	slimy	slow sign
sled dog	slingshot	slow-up
sleeky	slinking	sludgy
sleeper	slinky	sluggish
sleepers	slipknot	slumber
sleep-in	slipper	slurring
sleepless	slippers	________________
sleepwear	slither	________________
sleepy	sliver	________________
sleety	slobber	________________
sleeveless	slogan	________________
sleigh bells	sloping	________________
slender	sloppy	________________
slicer	sloshy	________________

SL /sl/ Initial—three syllables

slalom course	slide viewer	slow-witted
sledgehammer	sliding scale	sluggishness
sleeping bag	slip cover	slumberland
sleepwalking	slippery	slushiest
sleepyhead	slot machine	________________
slenderize	slovenly	________________
sliceable	slow-motion	________________
slide trombone	slow-moving	________________

SL /sl/ Medial—two syllables

asleep
bobsled
bracelet
bustling
crosslight
crossline
crossly
dislike
dislodge
dog sled
enslave
grand slam
hustling
jostling
juiceless
landslide
Lesley
loosely
nicely
North slope
onslaught
priceless
rustling
ski slope
snowslide
translate
tussling
useless
voiceless
Wesley
whistler
whistling
wrestler
wrestling
____
____
____
____
____

SL /sl/ Medial—three syllables

carelessly
cross-legged
dislocate
disloyal
enslavement
expressly
misleading
purposeless
purposely
super slide
translation
translative
translator
translocate
translucence
translucent
uselessly
wrestling camp
wrestling coach
wrestling match
wrestling shoes
wrestling team
____
____
____
____
____

SL /sl/ Medial—four syllables

dislocation
legislation
legislative
____
____
____
____
____
____

SL /sl/ Final—two syllables

axle
basal
bristle
bustle
capsule
castle
counsel
dorsal
fossil
gristle
jostle
missile
morsel
mussel
parcel
pencil
trestle
vessel
wrestle
____
____

SL /sl/ Final—three syllables

blood vessel	dismissal	utensil
carousel	dispersal	
colossal	rehearsal	

LS /ls/ Medial—two syllables

also	falsely	wholesome
balsam	hillside	
Elsa	pulsate	
elsewhere	Tulsa	
Elsie	ulcer	
falsehood	wholesale	

LS /ls/ Medial—three syllables

balsam fir	falsify	wholesaler
Coral Sea	quarrelsome	Wilson
falsetto	Uncle Sam	

LS /ls/ Final—one syllable

else		
false		
pulse		

LS /ls/ Final—two syllables

convulse		
impulse		
repulse		

SHL /ʃl/ Final—two syllables

bushel	marshal	spatial
crucial	partial	special
facial	racial	
glacial	social	

SHL /ʃl/ Final—three syllables

commercial	impartial	potential
essential	initial	provincial
financial	judicial	torrential
fire marshal	official	

SHL /ʃl/ Final—four syllables

antisocial
artificial
beneficial
consequential
differential
influential
nonessential
preferential
prejudicial
presidential
residential
____

SPL /spl/ Initial—one syllable

splash
splat
splay
spleen
splice
spliced
splint
split
splits
splotch
splurge
____

SPL /spl/ Initial—two syllables

splashdown
splash guard
splatter
splendid
splendor
splicer
splicing
splinter
split shift
splitting
splutter
____

SPL /spl/ Initial—three syllables

splintery
split entrance
split entry
split level
split second
____

LT /lt/ Medial—two syllables

alter
alto
Colton
cultist
delta
falter
faultless
filter
guilty
halter
hilltop
Hilton
melted
molten
poultry
quilting
salted
shelter
smelter
voltage
Walter
welter
yuletide
____

LT /lt/ Medial—three syllables

alternate
altitude
Central Time
cultism
cultivate
dial tone
faultfinding
loyalty
malted milk
multiple
multiply
multitude
novelty
penalty
resulting
revolted
royalty
saltshaker

specialty
voltmeter
welterweight
____
____
____

LT /lt/ Medial—four syllables

altimeter
altogether
cultivator
difficulty
multiplier
seat belt safety

LT /lt/ Final—one syllable

belt
bolt
built
colt
dealt
dwelt
fault
felt
guilt
halt
hilt
jilt
jolt
kilt
knelt
lilt
malt
melt
molt
pelt
quilt
salt
shalt
silt
smelt
spilt
stilt
tilt
vault
volt
Walt
welt
wilt
Wilt
____
____

LT /lt/ Final—two syllables

adult
asphalt
bank vault
black belt
blue belt
cobalt
consult
Corn Belt
default
exalt
exult
fan belt
farm belt
insult
pole vault
Renault
result
revolt
rock salt
seat belt
tumult
white belt
____
____

LT /lt/ Final—three syllables

difficult
garlic salt
leather belt
patchwork quilt
Roosevelt
somersault
thunderbolt
____
____

LTH /lθ/ Medial—two syllables

filthy
healthful
healthy
stealthy
Waltham
wealthy

LTH /lθ/ Medial—three syllables

filthiest	unhealthy	
stealthiest	wealthier	
unhealthful	wealthiest	

LTH /lθ/ Final—one syllable

filth	stealth	wealth
health	tilth	

LTS /lts/ Final—one syllable

belts	melts	tilts
bolts	molts	vaults
colts	pelts	welts
faults	quilts	wilts
jolts	salts	
kilts	silts	
malts	stilts	

LTS /lts/ Final—two syllables

adults	insults	revolts
consults	pole vaults	seat belts

TL /tl/ Medial—two syllables

atlas	outlet	potluck
butler	outline	settler
lightly	outlook	
outlaw	potlatch	

TL /tl/ Medial—three syllables

anciently	outlining	quietly
Atlanta	outlying	sedately
Atlantic	perfectly	
irately	politely	

TL /tl/ Final—three syllables

belittle	parental	skeletal
capital	pedestal	subtitle
entitle	rose beetle	
immortal	segmental	

TL /tl/ Final—four syllables

accidental
congenital
continental
elemental
fundamental
horizontal
incidental
monumental
noncommittal
oriental
sentimental
thermos bottle
tittle tattle
____
____

LV /lv/ Medial—two syllables

Alva
Alvin
Calvin
Cleveland
culvert
salvage
salvaged
salvo
shelving
silver
solvent
solving
velvet
____
____
____

LV /lv/ Medial—three syllables

Alvina
dissolving
evolvement
galvanic
galvanize
insolvent
involvement
involving
pulverize
quicksilver
resolving
revolving
salvation
silver fox
silver-plate
silversmith
silverware
silvery
solvable
Sylvia
velveteen
velvety
wolverine
____
____
____
____

LV /lv/ Final—one syllable

delve
salve
shelve
solve
twelve
valve
____
____
____

LV /lv/ Final—two syllables

absolve
bivalve
devolve
dissolve
evolve
involve
resolve
revolve
____

LVD /lvd/ Final—one syllable

delved
shelved
solved
____
____
____
____
____
____

LVD /lvd/ Final—two syllables

absolved
dissolved
evolved
involved
resolved
revolved
unsolved

LVZ /lvz/ Final—one syllable

delves
elves
selves
shelves
solves
valves
wolves

LVZ /lvz/ Final—two syllables

dissolves
evolves
involves
ourselves
resolves
revolves
themselves
yourselves

VL /vl/ Final—two syllables

bevel
civil
devil
gavel
gravel
hovel
level
marvel
navel
novel
oval
ravel
revel
rival
shovel
shrivel
swivel
weevil

VL /vl/ Final—three syllables

approval
arrival
boll weevil
carnival
festival
interval
removal
revival
steam shovel
unravel
upheaval

LY /lj/ Medial—two syllables

all year
billiards
billion
bouillon
bullion
coal yard
collier
Collier
Dahlia
failure
Julia
Julian
million
millionth
school yard
school year
stallion
trillion
valiant
value
valued
William
zillion

LY /lj/ Medial—three syllables

alienate
Amelia
Australia
Australian
azalea
battalion
billiard ball
billionaire
bouillon cube
Camellia
Centralia
Cornelia
cotillion
familial
familiar
four billion
magnolia
medallion
millionaire
rebellion
regalia
valiancy
valiantly
valuate
valueless
valuing
Vermillion
Williamsburg
____
____

LY /lj/ Medial—four syllables

billiard table
chameleon
familiarize
Julius Caesar
salutation
valuable
valuation
valuator
____

LZ /lz/ Medial—two syllables

bailsman
fool's cap
fool's gold
salesman
school zone
____
____
____
____

LZ /lz/ Final—one syllable

aisles
bails
bales
balls
bells
Bill's
bills
boils
bowls
calls
Charles
chills
coils
deals
dills
dolls
drills
eels
fails
falls
feels
files
fills
foals
foils
fools
fouls
frills
gales
gals
gills
goals
grills
growls
gulls
hails
halls
heels
hills
holes
hulls
jails
kneels
males
meals
miles
mills
moles

nails
oils
pails
peals
piles
pills
poles
polls
pools
pulls
quails
quills
rails
reels
roles
rolls
rules
sails
sales
scales
scowls
seals
sells
shrills
sills
skills
skulls
smells
smiles
snails
snarls
soils
soles
souls
spells
spills
spoils
spools
squalls
squeals
stalls
stools
strolls
styles
tails
tales
tells
thrills
tiles
toils
tolls
tools
walls
wells
whales
wheels
wills
wools
yells
____

LZ /lz/ Final—two syllables

angels
annals
ant hills
barrels
baseballs
battles
bluebells
bottles
bundles
bushels
camels
candles
capsules
carols
cattails
cradles
cymbals
dawdles
details
dwellers
eggshells
equals
females
fiddles
finals
footballs
formals
fossils
fuels
gruels
handles
hymnals
jewels
kindles
ladles
middles
needles
nettles
noodles
paddles
petals
poodles
portholes
pretzels
prevails
profiles
propels
pupils
quarrels
quetzals
rascals

rattles
rebels
recalls
refills
rentals
reptiles
retails
reveals
riddles
rivals
roll calls
saddles
sandals
sawmills
scandals
seagulls
seashells
settles
signals
Sioux Falls
skittles
snowballs
softballs
tadpoles
tattles
tittles
toadstools
toddles
toenails
tonsils
towels
windmills
____
____
____
____

LZ /lz/ Final—three syllables

aerials
animals
annuals
axials
basketballs
bass viols
Blue Angels
bookmobiles
burials
buttonholes
cannonballs
cardinals
Cardinals
carnivals
carousels
casseroles
cathedrals
coveralls
enamels
fairy tales
festivals
fingernails
generals
principals
projectiles
rehearsals
rituals
spectacles
syllables
utensils
volleyballs
____
____

ZL /zl/ Final—two syllables

chisel
damsel
dazzle
diesel
drizzle
easel
fizzle
frazzle
frizzle
fusil
grizzle
guzzle
Hazel
muzzle
nasal
nozzle
nuzzle
puzzle
schnozzle
sizzle
weasel
____
____
____

ZL /zl/ Final—three syllables

appraisal
arousal
disposal
embezzle
refusal
witch hazel

M

Pronounced: /m/
Spelled: m, mm, mn, mb, lm, gm, chm

M /m/ Initial—one syllable

Ma
Mac
mace
mad
made
Madge
maid
mail
mailed
main
maize
make
male
mall
malt
Mame
man
mane
mange
manned
map
mar
Marc
march
March
marched
mare
mark
Mark
marred
marsh
Marv
mash
mashed
mask
masked
mass
massed
mat
Mat
match
matched
mate
math
Matt
may
May
maze
mazed
me
meal
mean
meant
meat
meet
Mel
melt
men
mesh
meshed
mess
met
mice
mid
Midge
might
mike
Mike
mile
milk
milked
mill
milled
mime
mimed
mind
mine
mined
mint
mire
mired
miss
Miss
missed
mist
mite
mitt
mix
mixed
moan

moaned
mod
mode
mold
mole
Mom
monk
month
mood
moon
moor
moored
moose
mop
mope
moped
mopped
more
moss
most
moth
mount
mouse
mouth
mouthed
move
moved
much
mud
muff
muffed
mug
mull
mulled
mum
mush
muss
must
mutt
my
Myles
myrrh
myth
____
____

M /m/ Initial—two syllables

Mabel
macaw
machine
Madame
Madrid
maelstrom
Magi
magnet
mailman
Main Street
maintain
major
majored
malice
mammal
mammoth
mandate
Mandel
mankind
manner
manners
many
marbles
Marcus
Marie
marine
market
marriage
married
marrow
marry
Marshall
marten
Martha
martial
martin
Martin
Marty
martyr
Marvin
Mary
mascot
masher
mason
master
mastered
mattress
Maureen
Maurice
maybe
May Day
mayor
measure
measured
meaty
medal
member
membrane
mental
menu
merit
mermaid
merry
metal
meter
Mickey

middle
migraine
migrate
Milan
mildew
mildewed
mileage
milkmaid
milkman
milky
miller
Miller
Millie
Milton
minstrel
minute
mirror
mirrored
mister
Mitchell
mitten
mitzvah
model
modeled
modem
Molly
molten

Monday
money
monied
monkey
monkeyed
Monroe
monster
Monty
morbid
morose
Morris
Morse code
mother
motor
motored
mountain
moustache
mouthful
mouth guard
mouthwash
movement
movie
moving
Mr.
Mrs.
mudguard
mudhole

muffin
muffler
muggy
mukluk
mummy
mundane
Murray
muscle
mushing
mushroom
musk ox
muskrat
muslin
mustang
mustard
muster
mutton
muzzle
myna
Myrna
Myron
Myrtle
myself
mystic
mystique
____
____

M /m/ Initial—three syllables

MacArthur
machinate
machinist
mackerel
mackinaw
Mackintosh
macrograph
Madeline
Madison
Madonna

madrigal
magazine
magician
magistrate
magnitude
mailwoman
malfunction
management
manager
mandible

mandolin
maneuver
maneuvered
mannequin
manual
Manuel
marching band
March of Dimes
mariner
marital

marshmallow
Maryland
masculine
matronly
maverick
McKenzie
McKinley
meander
meandered
measurement
mechanic
mechanize
mechanized
medial
medieval
medium
melody
menial
Mercedes
mercury
Meredith
messenger
Messiah
meteor
Mexico
Miami
miasma
Micro Age
microfilm
microphone
microscope
microwave
Milky Way
millionaire
minister
ministry
Miranda
misfortune
Missouri
mobile home
moccasin
modulate
mollified
mollify
monitor
Montana
Monterey
Montpelier
monument
mortified
mortify
Mother's Day
motorbike
motorboat
motorcade
motorcar
motor home
motorist
motorize
multiplied
multiply
muscle-bound
musical
musician
musketeer
mussel crab
myopic
mystical
____
____
____
____

M /m/ Initial—four syllables

macaroni
machination
machinery
macroscopic
magnanimous
magnificent
malaria
mandibular
Manitoba
Massachusetts
mass emergy
medially
mediocre
melodrama
meticulous
metropolis
Mexican food
migratory
military
millinery
Minnesota
misadventure
misconception
miserable
misinterpret
misrepresent
Mississippi
modality
monastery
Mongolia
monotonous
monumental
morality
myopia
mysterious
mythology
____
____
____

M /m/ Initial—five syllables

Macedonia
magnification
major general
manipulation
manual training
manufacturer
mathematical
mechanization
Memorial Day
memorization
metropolitan
miscegenation
miscellaneous
misrepresented
Mississippian
misunderstanding
modification
monogenesis
monomania
monophobia
monoplegia
monotheism
monotonously
multiplication
musicology
mysteriously
____
____
____
____

M /m/ Medial—two syllables

aiming
almost
amen
amend
amends
amid
amidst
amiss
among
amount
Amy
asthma
beaming
bloomer
booming
camel
cement
chamois
checkmate
chimney
clamming
clammy
clamor
climate
climber
climbing
combing
comet
comic
coming
command
commend
commerce
common
damage
demand
dimmer
dimming
dreamer
dreaming
drummer
Edmond
Emma
famine
famous
flaming
foaming
foamy
grammar
grimace
grimy
gummy
hammer
hammock
hemlock
himself
homage
homely
homer
Homer
human
humid
humor
image
Jamey
Jamie
jasmine
jimmy
Jimmy
lament
layman
lemon
limeade
limit
Mama
Mamie
mammal
milkman

Mimi
moment
Mommy
naming
numbing
Omar
omen
pieman
pigmy
playmates
plumage
plumber
plummet
primer
Raymond
reamer
Remus
roomer
rumor
Sammy
scrimmage
seaman
segment
shammy
shimmer
simmer
Simon
skimmer
someone
stammer
steamer
steaming
streamer
submerge
summer
summit
swimmer
swimming
tamer
Tammy
Thomas
thumbing
timer
Timmy
tombstone
tomcat
Tommi
Tommy
trimmer
trimming
Truman
tumor
woman
women
yeoman
Yuma
____
____
____
____

M /m/ Medial—three syllables

adamant
admiral
admonish
a la mode
alchemist
Amanda
Amazon
Amelia
amethyst
amnesia
animal
argument
boomerang
camera
ceramic
cinnamon
circumstance
comedy
commission
committee
consumer
customer
demeanor
democrat
demonstrate
diminish
domestic
dominate
dominos
edema
Edmonton
emerald
emery
familiar
family
feminine
feminist
flamenco
flamingo
gamma ray
Gemini
hemisphere
homecoming
homemaker
homophone
humorous
imitate
imminent
infamous
laminate
laundromat

lawnmower
limerick
limited
memorize
memory
newcomer
numeral
numerous
ominous
optimist
persimmon
preempted
redeemer
salami
Samoa
Samoan
samovar
sediment
self-image
seminar
shoemaker
simulate
sledge hammer
somersault
submarine
submission
submissive
summerhouse
summer school
summer stock
summertime
supplement
symmetry
talisman
tamale
tenement
Timothy
tomato
tournament
ultimate
whimsical
Women's Club
Wyoming
____
____

M /m/ Medial—four syllables

accommodate
administer
admonition
Alabama
alimony
Amarillo
amaryllis
America
amphibian
anathema
animation
anomalous
anomaly
anonymous
Bohemian
catamaran
chameleon
climbing safety
commentator
commercially
commissioner
conglomerate
demolition
economist
eminently
gemologist
homophonous
humility
immensity
insomnia
insomniac
intimidate
magnanimous
monumental
noncommittal
panorama
paramedic
parameter
patrolwoman
phenomenon
predicament
proximity
public domain
seminary
timidity
unanimous
____
____

M /m/ Medial—five syllables

abominable
accommodation
administration
admonishingly
ameliorate
axiomatic
bimolecular
binomially
condominium
denomination
enumerated
geometrical

hippopotamus
immediately
innumerable
Memorial Day
momentarily
myringatomy
ramification
rudimentary

sedimentary
seminarian
simultaneous
unanimously
____
____
____
____

____
____
____
____
____
____
____
____

M /m/ Final—one syllable

aim
am
balm
beam
Bim
blame
bloom
boom
brim
broom
brougham
bum
calm
cam
came
chime
chrome
chum
clam
Clem
climb
comb
come
cram
cream
dam
dame
deem
dim

dime
dome
doom
dram
dream
drum
fame
flame
foam
frame
from
fume
game
gem
gleam
gloom
gnome
gram
grim
grime
groom
Guam
gum
gym
ham
hem
him
home
hum

hymn
I'm
jam
Jim
Kim
lam
lamb
lame
limb
lime
loam
loom
malm
Mame
Mom
mum
name
Nome
numb
ohm
palm
Pam
plum
plumb
pram
prim
prime
psalm
qualm

ram
ream
rhyme
rim
roam
Rome
room
Sam
same
scram
scream
seam
seem
sham
shame
skim
slam
slim
slime
slum
some
steam
stem
stream
strum
sum
swam
swim
tam
tame
team
teem
them
theme
thumb
thyme
Tim
time
Tom
tomb
tram
trim
vim
whim
whom
yam
zoom
____
____
____
____
____
____
____
____
____
____

M /m/ Final—two syllables

Adam
album
alum
annum
anthem
atom
balsam
bathroom
becalm
became
become
bedlam
bedroom
bedtime
Belgium
blossom
boredom
bottom
bridegroom
broadloom
brougham
buckram
carom
chartroom
chasm
checkroom
coatroom
condemn
courtroom
coxcomb
custom
daydream
daytime
defame
denim
dictum
doldrum
emblem
esteem
extreme
fathom
first name
flotsam
forum
frenum
gypsum
half time
heirloom
high time
homeroom
humdrum

ice cream
income
jetsam
last name
lifetime
madame
maxim
mayhem
modem
moonbeam
mushroom
phantom
phoneme
phylum
problem
random
redeem
salaam
spasm
springtime
sternum
Stockholm
stockroom
storeroom
sunbeam
supreme
symptom
system
tandem
theorem
twosome
wholesome
wigwam
William
wisdom

M /m/ Final—three syllables

Abraham
accustom
addendum
amalgam
anagram
anteroom
antonym
baptism
Bethlehem
Boulder Dam
bubble gum
Buckingham
buddhism
cablegram
calcium
Central Time
cerebrum
chewing gum
Christendom
cofferdam
decorum
diadem
diagram
dining room
elbowroom
facism
frolic
Hall of Fame
helium
homonym
honeycomb
Hoover Dam
jejunum
living room
maximum
minimum
monogram
overtime
pantomime
paradigm
pseudonym
radium
reading room
Rotterdam
sodium
soft-shell clam
sour cream
stadium
sugarplum
summertime
synonym
telegram
truism
wrestling team

M /m/ Final—four syllables

aluminum
aquarium
arboretum
beryllium
cerebellum
chauvinism
chrysanthemum
coliseum
compendium
consortium
family room
feudalism
gymnasium
heroism
hinduism
ideogram
Jerusalem
jingoism
journalism
Judaism
linoleum
mongolism
neoplasm
pacifism
paroxysm
petroleum
proscenium
realism
symposium
terrarium
video game

M /m/ Final—five syllables

Anglicanism
auditorium
behaviorism
Catholicism
condominium
crematorium
hesperidium
Protestantism
recidivism
romanticism
scholasticism
subjectivism

MB /mb/ Medial—two syllables

amber
Amber
Bambi
bamboo
Bombay
chamber
chambers
combine
combined
combo
combust
comeback
Dumbo
embank
embark
embed
ember
emboss
gambit
game bag
game bird
gumbo
imbibe
imbibed
Lambert
Lemberg
limber
Limberg
limbo
Lombard
lumbar
lumber
mambo
member
nameboard
number
numbered
Romberg
rumba
samba
slumber
slumbered
somber
tambour
timber
trombone
umber

MB /mb/ Medial—three syllables

ambition
bambino
bamboo shoots
bamboozle
Columbus
combustion
cucumber
cumbersome
December
embankment
embargo
embarrass
embassy
gamboling
hamburger
Kimberly
Limburger
lumbering
lumberjack
lumbermill
lumberyard
membership
November
numbering
numberline
ombudsman
outnumber
rambunctious
reimburse
remember
remembered
September
sombrero
somebody
tambourine
unnumbered
Zambezi
Zambia

MB /mb/ Medial—four syllables

ambassador
ambiguous
Cambodia
Columbia
combination
combustible
mumbo jumbo

MBER /mbɚ/ Final—two syllables

amber
Amber
chamber
ember
limber
lumber
member
number
slumber
somber
timber
umber

MBER /mbɚ/ Final—three syllables

cucumber
December
November
outnumber
remember
September

MER /mer/ /mɝ/ Medial—three syllables

admiral
armory
boomerang
emerald
emery
formerly
humorous
limerick
memory
numerate
numerous
somersault

MER /mer/ /mɚ/ Medial—four syllables

America	emergency	______
American	______	______

MER /mɚ/ Final—two syllables

armor	Homer	skimmer
clamor	humor	stammer
climber	murmur	steamer
drummer	plumber	streamer
Elmer	primer	summer
farmer	reamer	swimmer
former	roomer	tamer
grammar	rumor	tumor
hammer	shimmer	______
homer	simmer	______

MER /mɚ/ Final—three syllables

beachcomber	newcomer	sledgehammer
consumer	performer	______
customer	redeemer	______

ML /ml/ Final—two syllables

camel	mammal	______
dismal	normal	______
formal	thermal	______

ML /ml/ Final—three syllables

abnormal	decimal	subnormal
animal	enamel	______
caramel	informal	______

LM /lm/ Medial—two syllables

ailment	filmstrip	stalemate
Alma	hallmark	Talmud
almond	helmet	Thelma
Belmont	Palmer	trailman
Delmar	schoolmarm	Wilma
Elma	schoolmate	______
Elmer	Selma	______

LM /lm/ Medial—three syllables

almanac
almighty
almond paste
concealment
congealment
curtailment
derailment
enrollment
entailment
fulfillment
installment
instillment
palmetto
repealment
revealment
____
____
____

LM /lm/ Final—one syllable

elm
film
helm
realm
whelm
____

MP /mp/ Medial—two syllables

bumper
bumpy
campaign
camper
campground
camping
camp-out
campus
clamping
clumpy
compact
compare
compared
compass
compel
compete
complain
complaint
complete
complex
compound
compute
cramping
crimpy
crumple
crumply
dampen
dampened
dumping
dumpling
dumpster
dump truck
dumpy
empire
grumpy
hamper
impact
impair
impaired
impale
impaled
impart
impasse
impeach
impeached
impede
impel
impelled
impend
impose
jump ball
jumper
jumping
jump rope
jump seat
jump suit
jumpy
limpet
limpid
limping
lumpy
pamper
pampered
pampers
Pompey
pompous
primping
pumping
pumpkin
rampart
rumpling
sampan
sampler
scamper
scrimping
shrimping
skimpy
slumping

stamping
stumping
tamper
tampered
temper
tempered
tempest
template
temple
tempted
thumping
tramping
trumpet
trumping
vampire
whimper

MP /mp/ Medial—three syllables

accomplice
accomplish
amplify
assumption
attempted
bumper guard
bumper jack
camporee
compactor
companion
company
compassion
competent
component
composite
composure
computer
consumption
contemplate
decompose
decomposed
distemper
empower
encompass
example
exempted
exemption
high jumper
impacted
imported
imposter
jumping bean
jumping jack
No Dumping
Olympics
pompadour
preempted
presumption
pumpkin pie
redemption
resumption
tamper-proof
temperance
temperate
temptation

MP /mp/ Medial—four syllables

companionship
compensation
composition
contemplation
Humpty Dumpty
impalpable
imperious
intemperate
pomposity
pumpernickel
reimposing
temperament
temperature
temporary
unimportant

MP /mp/ Medial—five syllables

contemporary
impenetrable
imperishable
temperamental
temporization

MP /mp/ Final—one syllable

amp
blimp
bump
camp
champ
chump
clamp
clump
cramp
crimp
damp
dump
grump
hemp
hump
imp
jump
lamp
limp
lump
plump
primp
pump
ramp
romp
rump
scamp
shrimp
skimp
slump
stamp
stomp
stump
thump
tramp
trump
____
____
____

MP /mp/ Final—two syllables

boot camp
boys' camp
broad jump
encamp
floor lamp
gas pump
girls' camp
high jump
leg cramp
long jump
off ramp
on ramp
revamp
ski jump
sun lamp
tire pump
____
____

MP /mp/ Final—three syllables

Boy Scout camp
city dump
garbage dump
Girl Scout camp
postage stamp
rubber stamp
safety lamp
stomach cramp
sugar lump
summer camp
table lamp
wrestling camp
____
____
____

MPS /mps/ Final—one syllable

amps
blimps
bumps
champs
chumps
clamps
clumps
cramps
crimps
dumps
glimpse
imps
jumps
lamps
limps
lumps
mumps
primps
pumps
ramps
romps
shrimps
skimps
slumps

stamps
stumps
thumps
tramps
trumps
____
____
____
____

RM /rm/ Medial—two syllables

airmail
airman
armful
armhole
armor
armored
army
Burma
Burmese
Carmel
Carmen
charming
dormant
Erma
ermine
farm belt
farmer
farming
farmland
fireman
firemen
foreman
foremost
formal
format
former
garment
German
gourmet
harmful
harmless
hermit
hormone
Irma
mermaid
Norma
normal
Norman
permit
spearmint
sperm whale
surmise
surmount
termite
thermal
thermos
torment
turmoil
unarmed
vermin
Vermont
warmly
warm-up
wormwood
____
____
____

RM /rm/ Medial—three syllables

alderman
armament
armistice
armorer
armory
Bermuda
cormorant
enormous
farming land
fire marshall
firmament
formation
formula
Germany
germinate
harmonize
harmony
informal
marmalade
performance
performer
permanent
permission
pharmacist
pharmacy
Prince Charming
retirement
snake charmer
storm cellar
storm center
storm warning
storm window
terminal
terminate
thermostat
uniformed
vermillion
____
____

RM /rm/ Medial—four syllables

affirmative
armadillo
Armistice Day
army blanket
conformation
dormitory
fermentation
germination
harmonica
infirmary
infirmity
permanently
permeable
supermarket
termination
thermometer
uniformly
____

RM /rm/ Medial—five syllables

formalization
terminology
thermal barrier
uniformity
____
____
____

RM /rm/ Final—one syllable

arm
charm
dorm
farm
firm
form
germ
harm
squirm
storm
swarm
warm
worm
____
____

RM /rm/ Final—two syllables

affirm
alarm
bookworm
confirm
conform
cutworm
deform
dust storm
earthworm
hailstorm
inchworm
infirm
inform
perform
platform
rainstorm
reform
sandstorm
silkworm
snowstorm
tapeworm
windstorm
____
____

RM /rm/ Final—three syllables

angleworm
fire alarm
pachyderm
thunderstorm
uniform
____
____
____
____

SM /sm/ Initial—one syllable

smack
small
smart
smash
smear
smell
smelt
smile
smiled
smirch
smirk
smit

smite
smith
Smith
smock
smog
smoke
smoked
smooch
smooth
smote
smudge
smug

SM /sm/ Initial—two syllables

smacker
smacking
smaller
smallest
small fry
small game
smallpox
small talk
small-town
smarter
smartly
smartness
smart set
smash-up
smatter
smeary
smeller
smelling
smelly
smelter
smidgen
smiling
smirky
Smithville
smithy
smiting
smitten
smocking
smoggy
smokehouse
smoke screen
smokestack
Smoky
smolder
smoldered
smoother
smoothly
smother
smothered
smudgy
smugger
smuggest
smugly
smugness

SM /sm/ Initial—three syllables

smart aleck
smattering
smearier
smelling salts
smilingly
smithereens
smoke chaser
smoke jumper
smokier
smokiest
smoldering
smorgasbord
smothering
smudgily
smudginess

SM /sm/ Medial—two syllables

baseman
basement
blacksmith
Christmas
classman
classmate
dismay
dismiss
dismount
goldsmith
huntsman
iceman
locksmith
outsmart
placemat
pressman
tinsmith
transmit

SM /sm/ Medial—three syllables

businessman	first baseman	second baseman
Christmas card	locksmith shop	silversmith
Christmas Eve	Mr. Smith	third baseman
Christmas seals	pacemaker	______
Christmas tree	policeman	______
coppersmith	policemen	______

SM /sm/ Medial—four syllables

embarrassment	senior classman	______
junior classman	upper classman	______
lower classman	______	______

MY /mj/ Medial—two syllables

farmyard	______	______
______	______	______

MY /mj/ Medial—three syllables

amulet	simulate	stimulus
communist	stimulant	______
emulate	stimulate	______

MY /mj/ Medial—four syllables

Bohemian	______	______
stimulation	______	______

MZ /mz/ Medial—two syllables

doomsday	Jamestown	time zone
groomsman	thumbs down	______
helmsman	thumbs up	______

MZ /mz/ Final—one syllable

beams	comes	dims
bums	crams	domes
calms	creams	dooms
charms	crimes	drams
chimes	crumbs	dreams
clams	deems	drums
climbs	dimes	flames

foams
fumes
games
gems
gums
gyms
hams
hems
homes
hums
James
jams
Jim's
lambs
limbs
limes
looms
palms
Pam's
psalms
rams
reams
Reims
rhymes
rims
roams
rooms
Sam's
seems
shames
stems
sums
tames
teams
Thames
themes
thumbs
times
trams
trims
____
____

MZ /mz/ Final—two syllables

Adams
assumes
bedrooms
daydreams
exams
schoolrooms
windchimes
____
____

N

Pronounced: /n/
Spelled: n, nn, gn, kn, pn, ne

N /n/ Initial—one syllable

gnar
gnarl
gnarled
gnash
gnat
gnaw
gnome
gnu
knap
knave
knead
knee
kneel
knell
knew
knife
knight
knit
knob
knock
knoll
knot
know
known
nail

name
Nan
nap
Nash
Neal
neap
near
neat
neck
Ned
need
Neil
Nell
nerve
nest
net
new
news
next
nibs
nice
Nick
niece
night
Nile

nine
ninth
nip
nix
no
nod
noise
Nome
none
nook
noon
nor
North
nose
not
note
noun
now
numb
nun
nurse
nut
____
____
____

N /n/ Initial—two syllables

gnarling
gnarring
gnashing

gnathic
gnawing
gnomish

Gnostics
knapsack
knavish

kneecap
knee-deep
knee-high
knee-hole
knee-jerk
kneeler
kneepad
knickers
knickknack
knife-edge
knighthood
knightly
knitting
knockdown
knocker
knocking
knock-kneed
knockout
knockwurst
knothole
knotted
know-how
knowing
knowledge
knuckle
nail brush
nail file
naive
naked
nameboard
Nancy
Nanette
napkin
Naples
narrow
nasal
Nashville
natal
Nathan
nation
native
naughty
navy
nearly
nebbish
necklace
necktie
nectar
needle
neglect
Negus
neighbor
Neika
neither
Nellie
Nelson
Nemo
neon
nephew
nervy
network
neuter
neutral
neutron
never
Newark
Newman
New Year's
New York
Newark
Newman
nibble
nickel
nickname
Nicky
Nicole
nightfall
nightgown
night guard
nightmare
Nina
nineteen
ninety
Ninja
Nita
Nixon
Noah
noble
nobly
noel
Noel
noisy
nonsense
noodle
Norbert
Norma
normal
Norman
northern
North Pole
North Sea
North Shore
North Star
Norway
Norwich
nosebleed
nostril
nothing
notice
notion
nouveau
novel
novice
nowhere
nugget
number
nutmeg

nutty	________________	________________
nylon	________________	________________
pneuma	________________	________________

N /n/ Initial—three syllables

nail polish	negative	night watchman
Nairobi	negligee	nitrogen
nanogram	negligent	nobody
Nantucket	neighborhood	nocturnal
Naomi	nemesis	nomadic
narcissus	Netherlands	nominee
nasturtium	nether world	nostalgia
Natalie	networking	notary
national	neurosis	noteworthy
nationwide	Nevada	novelty
natively	New Delhi	November
natural	New England	nucleus
naturelike	newfangled	nursery
nausea	Newfoundland	nutcracker
nautical	New Hampshire	nutrition
Nautilus	New Jersey	pneumatic
Navajo	newspaper	pneumograph
Nebraska	New Year's Day	pneumonia
nectarine	New Year's Eve	________________
needlepoint	New Zealand	________________
needlework	nicety	________________

N /n/ Initial—four syllables

Nagasaki	nefarious	Nicaragua
Napoleon	negotiate	nobility
naturalist	neighborhood watch	nomenclature
naturalize	neolithic	noncommittal
navigation	neology	nonobjective
navigator	neurologist	nonresistant
Neanderthal	neurology	nonrestrictive
necessary	neurosurgeon	nonviolence
necessitate	neutrality	northwesterner
necessity	New Mexico	noticeable
necropolis	newspaperman	notorious

numerical
pneumococcus
pneumogastric
pneumothorax

N /n/ Medial—two syllables

Anna
any
banner
beanie
Benny
boner
bonnet
Bonnie
bonus
bunny
canal
canning
cannon
cannot
canoe
channel
Cheney
chimney
china
China
cleaner
cleaners
cleanup
Connie
cunning
Dana
Danish
Danny
Deming
Dena
denim
Dennis
deny
diner
dinner
donor
doughnut
downfall
drainage
Enid
Fannie
final
finer
finish
Finnish
Francis
frowning
funny
gainer
Gina
honey
honor
innate
inner
Janet
Jeanette
Jeanie
jennet
Jenny
Juneau
keener
kennel
Kenneth
Kenny
Lana
Lena
lightning
liner
lunar
manna
manner
mannered
manor
many
meaner
minor
minute
money
Nanette
Nannie
owner
panel
panic
panning
peanut
penny
Phoenix
plainer
planet
pony
pruning
rainbow
rainy
Reno
renowned
runner
running
schooner
sign-off
sign-up
Sinai
Sonny

sooner
Sooner
spinner
spinning
sunny
tanner
tanning
tennis
tenor
tinny
tiny
tonic
Venus
wiener
winner
Winnie
winning
____
____
____
____
____
____
____

N /n/ Medial—three syllables

Adonis
airliner
animal
Anita
Annabelle
another
banana
beginner
benefit
Benita
Canada
canary
chicken pox
China Sea
Chinatown
cinnamon
Denali
dinosaur
dishonor
dry cleaner
foreigner
funeral
Galena
Gemini
general
generous
gold panner
Hanukkah
honeybee
honeycomb
honeydew
honor roll
initial
initialed
inner ear
inner tube
innocent
Iron Age
Johnny Reb
juniper
Kennedy
kennel club
lanolin
lawnmower
lemonade
lineage
lioness
luncheonette
magnitude
maneuver
Manila
manual
Manuel
mariner
mineral
monitor
opener
pineapple
pinnacle
plenary
prisoner
questioner
roadrunner
Robin Hood
runner-up
scenery
serenade
sinister
strenuous
sunglasses
Sunnyvale
synagogue
teenager
tyranny
universe
venison
Vietnam
volcano
wagoner
Winnipeg
____
____
____
____
____
____
____
____

N /n/ Medial—four syllables

anatomy
Annapolis
Arizona
banana split
commissioner
continental
generation
generator
Honolulu
honorable
inaugurate
incandescent
initialize
machinery
manifesting
manipulate
manually
Mona Lisa
monastery
monopoly
monumental
municipal
peanut butter
poison ivy
practitioner
refinery
spontaneous
table tennis
unhappiness
unmannerly
vulnerable
Winnebago
____
____
____
____

N /n/ Medial—five syllables

animatedly
developmental
elementary
inability
inaccessible
inadequately
inarticulate
inordinately
manufacturing
mineralogist
miniaturize
Unitarian
veterinary
____
____

N /n/ Final—one syllable

an
Ann
ban
bean
been
Ben
bin
Blaine
blown
bone
brain
bran
brawn
brown
bun
can
cane
chain
chin
clan
clean
clown
coin
cone
crane
crown
Dan
dawn
Dawn
dean
Dean
den
dine
Don
done
down
drain
drown
dune
fan
fawn
fin
fine
Fran
fun
gain
Gene
glean
Glenn
gone
gown

grain
green
grin
groan
grown
hen
hone
in
inn
Jan
Jane
Jean
Jeanne
Joan
John
June
keen
Ken
kin
lane
Lane
lawn
lean
lien
line
loan
lone
loon
Lynn
main
Maine
man
mane
mean
men
mine
moon
Nan
nine
noon
noun
nun
on
one
own
pain
pan
pane
pawn
pen
phone
pin
pine
plain
plan
plane
prone
prune
pun
rain
ran
reign
rein
Rhine
Rhone
roan
Ron
run
sane
scan
scene
screen
seen
seine
Seine
Shane
Shawn
shin
shine
shone
shown
shrine
shun
sign
sin
skein
skin
son
soon
Spain
span
spawn
spin
spine
spoon
sprain
spun
stain
Stan
stone
sun
swan
swine
tan
ten
than
then
thin
throne
thrown
tin
tine
ton
tone
town
train
tune

twin
twine
vain
van
Van
vane
vein
vine
wane
when
whine
win
won
yawn
Zane
zone
____
____

N /n/ Final—two syllables

Aaron
adjoin
again
Aileen
airman
airplane
Akron
Alden
alone
atone
attain
baboon
backbone
bacon
bailsman
balloon
bargain
bassoon
bastion
baton
beacon
bearskin
began
begin
Berlin
Bethune
between
bonbon
Brian
bunyon
Burton
butane
button
cabin
caffeine
cake pan
Calvin
campaign
canteen
cartoon
Ceylon
Charline
chicken
children
chlorine
chow mein
Clifton
Clinton
clothespin
coastline
Colleen
cologne
Cologne
combine
common
complain
constrain
contain
convene
Dagan
Darlene
Dawson
deadline
deepen
define
deplane
design
divan
divine
Doreen
downtown
dragoon
Earlene
eighteen
Elaine
Elden
engine
Erin
Eugene
explain
fireman
flatten
foreseen
fortune
garden
gold mine
goose down
Gordon
hailstone
harpoon
headstone
Helen
Herman

Hilton
home run
homespun
human
humane
Irene
Jackson
Japan
Jason
Jensen
Johnson
Joline
Karen
key chain
limestone
Lincoln
lion
listen
log on
Lorin
Lorraine
lotion
Lyndon
machine
mailman
marine
Marine
martin
Martin
membrane
milestone
Milton
moisten
motion
mountain
napkin
nation
Nixon
Norman

notion
ocean
open
outshine
Owen
pecan
pie pan
pigeon
pigpen
pipeline
platoon
pontoon
postpone
praline
prison
puffin
raccoon
rattan
raven
ravine
recline
refine
refrain
regain
remain
rerun
resign
restrain
ribbon
Robbin
robin
Roman
rotten
ruin
run-in
Ryan
Saigon
salmon
sandman

satin
sealskin
seven
Sharon
Sheldon
shoeshine
sideline
soapstone
soybean
squirt gun
Steven
sunshine
suntan
Susan
Susanne
sustain
Sylvan
terrain
thirteen
topline
trombone
Truman
tycoon
unknown
urbane
Verlene
wagon
Waldon
Warren
Welden
whalebone
within
woman
women
yachtsman
yeoman
Zion
____
____

N /n/ Final—three syllables

Adaline
African
afternoon
Alison
allophone
Amazon
aspirin
attention
Audubon
autobahn
baritone
battalion
Bernadine
bobby pin
Buchanan
bus station
carnation
Caroline
Chinatown
chuck wagon
Cimarron
cinnamon
clergyman
collarbone
collation
collection
collegian
collision
confession
confusion
decision
derision
determine
dictaphone
discipline
division
Edison
emblazon
emotion
enlighten
entertain
evergreen
fire engine
fire station
firewoman
fisherman
formation
frying pan
gabardine
galleon
Galveston
gasoline
gas station
gelatin
gentleman
Geraldine
go-between
Halloween
Harrison
hurricane
hydroplane
ice-cream cone
Indian
Jackelyn
javelin
Jefferson
jellybean
Josephine
kerosene
location
log cabin
Madison
magazine
Magdalene
mailwoman
marathon
margarine
Mexican
mezzanine
Michigan
microphone
moccasin
monotone
overgrown
overran
overthrown
patrolman
pelican
Philippine
Phoenician
physician
policeman
porcupine
position
power line
putting green
read-a-thon
rejection
relation
religion
remission
reunion
reversion
roasting pan
safety pin
saxophone
scatterbrain
sea lion
Sheraton
signalman
skeleton
snowmachine
space station
spick and span

submarine
sugarcane
super fine
superman
Superman
suspension
tambourine
telephone
telethon
train station
triathlon
turpentine
unforeseen
unison
Van Buren
Vatican
venison
violin
vitamin
Washington
water crane
weather vane
windowpane
wolverine
xylophone
zeppelin
____
____
____
____

N /n/ Final—four syllables

adding machine
amputation
animation
benediction
chameleon
complication
Copenhagen
deviation
domination
elevation
fermentation
generation
germination
hibernation
hot-air balloon
indecision
lamination
lifeguard station
nomination
patrolwoman
patrolwomen
phenomenon
police station
policewoman
policewomen
politician
public domain
sanitation
satisfaction
supervision
syncopation
television
Victorian
____
____
____

ND /nd/ Medial—two syllables

Andy
bandage
bandstand
branding
Brandon
Brenda
bundle
Candace
candle
candy
Candy
cinder
Cindy
condemn
condor
dandy
fender
flounder
foundry
gander
Gandhi
Glenda
Glendale
grinder
grounded
grounder
handbag
handball
handbook
handcuff
handful
handle
handsaw
handshake
handsome
handspring
handy
hinder
Hindi

Hindu
hundred
indeed
indent
indulge
jaundiced
kindly
kindness
landing
landlord
landscape
landslide
Landy
launder
laundry
Linda
London
mandate
Mandy
Monday

plunder
ponder
Randolph
random
Randy
reindeer
render
rounded
rounding
round trip
roundup
sand crab
sandbox
sandbug
sandbur
sander
Sandy
sender
send-off
slander

slender
splendor
Sunday
sunder
tandem
tender
thunder
tundra
undamped
under
undone
undress
vendor
Wendy
window
windup
windy
wonder
____
____

ND /nd/ Medial—three syllables

Amanda
amendment
appendage
appendix
bandaging
candy bar
condition
conducive
conduction
conductor
endurance
handicap
handicraft
handiwork
handwriting
handwritten
Honduras

India
Indian
inundate
landlady
Laplander
laundromat
left-handed
London Bridge
mandarin
meander
plundering
sandalwood
sandbagging
sand dollar
sandpaper
sandpiper
storm window

Sunday School
sundial
tendency
tenderfoot
thunderbolt
thunderclap
thunderhead
thunderous
thunderstorm
thunderstruck
tinderbox
underbrush
underclothes
underdog
underfoot
underground
underline

undermine	understood	unfounded
underneath	undertake	wanderer
underpass	undertook	wanderlust
undersea	undertow	wonderful
undershirt	underwear	________
underside	underweight	________
understand	underwent	________
understate	underworld	________

ND /nd/ Medial—four syllables

candelabra	indelible	Indonesia
Cinderella	indentation	kindergarten
condemnation	independent	mendaciously
conditional	Indiana	mendacity
incandescent	indicative	undulating
indecently	indiscretion	________

ND /nd/ Medial—five syllables

appendicitis	indeterminate	underestimate
condominium	indiscriminate	underexposure
hypochondriac	industrialist	underprivileged
incandescently	Indy 500	understandingly
incendiary	serendipity	________
indefensible	underachiever	________
independency	underdeveloped	________

ND /nd/ Final—one syllable

and	end	hound
band	find	kind
bend	fined	land
bind	fond	lend
bland	found	mend
blend	fund	mind
blind	gland	mound
blond	grand	pond
bond	grind	pound
bound	ground	rend
brand	hand	rind
canned	hind	round

sand	stand	weaned
send	strand	wind
skinned	tend	wound
sound	trend	yawned
spanned	vend	________
spend	wand	________

ND /nd/ Final—two syllables

abound	expand	quicksand
aground	extend	Raymond
airbound	fairground	rebound
almond	farmland	refund
amend	Finland	remand
ascend	firebrand	remind
astound	foreground	respond
attend	grassland	right-hand
backbend	greyhound	Roland
background	headband	rotund
backhand	highland	second
bandstand	Holland	shorthand
behind	homeland	side band
beyond	husband	snowblind
bloodhound	inland	snowbound
Cleveland	intend	spellbound
combined	Ireland	stagehand
command	island	thousand
commend	jocund	unbind
compound	kickstand	unwind
confound	left-hand	up-end
contend	legend	upland
dachshund	longhand	waistband
dead end	mainland	woodland
defend	mankind	wristband
demand	Midland	________
depend	misspend	________
descend	offend	________
diamond	Portland	________
England	pretend	________
errand	profound	________

ND /nd/ Final—three syllables

apprehend
beforehand
comprehend
condescend
contraband
correspond
countermand
dividend
fairyland
Gila Bend
integrand
intertwined
marching band
Maryland
New England
Newfoundland
New Zealand
overland
recommend
Rhode Island
rhythm band
rubber band
savings bond
secondhand
Sugar Land
Sutherland
Switzerland
Tamarind
underground
underhand
understand
upper hand
vagabond
wonderland
wraparound
____

ND /nd/ Final—four syllables

merry-go-round
misunderstand
superintend
____
____
____
____
____
____

NER /nɚ/ Medial—three syllables

energy
funeral
general
generous
honor roll
inner ear
mineral
partnership
runnerup
scenery
spinneret
____

NER /nɚ/ Medial—four syllables

energetic
generation
generator
honorable
machinery
refinery
unmannerly
vulnerable
____

NER /nɚ/ Final—two syllables

banner
burner
cleaner
corner
diner
dinner
donor
gainer
gunner
honor
inner
liner
lunar
manner
manor
minor
owner
partner
plainer
runner
schooner
sooner
Sooner
spinner

tanner	Turner	____________
tenor	vintner	____________
turner	winner	____________

NER /nɚ/ Final—three syllables

airliner	foreigner	questioner
beginner	gold panner	roadrunner
container	governor	wagoner
dishonor	long liner	Westerner
dry cleaner	opener	____________
Easterner	prisoner	____________

NER /nɚ/ Final—four syllables

commissioner	____________	____________
mid-westerner	____________	____________
practitioner	____________	____________

NJ /ndʒ/ Medial—two syllables

angel	enjoin	pongee
banjo	enjoy	pungent
congeal	enjoyed	ranger
congealed	ginger	rangy
congest	ingest	sponges
conjure	inject	stranger
conjured	injure	tangent
danger	injured	unjust
dingy	lounger	vengeance
dungeon	manger	vengeful
engine	Ninja	____________

NJ /ndʒ/ Medial—three syllables

Angela	challenges	dangerous
angelfish	challenging	endanger
angelic	changeable	endangered
Angelus	congested	engendered
angina	congestion	engineer
avenger	conjecture	engineered
Blue Angels	conjugal	fire engine
Challenger	conjunction	ginger ale

gingerbread
gingerly
gingersnap
ingenious
injected
injection
injunction
injury
injustice
Lone Ranger
messenger
passenger
scavenger
tangerine
tangible

NJ /ndʒ/ Medial—four syllables

conjectural
conjugation
evangelic
evangelist
evangelize
injurious
intangible
meningitis

NJ /ndʒ/ Medial—five syllables

evangelical
ingenuity
laryngectomy

NJ /ndʒ/ Final—one syllable

change
flange
fringe
grange
hinge
lounge
lunge
mange
plunge
range
scrounge
singe
sponge
strange
tinge
twinge

NJ /ndʒ/ Final—two syllables

arrange
astringe
avenge
challenge
derange
downrange
estrange
exchange
expunge
impinge
lozenge
orange
revenge
scavenge
unhinge

NJ /ndʒ/ Final—three syllables

counter change
disarrange
interchange
prearrange
rearrange

NL /nl̩/ Final—two syllables

channel
colonel
final
flannel
funnel
hymnal
journal
kennel
panel
signal
spinal
tunnel
____
____
____

NL /nl̩/ Final—three syllables

arsenal
cardinal
criminal
doctrinal
eternal
external
fictional
fractional
functional
infernal
internal
marginal
maternal
national
nocturnal
nominal
optional
ordinal
paternal
personal
rational
seasonal
sectional
sentinel
terminal
____
____

NL /nl̩/ Final—four syllables

additional
congressional
diagonal
emotional
exceptional
irrational
nutritional
occasional
octagonal
original
provisional
sensational
____
____
____

RN /rn/ Medial—two syllables

Arnold
barnyard
Bernard
Bernice
burned-out
burner
burning
colonel
cornbread
corncob
Cornell
corner
cornered
cornet
cornfield
cornflakes
corn oil
cornstarch
darning
doorknob
earnest
earnings
Ernest
furnace
furnish
garnet
garnish
harness
horned toad
hornet
journal
journey
kernel
learning
Lorna
morning
mourning
Myrna
ornate

surname
tarnish
thorny
turncoat
turner
turnip
turnkey
turn on
turnout
turnpike
turnstile
varnish
Vernon
warning
worn-out
____
____
____

RN /rn/ Medial—three syllables

alternate
Bernadine
carnation
Carnegie
carnival
cornerstone
corn popper
Easterner
eternal
external
fraternal
furnishings
furniture
government
infernal
internal
internee
internist
internment
journalist
journeyman
maternal
nocturnal
ornament
paternal
returning
Southern Cross
Southerner
southernmost
storm warning
stubbornness
tornado
tournament
tourniquet
turnover
turntable
unfurnished
Westerner
westernmost
____
____
____
____
____
____

RN /rn/ Medial—four syllables

alternately
alternative
alternator
carnivorous
internalize
morning glory
returnable
vernacular
____

RN /rn/ Final—one syllable

barn
born
burn
churn
corn
darn
earn
fern
horn
learn
Lorne
mourn
scorn
stern
sworn
thorn
torn
turn
urn
Verne
warn
worn
yarn
yearn
____
____
____

RN /rn/ Final—two syllables

acorn
adjourn
adorn
airborne
auburn
Auburn
cavern
cistern
concern
eastern
fire thorn
fog horn
French horn
govern
Hawthorn
inborn
intern
iron
lantern
LaVerne
long horn
modern
newborn
pattern
popcorn
pronghorn
Rayburn
reborn
return
Saturn
shopworn
shorthorn
sojourn
southern
stubborn
sunburn
upturn
western
windburn

RN /rn/ Final—three syllables

Capricorn
southeastern
southwestern
unconcern
unicorn

NS /ns/ Medial—two syllables

answer
cancer
Cancer
censor
chancer
concede
concept
concern
concert
consent
console
consult
consume
council
dancer
denser
fancy
fencer
fencing
glancer
insert
inside
insist
insult
Jensen
Johnson
lancer
lonesome
mincemeat
monsoon
pencil
prancer
princess
Quincy
rancid
ransom
Sensei
senses
Spencer
sponsor
stencil
tensor
tinsel
tonsils
unsafe
unseal
unseen

NS /ns/ Medial—three syllables

advancement
advancer
agency
announcer
chancellor
commencement
concession
condenser
consider
consonant
consumer
consumption
counselor
currency
density
dispenser
enhancer
entrancer
fiancée
frequency
incentive
incident
insincere
insulate
insulted
linseed oil
nonsupport
offensive
one-sided
potency
principal
principle
reconcile
Regency
romancer
sensible
sensitive
transgressor
uncertain
unselfish
unsightly
vacancy

NS /ns/ Medial—four syllables

coincidence
consecutive
deficiency
emergency
insignia
intensity
peninsula
Pensacola
precedency
preconceiving
preconception
principalship
radiancy
reconsider
sensational
social science
unsatisfied
unsuitable
unsuspected
____
____

NS /ns/ Final—one syllable

bounce
chance
dance
dense
fence
France
glance
hence
lance
Lance
mince
once
ounce
pounce
prance
prince
rinse
sense
since
tense
thence
whence
wince
____

NS /ns/ Final—two syllables

absence
advance
announce
balance
commence
condense
conscience
Constance
convince

defense
denounce
dispense
distance
enhance
entrance
finance
Florence
fragrance
immense
incense
instance
intense
license
nonsense
nuisance
offense
past tense
patience
presence
pretense
pronounce
province
prudence
response
romance
science
sentence
sequence
silence
tuppence
twopence
vengeance
____
____
____
____
____
____

NS /ns/ Final—three syllables

abundance
acceptance
admittance
allegiance
alliance
allowance
ambulance
annoyance
appearance
appliance
audience
circumstance
common sense
conference
confidence
consequence
convenience
dependence
difference
disturbance
endurance
evidence
ignorance
impatience
importance
influence
innocence
insurance
maintenance
mispronounce
occurrence
performance
precedence
preference
prevalence
radiance
recurrence
redundance
reference
residence
resistance
reverence
subsistence
surveillance
tolerance
turbulence
utterance
variance
vigilance
____
____

NS /ns/ Final—four syllables

circumference
independence
indifference
inheritance
intelligence
obedience
predominance
preponderance
self-assurance
self-confidence
self-reliance
significance
____
____
____

SN /sn/ Initial—one syllable

snack
snacked
snag
snagged
snail
snake
snap
snapped
snare
snared
snarl
snatch
sneak
sneaked
sneer
sneeze
sneezed
snell
snelled
snide
snip
snipe
snipes
snipped
snitch
snob
snook
snoop
snoot
snooze
snore
snout
snow
snowed
snub
snubbed
snug

SN /sn/ Initial—two syllables

snack bar
snaffle
snagging
snaggy
snakebite
snake dance
snakeskin
snaky
snapback
snap bean
snapper
snapping
snappish
snappy
snapshots
snare drum
snatchy
snazzy
sneakers
sneaking
sneezy
snicker
sniffle
snippy
snobbish
snobby
snooper
Snoopy
snooty
snorkel
snowball
snowbank
snowbird
snow boots
snowbound
snow-capped
snowdrift
snowfall
snowflake
snow-go
snow job
snowman
snowplow
snowshoe
snowstorm
snowsuit
snow tires
Snow White
snubby
snuggle

SN /sn/ Initial—three syllables

snaggletooth
snaggletoothed
snake charmer
snakier
snapdragon
snappier
snappiness
snazzier
sneakiest
snickering
snout beetle
snowball fight

snow blindness
snowblower
snow bunting
snowmobile
snowy owl
____
____
____
____

SN /sn/ Initial—four syllables

snapping beetle
snapping turtle
snowy egret
____
____
____
____
____
____

NSER /nsɚ/ Final—two syllables

answer
cancer
Cancer
censor
chancer
dancer
denser
fencer
glancer
lancer
prancer
spencer
Spencer
sponsor
tensor
____
____
____

NSER /nsɚ/ Final—three syllables

advancer
announcer
condenser
dispenser
enhancer
entrancer
extensor
romancer
____

NT /nt/ Medial—two syllables

ante
antler
banter
cantor
center
centered
central
chanting
contempt
contend
content
contest
context
contort
contour
country
county
dainty
dental
dented
dentist
Denton
enter
entrance
entry
fainted
frantic
frontal
gentle
granted
grantor
hinted
hunter
hunting
huntress
into
junta
mantle
mental
mentor
minted
Monty
nineteen
ninety
onto
painted
painter
painting

pantry
plaintiff
plaintive
planter
planting
pointer
pointing
pontiff
printed
printer
printing
punted
quaintly
rental
rented
saintly
Santa
scented
shanty
slanted
splinter
squinted
squinter
syntax
tantrum
tinted
Trenton
vantage
vented
vintage
wanted
wanton
winter
____
____
____
____
____
____

NT /nt/ Medial—three syllables

advantage
Antarctic
Atlantic
attentive
carpenter
centerpiece
Centerville
Central Park
Central Time
consented
container
contented
contention
contentment
contestant
continent
continue
counterfeit
enchanted
encounter
enterprise
entertain
eventful
fantasy
gigantic
imprinted
incentive
indented
interact
intercede
intercept
intercom
interest
interface
interfere
interfold
intersect
interval
interview
invented
inventor
Kentucky
Kon Tiki
misprinted
parental
presenting
re-enter
repentant
repented
repenting
resented
resentful
resentment
romantic
Santa Claus
Santa Cruz
Santa Fe
self-centered
seventeen
seventy
storm center
tentative
tormentor
transplanting
wintergreen
wintertime
____
____
____
____
____
____

NT /nt/ Medial—four syllables

accidental
adventurer
antagonist
antagonize
antecedent
cantilever
commentary
contaminate
contemplating
continental
contingency
continual
continuous
continuum
conventional
departmental
differential
disadvantage
egocentric
governmental
horizontal
instrumental
integrity
interesting
intermission
intersection
intimidate
monumental
oriental
ornamental
pedimental
pigmentation
presentation
radiant heat
radiantly
regimental
representant
rudimental
sacramental
sentimental
supplemental
trans-Atlantic
transcendental
uneventful
unprevented
unrepentant
Valentine's Day
ventriloquist
yellow bunting
____
____

NT /nt/ Medial—five syllables

antibiotic
contaminated
contemporary
differentiate
disinterested
documentary
elementary
experiential
intermediate
international
involuntary
orientation
parliamentary
Protestantism
representation
supplementary
temperamental
testamentary
____
____
____

NT /nt/ Final—one syllable

ant
aunt
bent
blunt
brunt
bunt
can't
cent
chant
count
dent
don't
faint
feint
flint
front
gaunt
gent
grant
Grant
grunt
haunt
hint
hunt
jaunt
lent
lint
meant
mint
mount

paint
pant
pent
pint
plant
point
print
punt
quaint
quint
rant
rent
runt
saint
scant
scent
sent
shunt
slant
spent
sprint
squint
stunt
taunt
tent
tint
vent
want
went
won't
____
____
____

NT /nt/ Final—two syllables

absent
accent
account
affront
agent
ailment
amount
anoint
appoint
ascent
aslant
basement
Belmont
blueprint
brilliant
buoyant
cement
client
cogent
cold front
comment
consent
constant
content
descent
discount
distant
eggplant
enchant
entente
event
extent
ferment
foment
For Rent
frequent
gallant
garment
hydrant
imprint
indent
infant
instant
intent
invent
judgment
merchant
moment
movement
newsprint
oil paint
ointment
pageant
parchment
parent
patent
patient
pavement
payment
peasant
pennant
percent
pheasant
pigment
pinpoint
placement
pleasant
poignant
potent
preprint
present
prevent
prudent
quadrant
quotient
rampant
recent
recount

remnant
resent
rodent
sea front
segment
sergeant
serpent
servant
shipment
silent
spearmint
stagnant
standpoint
statement
strident
stringent
student
talent
tenant
torrent
transient
transplant
treatment
urgent
vacant
valiant
Vermont
vibrant
____
____
____

NT /nt/ Final—three syllables

abundant
accident
accountant
adjacent
adornment
advancement
affluent
allotment
amazement
amendment
amusement
announcement
apartment
apparent
appointment
arrangement
atonement
commencement
compartment
competent
compliment
component
consonant
contentment
continent
convenient
decedent
dependent
descendant
detergent
different
diligent
dissonant
document
dominant
efficient
elephant
elopement
emigrant
encroachment
enjoyment
enrollment
filament
ignorant
immigrant
implement
improvement
impudent
incident
indignant
inherent
innocent
insolvent
installment
instrument
investment
lenient
lieutenant
ligament
malignant
management
measurement
monument
nourishment
nutrient
occupant
operant
opponent
orient
ornament
palpitant
parliament
peppermint
permanent
persistent
petulant
precedent
president
prominent
Protestant
punishment

radiant
recurrent
refreshment
regiment
relevant
reluctant
represent
requirement
resentment
resident
resistant
respondent
restaurant
retirement
reverent
ruminant
sediment
sentiment
subjacent
subsequent
succulent
sufficient
supplement
sycophant
tenement
testament
tolerant
tournament
variant
vigilant
violent
wonderment

NT /nt/ Final—four syllables

accomplishment
adolescent
advertisement
apportionment
astonishment
determinant
entertainment
environment
equivalent
establishment
expedient
experiment
extravagant
independent
indifferent
ingredient
intelligent
intolerant
iridescent
magnificent
noncombatant
obedient
participant
precipitant
predicament
predominant
preponderant
presentiment
reinforcement
significant
single parent
subservient
superjacent
temperament
understatement
vice-president

NT /nt/ Final—five syllables

insignificant
interdependent
superintendent

NTH /nθ/ Medial—two syllables

anthem
anther
enthuse
enthused
menthol
monthly
panther
unthink

NTH /nθ/ Medial—three syllables

Anthony
Cynthia
Samantha
synthesis
synthesize
synthetic
unthankful
unthinking
unthoughtful

NTH /nθ/ Medial—four syllables

anthology
Corinthian
Corinthians
enthusiast
mentholated
parenthesis
pyracantha

NTH /nθ/ Final—one syllable

month
ninth
plinth
tenth

NTH /nθ/ Final—two syllables

billionth
Corinth
dozenth
eighteenth
fifteenth
fourteenth
millionth
nineteenth
seventh
sixteenth
thirteenth

NTH /nθ/ Final—three syllables

amaranth
eleventh
hyacinth
labyrinth
seventeenth

NGTH /ŋθ/ Medial—two syllables

lengthen
lengthways
lengthwise
lengthy
strengthen

NGTH /ŋθ/ Final—one syllable

length
strength

NGTH /ŋθ/ Final—two syllables

full-length
half-length
wave-length
whole-length

NY /nj/ Medial—two syllables

banyan
barnyard
bunion
Bunyan
canyon
Daniel
genial
genius
junior
Junior
Kenya
Kenyon
lanyard
minion
Muñoz
onion
Runnion
senior

senõr	Tanya	________
Spaniard	unused	________
spaniel	vineyard	________

NY /nj/ Medial—three syllables

ammonia	golden years	sinuate
annual	Grand Canyon	Virginia
banyan tree	ingenious	zinnia
begonia	lunula	________
Black Canyon	lunular	________
congenial	manuscript	________
convenience	minuet	________
convenient	monument	________
dominion	Paul Bunyan	________
geniuses	señora	________

NY /nj/ Medial—four syllables

annual wage	filet mignon	unusual
annually	gardenia	Virginia Beach
biannual	genuinely	West Virginia
Boulder Canyon	January	________
centennial	manufacture	________
cocker spaniel	monumental	________
continual	señorita	________
Dominion Day	triannual	________

NZ /nz/ Medial—two syllables

benzene	Kansas	________
Bronze Age	Wednesday	________
clansman	________	________
frenzy	________	________

NZ /nz/ Final—one syllable

bans	canes	coins
Benz	cans	cones
bins	chains	crowns
bones	chins	Dan's
bronze	cleans	deans
buns	clowns	dines

drains
fans
fines
fins
gains
grains
groans
jeans
lanes
lawns
leans
lines
loans
manes
mines
moans
moons
Nan's
nines
nouns
pains
pans
pens
phones
pines
pins
plains
planes
plans
prunes
puns
queens
rains
shines
shins
signs
skins
sons
spans
spins
spoons
stains
stones
swans
tans
teens
tens
thins
tins
tones
tons
trains
tunes
twins
vans
vines
wanes
wins
zones

NZ /nz/ Final—two syllables

balloons
batons
blue jeans
buttons
cake pans
cartoons
chickens
complains
detains
Great Plains
hailstones
heavens
kitchens
lions
machines
Marines
mountains
napkins
nations
notions
oceans
opens
outshines
pecans
pie pans
pigeons
platoons
puffins
ravens
remains
retains
ribbons
robins
sevens
sidelines
soybeans
swim fins
trombones
wagons

NDZ /ndz/ Final—one syllable

bends
binds
ends
finds
glands
grinds
hands
kinds
lands
lends
mends
minds
ponds
rends
rinds
sands
sends
sounds
spends
stands
tends
winds
____
____
____
____
____

NG

Pronounced: /ŋ/
Spelled: n, ng, ngue

NG /ŋ/ Medial—two syllables

anger
angle
angler
angling
anguish
Angus
banging
bangle
Bangor
Bengal
bongo
England
English
finger
fungus
gangplank
hanger
hunger
jangle
jingle
jungle
kingdom
kingly
linger
longer
mangle
mingle
mongoose
Ping Pong
ringer
singer
songster
springy
stringer
stronger
strongly
swinger
Tango
tingle
wrangler
wringer
younger
youngest
youngster
Youngstown
____
____
____
____
____
____
____
____
____
____
____
____

NG /ŋ/ Medial—three syllables

Anglican
Angola
angora
belonging
Buckingham
bungalow
chewing gum
dungaree
elongate
fingerling
fingernail
fingerpaint
fingerprint
fingertip
flamingo
hearing aid
heating pad
kangaroo
lingering
marching band
Singapore
untangled
Washington
____
____
____
____

NG /ŋ/ Final—one syllable

bang
Bing
bring
clang
cling
ding
dong
fang
fling
gang
gong
hang
hung
king
long
lung
Ming
pang
ping
pong
prong
rang
ring
rung
sang
sing
slang
sling
song
sprang
spring
sprung
sting
string
strong
stung
sung
swing
tang
thing
thong
throng
tong
tongue
wing
wring
wrong
____
____
____
____

NG /ŋ/ Final—two syllables

asking
baking
batting
beaming
bedding
being
belong
bending
biking
blessing
blinding
boating
booting
bowling
boxing
bucking
buckling
bullring
buying
buzzing
caring
carving
catching
charging
charming
chuckling
clamming
climbing
clowning
coming
cording
crackling
cramping
curling
cycling
dancing
ding-dong
dining
diving
docking
doing
driving
duckling
eating
evening
failing
falling
feeding
feeling
fencing
finding
fishing
fitting
flying
fouling
frying
giving

gliding
going
golfing
grabbing
greeting
guarding
guessing
guiding
Harding
having
hearing
helping
hiding
holding
Hong Kong
hopping
housing
jiving
jogging
judging
jumping
key ring
laughing
leading
leading
lifting
linking
living
loading
locking
lodging
looking
loving
making
morning
moving
paddling
painting
passing

Ping Pong
placing
playing
pounding
pressing
pulling
pushing
racing
raining
riding
ringing
roping
rounding
routing
rowing
ruling
running
sailing
saying
seeing
serving
setting
shaking
sharing
shining
shoestring
sitting
skating
skiing
sledding
sleeping
sleeting
sliding
snowing
sparring
speeding
standing
steering
stepping

stopping
stretching
surfing
swimming
tackling
talking
tanning
throwing
tingling
topping
touching
trailing
training
trotting
trying
tumbling
tying
wading
waiting
walking
watching
wearing
winning
wishing
working
wrestling
yachting
____
____
____
____
____
____
____
____
____
____
____
____

NG /ŋ/ Final—three syllables

arriving
awarding
backpacking
balancing
bandaging
bellowing
bobsledding
broadjumping
cancelling
canoeing
carousing
car racing
challenging
childbearing
coercing
collapsing
colluding
coloring
corroding
departing
dialing
dog mushing
dog sledding
drag racing
endearing
exciting
galloping
gardening
handwriting
hayriding
high diving
high jumping
hollering
homecoming
horse racing
hot rodding
ice skating
jump roping
kayaking
lassoing
listening
lumbering
marauding
measuring
performing
picnicking
place kicking
pole-vaulting
polishing
promoting
remaking
rewarding
rock climbing
skateboarding
skindiving
sky diving
snorkeling
spear fishing
square dancing
storm warning
sunbathing
surfboarding
tap dancing
Thanksgiving
tightroping
traveling
unfolding
unmaking
unmasking
visiting
wedding ring
weight lifting
windsurfing
Wyoming
____
____
____
____

NG /ŋ/ Final—four syllables

awakening
clarifying
classifying
coinciding
convalescing
deep sea fishing
exercising
figure skating
harmonizing
hockey skating
horseback riding
mountain climbing
pacifying
photographing
rectifying
river rafting
roller skating
salad dressing
salmon fishing
satisfying
scuba diving
stock car racing
televising
underlying
undertaking
verifying
water skiing
____
____
____

NGL /ŋl/ Medial—two syllables

angler	jingler	wrangling
angling	jingling	________
Anglo	jungly	________
England	mingling	________
English	wrangler	________

NGL /ŋl/ Medial—three syllables

Anglican	Englander	New England
anglicize	Englisher	________
anglify	English horn	________
drinking glass	Englishman	________

NGL /ŋl/ Final—two syllables

angle	mingle	wrangle
dangle	shingle	________
dingle	single	________
jangle	spangle	________
jingle	tangle	________
jungle	tingle	________

NGL /ŋl/ Final—three syllables

commingle	quadrangle	untangle
entangle	rectangle	________
Kris Kringle	right angle	________
left angle	triangle	________

NGTH /ŋθ/ Medial—two syllables

lengthen	lengthy	________
lengthways	strengthen	________
lengthwise	________	________

NGTH /ŋθ/ Final—one syllable

length	________	________
strength	________	________

NGTH /ŋθ/ Final—two syllables

full-length	wave-length	________
half-length	whole-length	________

NGZ /ŋz/ Final—one syllable

bangs	pangs	things
brings	pings	tongs
fangs	rings	wings
gangs	sings	wrongs
gongs	songs	
hangs	stings	
kings	swings	

NGZ /ŋz/ Final—two syllables

cravings	pavings	
drawings	savings	
paintings		

NK

Pronounced: **/ŋk/ and /nk/**
Spelled: nk, nch, nc

NK /nk/, /ŋk/ Medial—two syllables

anchor
anchored
ankle
Bangkok
bank draft
banker
banking
bank loan
bankrupt
blanket
blinker
blinking
bronco
Bronco
bunkbed
canker
cankered
chunky
clanking
clinker
concave
Concord
concur
conquer
cranking
dinky
donkey
drinker
drinking
encode
flanker
frankly
Hong Kong
honking
inkling
junket
junky
kinky
lanky
Lincoln
linkage
linking
linkup
monkey
pancake
ranking
rankle
rankled
shrinking
sinker
sinking
slinky
sprinkle
sprinkled
sprinkling
spunky
stinker
stinking
tanker
thank you
thinker
tinker
tinkle
tinkled
trinket
twinkle
twinkled
twinkling
winking
wrinkle
wrinkled
Yankee
yanking
____
____
____
____
____
____
____
____
____
____
____
____
____
____
____
____
____

NK /ŋk/ Final—one syllable

bank
blank
blink
brink
bunk
chink
chunk
clank
clink
crank
dank
drank
drink
dunk
flank
flunk
franc
frank
Frank
hank
Hank
honk
hunk
ink
junk
kink
lank
link
mink
monk
pink
plank
plunk
prank
punk
rank
rink
sank
shank
shrank
shrink
shrunk
sink
skink
skunk
slank
slink
slunk
spank
spunk
stank
stink
sunk
tank
thank
think
trunk
twink
wink
yank
Yank
zinc
____

NK /ŋk/ Final—two syllables

Burbank
chain link
chipmunk
embank
enrank
fruit drink
fuel tank
gas tank
lime drink
oil tank
outflank
outrank
out think
point-blank
prethink
soft drink
unlink
World Bank
____
____
____

NK /ŋk/ Final—three syllables

apple drink
bobolink
City Bank
countersink
grapefruit drink
interlink
kitchen sink
lemon drink
orange drink
pressure tank
river bank
savings bank
water tank
____
____

P

Pronounced: /p/
Spelled: p, pe, pp

P /p/ Initial—one syllable

pace
paced
pack
packed
pact
pad
page
Page
paged
paid
pail
pain
pained
paint
pair
paired
pal
pale
paled
pall
palled
palm
palmed
Pam
pan
Pan
pang
panned
pant
par
parch
parched
pare
pared
park
parked
part
pass
passed
past
paste
pat
Pat
patch
patched
pate
path
Paul
pause
paused
pave
paved
paw
pawed
pawn
pawned
pay
pea
peace
peach
peak
peaked
peal
pealed
pear
pearl
Pearl
pearls
pears
peat
peck
pecked
peek
peeked
peel
peeled
peep
peeped
peer
peered
peers
peg
Peg
pegged
pelt
pen
penned
pep
per
perch

perched
perk
Perk
pert
pet
Pete
pick
picked
pie
piece
pieced
pier
Pierce
pig
pike
pile
piled
pill
pills
pin
pinch
pinched
pine
pined
ping
pink
pinned
pint
pip
pipe
piped
pique
piqued

pit
pitch
pitched
Poe
point
poise
poised
poke
pole
poled
Polk
poll
polled
pond
pone
pool
pooled
poor
pop
Pop
popped
porch
pore
pork
port
pose
posed
post
pouch
pouched
pounce
pounced
pound

pounds
pour
poured
pout
pox
poxed
pub
puck
puff
pug
pull
pulled
pulp
pulse
pulsed
pun
punch
punk
punt
pup
purge
purged
purl
purled
purse
push
pushed
put
putt
pyre
____
____
____

P /p/ Initial—two syllables

paca
pacer
package
packaged

packer
packet
padded
paddle

paddy
padlock
padre
pagan

pageant
painful
painless
paintbrush
painted
painter
palace
palate
paleface
pallet
pallor
palsied
palsy
paltry
Pammy
pampas
pamper
pampered
pamphlet
pancake
panda
panel
paneled
panic
panicked
pansy
panther
pantry
pantsuit
papa
papal
paper
papered
papoose
pappy
parade
parboil
parboiled
parcel

pardon
pardoned
parent
parfait
paring
Paris
parish
parka
parking
parkway
parley
parlor
parole
parquet
parried
parrot
parry
parsley
parsnip
parson
partake
partial
partly
partner
partook
part-time
passage
passé
passing
passion
passive
passkey
passport
password
pasteboard
pastel
pastime
pastor
pastry

pasture
pastured
pasty
patchwork
patent
pathos
pathway
patience
patient
Patrick
patrol
patrolled
patron
Patsy
patter
pattered
pattern
patterned
patty
Patty
pauper
pavement
paving
pawnshop
payee
payment
payroll
peaceful
peacock
peanut
Peanuts
peasant
pebble
pebbled
pecan
pedal
pedaled
peddle
peddled

peeling
peephole
peevish
peewee
Peking
pellet
pelvis
penal
penance
penchant
pencil
penciled
pendant
pending
penguin
penknife
pennant
penny
pension
pensioned
pensive
penthouse
peon
people
peopled
pepper
peppered
perceive
perceived
percent
perfect
perform
performed
perfume
perfumed
perhaps
peril
periled
perish
perished
perjure
perjured
perky
permit
perplex
perplexed
Perry
Persia
persist
person
persuade
Peru
pesky
pester
pestered
petal
Peter
petite
petty
pewter
picket
pickle
pickled
pickup
picnic
picnicked
picot
picture
pictured
Pierre
pigeon
piggish
pigment
pigpen
pigskin
pigsty
pigtail
pigtailed
pilfer
pilgrim
pillage
pillar
pillared
pillow
pilot
pimple
pimpled
pincers
pinch-hit
pinchers
Ping Pong
pinhead
pinhole
pinkeye
pinkie
pinpoint
pinto
pin-up
pinwheel
pious
pipeline
piquant
pirate
Pisa
Pisces
piston
pitcher
pitchfork
pitfall
pithy
Pittsburgh
pity
pivot
pixy
pizza
pocket
pockmark

pockmarked
poem
poet
poignant
pointed
pointer
pointing
pointless
poison
poisoned
poker
pokey
poky
Poland
polar
polecat
police
policed
polish
polished
polite
polka
pollen
pollute
Polly
polo
polyp
pomade
pompon
pompous
poncho
ponder
pondered
pontiff
pontoon
pony
poodle
popcorn
Popeye

poplar
poplin
poppy
pop-up
porous
porpoise
porridge
portage
portal
porter
porthole
portion
Portland
portly
portrait
portray
portrayed
posse
possess
possessed
possum
postage
postal
postcard
posted
poster
postman
postmark
postpaid
postpone
postponed
posture
posy
potash
potent
pothook
potion
potlatch
potluck

pot roast
potter
poultice
poulticed
poultry
pouter
powder
powdered
Powell
power
powered
powwow
public
publish
published
pucker
puckered
pudding
puddle
puddled
pudgy
pueblo
Pueblo
puffball
puffin
puffy
pugnose
pugnosed
pullet
pulley
pulpit
pulsate
puma
pumice
pumiced
pumpkin
punch card
puncture
punctured

pungent
punish
punished
puppet
puppy
purchase
purchased
purloin
purple
purpose
pursue
pursued
pursuit
push-up
putter
puttered
putty
puzzle
pygmy
pylon
python
____
____
____

P /p/ Initial—three syllables

pachyderm
Pacific
pacifist
pacify
paddle wheel
pageantry
pagoda
pajamas
Pakistan
palatial
Palestine
palisade
pallbearer
palmetto
palmistry
palpable
palpitate
Pamela
Panama
pancreas
Pandora
paneling
panicky
pantaloon
pantomime
pantomimed
papaya
paperback
paperboy
paperweight
paprika
papyrus
parable
parachute
paradise
paradox
paraffin
paragon
paragraph
parakeet
parallel
paralleled
paralyze
paralyzed
paranoid
parapet
parasite
parasol
parental
parity
parsonage
Parthenon
particle
partition
partnership
passable
passably
passageway
Passaic
passenger
passerby
passionate
Passover
pasteurize
pasteurized
pastoral
paternal
Paterson
pathetic
patriarch
Patricia
patriot
patrolman
patronage
patronize
patronized
pawnbroker
Pearl Harbor
peccary
pectoral
peculiar
pedestal
pedigree
pemmican
penalize
penalized
penalty

penciling
pendulous
pendulum
penetrate
penitent
penmanship
penniless
pensioner
pentagon
peppermint
percentage
perception
percolate
percussion
perfection
perforate
performance
performing
perilous
period
periscope
perjury
permission
peroxide
persecute
persevere
persevered
persimmon
persistent
personal
personnel
persuasion
pertinent
peskiness
pessimist
pestilence
petition
petitioned
petrified

petrify
petticoat
pettiness
piano
picturesque
piggyback
piggy bank
pilgrimage
pillowcase
pimento
pinafore
pincushion
pineapple
pinfeather
pinnacle
pinochle
pinsetter
pioneer
piracy
pirouette
pitiful
pocketbook
pocketknife
pocket watch
podium
poetry
pogo stick
poisonous
polar bear
policeman
policy
polio
polishing
politics
polka dot
pollinate
polliwog
polygon
pompadour

pony ride
popover
popular
populate
porcelain
porcupine
portable
portico
portrayal
Portugal
position
positioned
positive
possession
possessive
possible
possibly
postage stamp
postglacial
posthumous
postmaster
postmortem
post office
potato
potential
potpourri
pottery
Poughkeepsie
poverty
powder puff
powdery
powerful
powerhouse
powerless
power line
power saw
publicize
publicized
publicly

public school
publisher
pugnacious
pulverize
pulverized
pumpkin pie
punching bag
punctual
punctuate
punishment
purveyor
pushover
pussyfoot
putting green
pyramid
___
___
___

P /p/ Initial—four syllables

pacifier
palomino
palpitation
panacea
panorama
panoramic
paralysis
parasitic
pardonable
paregoric
parenthesis
parishioner
parochial
participant
participate
participle
particular
Pasadena
paternity
pathology
patriotic
patrolwoman
peanut butter
pedestrian
pediatrics
pedodontist
Penelope
penetrable
penetration
penicillin
peninsula
perceptible
percolator
peremptory
perennial
perfectible
perfectionist
perfidious
performing arts
perfunctory
perimeter
periodic
periphery
perishable
periwinkle
permeable
permissible
perpetual
perpetuate
perplexity
perseverance
personable
personalize
personalized
personify
perspiration
pessimism
petroleum
piccalilli
pictorial
Pinnochio
pistachio
pitter-patter
pizzicato
podiatrist
poinsettia
poison ivy
police station
policewoman
policewomen
politician
Polynesia
polytechnic
pontifical
popularize
portulaca
potassium
potato chips
potentially
publication
public domain
publicity
Puerto Rico
pulmonary
pumpernickel
punctuation
punishable
purgatory
pussy willow
pyemia
pyorrhea
pyracantha
pyramidal

pyrogenic
pyrography
pyrolysis
pyrotechnic

P /p/ Initial—five syllables

Panama Canal
Pan American
pandemonium
parallelism
parallelogram
parliamentary
participial
particularly
pasteurization
Patagonia
paternalism
pathological
patriotism
pecuniary
pediatrician
penitentiary
Pennsylvania
perfectionism
perpendicular
personality
pianissimo
pituitary
polysyllabic
polysyllable
Pomeranian
possibility
punctuality
pyromania

P /p/ Medial—two syllables

apace
apart
apiece
appear
appeared
append
biped
blooper
Cape Cod
caper
capon
chipper
Chopin
chopper
chopping
choppy
clipper
clipping
copied
coping
copy
coupled
coupon
crackpot
creeper
crockpot
dapper
deeper
depart
depend
depict
depose
deposed
depot
dipper
dipping
dripping
dropout
dropping
dustpan
epic
epoch
flapper
flipper
gaping
gripper
groping
guidepost
happy
hippo
hippy
Hopi
hopper
hopping
Jaipur
Japan
jodhpurs
keeper
keep out
key punch
kopeck
leaping
leopard

Lopez
mapping
moping
moppet
mopping
napkin
napping
nipping
nippy
opah
opal
Opal
opaque
open
opened
opine
opined
oppose
opposed
Papa
paper
papered
papoose
pepper
peppered
peppy
pepsin
peptic
Ping Pong
piper
popcorn
poppy
pop-up
prepaid
proper
pupa
puppet
puppy
quipping

quipster
rapid
rapport
repaid
repair
repaired
repay
repeal
repealed
repeat
repel
repelled
repent
report
riper
riposte
ripper
roper
roping
scapegoat
scrapbook
scraper
scraping
scrapping
scrappy
seepage
seeping
shipper
shipping
sipping
skipper
slapping
sleeper
sleeping
slipper
slipping
soapbox
soapy
sopping

soppy
stepchild
stepson
stop-off
stopper
stopping
super
supper
suppose
supposed
taper
teapot
tepee
toothpaste
topping
toupee
trapeze
trapper
trapping
Trappist
two-piece
upbeat
upbraid
upbuild
update
updraft
upend
upgrade
upheave
upheld
uphill
uphold
uplift
upmost
upon
upper
vapor
whopper
wiper

wrapper
wrapping
wrap-up
zip code
zipper

P /p/ Medial—three syllables

apartment
apathy
apostle
apparel
apparent
appealing
appearing
appendix
appetite
apple pie
appointment
boarding pass
canape
canopy
capital
capitol
cherry pie
Chippewa
choppier
choppiest
chopping block
chopping wood
cooperage
Copper Age
copperhead
copybook
copyright
corn popper
crepe paper
deported
diaper
dissipate
drapery
emperor
epicure
epiderm
epigram
episode
floppy disk
frying pan
grasshopper
guinea pig
haphazard
hypocrite
inn keeper
Japanese
juniper
lollipop
newspaper
octopus
open door
opening
opera
operate
opinion
opponent
opposite
papaya
paperback
paper bag
paperboy
paper clip
paper dolls
papering
peppermint
Peter Pan
pineapple
popover
properly
property
recapping
recipe
repaying
repeated
repellent
repentance
repentant
repertoire
reporter
republic
repulsing
repulsion
repulsive
safety pin
sandpaper
sandpiper
separate
Singapore
skyscraper
slippery
soda pop
state trooper
stepping stone
stopover
stupendous
superman
Superman
supersede
superstar

supervise
timekeeper
Topeka
topical
tropical
typewriter
uppermost
vaporize
wallpaper
whippoorwill
Winnipeg
woodpecker
zeppelin
zoo keeper
____

P /p/ Medial—four syllables

Annapolis
apologize
apology
apparatus
apparition
appetizer
candy striper
capacity
capitulate
Copenhagen
depopulate
disappearance
disposable
epicanthus
epicenter
epidemic
epidermis
epiglottis
flipping a coin
handicapping
incipient
Lilliputian
litmus paper
manipulate
metropolis
monopoly
municipal
operator
paper cutter
paper towels
paratrooper
stapedial
superego
superficial
superior
superlative
supermarket
tissue paper
topography
vaporific
vaporizer
whippersnapper
Winnie-the-Pooh
wrapping paper
____
____
____
____

P /p/ Medial—five syllables

appendectomy
appendicitis
cosmopolitan
epicardium
epicurean
episcopalian
happy-go-lucky
hippopotamus
lapis lazuli
metropolitan
opinionated
opportunity
stapedectomy
unpopulated
____
____
____
____

P /p/ Final—one syllable

ape
beep
Bip
bop
cap
cape
chap
cheap
chip
chop
clap
clip
coop
cop
cope
coupe
creep
crepe

crop
croup
cup
deep
dip
drape
drip
droop
drop
flap
flip
flop
gap
gape
grape
grip
gripe
grope
group
hap
heap
hip
hoop
hop
hope
Hope
jeep
jump
keep
Kip
lap
leap
lip
loop
lope
map
mop
mope
nap
nape
neap
nip
peep
pep
pipe
plop
pop
Pope
prop
pup
rap
reap
rip
ripe
rope
sap
scoop
scope
scrap
scrape
scrip
seep
shape
sheep
ship
shop
sip
skip
Skip
slap
sleep
slip
sloop
slop
slope
snap
snip
snipe
soap
sop
soup
steep
step
stoop
stop
strap
strip
stripe
sup
swap
sweep
swipe
swoop
tap
tape
tip
top
trap
trip
troop
type
up
weep
whip
whoop
wipe
wrap
yap
yipe
zap
zip
____
____
____
____
____
____

P /p/ Final—two syllables

Aesop
airdrop
asleep
backdrop
backstop
backup
bagpipe
bean soup
bear trap
bebop
bishop
blow up
book drop
breakup
build-up
bus stop
carhop
catch-up
checkup
clean up
close-up
cold snap
co-op
cough drop
cowslip
doorstep
doorstop
dust mop
eavesdrop
elope
equip
escape
firetrap
flagship
flip-flop
flue pipe
footstep
gallop
gossip
grown-up
gumdrop
half-slip
hard up
hedgehop
hilltop
hookup
housetop
jump rope
ketchup
keyed up
landscape
makeup
markup
mishap
mousetrap
nightcap
pawn shop
peace pipe
pet shop
Phillip
pickup
polyp
pop-up
pork chop
post-op
pre-op
push-up
rag mop
rattrap
recoup
regroup
reship
round trip
roundup
sand trap
scallop
seascape
shipshape
shoeshop
shortstop
sign-up
sit-up
ski slope
sport shop
stopgap
stovepipe
subgroup
swap shop
syrup
teacup
tightrope
tip-top
toss-up
township
toy shop
tulip
turnip
unwrap
upkeep
warmed-up
warm-up
warship
whitecap
windpipe
windup
workshop
worship
wrap-up
write-up
____
____
____
____
____

P /p/ Final—three syllables

antelope
astroscope
baseball cap
bathing cap
battleship
beauty sleep
belly flop
buckle-up
buttercup
candy shop
cantaloupe
cassette tape
censorship
chicken coop
chimney sweep
city map
cityscape
coffee cup
develop
envelope
exhaust pipe
fellowship
fingertip
fire escape
floral shop
follow-up
Gaza Strip
gingersnap
gyroscope
handicap
horoscope
hula hoop
landing strip
laundry soap
leadership
linotype
lollipop
malaprop
marksmanship
masking tape
membership
microscope
misanthrope
mountaintop
onion dip
organ pipe
otoscope
overlap
overripe
oversleep
overstep
ownership
paper clip
partnership
penmanship
periscope
photo shop
pleasure trip
pogonip
prototype
rattletrap
runner-up
scholarship
seamanship
semi-ripe
sewer pipe
shoulder strap
soda pop
spectroscope
sponsorship
sportsmanship
stethoscope
stewardship
Sunset Strip
telescope
teletype
thunderclap
turboprop
U.S. map
water drop
weather strip
workmanship

P /p/ Final—four syllables

adhesive tape
audiotape
chocolate chip
cinemascope
citizenship
companionship
Cumberland Gap
curio shop
electroscope
electrotype
flippity-flop
guardianship
heliotrope
jet landing strip
kaleidoscope
laryngoscope
Little Bo Peep
measuring cup
measuring tape
novelty shop
potato chip

potato crop
stereotype
tomato soup
videotape

PER /pɚ/ Medial—three syllables

aspirin
Copper Age
copperhead
drapery
emperor
opera
paperback
paperclip
papering
peppermint
properly
property
slippery
superman
Superman
supersede
supervise
temperate
uppermost
vaporize

PER /pɚ/ Medial—four syllables

copper-plated
experiment
intemperate
operator
superego
superficial
temperative
vaporizer

PER /pɚ/ Final—two syllables

blooper
chipper
chopper
clipper
copper
creeper
dipper
flapper
flipper
gripper
helper
hopper
jasper
Jasper
keeper
paper
pepper
proper
riper
roper
scraper
shipper
skipper
slipper
stopper
stupor
super
supper
taper
trooper
upper
vapor
viper
whisper
whopper
wiper
wrapper
zipper

PER /pɚ/ Final—three syllables

crepe paper
diaper
grasshopper
improper
innkeeper
juniper
newspaper
sandpaper
sandpiper
skyscraper
state trooper
timekeeper
wallpaper

PER /pɚ/ Final—four syllables

candy striper	tissue paper	________
litmus paper	wrapping paper	________
paratrooper	writing paper	________

PL /pl/ Initial—one syllable

place	played	plowed
placed	plea	pluck
plaid	plead	plug
plain	please	plugged
plaint	pleased	plum
plait	pleat	plumb
plan	pledge	plume
plane	pledged	plumed
planed	plied	plump
plank	plight	plunge
planned	plink	plunged
plant	plinth	plunk
plants	plod	plus
plaque	plop	plush
plat	plopped	ply
plate	plot	________
play	plow	________

PL /pl/ Initial—two syllables

placard	planet	plated
place kick	plangent	plateful
place mat	planing	plate glass
place name	planking	platelet
placer	plankton	plate mark
placid	planner	plater
placing	planning	platform
placket	plantar	plating
plaintiff	planter	Plato
plaintive	plant food	platoon
Plainview	plasma	platter
Plainville	plaster	playback
planar	plastic	player
planer	plateau	playful

playground
playhouse
playmate
playoff
playpen
playroom
playsuit
playthings
playtime
playwear
playwright
plaza
pleaded
pleading
pleasant
pleasing
pleasure
pledger
plenty
pleural
plexus
pliant
pliers
plodded
plodder
plodding
plopping
plotted
plotter
plotting
plover
plower
plowshare
plugging
plug in
plumage
plumber
plumbing
plummet
plumpness
plunder
plunger
plunging
plural
plushy
plus sign
Pluto
plying
Plymouth
plywood
____

PL /pl/ Initial—three syllables

placebo
place hitter
place holder
place-kicker
placement test
placer gold
Placerville
plagiarize
plainclothesman
plainspoken
plaintively
planetoid
plantable
plantation
plasterboard
platinous
platinum
platonic
platypus
plausible
playacting
play-by-play
playfully
playing card
playing field
pleasantry
plenteous
plentiful
pleurisy
plexiglass
pliable
pliancy
plowable
plundering
pluralize
plutocrat
Plutonic
Plymouth Rock
____

PL /pl/ Initial—four syllables

plagiarism
planarian
planetary
planimeter
plasticity
platform rocker
Pleasant Island
pleasurable
plenipotent
plentifully
pleximeter
plotting paper
plurality
plutonium
____

PL /pl/ Initial—five syllables

planetarium
player piano
pledge of allegiance
plutonically
____
____

PL /pl/ Medial—two syllables

airplane
air plant
air plot
amply
aplite
aplomb
applaud
applause
applied
apply
birthplace
complain
complaint
complete
complex
comply
deplane
deplete
deplore
deploy
deplume
displace
display
displease
eggplant
employ
explain
explode
exploit
explore
fireplace
float plane
gangplank
grappling
home plate
hopeless
houseplant
ice plant
imply
jet plane
perplex
pipeline
poplar
replace
replant
replay
replete
reply
sapling
seaplane
simply
ski plane
sleepless
someplace
stapler
stoplight
supplant
supply
surplus
top line
upline
upload
____
____
____
____

PL /pl/ Medial—three syllables

accomplish
amplify
anyplace
appliance
applicant
appliqué
applying
complacent
complement
completion
complexion
complicate
compliment
contemplate
diploma
diplomat
discipline
double play
duplicate
employee
employment
explicit
explosion
explosive
heating plant
implement
incomplete
multiply
octuplet
quintuplet

replenish
resplendent
simplify
supplement
supplicant
triplicate
unemployed
unpleasant
water plant

PL /pl/ Medial—four syllables

amplifier
application
cassette player
complexity
explanation
exploration
multiplier
simplicity
unemployment

PL /pl/ Final—two syllables

ample
apple
chapel
couple
cripple
crumple
dimple
gospel
grapple
maple
opal
Opal
people
pimple
purple
ripple
rumple
sample
scalpel
scruple
simple
staple
steeple
temple
topple
triple
Whipple

PL /pl/ Final—three syllables

deep purple
disciple
example
free sample
multiple
pineapple
principal
principle
quadruple
quintuple
rose apple
____

PL /pl/ Final—four syllables

acne pimple
bottle nipple
candied apple
cornmeal scrapple
Episcopal
keep it simple
lovely dimple
mini-sample
more than ample
municipal
participle
rotten apple
spotted dapple
vice-principal
____

LP /lp/ Medial—two syllables

alpine
gulping
helper
helpful
helping
helpless
kelp crab
kelpfish
palpate
pulpit
scalpel
sculptor
sculpture
yelping
____

LP /lp/ Final—one syllable

alp
gulp
help
kelp
palp
pulp
scalp
whelp
yelp
____
____
____

MP /mp/ Medial—two syllables

bumper
bumpy
campaign
camper
campground
camping
camp-out
campus
clamping
clumpy
compact
compare
compared
compass
compel
compete
complain
complaint
complete
complex
compound
compute
cramping
crimpy
crumple
crumply
dampen
dampened
dumping
dumpling
dumpster
dump truck
dumpy
empire
grumpy
hamper
impact
impair
impaired
impale
impaled
impart
impasse
impeach
impeached
impede
impel
impelled
impend
impose
jump ball
jumper
jumping
jump rope
jump seat
jump suit
jumpy
limpet
limpid
limping
lumpy
pamper
pampered
pampers
Pompey
pompous
primping
pumping
pumpkin
rampart
rumpling
sampan
sampler
scamper
scrimping
shrimping
skimpy
slumping
stamping
stumping
tamper
tampered
temper
tempered
tempest
template
temple
tempted
thumping
tramping
trumpet
trumping
vampire
whimper
____
____

MP /mp/ Medial—three syllables

accomplice
accomplish
amplify
assumption
attempted
bumper guard
bumper jack
camporee
compactor
companion
company
compassion
competent
component
composite
composure
computer
consumption
contemplate
decompose
decomposed
distemper
empower
encompass
example
exempted
exemption
high jumper
impacted
imported
imposter
jumping bean
jumping jack
No Dumping
Olympics
pompadour
preempted
presumption
pumpkin pie
redemption
resumption
tamper-proof
temperance
temperate
temptation
____
____
____

MP /mp/ Medial—four syllables

companionship
compensation
composition
contemplation
Humpty Dumpty
impalpable
imperious
intemperate
pomposity
pumpernickel
reimposing
temperament
temperature
temporary
unimportant
____
____
____

MP /mp/ Medial—five syllables

contemporary
impenetrable
imperishable
temperamental
temporization
____
____
____
____

MP /mp/ Final—one syllable

amp
blimp
bump
camp
champ
chump
clamp
clump
cramp
crimp
damp
dump
grump
hemp
hump
imp
jump
lamp
limp
lump
plump

primp	shrimp	thump
pump	skimp	tramp
ramp	slump	trump
romp	stamp	________
rump	stomp	________
scamp	stump	________

MP /mp/ Final—two syllables

boot camp	girls' camp	revamp
boys' camp	high jump	ski jump
broad jump	leg cramp	sun lamp
encamp	long jump	tire pump
floor lamp	off ramp	________
gas pump	on ramp	________

MP /mp/ Final—three syllables

Boy Scout camp	rubber stamp	table lamp
city dump	safety lamp	wrestling camp
garbage dump	stomach cramp	________
Girl Scout camp	sugar lump	________
postage stamp	summer camp	________

MPS /mps/ Final—one syllable

amps	glimpse	romps
blimps	imps	shrimps
bumps	jumps	skimps
champs	lamps	slumps
chumps	limps	stamps
clamps	lumps	stumps
clumps	mumps	thumps
cramps	primps	tramps
crimps	pumps	trumps
dumps	ramps	________

PR /pr/ Initial—one syllable

Prague	pranced	prawn
praise	prank	prawns
praised	prate	pray
prance	Pratt	prayed

preach
preached
preen
press
pressed
prey
price
priced
pride
pried
pries
priest
prime
primed
primp
prince
print
prize
prized
pro
probe
probed
prod
prof
prom
prompt
prone
prong
proof
proofed
prop
propped
props
prose
proud
prove
prow
prowl
prude
prune
pruned
pry
____
____
____

PR /pr/ Initial—two syllables

practice
prairie
praline
pratique
prattle
prattler
preacher
precede
precept
precinct
precious
precise
preclude
predict
preempt
preface
prefect
prefer
prefix
prejudge
prelude
premier
premise
prepaid
prepare
prepared
prepay
preschool
prescribe
presence
present
presents
preserve
preshrunk
preside
press club
presser
pressing
pressman
pressroom
pressure
presswork
prestige
presto
presume
pretend
pretense
pretest
pretext
pretty
pretzel
prevail
prevent
preview
priceless
prickle
prickly
priesthood
primal
primate
primer
priming
primrose
princess
printed
printer

printing
printout
prior
prism
prison
pristine
private
probate
problem
proceed
proceeds
process
proclaim
proctor
Proctor
procure
produce
product
profess
profile
profit
profound
profuse
program
progress
project
prolong
promise
promote
prompted
prompter
promptly
pronghorn
pronoun
pronounce
pronounced
proofread
propel
proper
prophet
propose
propound
proscribe
prospect
prosper
protect
protein
protest
proton
protract
protrude
proverb
provide
province
provoke
prowess
proxy
prudence
Prudence
prudent
prudish
pruning
____
____
____
____

PR /pr/ Initial—three syllables

practical
prairie dog
preamble
prearrange
precaution
precedence
precedent
preceding
precipice
precision
precocious
preconceive
preconcert
precursor
predator
predestine
predicate
prediction
predispose
preemption
preexist
preference
preferment
prefigure
prejudice
premature
premiership
premium
prenatal
preordain
prescription
presently
preserver
president
pressurize
prestigious
presumption
pretentious
prevalence
prevention
previous
prickly pear
primary
primitive
principal

principle
printing press
prisoner
privacy
privately
privation
privilege
probable
probably
probation
proboscis
procedure
procession
processor
prodigal
prodigious
prodigy
producer
production
productive
profession
professor
proficient
profitee
profusion
progeny

prognosis
prognostic
progressive
prohibit
projected
projectile
projector
prolific
promenade
prominent
promising
promptitude
promulgate
pronouncement
propagate
propeller
proper name
property
prophecy
prophesy
prophetess
prophetic
propolis
proponent
proportion
proposal

propulsion
prosaic
prosecute
prosody
prospective
prosperous
protection
protective
protege
Protestant
protocol
protoplast
prototype
protractor
protrusion
provender
provided
providence
providing
provincial
provision
provoking
prudential
____
____
____

PR /pr/ Initial—four syllables

practicable
practical joke
practically
practical nurse
practitioner
prairie chicken
praying mantis
precarious
precedency
precipitant
precipitate

precipitous
preconception
predatory
predecessor
predetermine
predicament
predominance
predominant
preeminent
preexistence
preexistent

prefabricate
preferable
preferential
prefiguring
preformation
prefulfillment
pregalvanize
prehardener
preharmony
prehistoric
preholiday

preignition
preimposing
preinclining
preindicate
preinstruction
prejudicial
prematurely
premedical
premeditate
premonition
preoccupied
preparation
preponderance
preponderate
preposition
preposterous
prerequisite
prerogative
presentable
presentation
preservation
preservative
presidency
presidential
presumable
presumptuous
prevaricate
prima donna
primarily
prime minister
principally
priority
processional
proclamation
procrastinate
procreation
productively
professional
profitable
prohibition
prohibitive
proletary
proliferate
prolongation
promissory
promontory
propaganda
propensity
proportional
proposition
proprietor
proscenium
prosecution
prosperity
protuberance
protuberant
proverbial
provisional
provocation
provocative
proximity
____
____

PR /pr/ Initial—five syllables

precipitation
predestination
prehistorical
preliminary
premeditation
preparatory
prepositional
Presbyterian
principality
probability
productivity
prognostication
promissory note
pronunciation
____

PR /pr/ Medial—two syllables

appraise
appraised
apprize
approach
approved
April
apron
blueprint
bombproof
Capri
compress
culprit
cypress
Cypress
depress
depressed
deprive
deprived
dustproof
express
fireproof
footprint
impress
imprint
improve
oppress
rainproof

repress	shipwreck	surprise
reprieve	shipwrecked	surprised
reprint	soundproof	upright
reprise	sun proof	________
reproach	suppress	________
reprove	supreme	________

PR /pr/ Medial—three syllables

appraisal	expression	paprika
apprehend	expressive	represent
approval	expressway	repression
apricot	fingerprint	reprimand
April Fool	high pressure	reprinted
bulletproof	impression	reprisal
by-product	impressive	reprobate
capricious	imprison	reproduce
Capricorn	impromptu	soprano
comprehend	improper	tamper-proof
deprecate	improvement	unprepared
depressant	improvise	waterproof
depression	interpret	weatherproof
depressive	jet propelled	________
disapprove	low pressure	________
enterprise	mispronounce	________

PR /pr/ Medial—four syllables

appreciate	depreciate	reciprocate
apprehension	disapproval	reproduction
apprenticeship	impregnable	supremacy
approbation	impressionist	vice-president
appropriate	life preserver	word processor
approximate	proprietor	________
April Fools' Day	reciprocal	________

PR /pr/ Medial—five syllables

appreciation	impracticable	inappropriate
apprehensible	impressionable	interpretation
appropriation	impropriety	irrepressible
depreciation	improvisation	irreproachable

reprehensible	uncompromising	
representative	unprecedented	

RP /rp/ Medial—two syllables

airplane	perplex	tarpon
airport	porpoise	terpene
burping	purple	torpid
carpet	purpose	torpor
chirping	serpent	turpeth
fireplace	sharpen	war paint
hairpin	sharper	warpath
harping	surpass	warping
harpist	surplus	
harpoon	tarpan	

RP /rp/ Medial—three syllables

absorption	Scorpio	surplus store
carpenter	scorpion	tarpaulin
centerpiece	sharpener	torpedo
corporal	sharpening	turpentine
harpsichord	sharpshooter	unsharpened
power pack	sharpsighted	unsurpassed
purposely	sharpwitted	

RP /rp/ Medial—four syllables

caterpillar	perpetual	torpedo boat
incorporate	surpassable	

RP /rp/ Final—one syllable

burp	sharp	Thorpe
carp	slurp	twirp
chirp	tarp	warp
harp	thorp	

PS /ps/ Medial—two syllables

capsize	dip stick	hopscotch
capsule	dropsy	keepsake
chopsticks	gypsum	knapsack
deep South	gypsy	lapsing

lipstick
Mopsy
pipsqueak
slapstick
soapsuds
step stool
stop sign
tipsy
topsail
topside
topsoil
Topsy
typeset
upset
upstairs
upstart
upswing
____

PS /ps/ Medial—three syllables

asepsis
autopsy
biopsy
chop suey
collapsing
elapsing
ellipsis
Phillipsburg
relapsing
synopsis
tipsiness
tipsy cake
top secret
top sergeant
typesetter
typesetting
upsetting
upstanding
upsurging
upsweeping
upswelling
upswinging
____
____

PS /ps/ Medial—four syllables

epilepsy
topsy-turvy
upsettable
upside-down cake
upsy-daisy
____
____
____
____

PS /ps/ Final—one syllable

alps
Alps
caps
chaps
chips
chops
copes
crops
cups
dips
drapes
drips
drops
flaps
flips
flops
grapes
gripes
grips
gropes
groups
hopes
hops
jeeps
jumps
keeps
laps
lapse
leaps
lips
loops
maps
mops
naps
nips
peeps
pipes
pups
raps
reaps
rips
ropes
saps
scalps
scoops
scopes
scrapes
scraps

seeps
ships
shops
sips
skips
slaps
sleeps
slips
sloops
slopes
slumps
snaps
snipes
snips
steps
straps
stripes
swaps
tapes
taps
tips
tops
traps
trips
troops
weeps
whips
wipes
wraps
zips
____
____
____

PS /ps/ Final—two syllables

biceps
collapse
eclipse
elapse
ellipse
escapes
forceps
gallops
gossips
grown-ups
push-ups
raindrops
relapse
round trips
roundups
scallops
sit-ups
triceps
tulips
turnips
unwraps
wallops
____
____

PS /ps/ Final—three syllables

antelopes
cantaloupes
fire escapes
____
____
____
____
____
____

SP /sp/ Initial—one syllable

spa
space
spade
spake
span
spanned
spar
spare
spared
sparred
sparse
spat
spawn
speak
spear
speck
speech
spell
spelled
spend
spent
spice
spiced
spike
spill
spilled
spilt
spin
spine
spire
spit
spite
spitz

spoil
spoiled
spoke
spokes
sponge
sponged
spoof
spook
spool
spoon
spoor
sport
sports
spot
spouse
spout
spud
spun
spunk
spur
spurge
spurred
spurs
spurt
spy
____
____

SP /sp/ Initial—two syllables

space bar
spacecraft
space flight
spaceman
spaceport
spaceship
space suit
spacial
spacing
spacious
spadeful
spadework
spancel
spangle
Spaniard
spaniel
Spanish
spanner
spareribs
sparing
spark coil
sparker
sparkle
sparkler
sparkling
spark plug
sparring
sparrow
Spartan
spasm
spastic
spatial
spatter
spawning
speaker
speakers
speaking
spearfish
spearhead
spearmint
special
specie
specious
speckle
spectre
spectrum
speechless
speedboat
speedster
speedtrap
speedway
speedy
speed zone
spellbound
speller
spelling
spendthrift
sperm whale
spicy
spider
spiky
spillage
spilling
spillway
spinach
spinal
spindle
spindling
spineless
spinet
spinner
spinning
spin out
spinster
spiral
spirit
spitball
spiteful
spitfire
spittoon
spoilage
spoiling
spoken
spokesman

sponger
spongy
sponsor
spooky
spoon bread
spoonful
sportful
sporting
sports car
sportscast
sport shirt
sportsman
sportswear
sporty
spot check
spotlight
spotted
spotter
spotty
spun glass
spunky
Sputnik
sputter
spy glass
spying

SP /sp/ Initial—three syllables

space heater
space station
space writer
spaghetti
Spanish food
Spanish rice
sparable
sparrow hawk
spasmodic
spatula
speakable
spear fishing
specialist
specialize
specialty
specific
specify
specimen
spectacle
spectator
spectrogram
spectrograph
spectroscope
speculate
speedily
speed limit
spelling bee
spider web
spinal cord
spinal nerve
spinning wheel
spirited
spiritless
sponsoring
sponsorship
spookier
sporadic
sporting goods
sportscaster
sportsmanship
sportswriter
spunkier

SP /sp/ Initial—four syllables

spectacular
spectrometer
speech therapist
speech therapy
speedometer
spider monkey
spinal column
spiral notebook
spiritual
spirometer
spontaneous

SP /sp/ Initial—five syllables

Special Olympics
specialization
specifically
specification

SP /sp/ Medial—two syllables

aspen
Aspen
Casper
crispy
despair
despise
despised
despite
despoil
despoiled
dispatch
dispatched
dispel
dispose
dispute
gospel
grasping
high-speed
inspect
inspire
Jasper
larkspur
misplace
misspell
passport
peace pipe
prospect
prosper
respect
respire
respite
respond
response
Shakespeare
teaspoon
turnspit
waspish
waspy
whisper
____
____
____

SP /sp/ Medial—three syllables

aerospace
aspirin
baby spoon
desperate
disparate
disposal
hospital
inspection
Jasper Park
loudspeaker
mispronounce
outer space
outspoken
prospective
prospector
prosperous
respectful
respective
retrospect
suspenders
suspension
suspicion
suspicious
tablespoon
transparent
whispering
____

SP /sp/ Medial—four syllables

asparagus
conspiracy
correspondence
despairingly
desperado
desperation
despicable
dispensary
dispensation
disposable
disposition
disproportion
disputable
especially
espionage
high-spirited
hospitable
hospitalize
inspiration
litmus paper
low-spirited
perspicacious
perspiration
prosperity
respectable
respectively
respiration
respirator
responsible
tablespoonful
unspeakable
____
____

SP /sp/ Medial—five syllables

hospitality
indisputable
irresponsibly
respiratory

SP /sp/ Medial—six syllables

inspirationally
respectability
responsibility

SP /sp/ Final—one syllable

clasp
crisp
gasp
grasp
lisp
rasp
wasp
wisp

SPL /spl/ Initial—one syllable

splash
splat
splay
spleen
splice
spliced
splint
split
splits
splotch
splurge

SPL /spl/ Initial—two syllables

splashdown
splash guard
splatter
splendid
splendor
splicer
splicing
splinter
split shift
splitting
splutter

SPL /spl/ Initial—three syllables

splintery
split entrance
split entry
split level
split second

SPR /spr/ Initial—one syllable

sprain
sprang
sprawl
spray
spread
spree
sprig
spring
sprint
sprite
sprout
spruce
sprung
spry

SPR /spr/ Initial—two syllables

spraddle
sprayer
spray gun
spreader
spreadsheet
springboard
Springfield
springing
springtime
sprinkle
sprinkler
sprinkling
sprocket
____
____

SPR /spr/ Medial—two syllables

bedspread
hair spray
handspring
hot springs
Hot Springs
offspring
Rock Springs
____
____

SPR /spr/ Medial—three syllables

Brussels sprouts
ocean spray
shopping spree
Silver Spring
Union Springs
____

PT /pt/ Final—one syllable

chapped
chipped
chopped
clapped
clipped
crept
dipped
dripped
dropped
flapped
flipped
flopped
griped
gripped
heaped
hoped
hopped
kept
lapped
leaped
mapped
mopped
napped
nipped
peeped
piped
plopped
popped
propped
rapped
reaped
ripped
roped
scooped
scoped
scraped
scrapped
script
seeped
shipped
shopped
sipped
skipped
slept
slipped
snapped
snipped
stepped
stopped
strapped
swapped
swooped
taped
tapped
tipped
topped
trapped
tripped
typed
wept
wiped
wrapped
yipped
zapped
zipped
____

PT /pt/ Final—two syllables

abrupt
accept
adapt
adept
adopt
bankrupt
concept
corrupt
disrupt
Egypt
erupt
escaped
except
galloped
gossiped
postscript
precept
subscript
unwrapped
____
____

PT /pt/ Final—three syllables

intercept
non-adept
____
____
____
____

PY /pj/ Medial—two syllables

leap year
shipyard
____
____
____
____

PY /pj/ Medial—three syllables

deputize
deputy
impudence
impudent
populace
popular
populate
populous
stipulate
____
____
____

PY /pj/ Medial—four syllables

manipulate
popularize
popularly
popular song
popular vote
population
stipulation
unpopular
____
____
____
____

R

Pronounced: /r/
Spelled: r, rr, rh

R /r/ Initial—one syllable

race
rack
Rae
raft
rag
rage
raid
rail
rain
raise
rake
ram
rammed
ramp
Rams
ran
ranch
rang
range
ranged
rank
rant
rap
rapped
rash
rasp
rat
rate
rates
rats
rave
raw
ray
Ray
reach
read
real
realm
ream
reap
red
reed
Reed
reeds
reef
reel
reels
reign
rein
rent
rest
Rhine
rhyme
rib
ribbed
rice
rich
Rich
Rick
rid
ride
ridge
ridged
rig
rigged
right
rights
rim
rimmed
rims
rind
ring
rings
rink
rinse
rip
ripe
ripped
rise
risk
rite
road
roam
roast
robe
robed
rock
Rock
rocked
rocks

rod
Rod
rode
roe
rogue
role
Rolf
roll
rolls
Rome
Ron
roof
roofed
rook
room
rooms
roost
root
roots
Roots
rope
roped
rose
Rose
Ross
rot
rote

rough
round
rouse
rout
route
rove
row
rowed
Roy
rub
rubbed
rude
Rude
rue
ruff
rug
rule
ruled
rules
rump
run
rung
runt
rush
rushed
rust
rut

Ruth
rye
wrack
wraith
wrap
wrapped
wrath
wreath
wreck
wren
wrench
wrest
wretch
wring
wrist
writ
write
writhe
wrong
wrote
wrought
wrung
wry
____
____
____
____

R /r/ Initial—two syllables

rabbi
rabbit
rabid
rabies
raccoon
Rachel
racial
racing
racket
radish

raffle
rafting
ragged
ragtime
ragweed
railing
railway
raiment
rainbow
raincoat

rainfall
rainy
raisin
Raleigh
rally
ramble
rambling
rampage
rampant
rancid

Randolph
random
Randy
ranging
ransack
ransom
rapid
rapture
rascal
ratchet
rating
ratio
ration
rattan
rattle
ravage
ravel
raven
ravine
raving
rawhide
Rawlings
Raymond
rayon
react
reading
ready
Reagan
reason
Reba
rebate
rebel
rebirth
reborn
rebound
rebuild
rebuke
rebut
recall
recant
recede
receipt
receive
recent
recess
recite
reckless
reckon
reclaim
recline
recoil
recount
redeem
red hot
Redlands
Red Sea
Redskins
reduce
redwing
redwood
refill
refine
refined
reflect
refuge
refund
refuse
regain
regime
region
reject
rejoice
rejoiced
relapse
relate
relax
relaxed
relay
relayed
release
released
relic
relief
relieve
relieved
relish
rely
remains
remind
remnant
remote
remove
renew
repaid
repay
repeal
repeat
repel
replace
reply
reptile
request
rescue
rescued
resent
reset
resign
resist
resolve
resort
resound
respect
restless
result
retail
retain
retained

Reuben
reveal
revenge
review
revise
revive
revived
revoke
revolt
Rhea
rhinestone
Rhoda
Rhonda
rhythmic
ribbon
riches
Richie
ricksha
Ricky
ridden
riddle
rigging
righteous
right-hand
rigid
ringlet
ripen
Ripley
ripping
ripple
ripsaw
riptide
risking
Rita
rival
rivet
roadside
roadway
roasting

Robbin
robin
robot
robust
Rochelle
rocket
rockfish
Rockies
rocking
rock salt
Rockville
Rockwell
rocky
Rocky
rodent
Rodney
Roland
roll call
rollick
rolling
roll-out
Roman
romance
rompers
Ronald
roofing
rookie
roommate
roomy
rootbeer
rootstock
roping
Rosa
rosebud
rosebush
Roseland
Rosette
rosewood
rosin

Roslyn
rosy
rotate
rotten
rotund
roughage
roughen
rounded
roundhouse
rounding
roundup
routine
rowboat
rowdy
Roxanne
royal
rubbish
rubble
ruby
Ruby
ruddy
Rudolph
Rudy
ruffle
ruffled
Rugby
rugged
ruin
ruling
rumba
rummage
rummy
run-down
running
runoff
runway
rupee
Russell
Russia

Russian
rustic
rusty
Rusty
Ruth Ann
ruthful
Ruthie
ruthless
wrangle
wrangling
wrapping
wrap-up
wrathful
wreckage
wrestle
wrestling
wretched
wriggle
wrinkle
wrinkly
wrist watch
write-off
writeup
writing
written
wrongful
____
____
____
____

R /r/ Initial—three syllables

racquetball
radial
radiance
radiant
radiate
radical
radio
radium
radius
ramify
ramshackle
ratify
rational
rattlesnake
raveling
ravenous
reaction
readjust
ready-made
reagent
realign
realist
realize
really
rearrange
reascend
reasoning
reassume
Rebecca
rebellion
rebellious
receiving
reception
receptive
recession
recital
reckoning
recognize
recollect
recombine
recommend
recommit
recompense
reconcile
rectangle
rectify
rectitude
recumbent
recurrence
recurrent
recycle
redeeming
redemption
reduction
redundance
reelect
reflection
refugee
Regency
regiment
regulate
related
relation
relative
relatives
relaying
releasing
relevant
relief map
religion
religious
reluctant
remaining
remedy
removal
rendezvous
republic
resemblance
resemble
resentment
residence

resident
resistance
resonate
respectful
respective
retina
reunion
reunite
reveille
revenue
rheumatic
Rhode Island
ricochet
ridicule
right angle
right handed
ritual
road atlas
Robin Hood
rodeo
rolling pin
romantic
Roosevelt
rotation
Rowena
Roxana
royalty
rummage sale
runabout
runaway
runaways
running mate
wrestling camp
wrestling coach
wrestling match
wrestling shoes
wrestling team
wretchedness
wrongdoing
wrongfully

R /r/ Initial—four syllables

radiancy
rapidity
reactivate
reality
reasonable
reassemble
receivable
receptacle
recessional
recipient
recitation
reclamation
recognition
recognizance
recollection
reconnaissance
reconstitute
regulation
relationship
repetition
republican
reputation
residential
resolution
respectable
respectively
revolution
rhesus monkey
Rhodesia
ridiculous
riding safety
Rocky Mountains
Rosh Hoshanah
ruination
Rumanian
rutabaga

R /r/ Initial—five syllables

radioactive
rationality
reactionary
reawakening
recapitulate
reciprocity
recommendation
reconstituted
respiratory
roasting marshmallows
Roman Catholic
Roman numeral
rudimentary

R /r/ Initial—six syllables

reconciliation	________________	________________
reconsideration	________________	________________
Republican Party	________________	________________

R /r/ Medial—two syllables

Aaron
airy
arid
Aries
arise
arose
around
arouse
arrange
arranged
arrest
arrive
arrived
arrow
baron
barracks
barrage
barrel
barren
beret
berry
Berry
Beryl
boric
boring
borough
borrow
buried
burro
burrow
bury
Cairo
caring
carob
Carol
carols
carriage
Carrie
carried
carrot
carry
Cary
charades
cheery
Cheri
cherish
cherry
cherub
Cheryl
chorus
clearing
Cora
coral
Corey
corral
correct
corrode
corrupt
courage
currant
current
Cyril
dairy
daring
direct
Doreen
during
earring
eerie
era
erase
Eric
Erie
Erin
erode
errand
Europe
every
fairy
Far East
Farrah
fearing
ferry
firing
flooring
Flora
Florence
florist
flurry
foreign
forest
For Rent
forum
Four-H
furring
furrow
furry
fury
garage

Gary
Gerald
Geri
giraffe
glory
Harold
Harris
harrow
Harry
hayrack
hayride
hearing
herald
hero
heron
herring
high rise
hiring
hurrah
hurried
hurry
Ireland
iris
Iris
Irish
Jerry
joy ride
jury
Karen
key ring
Larry
Laura
laurel
Lawrence
Lorin
Lorraine
Lory
lyric
marine

maroon
marriage
married
marrow
marry
Mary
merit
merry
mirage
moral
morale
Morris
morrow
mural
narrate
narrow
narrows
nearing
nourish
oral
orange
parade
parent
Paris
parish
parole
parrot
payroll
peril
perish
Perry
Peru
Pharaoh
pirate
plural
porridge
quarrel
quarry
Sarah

sari
scurry
serene
series
sharing
Sharon
Sherese
sheriff
Sherrill
Sherry
siren
sorrow
sorry
spareribs
sparrow
spearing
spiral
spirit
squirrel
starry
steering
stirrup
storage
storeroom
stories
story
surrey
surround
syringe
syrup
tarring
Taurus
tearing
tea room
terrace
Terri
Terry
thorax
thorough

tiring
Torah
touring
tourist
tureen
turret
varied
vary
Vera
very
warrant
Warren
wary
weary
wiring
wiry
worried
worry
zero
Zorro
____
____
____
____

R /r/ Medial—three syllables

accurate
aerial
aerobics
aerospace
Anchorage
apparel
apparent
area
arena
aroma
arresting
arrival
arrowhead
arroyo
authorize
ball bearing
baritone
barricade
battery
bayberry
blackberry
blueberry
boundary
burial
calorie
camera
camporee
canary
caramel
caravan
caribou
Caroline
carry-all
casserole
celery
century
ceramics
cereal
chariot
Cherokee
cherry pie
Cherryvale
Cherryville
chokeberry
clarinet
clarity
coloring
copyright
Coral Sea
coral snake
correction
correspond
courageous
currency
daredevil
dewberry
diary
direction
director
dogberry
Dorothy
durable
duration
embarrass
emerald
encourage
everyday
everyone
everything
Fahrenheit
fairyland
fairytale
ferocious
Ferris wheel
fire engine
fire escape
fishing rod
Florida
furious
garrison
Gloria
glorify
glorious
glossary
godparent
gooseberry
gorilla

guarantee
gyroscope
hackberry
Harriet
Harrison
hearing aid
heritage
heroic
heroine
hickory
Honduras
horizon
horrible
horrify
hurricane
immoral
incorrect
indirect
inherent
inherit
inquiry
insurance
interrupt
Iron Age
irrigate
irritate
Israel
Israeli
Johnny Reb
juneberry
kangaroo
kerosene
Korea
lariat
luxury
lyrical
marigold
Marilyn
marimba
marina
Marine Corps
mariner
Marion
maritime
Maryland
masquerade
memorize
Missouri
mulberry
Nairobi
narration
narrative
nourishment
occurrence
occurring
operate
orangeade
Oregon
orient
origin
oriole
papyrus
parachute
parading
paradise
paraffin
parakeet
parallel
paralyze
parasite
parasol
parroting
period
periscope
pokeberry
pony ride
purify
Puritan
purity
pyramid
quandary
salary
saturate
señora
separate
serenade
serial
serious
Sheraton
skyrocket
snow flurry
sorrowful
spherical
storybook
summarize
summary
Syria
tambourine
teaberry
terrible
terrific
terrify
theorem
theorist
theorize
theory
therapist
Theresa
thoracic
thoroughfare
tomorrow
torrential
touring car
tyranic
tyrannize
tyranny
untiring

unwary
unwearied
Uranus
Uriah
Van Buren
variance
variant
various
veranda
verify
verily
very good
victory
waiting room
wearily
weariness
wearisome
wheelbarrow
worrisome
Zachary
____
____
____
____

R /r/ Medial—four syllables

aerophoto
Amarillo
amaryllis
America
American
Aquarius
area code
arithmetic
Arizona
artificial
aspiration
atmospheric
authority
baby carriage
ballerina
barracuda
category
ceremony
Colorado
comparison
compulsory
Costa Rica
curriculum
declaration
decoration
desirable
dictionary
encouragement
engineering
evaporate
everybody
geranium
heredity
horizontal
huckleberry
inaugurate
infuriate
inheritance
interruption
inventory
irrigation
January
legendary
loganberry
luxurious
macaroni
malaria
maple syrup
marionette
material
memorial
meridian
meteorite
military
minority
missionary
momentary
necessary
notorious
numerical
operating
operation
orangutan
oriental
original
originate
panorama
parachuting
paralysis
parenthesis
parochial
perimeter
perishable
sanctuary
secondary
security
seminary
seniority
señorita
separation
single parent
solitary
South Korea
stationary
stationery
tarantula
theoretic

therapeutic
tyrannical
variable
variation
variety
veritable
vicarious
Victoria
victorious
voluntary
waffle iron
____

R /r/ Medial—five syllables

auditorium
cafeteria
deteriorate
elementary
hieroglyphic
imaginary
inauguration
interrogative
irresistible
Memorial Day
necessarily
penitentiary
respiratory
rudimentary
Sagittarius
theoretical
unwarrantable
variegated
vegetarian
verification
vocabulary
voluntarily
____
____

R /r/ Medial—six syllables

Mediterranean
peculiarity
totalitarian
utilitarian
____
____

R /r/ Final—one syllable

air
are
bar
bare
bear
blare
blur
boar
bore
bur
Burr
car
care
cheer
choir
chore
clear
core
czar
dare
dear
deer
door
ear
fair
far
fare
fear
fir
fire
flair
floor
fore
four
fur
gear
glare
hair
hare
hear
heir
her
here
hire
hour
jar
lair
leer
lore
lure
mar
mare
mere
more
near
nor
oar

or
ore
our
pair
par
pare
pear
peer
pier
poor
pore
pour
pure
purr
scar
scare
score
share
shear
sheer
shore
sir
smear
snare
sneer
soar
sore
sour
spar
spare
spear
sphere
spire
spore
spur
square
squire
stair
star
stare
steer
stir
sure
swear
swore
tear
their
there
tire
tore
tour
veer
war
ware
wear
where
whir
wire
wore
year
your
you're
____
____
____
____

R /r/ Final—two syllables

acquire
adhere
admire
adore
afar
affair
afire
ajar
appear
ashore
aspire
assure
attire
aware
backfire
bazaar
before
beware
bizarre
bonfire
bookstore
boxcar
briar
campfire
cashier
cashmere
compare
conspire
contour
declare
demure
deplore
desire
despair
detour
devour
downpour
drugstore
eclair
elsewhere
empire
encore
endure
ensure
entire

esquire
expire
explore
Fillmore
flatcar
folklore
frontier
galore
guitar
half-hour
health fair
ignore
impair
implore
impure
indoor
inquire
inspire
insure
jaguar
killdeer
Lamar
larkspur
leap year
live wire
mature
memoir
mohair
monsieur
mule deer
New Year
nightmare
North Star
nowhere
obscure
occur
offshore
outdoor
outpour
outroar
outsoar
quasar
sapphire
satyr
seashore
secure
señor
Shakespeare
sincere
snack bar
software
somewhere
sonar
space bar
spitfire
squad car
stock car
stoneware
tambour
threescore
umpire
unfair
vampire
velour
veneer
welfare
____
____
____
____
____
____

R /r/ Final—three syllables

amateur
anywhere
atmosphere
Baltimore
billionaire
cable car
candy bar
cassimere
cavalier
caviar
chicken wire
commodore
Delaware
dinosaur
disappear
domineer
engineer
evening star
falling star
gondolier
handlebar
hemisphere
humidor
insecure
insincere
Leanor
manicure
matador
medicare
middle ear
millionaire
mountaineer
pinafore
pioneer
questionnaire
salad bar
seminar
shooting star
Singapore

solitaire
sophomore
souvenir
sycamore
Theodore
unaware
volunteer
____
____

R /r/ Final—four syllables

conquistador
El Salvador
U.S.S.R.
____
____
____
____
____
____

R /r/ Recurring—two syllables

career
carfare
clearer
dearer
error
fiercer
furor
horror
juror
mirror
nearer
racer
radar
rafter
railroad
rambler
rammer
ramrod
rancher
ranger
rapport
rater
rather
rattler
razor
reader
reamer
reaper
rector
recur
recurred
refer
reindeer
render
renter
repair
require
rerun
respire
restore
restroom
retire
rewrite
rider
rigger
ringer
riper
riser
river
roaster
robber
rocker
roller
roomer
rooster
root beer
Rory
roster
rotor
rover
Rover
rower
rubber
rudder
ruler
rumor
runner
rupture
rural
sheerer
tartar
terror
uproar
warfare
warrior
wrangler
wrapper
wrecker
wrestler
wringer
wrinkler
writer
____
____
____
____
____

R /r/ Recurring—three syllables

admirer
adorer
armorer
barrier
carrier
caterer
conjurer
conqueror
emperor
explorer
foreigner
furrier
hereafter
laborer
loiterer
lumberer
mariner
moreover
raspberry
reactor
realtor
reappear
reassure
recapture
receiver
recorder
recover
rectory
recurring
redeemer
reducer
referee
reference
register
regular
relay race
remainder
remember
remover
repairer
repeater
replier
requirement
requirer
rescuer
resider
resister
respecter
responder
responsor
restaurant
restorer
retailer
retainer
retirement
retiring
reverence
reverent
reverie
Rhone River
ring finger
ringleader
river boat
riverside
Riverside
roadrunner
rock 'n roll
rocking chair
roller skates
rookery
rosary
Rose Marie
Rose Mary
rotary
rubber band
rubber stamp
runner-up
rural route
terrier
thereafter
typewriter
underwear
wanderer
warrior
wherever
wonderer
wraparound
wrought iron
zero hour
____

R /r/ Recurring—four syllables

adventurer
barometer
candy wrapper
direct current
directory
exterior
inferior
interior
irregular
merry-go-round
radiator
rear admiral
receivership
reconsider
recovery
rectangular
recuperate
refinery

respiration
rhinoceros
roller coaster
Roman Empire
Rotarian
secretary
sound barrier
superior
territory
toreador
ulterior
wrapping paper

RB /rb/ Medial—two syllables

air base
airborne
air bus
arbor
barbed wire
barbells
barber
bareback
Burbank
carbon
choirboy
Corbet
Corbin
Corby
derby
disturbed
doorbell
Fairbanks
forbear
forbid
forborne
garbage
gerbil
harbor
Herbert
marble
morbid
nearby
orbit
sherbet
turban
turbid
turbine
turbot
urban
verbal
verbose
warble
warbler
yearbook
____
____

RB /rb/ Medial—three syllables

Ann Arbor
Barbara
barbaric
barbecue
barber chair
barber shop
fur bearer
harboring
orbital
overbear
tetherball
turbulence
turbulent
undisturbed
urbanite
urbanize
verbalize
verbally
verbatim
____
____

RB /rb/ Medial—four syllables

barbecue sauce
carbon paper
carburetor
orbicular
overbearing
roller derby
urbanity
verbosity
____

RB /rb/ Final—one syllable

barb
Barb
blurb
curb
garb
herb
Herb
verb
____

RB /rb/ Final—two syllables

absorb
adverb
disturb
exurb
potherb
proverb
rhubarb
suburb
superb

BR /br/ Initial—one syllable

brace
braced
brad
Brad
brag
bragged
braid
braille
brain
braise
braised
brake
brakes
bran
branch
brand
Brant
brash
brass
brat
brave
brawl
brawn
bray
brayed
braze
breach
breached
bread
breadth
break
breath
breathe
bred
breech
breed
breeze
Brent
Bret
brew
brewed
bribe
bribed
Brice
brick
bricked
bride
bridge
brief
briefed
brig
bright
brim
brimmed
brine
bring
brink
brisk
broach
broached
broad
brogue
broil
broiled
broke
Bronx
bronze
bronzed
brooch
brood
brook
Brooks
broom
broth
brought
brow
brown
browse
browsed
Bruce
bruise
bruised
brunch
brunt
brush
brushed
brusque
brute
Bryce

BR /br/ Initial—two syllables

bracelet
bracer
braces
bracing
bracken
bracket
brackish
Bradford
Bradley
braggart
Brahma
brainless
brainstorm
brainwash
brain wave
brainy
brakeage
brake drum
brake dye
brakeman
brake shoe
bramble
brandish
brandished
brand-new
brass band
brassy
bravo
brazen
brazier
Brazil
breadfruit
breakage
breakdown
breaker
breakfast
breakneck
breakup
breastbone
breastplate
breaststroke
breathing
breathless
breeches
breeder
breeding
breezy
Brenda
brethren
brewer
Brian
briar
brickbat
brickwork
brickyard
bridal
bridegroom
bridesmaid
bridge house
bridge lamp
Bridgeport
bridge sign
Bridget
Bridgeton
Bridge View
Bridgeville
bridgework
bridging
bridle
bridled
bridling
briefcase
briefing
briefly
briefness
brier
brigade
Brigham
brighten
brightened
brilliance
brilliant
brimful
brimstone
brindle
briny
brisket
bristle
bristled
Britain
British
brittle
broadcast
broadcloth
broaden
broadened
broad jump
broadloom
broadside
Broadway
brocade
brochure
brogan
broiler
broken
broker
bromide
bromine
bronchi
bronco
Bronze Age
brooded
brooder
brooding

brooklet
Brooklyn
broomstick
brother
browbeat
brownie
Brownie
brownish
brown rice
bruin
Bruins
brunette
brush fire
brush work
Brussels
Brutus
Bryan
Bryant
____
____
____

BR /br/ Initial—three syllables

bravado
bravery
Brazil nut
breakable
breakwater
breathtaking
brevity
bribery
bric-a-brac
bricklayer
bridle path
brigadier
brilliancy
bringing-up
British Isles
Britisher
broadcaster
broadcasting
broad jumper
broad-minded
broccoli
broken down
brokerage
bronchial
bronchitis
Brooklyn Bridge
brotherhood
brotherly
brouhaha
Brussels sprouts
____
____
____

BR /br/ Medial—two syllables

abrade
Abram
abreast
abridge
abridged
abroad
abrupt
cambric
Cambridge
clothes brush
cobra
cornbread
daybreak
Debra
debrief
debris
drawbridge
embrace
eyebrow
fabric
fibrous
float bridge
Gambrel
hairbrush
Hebrew
hybrid
inbred
Libra
membrane
nail brush
outbreak
paint brush
purebred
rye bread
sagebrush
sea breeze
shoebrush
sweetbread
toll bridge
toothbrush
vibrant
vibrate
whisk broom
white bread
windbreak
zebra
____
____
____
____
____

BR /br/ Medial—three syllables

Abraham
abrasive
abridgment
algebra
Brooklyn Bridge
celebrate
embracement
embracer
embrasure
embroider
Gabriel
gingerbread
Labrador
library
London Bridge
lubricate
Nebraska
paint brushes
pawnbroker
Rainbow Bridge
rebroadcast
scatterbrain
sombrero
thoroughbred
umbrella
unabridged
unbroken
underbrush
upbringing
vertebra
vertebral
vertebrate
vibration
whole wheat bread
____
____

BR /br/ Medial—four syllables

abbreviate
abranchial
abreaction
candelabra
celebrated
celebration
celebrity
embraceable
embracery
embroidery
Golden Gate Bridge
invertebrate
librarian
lubrication
Natural Bridge

RCH /rtʃ/ Medial—two syllables

archduke
archer
Archie
arching
archway
birch bark
churches
Churchill
fortune
kerchief
lurcher
lurching
marches
marching
merchant
nurture
nurtured
orchard
parchment
perchance
perches
perching
porches
purchase
purchased
researched
scorching
searchlight
starchy
surcharge
torchlight
virtue
____

RCH /rtʃ/ Medial—three syllables

archbishop
archdeacon
archduchess
archduchy
archerfish
archery
Archibald
arch support
cheddar cheese
departure
fortunate
handkerchief

interchange
marching band
March of Dimes
merchandise
misfortune
neckerchief
nurturing
orange orchard
overcharge
pear orchard
purchaser
purchasing
sea urchin
starchiest
virtual
____
____
____

RCH /rtʃ/ Medial—four syllables

apple orchard
archery set
birch bark basket
fortunately
fortune cookie
fortune hunter
fortuneteller
fortunetelling
grapefruit orchard
merchant marine
mortuary
purchasable
purchase order
torchlight parade
unfortunate
____
____
____

RCH /rtʃ/ Final—one syllable

arch
birch
church
lurch
march
March
parch
perch
porch
scorch
search
smirch
starch
torch
____

RCH /rtʃ/ Final—two syllables

blowtorch
cornstarch
out march
research
white birch
____

RCHT /rtʃt/ Final—one syllable

arched
marched
parched
perched
scorched
searched
starched
____
____

RD /rd/ Medial—two syllables

Airedale
birdhouse
birdie
birdseed
border
burden
card tricks
cardboard
cording
cordless
cordwood
garden
guarded
guardhouse
guardrail
hair-do
hard-boiled
harden
hardhead
Harding
hardly

hardship
hardware
hardwood
hardy
herdsman
hors d'oeuvre
hurdle
hurdler
ordain
ordeal
order
ordered
pardon
sturdy
tardy
third base
third class
Third World
Verde
warden
warder
wardrobe
yardage
yard light
yardstick
Zardax
____
____
____
____

RD /rd/ Medial—three syllables

bird watcher
borderline
cardinal
card table
concordance
concordant
corduroy
disorder
disordered
gabardine
gardener
Garden Grove
gardening
Garden State
guardian
Hoover Dam
Labor Day
ordering
orderly
ordinal
ordinance
ordinate
overdo
overdone
overdue
preordain
recorder
recording
regarding
regardless
reorder
rewording
rose garden
Saturday
standardize
standard time
stewardess
stewardship
unguarded
wardenship
____
____

RD /rd/ Medial—four syllables

accordion
coordinate
disorderly
Garden City
gardenia
garden party
guard of honor
guardianship
inboard motor
ordinary
ordination
outboard motor
standardizing
Verde River
____
____
____
____

RD /rd/ Medial—five syllables

coordination
guardian angel
ordinal number
ordinarily
overburdensome
____
____
____
____

RD /rd/ Final—one syllable

bard
beard
bird
board
bored
Byrd
card
chard
chord
cleared
cord
ford
Ford
gird
gourd
guard
hard
heard
herd
hoard
horde
lard
lord
moored
poured
roared
scared
scarred
scored
shared
spared
sparred
stared
steered
stirred
stored
third
toward
ward
weird
word
yard
____
____
____

RD /rd/ Final—two syllables

aboard
accord
afford
appeared
award
awkward
backboard
backward
backyard
barnyard
Bedford
Bernard
Big Bird
billboard
blackbird
blackboard
blizzard
bluebird
bombard
Buford
buzzard
cardboard
charge card
chessboard
Clifford
clipboard
Coast Guard
colored
Concord
cornered
courtyard
coward
cupboard
custard
dashboard
discard
eastward
Edward
flashcard
front yard
game bird
gizzard
graveyard
Harvard
hazard
Howard
inboard
inward
keyboard
kickboard
landlord
leeward
Leonard
leopard
lifeguard
lizard
Lombard
mallard
Maynard
measured
mouth guard
mud guard
mustard

nameboard
night guard
numbered
onward
orchard
outboard
outward
Oxford
pampered
password
postcard
prepared
punch card
Radford
rear guard
record
regard
reward
Rexford
Richard
rip cord
Ruford
safeguard
scoreboard
scorecard
seaboard
shepherd
shipyard
skateboard
skyward
songbird
southward
Spaniard
splattered
springboard
standard
Stanford
starboard
steward
stockyard
surfboard
switchboard
tagboard
tattered
thundered
timecard
tutored
unheard
upward
vineyard
wallboard
washboard
watchword
watered
wayward
westward
Willard
wizard

RD /rd/ Final—three syllables

aboveboard
afterward
birthday card
bodyguard
boulevard
checkerboard
Christmas card
color guard
cribbage board
disregard
diving board
drawing board
early bird
harpsichord
horned lizard
hummingbird
leotard
lumberyard
mockingbird
outnumbered
overboard
remembered
report card
Rocky Ford
room and board
rose-colored
rust-colored
Rutherford
Scotland Yard
shuffleboard
smorgasboard
spinal cord
substandard
thank-you card
union card
unnumbered
unwatered
Weatherford

RDZ /rdz/ Final—one syllable

bards
beards
birds
boards
cards
chords
cords
gourds
guards
hoards
lords
towards
wards
words
yards
______
______
______

RDZ /rdz/ Final—two syllables

backyards
blackbirds
bluebirds
buzzards
clipboards
cupboards
discards
flashcards
kick boards
leewards
leopards
lifeguards
lizards
orchards
postcards
punch cards
rear guards
rewards
score cards
shepherds
skateboards
songbirds
Spaniards
surfboards
timecards
vineyards
wizards
______
______
______

DR /dr/ Initial—one syllable

drab
draft
drag
drain
drake
Drake
dram
drank
drape
draped
draw
drawl
drawn
dread
dream
dreamed
dreams
dreamt
dredge
dredged
drench
dress
dressed
drew
dried
drift
drill
drilled
drink
drip
dripped
drive
droll
drone
drool
droop
drop
dropped
drought
drove
drown
drowse
drudge
drug
drum
drummed
drunk
drupe
dry
______
______
______
______
______

DR /dr/ Initial—two syllables

draftsman
drafty
dragging
dragnet
dragon
dragoon
drag race
drag strip
drainage
drainpipe
drama
drastic
drawback
drawbridge
drawer
drawing
drawstring
dreadful
dreamer
dreaming
dreamland
dreary
dredger
dredging
dresser
dressing
dribble
drier
driest
drifter
drifting
driftwood
drilling
drip-dry
drive-in
driven
driver
drive-through
driveway
drizzle
droopy
dropkick
droplet
droplight
dropping
drowsy
druggist
drugstore
druid
drummer
drumstick
dry cell
dry clean
drydock
dryer
dry goods
dry ice
dry milk
dryness
____
____
____
____
____
____
____

DR /dr/ Initial—three syllables

Dracula
draft dodger
dragonfly
Drakensburg
dramatic
dramatist
dramatize
drapery
drawing board
drawing card
drawing frame
drawing room
dreadfully
dreamily
dressmaker
dressing gown
dressing room
dressing up
drillmaster
drinkable
drive-in bank
driver's seat
driving range
drollery
drop kicker
dropsical
drop table
drowsiness
drudgery
drum major
drummer boy
dry cleaner
dry cleaning
dry goods store
dry measure
____
____
____
____
____
____
____

DR /dr/ Initial—four syllables

draconian
dramatical
dramaturgy
drastically
Dravidian
drawing table
dromedary
drosophila
dry battery
____
____
____

DR /dr/ Medial—two syllables

address
adrift
Andrew
Audrey
bass drum
bed rest
bedroll
bedroom
Cedric
children
coughdrop
dandruff
daydream
dewdrop
drip-dry
eardrop
eardrops
eardrum
eye drops
fire drill
foundry
fruit drink
gumdrop
headdress
hindrance
hum-drum
hundred
hundredth
hydrant
hydrate
hydro
laundry
lime drink
line drive
Madrid
Mildred
nose drops
Pedro
quadrant
quadrille
raindrops
Sandra
scoundrel
snare drum
snowdrift
soft drink
sundress
sun-dried
sundries
sundrops
sundry
tawdry
tendril
tundra
undress
withdraw
withdrawn
withdraws
withdrew
wondrous
Woodrow
____
____

DR /dr/ Medial—three syllables

Adrian
Andrea
apple drink
bongo drums
cathedral
dehydrate
eye dropper
Fredericksburg
grapefruit drink
hair dresser
hair dryer
hydraulics
hydrogen
hydrophone
hydroplane
kettle drum
lemon drink
line drawing
orange drink
overdrawn
overdrive
quadrangle
quadruped
quadruple
quadruplet
race driver
San Pedro

screwdriver
snapdragon
truck driver
withdrawal
withdrawing

DR /dr/ Medial—four syllables

adrenalin
dehydrated
driving safety
hydroponics
lemon-lime drink
melodrama
overdrawing
Padre Island
philodendron
photodrama
pineapple drink
quadrennial
quadruplicate
rhododendron
salad dressing
taxi driver

DR /dr/ Medial—five syllables

ambulance driver
hydrodynamics
hydrophobia
hypochondriac
quadrilateral

RF /rf/ Medial—two syllables

airfield
barefaced
barefoot
careful
cheerful
curfew
earful
earphone
fearful
forfeit
Garfield
orphan
parfait
perfect
perform
perfume
starfish
surface
surfboard
surfer
surfing

RF /rf/ Medial—three syllables

butterfat
carefully
carefulness
colorful
counterfeit
fire fighter
forfeiture
interface
interfere
interfold
labor force
orphanage
perfection
perfectly
perforate
performance
performer
performing
tenderfoot
underfoot
waterfall

RF /rf/ Medial—four syllables

butterfinger
imperfection
morphology
performing arts

FR /fr/ Initial—one syllable

frail
frame
Fran
franc
France
Frank
fraud
fray
freak
Fred
free
freeze
freight
French
fresh
fret
fried
friend
fright
frill
fringe
frisk
Fritz
frock
frog
from
frond
front
frost
froth
frown
froze
fruit
fry
phrase
____
____
____
____

FR /fr/ Initial—two syllables

fraction
fracture
fragile
fragment
fragrance
fragrant
framework
framing
Frances
franchise
Francis
Frankfurt
Franklin
frantic
Frazer
freakish
freckle
Freda
freedom
freefall
freehand
free-lance
free lunch
Freeport
freestyle
free throw
free time
freeway
free will
freezer
freighter
Fremont
French fries
French horn
French toast
Frenchman
frenum
frenzied
frenzy
frequent
freshen
freshman
fretful
friar
friction
Friday
Frieda
friendly
friendship
frigate
frighten
frigid
frisky
fritter
frizzy
frogman
frolic
frontage
frontal
fronted
frontier
front page
front room
frostbite
frosted
frosting
frosty
frozen
frugal

fruitcake	frustrate	frying
fruit cup	fryer	________

FR /fr/ Initial—three syllables

fractional	fricative	frost warning
fragmental	frictional	frostbitten
frankfurter	friction tape	fruitfulness
fraternal	friendliness	fruit salad
Frederica	frivolous	frustrating
Frederick	frizzier	frustration
Fredricksburg	frolicking	frying pan
freewheeling	frolicsome	phrenetic
frequency	frontal lobe	phrenitis
fresh water	front runner	________

FR /fr/ Initial—four syllables

fractionary	fraternity	phraseogram
fragility	fraternizing	phrenology
fragmentary	frighteningly	________

FR /fr/ Medial—two syllables

affray	confront	infringe
affront	deep freeze	Jack Frost
afraid	deepfry	Jeffrey
A-frame	defraud	leapfrog
Alfred	defray	refrain
befriend	defrost	refresh
belfry	fish fry	scot-free
boyfriend	girl friend	sea front
breadfruit	grapefruit	Wilfred
bullfrog	Hausfrau	Winfred
carefree	Humphrey	________
cold front	infract	________

FR /fr/ Medial—three syllables

affricate	defrosted	infraction
Africa	defroster	infrared
antifreeze	defrosting	infrequent
deep freezer	Good Friday	infringement

refreshing	unfriendly	Winifred
refreshments	unfrozen	________
sassafras	unfruitful	________
unafraid	waterfront	________

FR /fr/ Medial—four syllables

confrontation	refrigerate	unfrequented
infractible	San Francisco	unfriendliest
infrequently	South Africa	unfruitfulness
refreshingly	tutti frutti	________

FR /fr/ Medial—five syllables

infrangibleness	refrigeration	________
refractivity	refrigerative	________
refractometer	refrigerator	________

RG /rg/ Medial—two syllables

argue	gargle	stargaze
bargain	gurgle	target
Bergen	jargon	tour guide
cargo	Largo	Virgo
ergo	Morgan	________
forget	mortgage	________
forgive	organ	________
forgot	sorghum	________

RG /rg/ Medial—three syllables

argument	forgiven	organdy
burgundy	forgiveness	organic
cheeseburger	forgotten	organize
embargo	hamburger	pipe organ
forgetful	Limburger	undergo
forgetting	Margaret	________

RG /rg/ Medial—four syllables

burgomaster	forgivable	organizer
disorganize	kindergarten	undergarment
forget-me-not	organ grinder	unforgiven
forgettable	organism	________

RG /rg/ Medial—five syllables

organization	________	________
unforgettable	________	________

RG /rg/ Final—one syllable

berg	erg	________
burg	morgue	________

RG /rg/ Final—two syllables

Clarksburg	Lordsburg	Salzburg
Goldberg	Newberg	Strasbourg
Hamburg	Oldsberg	Strindberg
iceberg	Pittsburgh	Tilburg
Lemberg	Romberg	Youngberg
Lindberg	Roseburg	________

RG /rg/ Final—three syllables

Brandenburg	Luxembourg	Rosenburg
Cederberg	Oldenburg	Swedenborg
Edinburg	Petersburg	Williamsburg
Gettysburg	Phillipsburg	________
Heidelberg	Regensburg	________
Hindenburg	Reichenberg	________

RG /rg/ Final—four syllables

East Harrisburg	________	________
Johannesburg	________	________

GR /gr/ Initial—one syllable

grab	grant	graze
grace	Grant	grease
Grace	grape	great
grade	grapes	Greece
grades	graph	green
graft	grasp	greet
grain	grass	Greg
gram	grate	grew
grand	grave	grey
grange	gray	grid

grief
grieve
grill
grilled
grim
grime
grin
grind
grip
gripe
grit
groan
groom
groomed
groove
grooved
grope
gross
grouch
ground
grounds
group
grouse
grove
grow
growl
grown
growth
grub
grudge
gruff
grump
grunt
____
____
____

GR /gr/ Initial—two syllables

grabbing
graceful
gracious
grackle
grader
grade school
grading
grafting
Graham
grammar
grandad
grandeur
grandma
grandniece
grandpa
Grand Prix
grand slam
grandson
grandstand
grand tour
granite
grantee
grantor
granule
grapefruit
grapevine
graphic
graphite
grasping
grassland
grass snake
grassy
grateful
grating
gravel
graveyard
gravy
grazing
greasing
greasy
Great Dane
greater
greatest
Great Falls
Great Lakes
greatly
greedy
greenbacks
greenhouse
greeting
greetings
gremlin
Greta
Gretchen
greyhound
griddle
Griffin
Griffith
grillwork
grimace
grimy
grinder
grinding
grindstone
grinning
griping
gripping
gristle
gritty
grizzle
grizzled
grizzly
grocer
groggy
grooming

groomsman
grooving
groovy
groping
grotesque
grotto
grouchy
ground crew
grounder
ground floor
ground fog
groundhog
ground rules
ground wave
groundwire
groundwork
Grover
growing
grown-up
grubby
gruesome
grumble
grumpy
Grundy
grunion
____
____

GR /gr/ Initial—three syllables

gracias
graciously
gradual
graduate
granary
Grandberry
Grand Canyon
grandchildren
granddaughter
grandfather
grandiose
grand jury
grandmother
grandnephew
grandparents
granny knot
granulate
grasshopper
gratify
gratitude
gravity
Great Britain
Great Divide
Gregory
gridiron
Griselda
grizzly bear
groceries
grocery
ground cover
Ground Hog Day
grounds keeper
ground squirrel
ground zero
grueling
____

GR /gr/ Initial—four syllables

gradually
graduation
graduator
grammarian
grammatical
grandfather clock
Grand Old Party
grand piano
Granite City
graphology
gratifying
gratuitous
gravitation
great-grandparent
gregarious
grotesquerie
group therapy
____

GR /gr/ Medial—two syllables

aggrieve
aggrieved
agree
agreed
aground
angry
background
begrudge
bluegrass
blue-green
bridegroom
congress
degrade
degree
digress
disgrace
downgrade
egress

egret
engrave
engross
fairground
flagrant
foreground
fragrance
fragrant
hungry
ingrain
Ingram
ingrate
Ingrid
ingroup
land grant
migrate
mongrel
outgrow
outgrowth
Pilgrim
program
progress
regrade
regress
regret
regroup
school ground
tigress
upgrade
vagrant
______
______
______

GR /gr/ Medial—three syllables

aggregate
aggression
aggressive
agreement
allegro
anagram
au gratin
autograph
cablegram
centigrade
centigram
citrus grove
concord grapes
congregate
congressman
congruent
congruous
diagram
dictograph
disagree
disgraceful
disgruntle
emigrant
evergreen
Evergreen
filigree
homograph
immigrant
immigrate
ingrowing
integrate
kilogram
lettergram
Mardi Gras
migration
milligram
monogram
overgrown
overgrowth
paragraph
pedigree
phonograph
photograph
regression
Rio Grande
segregate
seismograph
study group
telegram
telegraph
underground
undergrown
undergrowth
ungraceful
ungracious
ungrateful
upgrading
vagrancy
wintergreen
______

GR /gr/ Medial—four syllables

aggravation
agriculture
allegretto
audiogram
biographer
biographic
biography
calligrapher
coffee grinder
conflagration
congratulate
congregation

congressional
congruity
disagreement
disintegrate
federal grant
geography
incongruent
incongruous
ingratiate
ingratitude
ingredient
integration
integrative
integrity
mimeograph
organ grinder
photographer
photography
regretfully
regrettable
retrogression
segregated
segregation
stenographer
subaggregate
subgranular
technography
telegrammic
telegrapher
telegraphic
telegraphy
tympanogram
typographer
typography
undergrading
ungraciously
ungrantable
ungraspable
____

GR /gr/ Medial—five syllables

agricultural
bibliography
biographical
diagrammatic
disagreeable
disintegrated
disintegration
geographical
incongruity
ingratiating
ingratiation
oceanographer
oceanographic
oceanography
topographical
undergraduate
ungrammatical
____

RJ /rdʒ/ Medial—two syllables

bargeman
barges
charge card
charger
Chargers
charging
clergy
cordial
forger
forging
Georgetown
Georgia
gorgeous
largely
larger
largest
Margie
margin
Margy
merger
merging
perjure
perjured
sergeant
splurging
sturgeon
surgeon
turgid
urgent
Virgil
____
____
____

RJ /rdʒ/ Medial—three syllables

allergic
allergy
chargeable
clergyman
convergence
converges
crackerjacks
detergent
discharges

divergent
emergent
energize
energy
enlargement
enlarger
forgery
insurgent
lethargic
lethargy
lumberjack
margarine
Margery
marginal
Marjorie
overjoy
overjoyed
perjury
recharger
recharging
surgery
surgical
urgency
Virginia
____
____
____

RJ /rdʒ/ Medial—four syllables

Argentina
emergency
energetic
reenlargement
supercharger
superjacent
Virgin Islands
Virgin Mary
West Virginia
____
____
____

RJ /rdʒ/ Final—one syllable

barge
charge
dirge
forge
George
gorge
gurge
large
Marge
merge
purge
scourge
serge
splurge
surge
urge
verge
____

RJ /rdʒ/ Final—two syllables

converge
discharge
diverge
emerge
engorge
enlarge
recharge
submerge
surcharge
upsurge
____
____

RK /rk/ Medial—two syllables

air-cool
arcade
archive
Arctic
barking
bearcat
Berkeley
carcass
charcoal
circle
circuit
circus
clerking
corkscrew
Corky
darken
darker
darkness
Dorcas
forecast
haircut
harken
jerkin
jerking

jerky
Larkin
larkspur
lurking
marker
market
marking
marquee
murky
orchid
parka
Parker
parking
parkway
perky
shirking
smirking
snorkle
spark plug
sparkle
sparkled
sparklers
sparkling
turkey
Turkey
Turkish
turquoise
workbench
workbook
working
workman
workmen
workroom
workshop
____
____

RK /rk/ Medial—three syllables

anarchist
anarchy
Antarctic
archaic
archangel
beef jerky
circular
circulate
darkener
embarking
encircle
marketing
Market Street
mazurka
mercury
Mercury
monarchist
monarchy
motorcade
motorcar
orchestra
overcame
overcast
overcoat
overcome
parking lights
parking lot
parking place
patchwork quilt
percolate
percussion
porcupine
remarking
sarcasm
sarcastic
Turkish bath
woodworking
workable
workmanship
work station
worktable
____
____
____
____

RK /rk/ Medial—four syllables

air-condition
altercation
Antarctica
Arcadia
Arctic Circle
Arctic Ocean
charcoal lighter
circuit breaker
disembarking
felt-tip marker
hierarchy
money market
orchestration
Park Avenue
parking meter
percolator
remarkable
semicircle
sheltered workshop
social worker
summer workshop
supermarket
turkey buzzard
____

RK /rk/ Final—one syllable

arc
ark
bark
Burke
Clark
clerk
cork
dark
Dirk
fork
hark
irk
jerk

Kirk
lark
lurk
marc
Marc
mark
Mark
park
perk
Perk
pork
quirk
shark

shirk
smirk
spark
stark
stork
torque
Turk
work
York

RK /rk/ Final—two syllables

birch bark
birthmark
bookmark
bridgework
check mark
debark
Denmark
earmark
embark
footmark
footwork
framework
frostwork

guesswork
hallmark
handwork
hayfork
homework
housework
landmark
loan shark
monarch
network
Newark
New York
patchwork

pitchfork
pockmark
postmark
remark
salesclerk
skylark
stonework
town clerk
trademark
uncork
woodwork

RK /rk/ Final—three syllables

baseball park
Central Park
city park
disembark
fancywork
handiwork
hierarchy
Jasper Park

meadowlark
needlework
Noah's Ark
overpark
overwork
patriarch
pencil mark
question mark

social work
Sunset Park
tuning fork
watermark
waterwork

RK /rk/ Final—four syllables

Denali Park
national park
quotation mark

________ ________
________ ________
________ ________

RKT /rkt/ Final—one syllable

arcked
barked
irked

jerked
marked
parked

sparked
worked
____

RKT /rkt/ Final—two syllables

embarked
postmarked
remarked

uncorked
unmarked
unworked

____
____
____

KR /kr/ Initial—one syllable

Chris
Christ
chrome
crab
craft
crag
Craig
cram
crammed
cramp
cramped
crane
crank
crash
crate
crave
craw
crawl
crawled
creak
cream
crease
creased

creed
creek
creep
crepe
crept
crest
Crete
crew
crib
cribbed
crick
cried
crime
crisp
crisped
croak
crock
crop
cross
crossed
crouch
croup
crow

crowd
crowed
crown
crowned
crude
cruise
cruised
crumb
crumbed
crumbs
crunch
crush
crust
crutch
cry
kraut
____
____
____
____
____
____
____

KR /kr/ Initial—two syllables

Christa
Christian
Christine
Christmas
Christy
chroma
Chrysler
Chrystal
crabby
cracker
cracking
crackling
cradle
cradled
craftsman
crafty
craggy
cramming
cramping
crater
crayfish
crayon
crazy
cream cheese
create
creature
credit
creeper
creeping
creepy
crescent
crevasse
crewel
crewman
crewmen
cribbage
cricket
crimson
cripple
crippled
crisis
crispy
crisscross
crochet
crock pot
crocus
crooked
crop dust
cropper
cropping
croquet
crossbow
crossing
crossroad
crosswalk
croutons
crowbar
crowded
crowdy
crowning
crow's nest
crucial
crude oil
cruel
cruise car
cruiser
cruise ship
cruising
crumble
crumbled
crumbly
crummy
crumple
crunchy
crusade
crushing
crystal
Kristi
____
____
____

KR /kr/ Initial—three syllables

Christina
Christmas card
Christmas Day
Christmas Eve
Christmas tree
Christopher
chromosome
chrysolite
crackerjack
craftsmanship
cranberry
crash helmet
Crater Lake
creation
creative
creator
credible
cremation
crepe paper
cribbage board
criminal
critical
criticize
crocheting
crockery
crocodile
Cro-Magnon

crop duster
cross-country
crossover
cross section
crucify
cruelty
crusader
crustacean
crystallize

KR /kr/ Initial—four syllables

chronology
chrysanthemum
cracker barrel
cranberry tree
creativeness
creditable
credit rating
credit union
criterion
critical mass
cross-country skis
cross reference
cross-country skis
crossword puzzle

KR /kr/ Medial—two syllables

accrete
accrue
accrued
acrid
across
aircraft
aircrew
Akron
bankrupt
book rack
cockroach
concrete
corn crib
decrease
decreased
decree
discrete
ecru
fulcrum
handcraft
increase
increased
king crab
macron
microbe
okra
packrat
pie crust
recruit
Red Cross
sacred
sand crab
scarecrow
sea crab
secret
secrete
spacecraft
stock room
tree crab
witchcraft
woodcraft

KR /kr/ Medial—three syllables

accredit
achromic
acrobat
acrylic
aircraftman
aircrewman
autocrat
bike crossing
deer crossing
democrat
doublecross
endocrine
giant crab
handcrafted
handicraft
hot cross buns
Hovercraft
hypocrite
increasing
increment
leather craft
microfilm
microphone
microscope
microwave
moose crossing
nutcracker
oyster crab
pancreas
pleasure craft

plutocrat
sacrifice
Santa Cruz
sauerkraut
secrecy
soft-shell crab
sour cream
synchronize
Veracruz
water craft

KR /kr/ Medial—four syllables

acrobatics
aristocrat
democracy
hypocrisy
increasingly
incredible
incredulous
incriminate
microscopic
plutocracy
railroad crossing
recreation
secretary

KR /kr/ Medial—five syllables

aircraft carrier
aristocratic
incriminating
microdetector

RL /rl/ Medial—two syllables

airlift
airline
Arlene
Arlon
barely
barley
Berlin
burlap
burly
careless
Carla
carload
Charlene
Charlie
Charline
Charlotte
clearly
curling
curly
Darlene
darling
Earlene
early
fairly
fearless
furlong
furlough
garland
garlic
Girl Scouts
Harlan
Harlem
Harley
heirloom
hourly
marlin
merely
Merlin
moorland
nearly
oarlock
parlor
pearly
poorly
scarlet
Shirley
squarely
starlight
starling
starlit
sterling
surely
swirly
Verlene
whirlpool
whirlwind
yearling
yearly

RL /rl/ Medial—three syllables

Arlington
Barley Green
barleycorn
blue marlin
brotherly
charlatan
charley horse
Charlottesville
Charlottetown
cheerleaders
curlicue
eagerly
early bird
entirely
fatherly
garlic bread
garlic salt
gingerly
Harlingen
hourly wage
Kimberly
mannerly
masterly
maturely
miserly
motherly
neighborly
northerly
obscurely
orderly
overland
overlap
overlay
overlie
overload
overlook
overly
Parliament
Pearl Harbor
power line
powerless
properly
quarterly
scholarly
securely
severely
sisterly
Sutherland
tenderly
utterly
whirlabout
whirligig
whirlpool bath
whirlybird
wonderland
____
____

RL /rl/ Medial—four syllables

curling iron
everlasting
New Orleans
northwesterly
sitting parlor
southeasterly
sterling silver
____
____

RL /rəl/ /ɝl/ Final—one syllable

Beryl
burl
Burl
Carl
curl
Earl
furl
girl
gnarl
hurl
Karl
Merle
pearl
Pearl
purl
skirl
snarl
swirl
twirl
whirl
whorl
____
____
____

RL /rəl/ /ɝl/ Final—two syllables

blue pearl
unfurl
untwirl
white pearl
young girl
____

RL /ɝl/ Final—three syllables

baby girl	knit and purl	___
baton twirl	Minnie Pearl	___
Campfire Girl	yellow pearl	___

REL /rəl/ Final—two syllables

barrel	mural	spiral
choral	oral	squirrel
coral	peril	sterile
floral	quarrel	___
moral	rural	___

REL /rəl/ Final—three syllables

admiral	imperil	pastoral
apparel	lateral	sculptural
corporal	liberal	several
cultural	mackerel	___
funeral	mineral	___
general	natural	___
immoral	numeral	___

REL /rəl/ Final—four syllables

bilateral	inaugural	unnatural
collateral	intramural	vice-admiral
conjectural	rear admiral	___

RLZ /rlz/ Final—one syllable

Charles	pearls	whorls
curls	purls	___
Earl's	snarls	___
girls	swirls	___
gnarls	twirls	___
hurls	whirls	___

LR /lr/ Medial—two syllables

all right	seal ring	___
ballroom	toll road	___
railroad	walrus	___
schoolroom	___	___

LR /lr/ Medial—three syllables

already
cavalry
civil rights
coral reef
cradle roll
gravel road
jewelry
middle ring
rivalry
____
____
____

RM /rm/ Medial—two syllables

airmail
airman
armful
armhole
armor
armored
army
Burma
Burmese
Carmel
Carmen
charming
dormant
Erma
ermine
farm belt
farmer
farming
farmland
fireman
firemen
foreman
foremost
formal
format
former
garment
German
gourmet
harmful
harmless
hermit
hormone
Irma
mermaid
Norma
normal
Norman
permit
spearmint
sperm whale
surmise
surmount
termite
thermal
thermos
torment
turmoil
unarmed
vermin
Vermont
warmly
warm-up
wormwood
____
____
____

RM /rm/ Medial—three syllables

alderman
armament
armistice
armorer
armory
Bermuda
cormorant
enormous
farming land
fire marshal
firmament
formation
formula
Germany
germinate
harmonize
harmony
informal
marmalade
performance
performer
permanent
permission
pharmacist
pharmacy
Prince Charming
retirement
snake charmer
storm cellar
storm center
storm warning
storm window
terminal

terminate
thermostat
uniformed
vermillion

RM /rm/ Medial—four syllables

affirmative
armadillo
Armistice Day
army blanket
conformation
dormitory
fermentation
germination
harmonica
infirmary
infirmity
permanently
permeable
supermarket
termination
thermometer
uniformly

RM /rm/ Medial—five syllables

formalization
terminology
thermal barrier
uniformity

RM /rm/ Final—one syllable

arm
charm
dorm
farm
firm
form
germ
harm
squirm
storm
swarm
warm
worm

RM /rm/ Final—two syllables

affirm
alarm
bookworm
confirm
conform
cutworm
deform
dust storm
earthworm
hailstorm
inchworm
infirm
inform
perform
platform
rainstorm
reform
sandstorm
silkworm
snowstorm
tapeworm
windstorm

RM /rm/ Final—three syllables

angleworm
fire alarm
pachyderm
thunderstorm
uniform

RN /rn/ Medial—two syllables

Arnold
barnyard
Bernard
Bernice
burned-out
burner
burning
colonel
cornbread
corncob
Cornell
corner
cornered
cornet
cornfield
cornflakes
corn oil
cornstarch
darning
doorknob
earnest
earnings
Ernest
furnace
furnish
garnet
garnish
harness
horned toad
hornet
journal
journey
kernel
learning
Lorna
morning
mourning
Myrna
ornate
surname
tarnish
thorny
turncoat
turner
turnip
turnkey
turn on
turnout
turnpike
turnstile
varnish
Vernon
warning
worn-out

RN /rn/ Medial—three syllables

alternate
Bernadine
carnation
Carnegie
carnival
cornerstone
corn popper
Easterner
eternal
external
fraternal
furnishings
furniture
government
infernal
internal
internee
internist
internment
journalist
journeyman
maternal
nocturnal
ornament
paternal
returning
Southern Cross
Southerner
southernmost
storm warning
stubbornness
tornado
tournament
tourniquet
turnover
turntable
unfurnished
Westerner
westernmost

RN /rn/ Medial—four syllables

alternately
alternative
alternator
carnivorous
internalize
morning glory
returnable
vernacular
____

RN /rn/ Final—one syllable

barn	learn	urn
born	Lorne	Verne
burn	mourn	warn
churn	scorn	worn
corn	stern	yarn
darn	sworn	yearn
earn	thorn	________
fern	torn	________
horn	turn	________

RN /rn/ Final—two syllables

acorn	Hawthorn	return
adjourn	inborn	Saturn
adorn	intern	shopworn
airborne	iron	shorthorn
auburn	lantern	sojourn
Auburn	LaVerne	southern
cavern	long horn	stubborn
cistern	modern	sunburn
concern	newborn	upturn
eastern	pattern	western
fire thorn	popcorn	windburn
fog horn	pronghorn	________
French horn	Rayburn	________
govern	reborn	________

RN /rn/ Final—three syllables

Capricorn	southwestern	unicorn
southeastern	unconcern	________

RP /rp/ Medial—two syllables

airplane	harping	serpent
airport	harpist	sharpen
burping	harpoon	sharper
carpet	perplex	surpass
chirping	porpoise	surplus
fireplace	purple	tarpan
hairpin	purpose	tarpon

terpene
torpid
torpor
turpeth
war paint
warpath
warping

RP /rp/ Medial—three syllables

absorption
carpenter
centerpiece
corporal
harpsichord
power pack
purposely
Scorpio
scorpion
sharpener
sharpening
sharpshooter
sharpsighted
sharpwitted
surplus store
tarpaulin
torpedo
turpentine
unsharpened
unsurpassed

RP /rp/ Medial—four syllables

caterpillar
incorporate
perpetual
surpassable
torpedo boat

RP /rp/ Final—one syllable

burp
carp
chirp
harp
sharp
slurp
tarp
thorp
Thorpe
twirp
warp

PR /pr/ Initial—one syllable

Prague
praise
praised
prance
pranced
prank
prate
Pratt
prawn
prawns
pray
prayed
preach
preached
preen
press
pressed
prey
price
priced
pride
pried
pries
priest
prime
primed
primp
prince
print
prize
prized
pro
probe
probed
prod
prof
prom
prompt
prone

prong
proof
proofed
prop
propped
props
prose
proud
prove
prow
prowl
prude
prune
pruned
pry
____
____
____

PR /pr/ Initial—two syllables

practice
prairie
praline
pratique
prattle
prattler
preacher
precede
precept
precinct
precious
precise
preclude
predict
preempt
preface
prefect
prefer
prefix
prejudge
prelude
premier
premise
prepaid
prepare
prepared
prepay
preschool
prescribe
presence
present
presents
preserve
preshrunk
preside
press club
presser
pressing
pressman
pressroom
pressure
presswork
prestige
presto
presume
pretend
pretense
pretest
pretext
pretty
pretzel
prevail
prevent
preview
priceless
prickle
prickly
priesthood
primal
primate
primer
priming
primrose
princess
printed
printer
printing
printout
prior
prism
prison
pristine
private
probate
problem
proceed
proceeds
process
proclaim
proctor
Proctor
procure
produce
product
profess
profile
profit
profound
profuse
program
progress
project
prolong

promise
promote
prompted
prompter
promptly
pronghorn
pronoun
pronounce
pronounced
proofread
propel
proper
prophet
propose
propound
proscribe
prospect
prosper
protect
protein
protest
proton
protract
protrude
proverb
provide
province
provoke
prowess
proxy
prudence
Prudence
prudent
prudish
pruning
____
____
____
____

PR /pr/ Initial—three syllables

practical
prairie dog
preamble
prearrange
precaution
precedence
precedent
preceding
precipice
precision
precocious
preconceive
preconcert
precursor
predator
predestine
predicate
prediction
predispose
preemption
preexist
preference
preferment
prefigure
prejudice
premature
premiership
premium
prenatal
preordain
prescription
presently
preserver
president
pressurize
prestigious
presumption
pretentious
prevalence
prevention
previous
prickly pear
primary
primitive
principal
principle
printing press
prisoner
privacy
privately
privation
privilege
probable
probably
probation
proboscis
procedure
procession
processor
prodigal
prodigious
prodigy
producer
production
productive
profession
professor
proficient
profitee
profusion
progeny
prognosis

prognostic
progressive
prohibit
projected
projectile
projector
prolific
promenade
prominent
promising
promptitude
promulgate
pronouncement
propagate
propeller
proper name
property
prophecy
prophesy
prophetess
prophetic
propolis
proponent
proportion
proposal
propulsion
prosaic
prosecute
prosody
prospective
prosperous
protection
protective
protege
Protestant
protocol
protoplast
prototype
protractor
protrusion
provender
provided
providence
providing
provincial
provision
provoking
prudential
____
____
____

PR /pr/ Initial—four syllables

practicable
practical joke
practically
practical nurse
practitioner
prairie chicken
praying mantis
precarious
precedency
precipitant
precipitate
precipitous
preconception
predatory
predecessor
predetermine
predicament
predominance
predominant
preeminent
preexistence
preexistent
prefabricate
preferable
preferential
prefiguring
preformation
prefulfillment
pregalvanize
prehardener
preharmony
prehistoric
preholiday
preignition
preimposing
preinclining
preindicate
preinstruction
prejudicial
prematurely
premedical
premeditate
premonition
preoccupied
preparation
preponderance
preponderate
preposition
preposterous
prerequisite
prerogative
presentable
presentation
preservation
preservative
presidency
presidential
presumable
presumptuous
prevaricate

prima donna
primarily
prime minister
principally
priority
processional
proclamation
procrastinate
procreation
productively
professional
profitable
prohibition
prohibitive
proletary
proliferate
prolongation
promissory
promontory
propaganda
propensity
proportional
proposition
proprietor
proscenium
prosecution
prosperity
protuberance
protuberant
proverbial
provisional
provocation
provocative
proximity
____
____
____
____
____

PR /pr/ Initial—five syllables

precipitation
predestination
prehistorical
preliminary
premeditation
preparatory
prepositional
Presbyterian
principality
probability
productivity
prognostication
promissory note
pronunciation
____

PR /pr/ Medial—two syllables

appraise
appraised
apprize
approach
approved
April
apron
blueprint
bombproof
Capri
compress
culprit
cypress
Cypress
depress
depressed
deprive
deprived
dustproof
express
fireproof
footprint
impress
imprint
improve
oppress
rainproof
repress
reprieve
reprint
reprise
reproach
reprove
shipwreck
shipwrecked
soundproof
sun proof
suppress
supreme
surprise
surprised
upright
____
____
____
____
____
____
____
____
____

PR /pr/ Medial—three syllables

appraisal	expression	paprika
apprehend	expressive	represent
approval	expressway	repression
apricot	fingerprint	reprimand
April Fool	high pressure	reprinted
bulletproof	impression	reprisal
by-product	impressive	reprobate
capricious	imprison	reproduce
Capricorn	impromptu	soprano
comprehend	improper	tamper-proof
deprecate	improvement	unprepared
depressant	improvise	waterproof
depression	interpret	weatherproof
depressive	jet propelled	________________
disapprove	low pressure	________________
enterprise	mispronounce	________________

PR /pr/ Medial—four syllables

appreciate	depreciate	reciprocate
apprehension	disapproval	reproduction
apprenticeship	impregnable	supremacy
approbation	impressionist	vice-president
appropriate	life preserver	word processor
approximate	proprietor	________________
April Fools' Day	reciprocal	________________

PR /pr/ Medial—five syllables

appreciation	impropriety	reprehensible
apprehensible	improvisation	representative
appropriation	inappropriate	uncompromising
depreciation	interpretation	unprecedented
impracticable	irrepressible	________________
impressionable	irreproachable	________________

RS /rs/ Medial—two syllables

arson	cursor	fireside
corsage	dorsal	forceps
cursive	firesale	foresaw

foresee
foreseen
foresight
forsake
for sale
forsook
herself
horseback
horsefly
horseman
horseshoe
horse show
mercy
morsel
Morse Code
ourselves
parcel
parsley
parsnip
parson
perceive
percent
person
perspire
pursue
pursuit
scarcely
tiresome
torso
verso
versus
Warsaw
yourself

RS /rs/ Medial—three syllables

arsenal
arsenic
cumbersome
diversely
fire safety
forsaken
horsepower
intercede
Jefferson
lumbersome
Mercedes
narcissus
near-sighted
nursery
overseas
oversight
overstate
parcel post
parsonage
percentage
persecute
persimmon
persistent
personal
personnel
porcelain
power saw
precursor
rehearsal
rehearsing
reverses
reversing
riverside
Riverside
salesperson
somersault
supersede
supervise
underset
unforeseen
varsity
versatile
versify

RS /rs/ Medial—four syllables

adversary
controversy
diversity
impersonate
marsupial
nursery rhymes
nursery school
persecution
personally
supersonic
superstition
universal
unmerciful
versifier
vice versa
water safety

RS /rs/ Medial—five syllables

anniversary
diversifying
personality
universally
university
versatility
versification
____
____

RS /rs/ Final—one syllable

coarse
course
curse
fierce
force
hearse
hoarse
horse
nurse
pierce
Pierce
purse
scarce
source
sparse
verse
worse
____
____
____
____

RS /rs/ Final—two syllables

adverse
Air Force
averse
coerce
concourse
converse
disburse
disperse
diverse
divorce
endorse
enforce
golf course
imburse
immerse
inverse
race course
recourse
rehearse
remorse
resource
reverse
saw horse
school nurse
sea horse
submerse
transverse
traverse
____
____
____
____
____

RS /rs/ Final—three syllables

charley horse
fire safety
first aid course
hobby horse
intersperse
labor force
office nurse
police force
quarter horse
reinforce
rocking horse
slalom course
student nurse
universe
____

RSH /rʃ/ Medial—two syllables

airship
earshot
Marsha
marshal
martial
partial
portion
warship
worship
____
____
____

RSH /rʃ/ Medial—three syllables

censorship	martial law	proportion
commercial	membership	scholarship
contortion	overshade	sponsorship
distortion	overshine	undershirt
fire marshal	overshoes	undershot
foreshadow	overshoot	undershrub
leadership	overshot	watershed
Marshal Sea	ownership	________
marshmallow	partnership	________
martial arts	pastorship	________

RSH /rʃ/ Medial—four syllables

antique airship	overshadow	treasurership
chancellorship	thundershower	undersheriff
Marshall Islands	torsionally	________

RSH /rʃ/ Final—one syllable

harsh	________	________
kirsch	________	________
marsh	________	________

SHR /ʃr/ Initial—one syllable

shrank	shrill	shrub
shred	shrimp	shrug
shrew	shrine	shrugged
shrewd	shrines	shrugs
shrews	shrink	shrunk
shriek	shrive	________
shrift	shroud	________
shrike	shrove	________

SHR /ʃr/ Initial—two syllables

shredded	shrimp boat	shriveled
Shreveport	shrimper	shriven
shrewdly	Shriners	shrubby
shrewdness	shrinkage	shrugging
shrewish	shrinking	shrunken
shrillest	shrivel	________

SHR /ʃr/ Initial—three syllables

shriveling
shrubbery
____
____
____
____

SHR /ʃr/ Medial—two syllables

enshrine
mushroom
preshred
preshrink
preshrunk
unshred
washrag
washroom
____

SKR /skr/ Initial—one syllable

scram
scrap
scrape
scratch
scrawl
scream
screech
screen
screw
scribe
scrimp
script
scroll
Scrooge
scrub
scrunch
____
____

SKR /skr/ Initial—two syllables

scraggly
scramble
scrambled
scrapbook
scraper
scrapper
scratchy
scrawny
screening
screenplay
screentest
screwball
scribble
scribbled
scrimmage
scripture
scrub nurse
scrumptious
scruple
____
____

SKR /skr/ Initial—three syllables

screen writer
screwdriver
scrupulous
scrutinize
scrutiny
____
____
____
____

SKR /skr/ Medial—two syllables

ascribe
ascribed
corkscrew
describe
described
discreet
escrow
ice cream
inscribe
muskrat
postscript
prescribe
prescribed
silkscreen
subscribe
subscribed
subscript
transcribe
transcribed
____
____

SKR /skr/ Medial—three syllables

description	inscription	subscription
descriptive	manuscript	________
ice-cream man	prescription	________
ice-cream truck	skyscraper	________

SPR /spr/ Initial—one syllable

sprain	spree	sprout
sprang	sprig	spruce
sprawl	spring	sprung
spray	sprint	spry
spread	sprite	________

SPR /spr/ Initial—two syllables

spraddle	springboard	sprinkler
sprayer	Springfield	sprinkling
spray gun	springing	sprocket
spreader	springtime	________
spreadsheet	sprinkle	________

SPR /spr/ Medial—two syllables

bedspread	hot springs	Rock Springs
hair spray	Hot Springs	________
handspring	offspring	________

SPR /spr/ Medial—three syllables

Brussels sprouts	Silver Spring	________
ocean spray	Union Springs	________
shopping spree	________	________

STR /str/ Initial—one syllable

straight	straw	stressed
strain	stray	stretch
strained	strayed	stretched
strait	streak	strict
strand	stream	stride
strange	street	strike
strap	strength	string
strapped	stress	strip

stripe
stripped
strive
strobe
stroke
strokes
stroll
strolled
strong
strove
struck
strum
strung
strut

STR /str/ Initial—two syllables

straggle
stranger
strapping
streaking
streamer
streamline
streetcar
strengthen
stressing
stretcher
stretching
stretch-out
stretchy
stricken
strident
strike out
strike zone
string beans
stringent
stringing
stringy
stripping
striving
strobe lamp
stroller
strolling
strongbox
stronghold
strongly
structure
strudel
struggle
strumming
strutting
strychnine

STR /str/ Initial—three syllables

straightforward
strait jacket
strategy
stratosphere
strawberry
strenuous
string quartet
stroboscope
structural

STR /str/ Initial—four syllables

streptococcus
streptomycin
stringed instruments

STR /str/ Medial—two syllables

abstract
airstrip
astray
astride
backstroke
bloodstream
bowstring
breaststroke
constrict
construct
destroy
distract
distress
downstream
frustrate
gold stream
high-strung
instruct
minstrel
mistreat
mistress

monstrous
nostril
obstruct
ostrich
pastry
restrain
restrict
rostrum
seamstress
shoestring
side street
sidestroke
upstream
vestry
____

STR /str/ Medial—three syllables

Astrodome
astronaut
Australia
Austria
chemistry
comic strip
construction
demonstrate
destroyer
destruction
destructive
distraction
distribute
doll stroller
Gaza Strip
illustrate
industry
instruction
instructor
instrument
orchestra
reconstruct
restraining
restricting
restriction
Sunset Strip
tapestry
____
____
____

STR /str/ Medial—four syllables

apostrophe
astrology
astronomer
astronomy
baby stroller
band instruments
candy striper
catastrophe
catastrophic
demonstration
distribution
illustration
industrial
industrious
instrumental
orchestra pit
pedestrian
reconstruction
string orchestra
____
____

STR /str/ Medial—five syllables

administration
astronomical
boa constrictor
instrumentalist
____
____

RT /rt/ Medial—two syllables

artful
artist
barter
Bertram
Burton
Carter
carton
cartoon
cartridge
cartwheel
certain
charter
Cortez
courthouse
courtyard
curtain
Curtis
dirty
fertile
forty
fourteen

garter
Gertrude
hearty
martin
Martin
Marty
martyr
mortal
mortar
Myrtle
partake
parted
parting
partly
partner
partridge
part-time
party
pertain
portage
Portage
porter
Porter
porthole
Portland
portrait
portray
quarter
quartet
quart jar
quarto
shortage
shortcake
short-changed
short-cut
shorten
shorthand
shorthorn
shortly
shortstop
shortwave
Shorty
smarter
smartly
sorting
sport car
sporting
sportive
sportsman
sporty
squirting
started
starter
startle
thirteen
thirteenth
thirty
tortoise
turtle
vertex
warthog
wiretap
____

RT /rt/ Medial—three syllables

advertise
Alberta
aorta
apartment
artichoke
article
artifact
artisan
assortment
bartering
cartilage
certainty
certified
certify
chartering
compartment
courtesy
departed
department
deportment
fertilize
fortieth
fortify
garter snake
Gilberta
headquarters
heartbroken
heartily
immortal
importance
important
liberty
light-hearted
particle
partition
partnership
portable
property
quarterback
report card
reporter
reporting
Roberta
Roquefort cheese
short circuit
shortening
short-handed
short-sighted

short story
soft-hearted
sportsmanlike
sportsmanship
sportswoman
sportswriter
summertime
support group
support staff
thirtieth
tortilla
turtledove
vertebra
vertebral
vertical
vertigo
____
____

RT /rt/ Medial—four syllables

advertisement
articulate
artificial
certificate
certified check
certified mail
comfortable
convertible
departable
fertility
invertebrate
Liberty Bell
participate
participle
particular
porterhouse steak
portfolio
property tax
Puerto Rico
refertilize
reportedly
self-imparting
short division
short-handedness
short-sightedness
smart-alecky
unfortified
unimportant
unsportsmanlike
well-fortified
well-supported
____
____

RT /rt/ Medial—five syllables

false advertising
opportunity
past participle
pertinacity
quarterly report
uncomfortable
____
____
____

RT /rt/ Final—one syllable

art
Bart
Bert
blurt
cart
carte
chart
court
Curt
dart
dirt
flirt
fort
girt
heart
hurt
Kurt
mart
part
pert
port
quart
quirt
shirt
short
skirt
smart
snort
sort
sport
spurt
squirt
start
tart
thwart
wart
____
____
____

RT /rt/ Final—two syllables

advert	escort	pushcart
airport	evert	report
Albert	exert	resort
alert	expert	revert
apart	export	Robert
assert	extort	seaport
athwart	filbert	Shreveport
avert	Gilbert	sportshirt
comfort	go-cart	stalwart
concert	Head Start	subvert
convert	Herbert	support
Delbert	Hubert	sweatshirt
depart	impart	sweetheart
deport	import	transport
desert	inert	transvert
dessert	insert	T-shirt
distort	invert	unhurt
divert	Lambert	yogurt
dress shirt	outsmart	________________
effort	oxcart	________________
Elbert	passport	________________

RT /rt/ Final—three syllables

a la carte	introvert	shopping cart
counterpart	liverwort	tennis court
davenport	martial art	trailer court
disconcert	miniskirt	undershirt
extrovert	preconcert	________________
hula skirt	retrovert	________________

TR /tr/ Initial—one syllable

trace	trail	tramp
traced	trailed	tramped
track	trails	trance
tracked	train	trap
tract	trained	trapped
trade	trait	trash
trades	tram	trawl

tray
tread
treat
treats
tree
trek
trench
trend
Trent
tress
tribe
trice
trick
tried
tries
trill
trim
trimmed
trip
tripe
tripped
Trish
trite
trod
troll
troop
troops
trot
troth
trough
trounce
trout
trow
Troy
truce
truck
trucked
trudge
true
trump
trumped
trunk
trunks
truss
trust
truth
truths
try
____
____
____

TR /tr/ Initial—two syllables

tracing
tracker
tracking
trackless
track meet
traction
tractor
Tracy
trademark
trade name
tradesman
trade wind
trading
traduce
traffic
tragic
trailer
trainee
trainer
training
trainman
traitor
tramcar
tramline
trammel
tramper
trample
trampler
trampling
tramway
tranquil
transact
transcend
transcribe
transcript
transept
transfer
transfix
transform
transfuse
transgress
transient
transit
translate
transmit
transmute
transom
transpire
transplant
transport
transpose
transverse
trapdoor
trapeze
trapper
trapping
trappings
trash can
travel
traveled

traverse
trawler
treadle
treadmill
treason
treasure
treating
treatment
treaty
treble
tree house
trekking
trellis
tremble
trembling
tremor
trenchant
trencher
Trenton
trespass
trestle
triad
trial
tribal
tribesman
tribesmen
tribune
tribute
trickle
trickster

tricky
trident
trifle
trifler
trifling
trigger
trillion
trimmer
trimming
trimmings
trinket
trio
triple
triplet
triplex
tripod
tripping
triumph
trivet
trodden
Trojan
trolley
trombone
trooper
troopship
trophy
tropic
trotter
trotting
trouble

troubled
troubling
troublous
trouncing
trousers
trousseau
trowel
truant
trucking
truckle
truckled
truck route
truck stop
Trudy
truffle
truly
Truman
trumpet
trundle
trustee
trustees
trustful
trusting
trusty
truthful
trying
tryout
____
____
____

TR /tr/ Initial—three syllables

traceable
trachea
trackable
tractable
trade union
trading post
tradition

traducement
traducer
tragedy
tragical
trailblazer
trailer camp
trailer court

trailer park
train station
trainable
training aid
training school
traitorous
trammeling

trampoline
tranquilest
tranquilize
transaction
transcendent
transcribing
transcription
transference
transferring
transfigured
transformer
transfusion
transgression
transgressor
transition
transitive
translation
translator
translucent
transmission
transmitter

transonic
transparent
transpolar
trapezoid
traveler
treacherous
treasure chest
treasure house
treasure hunt
treasure map
treasurer
treasury
tremendous
tremulous
trespassing
triangle
triathlon
tribunal
trickery
tricolor
tricycle

trilogy
Trinidad
trinity
triplicate
triumphal
triumphant
trivial
tropical
troubadour
troublesome
truculence
truculent
truism
trumpery
trumpeter
trundle bed
trustworthy
truthfulness
____
____
____

TR /tr/ Initial—four syllables

tracking station
traditional
tragedian
tragedienne
tragically
trajectory
tranquility
tranquilizer
trans-Andean
transatlantic
transcendental

transferable
transferential
transforamtion
transitional
transitory
transmigration
transmutation
transparency
transplantation
transportation
treasonable

trepidation
triangular
tribulation
tributary
triennial
triplicating
triumphal arch
____
____
____
____

TR /tr/ Initial—five syllables

tracheotomy
traditionally
transcendentalist

transcontinental
transfiguration
triangulation

trigonometry
triviality
____

TR /tr/ Medial—two syllables

actress
attract
betray
central
citrus
contract
control
country
detract
detrain
Detroit
doctrine
dog track
entrance
entry
extra
extract
extreme
field trip
firetrap
fire truck
horse trail
intrigue
matrix
matron
mattress
metric
neutral
neutron
nitrate
pantry
partridge
Patrick
patrol
patrolled
patron
pine tree
portrait
portray
poultry
protract
protrude
race track
retract
retreat
retrieve
round trip
sentry
ski trail
spectrum
subtract
sultry
tantrum
tightrope
untried
untrue
untruth
waitress
____
____

TR /tr/ Medial—three syllables

attraction
attractive
Australia
Beatrice
Central Park
concentrate
contraction
contradict
contrary
country club
countryside
detraction
detriment
electric
electron
extremely
infantry
inside track
intricate
introduce
maple tree
matriarch
metrical
metronome
nitrogen
nutrient
nutrition
nutritious
orchestra
outrageous
patriarch
Patricia
patriot
Patriots
patrolman
penetrate
petrify
poetry
postmistress
protractor
railroad track
rainbow trout
reentry
retraction
retrenchment
retrieval
retriever
retrieving

retrograde
retrogress
retrospect
ski patrol
spectroscope
state trooper
subcontract
subtraction
subtropics
untruthful
victrola

TR /tr/ Medial—four syllables

catastrophe
concentration
contribution
control tower
controversy
electrical
electrician
electronics
entrepreneur
extravagance
extravagant
geometry
illustrated
introduction
matriarchy
matriculate
matrimony
metric system
metropolis
no trespassing
paratrooper
patriotic
patrolwoman
pedestrian
petrified wood
petroleum
remote control
retribution
retroactive
retroflexion
retrogression
retroversion
St. Patrick's Day
subtropical
ultrasonic
unobtrusive
ventriloquist

TR /tr/ Medial—five syllables

electricity
metropolitan
pediatrician

RTS /rts/ Final—one syllable

arts
blurts
carts
charts
courts
darts
flirts
forts
hearts
parts
ports
quarts
shirts
shorts
skirts
sorts
sports
spurts
squirts
warts

RTS /rts/ Final—two syllables

airports
alerts
concerts
departs
deserts
desserts
distorts
experts
exports
imports
inserts
inverts

passports	seaports	________
reports	supports	________
resorts	transports	________
reverts	________	________

RST /rst/ Final—one syllables

burst	hurst	thirst
cursed	Hurst	worst
first	nursed	________
forced	pierced	________

RST /rst/ Final—two syllables

airburst	enforced	sunburst
cloudburst	imbursed	unversed
coerced	immersed	________
dispersed	outburst	________
divorced	rehearsed	________
endorsed	reversed	________

RTH /rð/ Medial—two syllables

farther	norther	________
farthest	northern	________
farthing	swarthy	________
further	worthy	________

RTH /rð/ Medial—three syllables

airworthy	northernmost	worthiest
blameworthy	noteworthy	worthily
farthermost	seaworthy	worthiness
furthermore	swarthier	Worthington
northerly	thankworthy	________
Northern Cross	trustworthy	________
northern lights	unworthy	________
Northerner	worthier	________

RTH /rð/ Medial—four syllables

nevertheless	________	________
unseaworthy	________	________
unworthiness	________	________

RTH /rθ/ Medial—two syllables

Arthur
Bertha
birthday
birthmark
birthplace
birthrate
birthright
Carthage
Eartha
earthborn
earthbound
earthen
earthling
earthly
earthnut
earthquake
earthward
earthworm
earthy
forethought
forthright
forthwith
fourth grade
hearthstone
Martha
Northcutt
northeast
northland
North Pole
Northport
North Shore
North Slope
North Star
northward
northwest
Swarthmore
Swarthout
unearthed
worthless
worthwhile
____
____
____
____
____

RTH /rθ/ Medial—three syllables

afterthought
arthritic
arthritis
birthday card
earthenware
earth science
earthshaking
forthcoming
MacArthur
northeastern
northeastward
Northampton
northwestern
Northwestern
orthodox
orthoscope
overthrow
Parthenon
Port Arthur
unearthing
unearthly
____
____
____

RTH /rθ/ Medial—four syllables

birthday party
earth satellite
Happy Birthday
Martha's Vineyard
merthiolate
North Africa
North Dakota
orthodontics
orthodontist
orthogenic
orthographic
orthography
orthopedic
orthopedics
unearthliness
____
____
____

RTH /rθ/ Medial—five syllables

North America
North American
North Carolina
orthochromatic
orthodontia
orthogenesis
orthogenetic
orthographical
____

RTH /rθ/ Final—one syllable

berth
birth
dearth
earth
firth
forth
fourth
girth
hearth
mirth
north
swarth
worth
____
____

RTH /rθ/ Final—two syllables

childbirth
Ellsworth
Emsworth
Fort Worth
henceforth
Kenworth
rebirth
thenceforth
unearth
Wadsworth
Wentworth
Woolworth
____
____
____

THR /θr/ Initial—one syllable

thrall
thrash
thread
threads
threat
three
thresh
threw
thrice
thrift
thrill
thrilled
thrills
thrive
thrived
throat
throb
throbbed
throne
throned
throng
through
throve
throw
thrown
thrum
thrummed
thrush
thrust
____

THR /θr/ Initial—two syllables

thralldom
thrasher
thrashing
threadbare
threaded
threader
threading
threadlike
thread mark
thready
threaten
threefold
threepence
three-ply
threescore
threesome
threesquare
thresher
threshold
thriftless
thrift shop
thrift store
thrifty
thriller
thrilling
thriver
thriving
throaty
throbbing
thrombus
throttle
throttling
throughout
through street
throwback
thrower

throw in	thrumming	________
throwing	thrusting	________
throw rug	thruway	________

THR /θr/ Initial—three syllables

threatening	three-wheeler	throatier
three-bagger	thresher shark	throatiest
three-base hit	thriftier	thrombosis
three-decker	thriftiest	throwaway
three-quarters	thriftily	________

THR /θr/ Initial—four syllables

threateningly	three-ring circus	throat microphone
three-legged race	threshing machine	________

THR /θr/ Medial—two syllables

anthrax	free throw	spendthrift
bathrobe	Guthrie	unthread
bathroom	heartthrob	unthrone
cutthroat	Jethro	walk-through
drive-through	look-through	Winthrop
enthrall	outthrew	wood thrush
enthrone	outthrow	________

THR /θr/ Medial—three syllables

anthracite	brown thrasher	overthrow
anthropoid	flamethrower	Plymouth Rock
arthritic	follow-through	unthreaded
arthritis	hermit thrush	________

THR /θr/ Medial—four syllables

erythrocyte	misanthropic	________
javelin throw	philanthropist	________

RV /rv/ Medial—two syllables

carver	dervish	harvest
carving	fervid	Harvey
carvings	fervor	Irving
corvette	Harvard	Kerrville

larva	servant	swerving
marvel	server	________
Marvin	service	________
Mervin	serving	________
nervous	starving	________
perverse	survey	________
scurvey	survive	________

RV /rv/ Medial—three syllables

Centerville	observing	survey crew
conserver	preserver	surveying
conserving	preserving	surveyor
deserver	reserving	survival
deserving	reservoir	surviving
enervate	self-service	survivor
fervently	serviceman	survivors
marveling	servicemen	unnerving
marvelous	services	Waterville
Minerva	servicing	wood carving
observance	servitude	________
observant	starvation	________
observer	supervise	________

RV /rv/ Medial—four syllables

conservation	observation	soapstone carvings
conservative	perseverence	subservient
conservator	preservation	survey party
effervescent	reservation	survival kit
enervated	reservations	survivorship
enervation	serviceable	topsy-turvy
intervention	service station	________
life preserver	servicewoman	________
nervous system	servicewomen	________

RV /rv/ Final—one syllable

carve	starve	________
curve	swerve	________
nerve	verve	________
serve	________	________

RV /rv/ Final—two syllables

conserve	observe	self-serve
deserve	preserve	________
hors d'oeuvre	reserve	________

RVD /rvd/ Final—one syllable

carved	starved	________
curved	swerved	________
served	________	________

RVD /rvd/ Final—two syllables

deserved	preserved	unnerved
observed	reserved	________

RVZ /rvs/ Final—one syllable

carves	scarves	turves
dwarves	serves	wharves
nerves	starves	________

RVZ /rvs/ Final—two syllables

conserves	observes	________
deserves	preserves	________

RW /rw/ Medial—two syllables

airways	fairway	Norway
careworn	farewell	Sherwood
carwash	fireweed	shoreward
carwax	firewood	therewith
Corwin	fireworks	________
doorway	forward	________
Erwin	Irwin	________

RW /rw/ Medial—three syllables

afterword	thenceforward	underworld
afterworld	underwaist	waterways
netherward	underwear	water wings
silverware	underweight	waterworks
spiderweb	underwent	wonder-world
straightforward	underwood	________

RW /rw/ Medial—four syllables

underwater ________ ________

RY /rj/ Medial—three syllables

lumberyard	solar year	________
lunar year	yesteryear	________

RY /rj/ Medial—four syllables

labor union ________ ________

RZ /rz/ Final—one syllable

airs	gears	scores
bars	glares	scours
bears	hares	shares
blares	hears	shears
blurs	heirs	shirrs
bores	hers	shores
burrs	hires	sirs
cares	hours	slurs
cars	jars	smears
chairs	jeers	snares
cheers	lures	snores
choirs	mares	soars
chores	mars	sores
clears	Mars	sours
cores	nears	spares
dares	oars	spars
doors	ours	spears
ears	pairs	spurs
errs	pears	squares
fairs	peers	stairs
fares	piers	stares
fears	pores	stars
fires	pours	steers
firs	purrs	stirs
flares	rears	tears
floors	roars	theirs
fours	scares	tires
furs	scars	tours

wares	wires	________
wars	years	________
wears	yours	________

RZ /rz/ Final—two syllables

admires	campers	filters
affairs	campfires	fingers
allures	captors	fixtures
altars	captures	Flanders
anchors	carvers	flatcars
angers	cashiers	flickers
answers	casters	fliers
antlers	catchers	flippers
appears	cedars	flounders
arbors	checkers	flowers
aspires	colors	founders
Azores	compares	fractures
backfires	crackers	glaciers
badgers	declares	guitars
barbers	devours	ignores
batters	diners	indoors
bazaars	dinners	lathers
beavers	dippers	matures
beggars	divers	members
bidders	doctors	minors
binders	dollars	molars
bleachers	downstairs	movers
blisters	drawers	odors
boilers	dressers	outdoors
bookstores	drivers	pillars
borders	drummers	pliers
boulders	empires	poplars
boxers	errors	posters
breakers	explores	powders
brokers	farmers	powers
builders	fenders	quarters
burners	fielders	rangers
buzzers	figures	razors
callers	fillers	readers

refers
rivers
rockers
rollers
rompers
roosters
rulers
rumors
scissors
seashores
showers
sisters
slippers
slivers
sneakers
sparklers
speakers
squad cars
tankers
tweezers
umpires
upstairs
vampires
velours
vespers
wafers
____

RZ /rz/ Final—three syllables

adventures
amateurs
ancestors
announcers
anteaters
beginners
bystanders
calendars
campaigners
candy bars
carpenters
carriers
diapers
dinosaurs
disappears
discovers
engineers
erasers
fasteners
firecrackers
foreigners
horse lovers
leftovers
loudspeakers
managers
polar bears
professors
propellers
receivers
recorders
recovers
registers
remainders
reporters
sandpipers
screwdrivers
state troopers
studded tires
teenagers
unawares
volunteers
____

ER /ɚ/ Medial—three syllables

lowering
lowermost
powerboat
powerful
showering
towering
____
____
____

ER /ɚ/ Final—two syllables

brier
buyer
drier
flier
flower
grower
layer
lower
mayor
player
plower
power
rower
sewer
shower
slower
thrower
tower
viewer
____
____

ER /ɚ/ Final—three syllables

ballplayer	Mayflower	wallflower
flamethrower	rain shower	watchtower
horsepower	sandflower	widower
lawnmower	slide viewer	willpower
light tower	sunflower	________
manpower	tax payer	________

ER /ɚ/ Final—four syllables

cassette player	overpower	________
control tower	thundershower	________
Eisenhower	wholesale buyer	________

IER /iɚ/ Final—three syllables

barrier	lovelier	terrier
carrier	luckier	thriftier
courier	merrier	tidier
flightier	meteor	wealthier
furrier	smearier	________
linear	snazzier	________

IER /iɚ/ Final—four syllables

air carrier	inferior	ulterior
anterior	interior	unhappier
exterior	superior	________

IER /iɚ/ Final—five syllables

aircraft carrier	thermal barrier	________
letter carrier	________	________

BER /bɚ/ Medial—three syllables

cheeseburger	liberate	numbering
fiberglass	liberty	number line
gabardine	limburger	rubber band
hamburger	lumbering	rubber stamp
harboring	lumberjack	shrubbery
hibernate	lumberyard	slumberer
Kimberly	membership	tubercle
liberal	neighborhood	tuberous

BER /bɚ/ Medial—four syllables

deliberate	tubercular	______
remembering	______	______

BER /bɚ/ Final—two syllables

barber	labor	slobber
blubber	neighbor	sober
clobber	rubber	tuber
fiber	saber	______

BER /bɚ/ Final—three syllables

belabor	October	______
foam rubber	______	______

MBER /mbɚ/ Final—two syllables

amber	lumber	timber
Amber	member	umber
chamber	number	______
ember	slumber	______
limber	somber	______

MBER /mbɚ/ Final—three syllables

cucumber	November	remember
December	outnumber	September

CHER /tʃɚ/ Medial—three syllables

archery	futurism	______
cultural	futurist	______
futureless	rupturing	______

CHER /tʃɚ/ Medial—four syllables

naturalist	______	______
naturally	______	______

CHER /tʃɚ/ Final—two syllables

archer	catcher	facture
bleacher	clincher	feature
butcher	creature	fixture
capture	culture	flincher

fracture
future
gesture
launcher
leacher
lecture
luncher
lurcher
mixture
moisture
nature
pasture
picture
pitcher
posture
preacher
puncture
rancher
richer
rupture
rupture
stature
teacher
Thatcher
venture
voucher
watcher
____
____
____
____
____
____

CHER /tʃɚ/ Final—three syllables

adventure
back scratcher
bird watcher
departure
dogcatcher
flycatcher
furniture
indenture
ligature
overture
signature
____

CHER /tʃɚ/ Final—four syllables

agriculture
legislature
literature
manufacture
miniature
temperature
____
____
____

DER /dɚ/ Medial—three syllables

elderish
elderly
eldermost
orderly
powderhorn
powdering
powdery
spider web
tenderfoot
thunderbolt
thunderclap
thunderhead
thunderous
thunderstorm
thunderstruck
tinderbox
underbrush
underclothes
underdog
underfoot
underground
underling
undermine
underneath
underpass
undersea
undershirt
underside
understand
understood
undertake
undertook
underwear
underweight
underwent
wanderer
wandering
wanderlust
wanderoo
wilderness
wonderful
____
____
____
____

DER /dɚ/ Medial—four syllables

elderberry	powdering tub	understanding
elder statesman	powder monkey	undertaker
kindergarten	thundershower	undertaking
misunderstand	undercover	underwater
misunderstood	undergarment	________
orderliness	underlying	________

DER /dɚ/ Final—two syllables

alder	folder	rudder
bidder	gander	sander
binder	glider	sender
bladder	grinder	shudder
bleeder	grounder	slander
blender	herder	slender
blinder	hinder	speeder
blunder	ladder	spider
border	launder	splendor
boulder	leader	spreader
chowder	louder	tender
cider	odor	threader
cinder	order	thunder
colder	plodder	tinder
condor	plunder	udder
elder	powder	under
Elder	raider	weeder
fender	reader	________
fielder	render	________
flounder	rider	________

DER /dɚ/ Final—three syllables

asunder	disorder	outsider
bewilder	embroider	remainder
calendar	faultfinder	reminder
cheerleader	free-loader	ringleader
commander	insider	shareholder
consider	islander	stepladder
crusader	lavender	________
cylinder	left-hander	________

DER /dɚ/ Final—four syllables

Alexander	ice cream vendor	________
ambassador	winter splendor	________

FER /fɚ/ Medial—three syllables

afferent	inference	reference
conference	offering	referent
difference	phosphorus	suffering
different	preference	________

FER /fɚ/ Medial—four syllables

indifference	long-suffering	referable
indifferent	preferable	referential
inferential	preferential	reoffering

FER /fɚ/ Final—two syllables

buffer	gopher	safer
camphor	infer	scoffer
chauffeur	loader	suffer
confer	loafer	sulphur
deafer	offer	transfer
defer	prefer	wafer
differ	refer	zephyr
gaffer	roofer	________
golfer	rougher	________

FER /fɚ/ Final—three syllables

bus transfer	________	________
decipher	________	________

GER /gɚ/ Medial—three syllables

rigorous	________	________
vigorous	________	________

GER /gɚ/ Final—two syllables

beggar	dagger	leaguer
bigger	eager	logger
chigger	jigger	lugger
cougar	lager	meager

rigor	tiger	________________
stagger	vigor	________________

GER /gɚ/ Final—three syllables

cheeseburger	Limburger	vinegar
hamburger	outrigger	________________

NGER /ŋgɚ/ Medial—three syllables

fingerling	fingerprint	lingering
fingernail	fingerspell	________________

NGER /ŋgɚ/ Final—two syllables

finger	longer	wringer
hanger	ringer	younger
hunger	singer	________________
linger	swinger	________________

JER /dʒɚ/ Medial—three syllables

dangerous	gingerly	majorette
ginger ale	gingersnap	________________
gingerbread	injury	________________

JER /dʒɚ/ Medial—four syllables

belligerent	gingerliness	________________
exaggerate	major-domo	________________

JER /dʒɚ/ Final—two syllables

badger	larger	pledger
danger	ledger	ranger
dodger	lodger	Roger
dredger	lounger	soldier
ginger	major	stranger
Ginger	manger	wager
injure	merger	________________

JER /dʒɚ/ Final—three syllables

avenger	Lone Ranger	passenger
drum major	manager	procedure
endanger	messenger	scavenger

teenager	________	________
villager	________	________
voyager	________	________
Voyager	________	________

JER /dʒɚ/ Final—four syllables

astrologer	________	________
supercharger	________	________
train passenger	________	________

KER /kɚ/ Medial—three syllables

acreage	discourage	rookery
Anchorage	handkerchief	snickering
bakery	licorice	soccer ball
brokerage	mackerel	wickerwork
checkerboard	neckerchief	________

KER /kɚ/ Final—two syllables

acre	flicker	soccer
anchor	hiker	speaker
baker	kicker	stocker
banker	knocker	sucker
bicker	locker	tanker
blocker	looker	tucker
breaker	poker	wicker
broker	Quaker	wrecker
canker	rocker	________
choker	seeker	________
clinker	shaker	________
conquer	slicker	________
cracker	sneaker	________
flanker	snicker	________

KER /kɚ/ Final—three syllables

backpacker	loudspeaker	shoemaker
dressmaker	nutcracker	watchmaker
hitch-hiker	pact maker	windbreaker
homemaker	pawnbroker	woodpecker
linebacker	saltshaker	________

LER /lɚ/ Medial—three syllables

allergic	gallery	scholarship
allergy	polar bear	tolerance
celery	polarize	tolerant
collarbone	polar lights	________
colorful	roller skates	________
coloring	salary	________

LER /lɚ/ Medial—four syllables

artillery	polar axis	tolerable
capillary	polar region	tolerably
intolerant	roller skating	________

LER /lɚ/ Medial—five syllables

intolerable	roller skating rink	________
polarization	similarity	________
popularity	________	________

LER /lɚ/ Final—two syllables

antler	jailer	smaller
baler	mailer	smeller
Baylor	miller	solar
bowler	Miller	speller
broiler	molar	sprawler
caller	parlor	squealer
cellar	peddler	stroller
collar	piler	tailor
color	pillar	taller
cooler	polar	Taylor
crawler	poler	teller
dealer	poplar	thriller
dollar	roller	tiller
driller	ruler	trailer
drooler	sailor	trawler
duller	scaler	troller
dweller	scholar	Tyler
feeler	sealer	whaler
healer	seller	________
heeler	shriller	________

LER /lɚ/ Final—three syllables

angular	modular	secular
bachelor	muscular	similar
consoler	ocular	singular
controller	patroller	three-wheeler
counselor	popular	tricolor
discolor	propeller	tubular
four-wheeler	regular	two-wheeler
jeweler	retailer	wholesaler
littler	sand dollar	________

LER /lɚ/ Final—four syllables

caterpillar	particular	twin propeller
fortuneteller	semitrailer	unpopular
irregular	spectacular	watercolor
lenticular	storm cellar	________
multicolor	technicolor	________

MER /mɚ/ Medial—three syllables

admiral	emery	memory
armory	formerly	numerate
boomerang	humorous	numerous
emerald	limerick	somersault

MER /mɚ/ Medial—four syllables

America	emergency	________
American	________	________

MER /mɚ/ Final—two syllables

armor	Homer	skimmer
clamor	humor	stammer
climber	murmur	steamer
drummer	plumber	streamer
Elmer	primer	summer
farmer	reamer	swimmer
former	roomer	tamer
grammar	rumor	tumor
hammer	shimmer	________
homer	simmer	________

MER /mɚ/ Final—three syllables

beachcomber	newcomer	sledgehammer
consumer	performer	______
customer	redeemer	______

NER /nɚ/ Medial—three syllables

energy	honor roll	runnerup
funeral	inner ear	scenery
general	mineral	spinneret
generous	partnership	______

NER /nɚ/ Medial—four syllables

energetic	honorable	unmannerly
generation	machinery	vulnerable
generator	refinery	______

NER /nɚ/ Final—two syllables

banner	inner	schooner
burner	liner	sooner
cleaner	lunar	Sooner
corner	manner	spinner
diner	manor	tanner
dinner	minor	tenor
donor	owner	turner
gainer	partner	Turner
gunner	plainer	vintner
honor	runner	winner

NER /nɚ/ Final—three syllables

airliner	foreigner	questioner
beginner	gold panner	roadrunner
container	governor	wagoner
dishonor	long liner	Westerner
dry cleaner	opener	______
Easterner	prisoner	______

NER /nɚ/ Final—four syllables

commissioner	practitioner	______
mid-westerner	______	______

PER /pɚ/ Medial—three syllables

aspirin
Copper Age
copperhead
drapery
emperor
opera
paperback
paperclip
papering
peppermint
properly
property
slippery
superman
Superman
supersede
supervise
temperate
uppermost
vaporize
____

PER /pɚ/ Medial—four syllables

copper-plated
experiment
intemperate
operator
superego
superficial
temperative
vaporizer
____

PER /pɚ/ Final—two syllables

blooper
chipper
chopper
clipper
copper
creeper
dipper
flapper
flipper
gripper
helper
hopper
jasper
Jasper
keeper
paper
pepper
proper
riper
roper
scraper
shipper
skipper
slipper
stopper
stupor
super
supper
taper
trooper
upper
vapor
viper
whisper
whopper
wiper
wrapper
zipper
____

PER /pɚ/ Final—three syllables

crepe paper
diaper
grasshopper
improper
innkeeper
juniper
newspaper
sandpaper
sandpiper
skyscraper
state trooper
timekeeper
wallpaper
____
____

PER /pɚ/ Final—four syllables

candy striper
litmus paper
paratrooper
tissue paper
wrapping paper
writing paper

RER /rɚ/ Final—two syllables

barer	juror	wearer
carer	mirror	________
error	sheerer	________
horror	terror	________

RER /rɚ/ Final—three syllables

admirer	conqueror	lumberer
adorer	emperor	usurper
armorer	explorer	wanderer
caterer	laborer	________
conjurer	loiterer	________

SER /sɚ/ Medial—three syllables

glossary	nursery	Switzerland
grocery	sponsorship	ulcerate

SER /sɚ/ Medial—four syllables

accessory	nursery school	________
nursery man	rhinoceros	________

SER /sɚ/ Final—two syllables

bracer	kisser	racer
chaser	lacer	saucer
closer	leaser	slicer
creaser	lesser	splicer
crosser	nicer	tracer
dicer	pacer	ulcer
dresser	piercer	________
grocer	placer	________
guesser	presser	________

SER /sɚ/ Final—three syllables

aggressor	eraser	professor
assessor	horse racer	progressor
compressor	officer	reducer
conducer	oppressor	successor
embosser	possessor	transgressor
enticer	producer	________

SER /sɚ/ Final—four syllables

dog sled racer	predecessor	________
interlacer	reproducer	________

NSER /nsɚ/ Final—two syllables

answer	denser	Spencer
cancer	fencer	sponsor
Cancer	glancer	tensor
censor	lancer	________
chancer	prancer	________
dancer	spencer	________

NSER /nsɚ/ Final—three syllables

advancer	dispenser	extensor
announcer	enhancer	romancer
condenser	entrancer	________

SHER /ʃɚ/ Medial—three syllables

fisherman	fishery	________
fishermen	pressuring	________

SHER /ʃɚ/ Final—two syllables

crusher	plusher	usher
glacier	pressure	washer
gusher	rusher	________
kosher	squasher	________
lasher	thrasher	________
masher	thresher	________

SHER /ʃɚ/ Final—three syllables

blood pressure	kingfisher	publisher
Britisher	low-pressure	trash masher
high-pressure	New Hampshire	________

STER /stɚ/ Medial—three syllables

asterisk	masterpiece	yesterday
castor oil	mastery	________
history	oyster crab	________
mastering	westerly	________

STER /stɚ/ Medial—four syllables

master-at-arms	preposterous	upholstery
masterfully	sister-in-law	__________
prehistory	southeasterly	__________

STER /stɚ/ Final—two syllables

aster	Foster	roadster
blister	hamster	roaster
booster	holster	rooster
Buster	lobster	roster
caster	luster	sister
Chester	master	spinster
cluster	mister	tester
coaster	monster	thruster
Custer	muster	toaster
duster	oyster	twister
Easter	pastor	Webster
faster	pester	youngster
fluster	plaster	__________
foster	poster	__________

STER /stɚ/ Final—three syllables

adjuster	half-sister	sinister
ancestor	minister	Sylvester
bandmaster	postmaster	taskmaster
canister	register	toastmaster
disaster	resister	upholster
forecaster	scoutmaster	Worcester
gangbuster	semester	__________
Grand Master	shipmaster	__________

STER /stɚ/ Final—four syllables

administer	Gila monster	quartermaster
flabbergaster	prime minister	roller coaster

TER /tɚ/ Medial—three syllables

aftermath	artery	butterfly
afterward	attorney	butterscotch
alternate	buttercup	counterfeit

determine
enterprise
entertain
eternal
external
factory
interact
interblend
intercede
intercept
intercom
interest
interfere
interpret
intersect
interval
interview
lateral
lettergram
letterhead
lettering
loitering
lottery
motorboat
motorhome
nectarine
outer space
pottery
quarterback
quarterly
shutterbug
smattering
splintery
utterance
utterly
uttermost
veteran
water bed
waterbird
water bug
watercress
water hole
waterfall
waterfowl
waterfront
waterline
waterlogged
watermark
water plant
waterproof
water rat
watertight
waterway
waterwheel
waterworks
yesterday
____

TER /tɚ/ Medial—four syllables

alternative
directory
eternity
externalize
illiterate
interesting
intermission
intersection
literature
motorcycle
predetermine
quartermaster
quartersection
watercolor
watering place
water lily
watermelon
water polo
water skiing
____
____

TER /tɚ/ Medial—five syllables

disinterested
distributorship
intermediate
international
literarily
uninterrupted
unutterable
veterinary
water buffalo

TER /tɚ/ Final—two syllables

batter
beater
better
bitter
bloater
blotter
brighter
butter
canter
chatter
cheater
clatter

clutter
crater
critter
cutter
daughter
eater
fatter
fighter
flatter
floater
flutter
freighter
fritter
glitter
grater
greater
gutter
heater
hitter
hotter
later
latter
letter
lighter
liter
litter
loiter
matter
meter
motor
mutter
neater
otter
patter
pewter
platter
plotter
potter
putter
quitter
quoter
rotor
scatter
setter
shatter
shutter
sitter
skater
slaughter
smatter
spatter
splatter
spotter
sputter
squatter
stutter
sweater
tighter
traitor
tutor
twitter
utter
voter
waiter
water
whiter
writer
____
____
____
____
____

TER /tɚ/ Final—three syllables

anteater
auditor
beanshooter
chain letter
computer
creator
dictator
editor
equator
fire fighter
gas meter
globe trotter
high water
janitor
Jupiter
locater
monitor
narrator
newsletter
predator
promoter
saltwater
Senator
shot-putter
spectator
stonecutter
storm center
theater
tidewater
transistor
translator
typesetter
typewriter
visitor
wood cutter
____
____
____
____

TER /tɚ/ Final—four syllables

agitator	duplicator	numerator
alligator	educator	operator
alma mater	elevator	parking meter
altimeter	escalator	peanut butter
aviator	excavator	percolator
calculator	generator	perimeter
centimeter	incubator	radiator
commentator	kilometer	thermometer
competitor	legislator	____________
cultivator	liberator	____________
decorator	moderator	____________
demonstrator	navigator	____________
diameter	nominator	____________

TER /tɚ/ Final—five syllables

accelerator	anemometer	____________
amphitheater	denominator	____________

THER /θɚ/ Final—two syllables

Arthur	Luther	____________
author	panther	____________
ether	Reuther	____________

THER /ðɚ/ Medial—three syllables

bothering	lathering	tetherball
bothersome	leatherneck	weathercock
brotherhood	leatherwork	Weatherford
brotherly	Netherlands	weatherglass
furtherance	otherwise	weather vane
furthermore	Rutherford	____________
furthermost	smithereens	____________
gathering	smothering	____________
heathery	southerly	____________

THER /ðɚ/ Medial—four syllables

father-in-law	weatherbeaten	____________
leather jacket	wool gathering	____________
mother-in-law	____________	____________

THER /ðɝ/ Final—two syllables

bother	heather	smother
breather	Heather	tether
brother	lather	thither
dither	leather	weather
either	mother	whether
farther	neither	whither
father	other	wither
feather	rather	zither
further	slither	________
gather	smoother	________

THER /ðɝ/ Final—three syllables

another	grandmother	stepfather
godfather	half brother	stepmother
godmother	housemother	together
grandfather	stepbrother	________

THER /ðɝ/ Final—four syllables

altogether	shaving lather	________
patent leather	stormy weather	________

VER /vɚ/ Medial—three syllables

advertise	overalls	overlook
average	overboard	overnight
beverage	overcast	overpass
Beverly	overcoat	overrun
bravery	overcome	overseas
conversion	overdo	overshoe
coverage	overdraft	oversight
covering	overdue	overtake
diversion	overflow	overtime
evergreen	overgrow	overture
favorite	overhand	overweight
flavoring	overhaul	overwhelm
Hoover Dam	overhead	overwork
ivory	overhear	overwrite
leverage	overjoy	poverty
liverwurst	overlap	reverence

reverent
several
Silver Age
silverware
silvery
slavery
subversive
thievery
wolverine
____
____
____

VER /vɚ/ Medial—four syllables

Beverly Hills
controversy
conversation
covered wagon
delivery
discovery
diversity
favorable
invertebrate
nevertheless
overpower
receivership
recovery
universal
____

VER /vɚ/ Final—two syllables

beaver
cleaver
clever
clover
cover
Denver
diver
driver
ever
favor
fever
flavor
giver
Grover
Hoover
hover
lever
liver
louver
lover
mover
never
over
plover
quaver
quiver
river
rover
Rover
savor
sever
shiver
sliver
unfavorable
waiver
waver
weaver
____
____
____
____
____

VER /vɚ/ Final—three syllables

deliver
discover
endeavor
forever
hay fever
however
leftover
maneuver
moreover
Passover
preserver
quicksilver
receiver
recover
retriever
Rhone River
screwdriver
skin diver
stopover
turn over
uncover
Vancouver
whatever
whenever
wherever
whichever
whoever
whomever
whyever
____

VER /vɚ/ Final—four syllables

life preserver
redeliver
scuba diver
whatsoever
whensoever
whosoever

YER /jɚ/ Medial—three syllables

figure eight
figurehead
figurine

YER /jɚ/ Final—two syllables

failure
figure
junior
lawyer
savior
senior

YER /jɚ/ Final—three syllables

behavior
employer
familiar
peculiar
refigure
Tom Sawyer

YER /jɚ/ Final—four syllables

misbehavior
power failure
trial lawyer
unfamiliar

ZER /zɚ/ Medial—three syllables

misery
observing
reservoir

ZER /zɚ/ Medial—four syllables

miserable
miserably
observation
preservation
reservation

ZER /zɚ/ Final—two syllables

blazer
bruiser
buzzer
Caesar
cleanser
cruiser
freezer
geyser
hawser
laser
loser
miser
quizzer
razor
riser
squeezer
user
visor
Windsor

ZER /zɚ/ Final—three syllables

accuser	composer	incisor
adviser	deep freezer	trailblazer
bulldozer	divisor	________

ZER /zɚ/ Final—four syllables

appetizer	polarizer	________
atomizer	stabilizer	________
fertilizer	vaporizer	________

ZHER /ʒɚ/ Medial—three syllables

azurite	measurement	treasury
glaziery	measuring	________
leisurely	treasurer	________

ZHER /ʒər/, /ʒɚ/ Medial—four syllables

measuring cup	pleasurable	________
measuring tape	Treasure Island	________

ZHER /ʒɚ/ Final—two syllables

closure	pleasure	________
leisure	treasure	________
measure	________	________

ZHER /ʒɚ/ Final—three syllables

composure	exposure	________
displeasure	foreclosure	________
enclosure	remeasure	________

S

Pronounced: /s/
Spelled: s, ss, sc, sch, c, ce, sw, sp, ps, z, x

S /s/ Initial—one syllable

cell
cells
cent
cinch
cite
psalms
psyched
sack
sacked
sad
safe
sag
sage
said
sail
sailed
saint
sake
sale
sales
salt
salve
Sam
same
sand
sane
sang
sank
sap
sapped
sash
sat
Saul
save
saved
saw
say
scene
scent
sea
seal
sealed
seals
seam
sear
search
searched
seat
see
seed
seeds
seek
seem
seemed
seen
seep
seine
seize
seized
self
sell
send
sent
serf
serve
served
set
Seth
sew
sewn
sick
Sid
side
sides
siege
sieve
sift
sigh
sight
sign
signed
signs
silk
sill
silt
sin
sing
singe
sink
sinned

Sioux
sip
sips
sir
sit
site
sites
size
so
soak
soaked
soap
soar
sob
sobbed
sock
sod
soft
soil
sold
sole
solve
some
son
song
soon
soot
soothe
sop
sore
sort
sought
soul
sound
sounds
soup
sour
south
sow
sown
soy
sub
subbed
such
suck
suds
sue
Sue
sued
suit
suite
sulk
sum
summed
sun
sung
sunk
sunned
surf
surge
____
____
____

S /s/ Initial—two syllables

cedar
ceiling
cellar
cement
center
central
certain
Ceylon
cider
cinder
Cindy
circle
circled
circuit
cited
city
civet
civic
civil
cycle
cycling
cyclone
cymbals
Cyril
pseudo
psyched-up
Sabbath
saber
sable
sachet
sacred
sadder
saddle
sadly
safer
safety
saga
sagebrush
sailboat
sailfish
sailing
sailor
saintly
salaam
salad
salesclerk
salesman
Sally

salmon
salon
salty
salute
salvage
Sammy
sampan
sample
sampler
sandal
sandbag
sandbar
sandbug
sandbur
sand crab
sandman
sandpail
sandpile
sandwich
sandy
Sandy
sapling
sapphire
sappy
sardine
sari
satchel
satin
Saturn
sauna
saunter
saute
savage
saving
savings
savor
sawing
sawmill
saying

scenic
scented
scepter
scissors
Seabee
sea breeze
seafood
sea front
sea gull
sealer
seaplane
seaport
searchlight
seashell
seashore
season
seat belt
sea trout
seaward
seaway
seaweed
Sea World
seclude
second
secret
section
sector
secure
sedan
sedate
seedling
seeing
seeming
segment
seldom
select
selfish
semi
senate

senile
senior
señor
sentry
serene
sergeant
series
sermon
serpent
serum
servant
serving
session
setter
setting
settle
set-up
seven
seventh
sever
severe
sewage
sewer
sewing
Sibyl
sickle
side band
sided
sideline
sideshow
sidewalk
sideways
siding
signal
signing
sign-off
sign-up
silent
silkworm

silky
silly
silo
silver
simmer
simple
Sinai
singer
singing
single
Sioux Falls
siphon
siren
sitting
sit-up
sizzle
soapy
soccer
social
socked-in
socket
soda
sofa
softball
soften
software
soggy
solar
soldier
solemn
solid
solo
somber
someday
somehow
someone
something
sometime
sometimes
somewhere
sonar
songbird
Sonja
sonnet
Sonny
sooner
Sooner
sopping
soppy
sorrow
sorry
souffle´
sounding
soundly
soundproof
soundwaves
soupy
sourdough
South Bridge
southern
southpaw
South Pole
southward
soybean
St. Paul
subbing
subdue
subgroup
subject
sublet
sublime
submerge
submerse
submit
subtle
subtract
suburb
subway
succumb
sucker
suckling
suction
Sudan
sudden
suet
Suez
suffer
suffice
suited
suitor
sulfur
sulky
sullen
sultry
summer
summit
summon
summons
sun bath
sun bathe
sunbeam
sunburn
sundae
Sunday
sun deck
sunder
sundown
sundries
sunfish
sunken
sun lamp
sunlight
sunlit
sunny
sun proof
sunrise
sunshine

sun tan
super
superb
supine
supper
supplied
supplies
supply
support
suppose
supreme
surcharge
surfboard
surfer
surfing
surgeon
surmise
surmount
surname
surprise
surrey
surround
survey
survive
Susan
Susie
suture
Suzanne
swordfish
Sydney
symbol
symptom
syphon
syringe
syrup
____
____
____
____

S /s/ Initial—three syllables

celebrate
celery
cellophane
Centerville
centigrade
centipede
Central Park
Central Time
century
cereal
certainly
certified
certify
cinema
cinnamon
circular
circulate
citizen
city hall
civilian
civilize
Civil War
cylinder
Cynthia
sabotage
saboteur
saccharin
sacrament
safety belt
safety pin
safflower
salad bar
salad oil
salami
salary
saleswoman
saliva
salvation
Samoa
Samoan
sand dollar
sand piper
sandalwood
sandpaper
sanity
San Pedro
Santa Claus
Santa Cruz
Santa Fe
satellite
Saturday
sauerkraut
Savannah
savings bond
savory
scenery
seafaring
sea level
sea lion
seamanship
sea otter
seasoning
sea urchin
seaworthy
second hand
sectional
secular
sedative
sediment
segregate
seismograph
selection

self-assured
self-composed
self-contained
self-control
self-giving
self-glory
self-image
self-imposed
self-pity
self-regard
self-reproach
semaphore
senator
señora
sentiment
separate
September
sequoia
serape
serenade
serial
settlement
seventeen
seventeenth
seventy
several
signature
sign language
silhouette
Silver Age
silverware
similar
simplify
Singapore
singular
situate
soccerball
soccerfield
sociable
socialize
social work
soda pop
sodium
soft-hearted
soft-shell crab
solar heat
solitaire
solitude
soluble
solution
sombrero
somebody
sonata
sonic boom
son-in-law
sophomore
soprano
sorrowful
soundproofing
sour cream
sousaphone
southerly
Southerner
souvenir
Soviet
subcontract
subdivide
subjection
subjective
subjunctive
submarine
subnormal
subpoena
subtitle
suburban
succotash
succulent
suffering
sufficient
sufficing
suffocate
suggestion
suitable
sulfuric
summarize
summary
summation
summer camp
summertime
sun bathing
sun dial
sunflower
Sunnyvale
Sun Valley
superman
Superman
supplement
supportive
Supreme Court
surrender
surroundings
surveying
Sutherland
sycamore
sycophant
syllable
Sylvia
symbolic
symbolize
symmetry
sympathize
sympathized
sympathy
symphonic
symphony
synagogue
synchronize

syncopate
synonym
synthetic
Syria
syrupy

S /s/ Initial—four syllables

celebration
celebrity
cemetery
centimeter
ceremony
certificate
certified check
certified mail
Cinderella
circulation
citizenship
psychology
safety glasses
safety helmet
salamander
satellite dish
seasonable
secondary
secretary
sectarian
seeing-eye dog
self-appointed
self-determined
self-directed
self-evident
semicolon
seminary
señorita
sentimental
separation
seventieth
sewing machine
single parent
social-minded
social welfare
social worker
soda fountain
South Korea
South Vietnam
subcommittee
subcontinent
subdivision
subjectively
subliminal
subordinate
Suez Canal
sukiyaki
supercharger
superego
superficial
super highway
superimpose
superior
supermarket
supervision
supremacy
symbolical
symmetrical
sympathetic
sympathizer
sympathizing
symposium
symptomatic
syncopation
synonymous
systematize

S /s/ Initial—five syllables

civilization
psychological
Sagittarius
sedimentary
self-analysis
subcutaneous
submicroscopic
subminiature
subsidiary
subterranean
sulfanilamide
superintendent
supervisory

S /s/ Initial—six syllables

subequatorial
subminiaturize
supernumerary
systematically

S /s/ Medial—two syllables

acid
ascend
ascent
aside
assert
assign
assume
basic
basin
bassoon
beside
besiege
Bessie
bison
blessing
blossom
bosses
bossy
bracelet
bracer
braces
Brussels
bussing
Casey
cassette
castle
chasing
classic
classy
closer
creaser
crescent
crosser
crossing
crusade
Dawson
deceit
deceive
decent
decide
descend
descent
dicer
dissect
dresser
dressing
dress up
essay
eyesight
facet
facing
faucet
Flossie
flossing
fossil
fussing
fussy
gases
glasses
glisten
glossy
gossip
grassy
grocer
guesser
guessing
hassock
hayseed
high sea
hissing
icing
icy
Jason
Jaycees
kissing
lacer
lacing
lacy
Lassie
lasso
leaser
leasing
lessen
lesser
lesson
Lisa
listen
loosen
Lucille
Lucy
mason
massage
massive
message
messy
missing
mossy
muscle
muscled
mussel
myself
Osage
pacer
pacing
passage
passing
peso
piecer
pieces
Pisces
placer
placid
placing
posse

possum
precede
precept
precinct
presser
pressing
pricing
proceed
proceeds
racer
racing
recede
receipt
receive
recent
recite
reset
Russell
tassel
tossing
toss-up
tracer
tracing
Tracy
trestle
Tucson
tussle
two-some
usage
vessel
voices
voicing
wayside
whistle
____
____

S /s/ Medial—three syllables

aerosol
aggressor
Alison
Alissa
Arkansas
assembly
assortment
assumption
asylum
babysit
bathing suit
Bay City
bicycle
bus safety
casino
casserole
Chicasaw
China Sea
classical
classify
compressor
conducer
courtesy
crossover
crusader
cul-de-sac
Dawson Creek
December
deceptive
decibel
decided
decimal
decipher
decision
descendant
desecrate
desolate
dinosaur
disable
disagree
disappear
disciple
discipline
disinfect
disobey
disorder
Edison
embassy
embosser
enticer
episode
eraser
essential
fantasy
Ferris wheel
field glasses
garrison
gasoline
glossary
gooseberry
grasshopper
grocery
hairdresser
Harrison
heavyset
high-sounding
icicle
innocent
isolate
jealousy
kerosene
legacy
lesson plan
lyceum
Madison

medicine
messenger
moccasin
molasses
mussel crab
oasis
ocelot
officer
opossum
oppressor
pacemaker
Pacific
parasite
parasol
passageway
passenger
Passover
pharmacy
policeman
policy
possessor
precedent
preceding
preceptor
precipice
principal
principle
procedure
producer
professor
progressor
promising
prophecy
prophesy
racing car
receiver
reception
receptive
recipe
recital
recycle
reducer
rejoicing
tendency
Tennessee
tennis court
tennis shoes
Teresa
tricycle
two-cycle
two-sided
U.S.A.
U.S.N.
Uncle Sam
unfasten
unison
unloosen
vacillate
windowsill
worrisome
____
____
____

S /s/ Medial—four syllables

accuracy
ambassador
antecedent
antiseptic
associate
capacity
cassette player
classified ad
coliseum
commissary
desegregate
disadvantage
facilitate
Fantasy Land
hacienda
impossible
increasingly
interlacer
jealousy
kilocycle
Minnesota
municipal
nervous system
participate
participle
penicillin
philosopher
philosophy
policewoman
potassium
precipitant
precipitate
presidency
pussy willow
receivable
receivership
receptacle
reciprocal
reproducer
rhesus monkey
U.S.A.F.
U.S.M.C.
U.S.S.R.
ultrasonic
undecided
unicycle
vacillation
velocity

vice-president	vitamin C	________
vicinity	Yosemite	________
virtuoso	________	________

S /s/ Medial—five syllables

animosity	disobedient	promissory note
association	electricity	unnecessary
classification	miscellaneous	unprecedented
confederacy	necessarily	vice presidency
curiosity	potato salad	water moccasin
data processing	precipitation	________

S /s/ Final—one syllable

ace	fuss	louse
base	gas	mace
bass	geese	mass
Bess	glass	mess
bless	gloss	mice
bliss	goose	miss
blouse	grace	Miss
boss	Grace	moose
brace	grass	moss
brass	grease	mouse
Bruce	Greece	nice
Bryce	grouse	niece
bus	guess	noose
case	Gus	pace
chase	hiss	pass
chess	house	peace
Chris	ice	piece
class	Joyce	place
crease	juice	plus
cross	kiss	press
dice	lace	price
dose	lass	race
dress	lease	rice
face	less	Ross
fleece	lice	Russ
floss	loose	this

thus
toss
trace
twice
us
vase
vice
vise
voice
yes
____
____

S /s/ Final—two syllables

access
across
actress
address
advice
Agnes
aimless
air base
air bus
alas
Alice
amiss
anxious
apiece
Bernice
bias
birdhouse
birthplace
blue grass
boat house
bonus
bookcase
breathless
briefcase
business
bypass
caboose
cactus
campus
Candice
canvas
carcass
careless
caress
Carlos
cautious
Cayuse
chorus
Clovis
compass
compress
concise
confess
congress
cordless
countless
courthouse
Curtis
Dallas
decrease
deface
Denise
Dennis
depress
device
displace
doghouse
dollhouse
Doris
doubtless
Douglas
dry ice
duchess
emboss
embrace
endless
erase
Eunice
express
famous
firehouse
fireplace
fitness
focus
fungus
furnace
genius
goodness
gorgeous
gracious
greenhouse
harness
Harris
headdress
heiress
helpless
Highness
hopeless
hot house
hour glass
ice house
illness
impress
increase
invoice
iris
Iris
Janice
jealous

joyous
Kansas
kindness
lattice
lettuce
Lewis
lifeless
lighthouse
likeness
Linus
Lois
lotus
Lucas
malice
mattress
menace
minus
mongoose
Morris
mouthpiece
mucus
necklace
needless
nervous
notice
novice
obese
office
oppress
palace
pampas
papoose
Paris
penthouse
Phyllis
playhouse
police
porpoise
possess
practice
precious
precise
preface
premise
process
produce
profess
profuse
progress
promise
pump house
purchase
purpose
rebus
Red Cross
reduce
release
replace
righteous
roundhouse
Rufus
ruthless
schoolhouse
shameless
shapeless
shoelace
sickness
Taurus
tennis
terrace
thermos
thickness
Thomas
thoughtless
tigress
timepiece
toolhouse
toothless
tortoise
townhouse
treehouse
trellis
two-piece
undress
unlace
unless
useless
Venice
vicious
waitress
Wallace
walrus
warehouse
weakness
White House
witless
witness
wondrous
wordless
workplace
worthless
____

S /s/ Final—three syllables

about face
accomplice
adios
alias
ambitious
anyplace
apple juice
arthritis
Beatrice

boarding pass
Chilkoot Pass
cleanliness
coffeehouse
Columbus
contagious
courageous
courteous
curious
dangerous
data base
delicious
dental floss
doublecross
embarrass
encompass
enormous
eye witness
fabulous
fiberglass
furious
generous
glorious
happiness
hideous
hiding place
Honduras
horrendous
humorous
igneous
impetus
infectious
ingenious
interface
introduce
lemon juice
lioness
luminous
marvelous
momentous
Mother Goose
mountainous
nautilus
nucleus
numerous
nutritious
obvious
octopus
ominous
open house
orange juice
outrageous
overpass
pancreas
papyrus
paradise
pillowcase
platypus
poisonous
populous
powerhouse
powerless
precipice
precocious
prejudice
previous
printing press
radius
ravenous
rebellious
relay race
religious
reproduce
tedious
tetanus
thoroughness
tidiness
underpass
unkindness
Uranus
various
venturous
vigorous
villainous
virtuous
vivacious
wilderness
wordiness
____
____

S /s/ Final—four syllables

adventurous
amaryllis
ambiguous
amphibious
Annapolis
anonymous
apparatus
Aquarius
camera case
continuous
diabetes
diagnosis
hilarious
incredulous
loving kindness
metropolis
miraculous
nevertheless
notorious
opera house
paddle tennis

praying mantis
precarious
ridiculous
table tennis
tomato juice

tumultuous
unanimous
vicarious
victorious
voluminous

S /s/ Final—five syllables

appendicitis
hippopotamus
magnifying glass

metamorphosis
simultaneous
tuberculosis

S /s/ Recurring—one syllable

cease
sauce
sense

since
sis

S /s/ Recurring—two syllables

assess
basis
biceps
cease fire
ceaseless
Cecil
censor
census
Christmas
circus
citrus
crisis
criss cross
cypress
Cypress
decease
Francis
glass house
incense
license
priceless
recess

sack race
sassy
saucepan
saucer
saucy
sausage
sawhorse
scentless
seaside
secede
seesaw
sentence
sequence
service
sickness
silence
sincere
sinus
sissy
sister
so-so
soapsuds

solace
South Seas
subset
subside
subsoil
succeed
sucrose
suitcase
sunset
suppress
surface
surpass
surplus
suspect
suspense
system
thesis
voiceless

S /s/ Recurring—three syllables

assessor
Cecilia
cellulose
Celsius
censorship
centerpiece
chili sauce
Christmas card
Christmas Day
Christmas Eve
Christmas tree
emphasis
five senses
gaseous
narcissus
processor
sacrifice
sassafras
satisfy
sea sickness
secession
self-addressed
self-conscious
self-defense
self-esteem
self-righteous
self-searching
self-support
sensation
sensible
sensitive
serious
serviceman
solar house
solicit
S.O.S.
Southern Cross
St. Louis
subconscious
subjacent
subsequent
subsidize
subsidy
subsistence
subsonic
successor
summer house
sumptuous
sunglasses
suppressor
surfacing
synopsis
synthesis
systemize
taco sauce
trespassing
unconscious
usefulness
____
____
____
____
____

S /s/ Recurring—four syllables

accessory
analysis
assessable
Civil Service
dissatisfied
flying saucer
insecticide
Massachusetts
necessary
necessity
no trespassing
paralysis
parenthesis
precipitous
predecessor
rhinoceros
salad dressing
seat belt safety
self-discipline
self-sacrifice
self-sufficient
self-supporting
semicircle
sensational
South China Sea
South Pacific
susceptible
suspension bridge
synonymous
word processor
____
____
____

SF /sf/ Initial—one syllable

sphere
sphinx
____
____
____
____

SF /sf/ Initial—two syllables

spheric
spheroid

SF /sf/ Initial—three syllables

spherical

SF /sf/ Initial—four syllables

spherically

SF /sf/ Medial—two syllables

asphalt
blaspheme
cat's fur
forceful
graceful
henceforth
houseful
peaceful
thenceforth
transfer
transfix
transform
transfuse
useful

SF /sf/ Medial—three syllables

atmosphere
blasphemer
blasphemous
blasphemy
disfavor
disfigure
gas fixture
gas furnace
hemisphere
lithosphere
misfortune
phosphorus
satisfy
stratosphere
transference
transfigure
transformer
transfusion
usefulness

SF /sf/ Medial—four syllables

asphyxiate
dysphasia
satisfaction
transferable
transformation
transfusible

FS /fs/ Medial—three syllables

cough syrup
life cycles
lifesaving

FS /fs/ Final—one syllable

beefs
bluffs
briefs
buffs
chefs
chiefs
cliffs
coughs
cuffs
fluffs
goofs
huffs

Jeff's
muffs
proofs
puffs
reefs
roofs
ruffs
scoffs
scuffs
spoofs
staffs
stuffs
whiffs

FS /fs/ Final—two syllables

beliefs
cast offs
cutoffs
giraffes
handcuffs
kerchiefs
layoffs
play-offs
show-offs
takeoffs
tariffs

FS /fs/ Final—three syllables

photographs
powder puffs
telegraphs

SK /sk/ Initial—one syllable

scab
scald
scale
scaled
scamp
scan
scanned
scant
scar
scarce
scare
scared
scarf
scarred
scat
scheme
schemed
school
scoff
scold
scoop
scooped
scoot
scope
scorch
scorched
score
scored
scorn
scorned
Scotch
Scott
scour
scoured
scout
scouts
scowl
scowled
scuff
scum
skate
skeet
sketch
ski
skid
skiff
skill
skilled
skim
skimmed
skimp
skimped
skin
skinned
skip
skipped
skirt
skit
skulk
skull
skunk
skunked
sky

SK /sk/ Initial—two syllables

scabbard
scabby
scaffold
scallion
scallop
scalloped
scallops
scalpel
scamper
scandal
scanty
scapegoat
scarcely
scarecrow
scarlet
scary
scatter
scattered
schedule
scheduled
scholar
schoolboy
school bus
schoolgirl
schoolhouse
schooling
schoolmarm
schoolmate
schoolroom
schooner
scolding
scooter
scorcher
scoreboard
scorecard
scornful
scot-free
Scotland
Scotsman
Scottie
Scottish
Scottsdale
Scottsville
Scotty
scoundrel
scouting
scuba
scuffle
scuffled
sculptor
sculpture
sculptured
scurried
scurry
scurvy
scuttle
Skagway
skateboard
skated
skater
skating
skeptic
sketchbook
sketchy
skidding
skier
skiing
ski jump
ski lift
skillet
skillful
skinny
skunkweed
sky blue
skyborn
skydive
Skylab
skylark
skyline
skyward
skyway
skywrite
____
____

SK /sk/ Initial—three syllables

scandalize
scapula
scatterbrain
scattering
scatter rug
scavenger
schematic
scholarship
scholastic
scorekeeper
Scorpio
scorpion
Scotland Yard
Scott City
scoutmaster
scuttlebutt
skate-a-thon
skatemobile
skeleton
ski-a-thon
skin diving
ski patrol
sky cover
sky diving

sky rocket	skywriter	________
skyscraper	skywriting	________

SK /sk/ Medial—two syllables

asking	frisky	night school
basket	gasket	oilskin
basking	Girl Scouts	Oscar
biscuit	grade school	outskirts
Boy Scouts	grass skirt	pesky
brisket	Haskell	pigskin
buckskin	high school	plaid skirt
calfskin	hopscotch	preschool
cascade	husking	Redskins
casket	husky	rescue
cub Scout	Husky	risky
day school	ice skate	sealskin
discard	kidskin	sheepskin
discount	landscape	threescore
discourse	mascot	tuskless
discuss	miscount	whiskbroom
diskette	muskegs	whisker
dusky	musk ox	whiskers
escape	muskrat	________
escort	musky	________

SK /sk/ Medial—three syllables

Alaska	discordance	hockey skate
basketball	discourage	horoscope
basketful	discouraged	hula skirt
basket weave	discover	huskiness
basketwork	discovered	ice skating
breadbasket	discussion	mascara
butterscotch	escapade	masculine
confiscate	escapement	masquerade
discolor	escarpment	May basket
discomfort	Eskimo	microscope
disconcert	fire escape	misconstrue
disconnect	gyroscope	mosquito
discontent	hibiscus	muscular

musketeer	spectroscope	whiskery
muskmelon	stethoscope	Wisconsin
musk oxen	Stravinsky	________
Nebraska	summer school	________
onionskin	Sunday School	________
periscope	telescope	________
public school	wastebasket	________
roller skates	whiskerless	________

SK /sk/ Medial—four syllables.

baleen basket	Episcopal	private schooling
birch bark basket	escalator	roller skating
disconsolate	figure skater	San Francisco
discontented	figure skating	________
discontinue	kaleidoscope	________
discovery	microscopic	________
Easter basket	picnic basket	________

SK /sk/ Final—one syllable

ask	dusk	rusk
bask	flask	task
bisque	frisk	tusk
brisk	husk	whisk
brusque	mask	________
cask	mosque	________
desk	musk	________
disk	risk	________

SK /sk/ Final—two syllables

corn husk	grotesque	unmask
face mask	mollusk	________
file disk	school desk	________
gas mask	swim mask	________

SK /sk/ Final—three syllables

asterisk	office desk	________
data disk	picturesque	________
floppy disk	reading desk	________
mammoth tusk	________	________

KS /ks/ Medial—two syllables

accent
accept
access
axis
axle
bake sale
boxcar
boxer
boxful
boxing
boxwood
dachshund
Dexter
dextrose
Dixie
Dixon
exceed
excel
except
excerpt
excess
exchange
exchanged
excise
excite
excuse
excused
exhale
exhaled
expand
expanse
expect
expel
expelled
expend
expense
expert
expire
Expo
export
expose
exposed
expound
extant
extend
extern
extinct
extol
extort
fixate
fixing
fixture
foxhole
foxhound
Jackson
Knoxville
Maxine
mixer
mixing
mixture
mix-up
Nixon
oxcart
oxen
Oxford
oxide
perplexed
pixy
proxy
quicksand
Roxanne
sextet
sexton
sixpence
sixteen
sixteenth
sixth sense
sixty
succeed
success
taxi
Texas
toxic
toxin
vaccine
waxy
____
____
____
____

KS /ks/ Medial—three syllables

axiom
complexion
dexterous
dioxide
excavate
exceeding
excellence
excellent
excepting
exception
exceptive
excerption
excessive
exchequer
excision
excitant
excited
excitement

exciter
exciting
excursion
excursive
execute
exercise
exercised
exhalant
exlibris
exodus
exogen
exorcise
expanded
expansion
expansive
expectant
expedite
expensive
exponent
exporter
exposure
expulsion
extended
extension
extensive
extensor
external
extinction
extinctive
extinguish
extortion
exudate
flexible
galaxy
hexagon
Jacksonville
Lexington
luxury
maximum
Mexican
Mexico
oxidize
oxygen
quicksilver
saxophone
successful
succession
successive
successor
taxable
taxation
taxicab
taxpayer
vaccinate
vexation
____
____
____
____
____

KS /ks/ Medial—four syllables

accelerate
Alexander
approximate
complexity
excavation
excavator
exceedingly
excellency
excelsior
exceptional
excessively
exchangeable
excisable
excitable
excitation
excusable
execution
executor
exerciser
exfoliate
exhalation
exhibition
exotoxin
expectancy
expectation
expectorant
expedience
expedient
expendable
expenditure
experience
experiment
expiration
exportation
exposition
expositor
extendible
exterior
exterminate
externalize
extinguisher
fox terrier
index finger
luxuriant
luxurious
Mexican food
New Mexico
Old Mexico
proximity
relaxation
Route 66

St. Patrick's Day
success story
Texas Rangers
unexpected
vaccination
____
____
____
____

KS /ks/ Medial—five syllables

exceptionable
exceptionably
excitableness
excitatory
excommunicate
executable
exfoliation
exhibitioner
exhibitionist
ex officio
expediency
experimental
expiratory
extemporary
extenuation
extermination
Mexican Hat Dance
Mexico City
____
____
____

KS /ks/ Final—one syllable

aches
ax
backs
bakes
beaks
bikes
blacks
blocks
books
box
brakes
breaks
bricks
Bronx
brooks
Brooks
bucks
Bucks
cakes
checks
cheeks
chicks
chokes
chucks
clicks
cloaks
clocks
coax
cokes
cooks
Cox
cracks
creaks
creeks
croaks
crocks
crooks
decks
dikes
docks
drakes
ducks
dukes
fakes
fix
flakes
flax
flecks
flex
flicks
flocks
flukes
folks
fox
francs
freaks
frocks
Greeks
hawks
hex
hikes
hoax
hocks
hooks
irks
Jack's
jacks
Jake's
jinx
jokes
kicks
knacks
knocks
lacks
lakes

lax
likes
locks
looks
lox
lux
lynx
makes
minx
mix
necks
ox
picks
pox
racks
ranks
rex
Rex
rocks
sacks
seeks
shakes
shocks
six
slacks
smocks
smokes
snacks
snakes
socks
sphinx
spikes
spooks
squeaks
stacks
steaks
sticks
tacks
tax
Tex
ticks
tracks
tricks
trucks
tucks
vex
wakes
wax
weeks
whacks
wrecks
yaks
____
____

KS /ks/ Final—two syllables

affix
Alex
annex
antiques
apex
attacks
attics
Aztecs
bandbox
barracks
basics
beefsteaks
beeswax
black snakes
borax
classics
clinics
coin box
comics
complex
convex
cornflakes
critics
daybreaks
deluxe
Derrick's
derricks
duplex
epics
epochs
ethics
fabrics
Felix
garlics
hat box
icebox
index
influx
invokes
kayaks
larynx
latex
lyrics
mailbox
mistakes
musk ox
notebooks
padlocks
peacocks
perplex
Phoenix
physics
pillbox
prefix
race tracks
relax
sandbox

scrapbooks
shamrocks
silex
smallpox
snowflakes
sound box
suffix
surtax
sweepstakes
syntax
thorax
thumbtacks
toothpicks
triplex
woodchucks
wordbooks
workbooks
yardsticks
____
____
____

KS /ks/ Final—three syllables

aerobics
almanacs
appendix
artichokes
candlesticks
ceramics
chicken pox
comic books
elastics
equinox
garter snakes
income tax
lumberjacks
motorbikes
orthodox
paperbacks
pogo sticks
politics
railroad tracks
storybooks
____
____
____
____

KS + Adjoining Clusters, Medial—two syllables

exclaim
exclaimed
exclude
excrete
explain
explode
exploit
explore
express
expressed
extra
extract
extreme
extrude
foxglove
foxtrot
____
____

KS + Adjoining Clusters, Medial—three syllables

ecstasy
ecstatic
exclusion
exclusive
expletive
explicit
explorer
explosion
explosive
expressage
expression
expressive
expressly
expressman
express train
expressway
exquisite
extra bold
extraction
extractor
extradite
extravert
extremely
extremist
extricate
extrinsic
extrovert
extrusion
____
____
____
____
____
____
____
____

KS + Adjoining Clusters, Medial—four syllables

exclamation
exclusively
excruciate
explanation
exploitation
explorative
expropriate
extractable
extradition
extraneous
extrapolate
extravagance
extravagant
extraversion
extremity
extroversion
____
____

KS + Adjoining Clusters, Medial—five syllables

exclamation mark
exclamatory
explanatory
exploratory
expropriation
extrajudicial
extrasensory
extravascular
____

SL /sl/ Initial—one syllable

slab
slack
slacks
slam
slang
slant
slap
slash
slat
slate
slave
slaw
sled
sleek
sleep
sleet
sleeve
sleigh
sleight
slept
slew
slick
slid
slide
slides
slight
slim
slime
sling
slip
slit
sloop
slope
slot
sloth
slouch
slow
sludge
slug
slugs
sluice
slum
slump
slung
slunk
slur
slurp
slush
sly
____
____

SL /sl/ Initial—two syllables

slacken
slacker
slalom
slapstick
slashing
sledder
sledding
sled dog
sleeky
sleeper
sleepers
sleep-in
sleepless
sleepwear
sleepy
sleety
sleeveless
sleigh bells

slender
slicer
slicing
slicker
slide rule
sliding
slighting
slightly
slimy
slingshot
slinking
slinky
slipknot
slipper
slippers
slither
sliver
slobber
slogan
sloping
sloppy
sloshy
sloth bear
slothful
slouchy
Slovak
slowdown
slowpoke
slow sign
slow-up
sludgy
sluggish
slumber
slurring

SL /sl/ Initial—three syllables

slalom course
sledgehammer
sleeping bag
sleepwalking
sleepyhead
slenderize
sliceable
slide trombone
slide viewer
sliding scale
slip cover
slippery
slot machine
slovenly
slow-motion
slow-moving
slow-witted
sluggishness
slumberland
slushiest

SL /sl/ Medial—two syllables

asleep
bobsled
bracelet
bustling
crosslight
crossline
crossly
dislike
dislodge
dog sled
enslave
grand slam
hustling
jostling
juiceless
landslide
Lesley
loosely
nicely
North slope
onslaught
priceless
rustling
ski slope
snowslide
translate
tussling
useless
voiceless
Wesley
whistler
whistling
wrestler
wrestling

SL /sl/ Medial—three syllables

carelessly
cross-legged
dislocate
disloyal
enslavement
expressly
misleading
purposeless
purposely
super slide
translation
translative
translator
translocate
translucence
translucent
uselessly
wrestling camp
wrestling coach
wrestling match
wrestling shoes
wrestling team

SL /sl/ Medial—four syllables

dislocation
legislation
legislative

SL /sl/ Final—two syllables

axle
basal
bristle
bustle
capsule
castle
counsel
dorsal
fossil
gristle
jostle
missile
morsel
mussel
parcel
pencil
trestle
vessel
wrestle

SL /sl/ Final—three syllables

blood vessel
carousel
colossal
dismissal
dispersal
rehearsal
utensil

LS /ls/ Medial—two syllables

also
balsam
Elsa
elsewhere
Elsie
falsehood
falsely
hillside
pulsate
Tulsa
ulcer
wholesale
wholesome

LS /ls/ Medial—three syllables

balsam fir
Coral Sea
falsetto
falsify
quarrelsome
Uncle Sam
wholesaler
Wilson

LS /ls/ Final—one syllable

else		
false		
pulse		

LS /ls/ Final—two syllables

convulse		
impulse		
repulse		

SM /sm/ Initial—one syllable

smack	smirk	smooth
small	smit	smote
smart	smite	smudge
smash	smith	smug
smear	Smith	
smell	smock	
smelt	smog	
smile	smoke	
smiled	smoked	
smirch	smooch	

SM /sm/ Initial—two syllables

smacker	smeller	Smoky
smacking	smelling	smolder
smaller	smelly	smoldered
smallest	smelter	smoother
small fry	smidgen	smoothly
small game	smiling	smother
smallpox	smirky	smothered
small talk	Smithville	smudgy
small-town	smithy	smugger
smarter	smiting	smuggest
smartly	smitten	smugly
smartness	smocking	smugness
smart set	smoggy	
smash-up	smokehouse	
smatter	smoke screen	
smeary	smokestack	

SM /sm/ Initial—three syllables

smart aleck
smattering
smearier
smelling salts
smilingly
smithereens
smoke chaser
smoke jumper
smokier
smokiest
smoldering
smorgasbord
smothering
smudgily
smudginess
____
____
____

SM /sm/ Medial—two syllables

baseman
basement
blacksmith
Christmas
classman
classmate
dismay
dismiss
dismount
goldsmith
huntsman
iceman
locksmith
outsmart
placemat
pressman
tinsmith
transmit
____
____
____

SM /sm/ Medial—three syllables

businessman
Christmas card
Christmas Eve
Christmas seals
Christmas tree
coppersmith
first baseman
locksmith shop
Mr. Smith
pacemaker
policeman
policemen
second baseman
silversmith
third baseman
____
____
____

SM /sm/ Medial—four syllables

embarrassment
junior classman
lower classman
senior classman
upper classman
____

SN /sn/ Initial—one syllable

snack
snacked
snag
snagged
snail
snake
snap
snapped
snare
snared
snarl
snatch
sneak
sneaked
sneer
sneeze
sneezed
snell
snelled
snide
snip
snipe
snipes
snipped
snitch
snob
snook

snoop	snow	______
snoot	snowed	______
snooze	snub	______
snore	snubbed	______
snout	snug	______

SN /sn/ Initial—two syllables

snack bar	sneakers	snowdrift
snaffle	sneaking	snowfall
snagging	sneezy	snowflake
snaggy	snicker	snow-go
snakebite	sniffle	snow job
snake dance	snippy	snowman
snakeskin	snobbish	snowplow
snaky	snobby	snowshoe
snapback	snooper	snowstorm
snap bean	Snoopy	snowsuit
snapper	snooty	snow tires
snapping	snorkel	Snow White
snappish	snowball	snubby
snappy	snowbank	snuggle
snapshots	snowbird	______
snare drum	snow boots	______
snatchy	snowbound	______
snazzy	snow-capped	______

SN /sn/ Initial—three syllables

snaggletooth	snazzier	snow bunting
snaggletoothed	sneakiest	snowmobile
snake charmer	snickering	snowy owl
snakier	snout beetle	______
snapdragon	snowball fight	______
snappier	snow blindness	______
snappiness	snowblower	______

SN /sn/ Initial—four syllables

snapping beetle	______	______
snapping turtle	______	______
snowy egret	______	______

NS /ns/ Medial—two syllables

answer
cancer
Cancer
censor
chancer
concede
concept
concern
concert
consent
console
consult
consume
council
dancer
denser
fancy
fencer
fencing
glancer
insert
inside
insist
insult
Jensen
Johnson
lancer
lonesome
mincemeat
monsoon
pencil
prancer
princess
Quincy
rancid
ransom
Sensei
senses
Spencer
sponsor
stencil
tensor
tinsel
tonsils
unsafe
unseal
unseen
____

NS /ns/ Medial—three syllables

advancement
advancer
agency
announcer
chancellor
commencement
concession
condenser
consider
consonant
consumer
consumption
counselor
currency
density
dispenser
enhancer
entrancer
fiancee′
frequency
incentive
incident
insincere
insulate
insulted
linseed oil
nonsupport
offensive
one-sided
potency
principal
principle
reconcile
Regency
romancer
sensible
sensitive
transgressor
uncertain
unselfish
unsightly
vacancy

NS /ns/ Medial—four syllables

coincidence
consecutive
deficiency
emergency
insignia
intensity
peninsula
Pensacola
precedency
preconceiving
preconception
principalship

radiancy
reconsider
sensational
social science
unsatisfied
unsuitable
unsuspected
____
____

NS /ns/ Final—one syllable

bounce
chance
dance
dense
fence
France
glance
hence
lance
Lance
mince
once
ounce
pounce
prance
prince
rinse
sense
since
tense
thence
whence
wince
____

NS /ns/ Final—two syllables

absence
advance
announce
balance
commence
condense
conscience
Constance
convince
defense
denounce
dispense
distance
enhance
entrance
finance
Florence
fragrance
immense
incense
instance
intense
license
nonsense
nuisance
offense
past tense
patience
presence
pretense
pronounce
province
prudence
response
romance
science
sentence
sequence
silence
tuppence
twopence
vengeance
____
____
____

NS /ns/ Final—three syllables

abundance
acceptance
admittance
allegiance
alliance
allowance
ambulance
annoyance
appearance
appliance
audience
circumstance
common sense
conference
confidence
consequence
convenience
dependence
difference
disturbance
endurance

evidence
ignorance
impatience
importance
influence
innocence
insurance
maintenance
mispronounce
occurrence
performance
precedence
preference
prevalence
radiance
recurrence
redundance
reference
residence
resistance
reverence
subsistence
surveillance
tolerance
turbulence
utterance
variance
vigilance
____
____

NS /ns/ Final—four syllables

circumference
independence
indifference
inheritance
intelligence
obedience
predominance
preponderance
self-assurance
self-confidence
self-reliance
significance
____
____
____

SP /sp/ Initial—one syllable

spa
space
spade
spake
span
spanned
spar
spare
spared
sparred
sparse
spat
spawn
speak
spear
speck
speech
spell
spelled
spend
spent
spice
spiced
spike
spill
spilled
spilt
spin
spine
spire
spit
spite
spitz
spoil
spoiled
spoke
spokes
sponge
sponged
spoof
spook
spool
spoon
spoor
sport
sports
spot
spouse
spout
spud
spun
spunk
spur
spurge
spurred
spurs
spurt
spy
____
____

SP /sp/ Initial—two syllables

space bar
spacecraft
space flight
spaceman
spaceport
spaceship
space suit
spacial
spacing
spacious
spadeful
spadework
spancel
spangle
Spaniard
spaniel
Spanish
spanner
spareribs
sparing
spark coil
sparker
sparkle
sparkler
sparkling
spark plug
sparring
sparrow
Spartan
spasm
spastic
spatial
spatter
spawning
speaker
speakers
speaking
spearfish
spearhead
spearmint
special
specie
specious
speckle
spectre
spectrum
speechless
speedboat
speedster
speedtrap
speedway
speedy
speed zone
spellbound
speller
spelling
spendthrift
sperm whale
spicy
spider
spiky
spillage
spilling
spillway
spinach
spinal
spindle
spindling
spineless
spinet
spinner
spinning
spin out
spinster
spiral
spirit
spitball
spiteful
spitfire
spittoon
spoilage
spoiling
spoken
spokesman
sponger
spongy
sponsor
spooky
spoon bread
spoonful
sportful
sporting
sports car
sportscast
sport shirt
sportsman
sportswear
sporty
spot check
spotlight
spotted
spotter
spotty
spun glass
spunky
Sputnik
sputter
spy glass
spying
____
____
____
____
____

SP /sp/ Initial—three syllables

space heater	specific	spinning wheel
space station	specify	spirited
space writer	specimen	spiritless
spaghetti	spectacle	sponsoring
Spanish food	spectator	sponsorship
Spanish rice	spectrogram	spookier
sparable	spectrograph	sporadic
sparrow hawk	spectroscope	sporting goods
spasmodic	speculate	sportscaster
spatula	speedily	sportsmanship
speakable	speed limit	sportswriter
spear fishing	spelling bee	spunkier
specialist	spider web	________
specialize	spinal cord	________
specialty	spinal nerve	________

SP /sp/ Initial—four syllables

spectacular	speedometer	spiritual
spectrometer	spider monkey	spirometer
speech therapist	spinal column	spontaneous
speech therapy	spiral notebook	________

SP /sp/ Initial—five syllables

Special Olympics	specifically	________
specialization	specification	________

SP /sp/ Medial—two syllables

aspen	dispatched	misplace
Aspen	dispel	misspell
Casper	dispose	passport
crispy	dispute	peace pipe
despair	gospel	prospect
despise	grasping	prosper
despised	high-speed	respect
despite	inspect	respire
despoil	inspire	respite
despoiled	Jasper	respond
dispatch	larkspur	response

Shakespeare	waspish	________
teaspoon	waspy	________
turnspit	whisper	________

SP /sp/ Medial—three syllables

aerospace	mispronounce	suspension
aspirin	outer space	suspicion
baby spoon	outspoken	suspicious
desperate	prospective	tablespoon
disparate	prospector	transparent
disposal	prosperous	whispering
hospital	respectful	________
inspection	respective	________
Jasper Park	retrospect	________
loudspeaker	suspenders	________

SP /sp/ Medial—four syllables

asparagus	disputable	respectable
conspiracy	especially	respectively
correspondence	espionage	respiration
despairingly	high-spirited	respirator
desperado	hospitable	responsible
desperation	hospitalize	tablespoonful
despicable	inspiration	unspeakable
dispensary	litmus paper	________
dispensation	low-spirited	________
disposable	perspicacious	________
disposition	perspiration	________
disproportion	prosperity	________

SP /sp/ Medial—five syllables

hospitality	respiratory	________
indisputable	________	________
irresponsibly	________	________

SP /sp/ Medial—six syllables

inspirationally	________	________
respectability	________	________
responsibility	________	________

SP /sp/ Final—one syllable

clasp
crisp
gasp
grasp
lisp
rasp
wasp
wisp

PS /ps/ Medial—two syllables

capsize
capsule
chopsticks
deep South
dip stick
dropsy
gypsum
gypsy
hopscotch
keepsake
knapsack
lapsing
lipstick
Mopsy
pipsqueak
slapstick
soapsuds
step stool
stop sign
tipsy
topsail
topside
topsoil
Topsy
typeset
upset
upstairs
upstart
upswing

PS /ps/ Medial—three syllables

asepsis
autopsy
biopsy
chop suey
collapsing
elapsing
ellipsis
Phillipsburg
relapsing
synopsis
tipsiness
tipsy cake
top secret
top sergeant
typesetter
typesetting
upsetting
upstanding
upsurging
upsweeping
upswelling
upswinging

PS /ps/ Medial—four syllables

epilepsy
topsy-turvy
upsettable
upside-down cake
upsy-daisy

PS /ps/ Final—one syllable

alps
Alps
caps
chaps
chips
chops
copes
crops
cups
dips
drapes
drips
drops
flaps
flips
flops
grapes
gripes
grips
gropes
groups

hopes
hops
jeeps
jumps
keeps
laps
lapse
leaps
lips
loops
maps
mops
naps
nips
peeps
pipes
pups
raps
reaps
rips
ropes
saps
scalps
scoops
scopes
scrapes
scraps
seeps
ships
shops
sips
skips
slaps
sleeps
slips
sloops
slopes
slumps
snaps
snipes
snips
steps
straps
stripes
swaps
tapes
taps
tips
tops
traps
trips
troops
weeps
whips
wipes
wraps
zips
____
____
____

PS /ps/ Final—two syllables

biceps
collapse
eclipse
elapse
ellipse
escapes
forceps
gallops
gossips
grown-ups
push-ups
raindrops
relapse
round trips
roundups
scallops
sit-ups
triceps
tulips
turnips
unwraps
wallops
____
____

PS /ps/ Final—three syllables

antelopes
cantaloupes
fire escapes
____
____
____

RS /rs/ Medial—two syllables

arson
corsage
cursive
cursor
dorsal
firesale
fireside
forceps
foresaw

foresee
foreseen
foresight
forsake
for sale
forsook
herself
horseback
horsefly
horseman
horseshoe
horse show
mercy
morsel
Morse Code
ourselves
parcel
parsley
parsnip
parson
perceive
percent
person
perspire
pursue
pursuit
scarcely
tiresome
torso
verso
versus
Warsaw
yourself
____
____
____
____
____
____

RS /rs/ Medial—three syllables

arsenal
arsenic
cumbersome
diversely
fire safety
forsaken
horsepower
intercede
Jefferson
lumbersome
Mercedes
narcissus
near-sighted
nursery
overseas
oversight
overstate
parcel post
parsonage
percentage
persecute
persimmon
persistent
personal
personnel
porcelain
power saw
precursor
rehearsal
rehearsing
reverses
reversing
riverside
Riverside
salesperson
somersault
supersede
supervise
underset
unforeseen
varsity
versatile
versify
____
____
____
____
____

RS /rs/ Medial—four syllables

adversary
controversy
diversity
impersonate
marsupial
nursery rhymes
nursery school
persecution
personally
supersonic
superstition
universal
unmerciful
versifier
vice versa
water safety
____
____

RS /rs/ Medial—five syllables

anniversary	universally	versification
diversifying	university	
personality	versatility	

RS /rs/ Final—one syllable

coarse	hoarse	scarce
course	horse	source
curse	nurse	sparse
fierce	pierce	verse
force	Pierce	worse
hearse	purse	

RS /rs/ Final—two syllables

adverse	endorse	resource
Air Force	enforce	reverse
averse	golf course	saw horse
coerce	imburse	school nurse
concourse	immerse	sea horse
converse	inverse	submerse
disburse	race course	transverse
disperse	recourse	traverse
diverse	rehearse	
divorce	remorse	

RS /rs/ Final—three syllables

charley horse	labor force	rocking horse
fire safety	office nurse	slalom course
first aid course	police force	student nurse
hobby horse	quarter horse	universe
intersperse	reinforce	

ST /st/ Initial—one syllable

stack	stain	stalk
stacked	stair	stall
staff	stairs	stalled
stag	stake	stamp
stage	staked	stamped
staged	stale	stand

star
starch
stare
stared
start
state
states
stave
stay
steak
steam
steed
steel
steep
steer
stem
stemmed
step
stepped
stern
stew
stick
stiff
still
stilt
sting
stink
stir
stirred
stitch
stock
stocks
stoke
stole
stomp
stone
stood
stool
stoop
stop
stopped
store
stored
stork
storm
stout
stove
stow
stub
stubbed
stud
stuff
stump
stun
stung
stunk
stunned
stunt
sty
style
____
____
____

ST /st/ Initial—two syllables

stable
stagecoach
stagger
staircase
stallage
stallion
stammer
stampede
standard
Stanford
Stanley
stanza
staple
starboard
starfish
starling
statement
statesman
static
station
statue
steadfast
steady
steamboat
steamer
steamship
steeple
steerage
steel wool
sterling
Steven
steward
Stewart
sticky
stifle
stinger
stingray
stirrup
stock car
stocker
Stockholm
stocking
stockroom
stocky
stockyard
stolen
stomach
Stone Age

stoneware
stonework
stoplight
stop-off
stoppage
stopper
stopping
stopwatch
storage
storehouse
storeroom
stories
stormy
story
stovepipe
stowage
stubble
stubborn
stubby
stuck-up
student
studied
study
stuffing
stuffy
stumble
stunning
sturdy
sturgeon
stutter
stylish
stylist
stylize
stylus
stymied
____

ST /st/ Initial—three syllables

stadium
stalactite
stalagmite
stateswoman
statistics
steam engine
steam shovel
stepbrother
stepfather
stepladder
stepmother
stepping stone
stereo
sterilize
stethoscope
stimulate
stimulus
stock exchange
stock market
stomach ache
stonecutter
stopover
storm cellar
storm center
storm warning
storm window
storybook
stowaway
studio
studious
study group
study hall
stumbling block
stupendous
stuttering
____

ST /st/ Initial—four syllables

stationary
stationery
station master
station wagon
____
____

ST /st/ Medial—two syllables

abstain
bandstand
beefsteak
breastbone
bus stop
cast iron
castoff
Chester
chestnut
chopsticks
coastal
Coast Guard
coastline
constant
costume
crystal
Crystal
custom
destine
distal
distance

distant
distaste
distend
distill
distinct
distort
disturb
drugstore
drumstick
dustcloth
Easter
eastern
eastward
Einstein
estate
Estelle
Ester
footstep
footstool
frostbite
frosting
ghastly
ghost town
grandstand
grindstone
hailstone
hailstorm
hasty
haystack
head start
headstone
homestead
hostage
hostel
hostess
hostile
housetop
Houston
iced tea

install
instance
instant
instead
instep
instinct
justice
keystone
lasting
limestone
lipstick
livestock
milestone
mistake
mister
mistook
misty
mostly
mustang
nasty
North Star
pastel
pastels
pastime
pastor
pester
piston
postage
postal
postcard
posted
posting
postman
postmark
postpaid
postpone
postscript
question
restless

rhinestone
rustic
rusty
Rusty
sandstorm
shoe store
shortstop
smokestack
substance
sustain
sweepstakes
tasty
test tube
toadstool
tombstone
tungsten
turnstile
two-step
vista
waistband
western
West Point
westward
withstand
withstood
wristband
yardstick
____
____
____
____
____
____
____
____
____
____
____
____

ST /st/ Medial—three syllables

accustom
adjustment
armistice
artistic
asbestos
assistance
assistant
astonish
bus station
bystander
candlestick
castanets
castaway
consistent
constitute
contestant
crop duster
custody
customer
destiny
destitute
devastate
distasteful
distemper
distiller
distinction
distinguish
establish
estimate
existence
fantastic
festival
fiesta
gas station
gymnastics
high-stepping
historic
hockey stick
honesty
injustice
installment
instantly
institute
intestine
investment
justify
Lone Star State
long distance
majestic
majesty
mastodon
mistaken
northwestern
Northwestern
obstacle
outstanding
pasteurize
pedestal
persistent
photostat
pogo stick
postage stamp
postmaster
post office
postmistress
predestine
Protestant
questioner
question mark
questionnaire
resistance
sarcastic
shooting star
siesta
southeastern
space station
substandard
substantial
substation
substitute
summer stock
superstar
sustenance
testament
testify
thermostat
tossed salad
tostada
train station
understand
understood
vestibule
youth hostel
____
____
____

ST /st/ Medial—four syllables

consistency
constituent
constitution
Costa Rica
custodian
customary
establishment
grocery store
historian
hysterical
institution
interesting

investigate	questionable	T.V. station
misunderstand	readjustment	testimony
misunderstood	realistic	unaccustomed
optimistic	relay station	understanding
pessimistic	solar system	United States
posterior	superstition	________________

ST /st/ Medial—five syllables

constituency	postmeridian	unquestionable
investigative	predestination	________________

ST /st/ Final—one syllable

baste	gust	pressed
beast	haste	priest
best	hoist	quest
blast	host	raced
blest	iced	rest
boast	jest	roast
boost	just	roost
bussed	last	rust
bust	least	taste
cast	lest	test
chest	list	thrust
coast	lost	toast
cost	mast	twist
crest	messed	vast
crossed	midst	versed
crust	missed	vest
dressed	mist	voiced
dust	moist	waist
east	most	waste
faced	must	west
fast	nest	wist
feast	passed	wrest
fist	past	wrist
frost	paste	yeast
fussed	pest	zest
ghost	placed	________________
guest	post	________________

ST /st/ Final—two syllables

abreast
adjust
against
almost
amidst
arrest
artist
assist
August
Baptist
bed rest
biggest
breakfast
broadcast
chemist
choicest
combust
compost
conquest
consist
contest
contrast
cutest
cyclist
deepest
defrost
dentist
detest
digest
driest
druggist
earnest
eldest
embossed
enlist
ernest
exhaust
exist
Far East
farthest
flautist
florist
forecast
forest
French toast
furthest
gatepost
greatest
gymnast
half-mast
harvest
honest
inquest
insist
invest
Key West
largest
locust
longest
loosest
loudest
low-cost
lyrist
Midwest
milepost
modest
nearest
neatest
newest
newscast
nicest
Northeast
Northwest
oldest
outpost
poorest
post-test
pre-test
pronounced
protest
request
resist
richest
ripest
robust
safest
sandblast
sand-cast
sawdust
sheerest
shrillest
signpost
sleekest
slickest
slowest
slyest
smallest
smartest
smoothest
Southeast
Southwest
steadfast
strongest
stylist
subsist
suggest
tempest
thinnest
toothpaste
tourist
trimmest
truest
typist
unjust

unrest	widest	______
upmost	youngest	______
utmost	______	______

ST /st/ Final—three syllables

activist	luckiest	scientist
amethyst	Middle East	silliest
analyst	monarchist	skinniest
atheist	narrowest	smelliest
bassoonist	naughtiest	soggiest
classicist	novelist	soloist
daintiest	optimist	specialist
dramatist	organist	stockiest
fuzziest	overcast	theorist
happiest	parcel post	therapist
hornet's nest	pessimist	thriftiest
hungriest	pharmacist	tidiest
idealist	physicist	trombonist
immodest	pianist	unbalanced
interest	prettiest	unnoticed
journalist	quietist	uppermost
kindliest	rebroadcast	vocalist
littlest	roomiest	wealthiest
loveliest	satirist	______

ST /st/ Final—four syllables

antagonist	naturalist	rhinologist
apologist	nonconformist	unhappiest
autonomist	orthodontist	urologist
biologist	otologist	ventriloquist
economist	pathologist	violinist
enthusiast	philanthropist	______
geologist	psychiatrist	______
iconoclast	psychologist	______

ST /st/ Final—five syllables

audiologist	entomologist	ornithologist
audiometrist	etymologist	______
cardiologist	ophthalmologist	______

TS /ts/ Medial—two syllables

batsman
Betsy
Datsun
gutsy
itself
jet set
jetsam
Matson
Mezzo
Nazi
outsell
outset
outside
outsing
outsit
outsize
outsold
outsole
Patsy
pit saw
pizza
pretzel
quartzlike
quetzal
ritzy
schizo
schizoid
schnitzel
Scotsman
Scottsville
sitz bath
Watson
yachtsman
____
____
____

TS /ts/ Medial—three syllables

Fitzgerald
gutsiness
outselling
outsider
pit sample
ritzier
ritziest
____
____

TS /ts/ Medial—four syllables

outsettlement
pizzeria
pizzicato
schizophrenic
____
____

TS /ts/ Final—one syllable

ants
aunts
baits
bats
bites
bits
blitz
blots
boats
boots
cats
cheats
chutes
cleats
crates
cuts
dates
debts
eats
fates
fights
fits
Fitz
flats
fleets
flits
floats
flutes
fruits
gates
gents
gnats
goats
grates
greets
grits
guts
hoots
huts
jets
kites
knits
knots
let's
lights

loots
lots
lutes
mates
mats
meats
meets
mites
mitts
mutes
nets
nights
notes
nuts
oats
pants
pats
pets
pits
plates
pleats
pots
putts
quits
quotes
rates
rats
rights
roots
rots
routes
routs
ruts
scouts
Scouts
seats
sets
sheets
shoots
shorts
sights
sites
sits
skates
skits
slates
slats
slits
slots
spits
splits
sports
spots
spouts
states
threats
tights
toots
totes
vats
votes
waits
wants
weights
wits
writes
yachts
____
____

TS /ts/ Final—two syllables

acquits
admits
ballots
biscuits
bonnets
brackets
buckets
cadets
carrots
cold cuts
comets
commits
commutes
cornets
cutlets
debates
defeats
denotes
dictates
diets
digits
doughnuts
duets
eaglets
edits
emits
equates
faucets
footlights
footnotes
forfeits
garnets
giants
Giants
giblets
Girl Scouts
goblets
hatchets
ice boats
ice skates
ignites
inlets

insights
invites
jackets
jackpots
kumquats
lifeboats
limits
locates
lockets
lookouts
magnets
mallets
markets
mascots
merits
midgets
minutes
muskets
muskrats
narrates
nuggets
omits
orbits
outfits
outwits
pamphlets
parrots
peanuts
pellets
permits
pheasants
pilots
pirates
pivots
planets
playmates
pockets
poets
polecats
portraits
primates
profits
promotes
pullets
pulpits
puppets
quintets
rabbits
rackets
raincoats
rebates
receipts
recites
recruits
red-hots
regrets
repeats
retreats
ringlets
riots
rivets
robots
rockets
roommates
rotates
rowboats
sailboats
salutes
secrets
senates
skillets
slingshots
snapshots
sockets
speedboats
spirits
spotlights
steamboats
tablets
targets
termites
thickets
tickets
tidbits
tomcats
tugboats
two-bits
unites
units
visits
wallets
whaleboats
whole notes
____
____
____

TS /ts/ Final—three syllables

copyrights
dominates
elevates
estimates
irrigates
irritates
isolates
kilowatts
minuets
motorboats
nominates
ocelots
omelets
opposites
overcoats

parachutes
parakeets
parasites
patriots
penetrates
powerboats
prohibits
radiates
regulates
roller skates
satellites
separates
shelled walnuts
silhouettes
skyrockets
statuettes
tolerates
violets
____
____
____

TS /ts/ Final—four syllables

initiates
marionettes
Massachusetts
originates
participates
____

SW /sw/ Initial—one syllable

suave
suede
suite
swab
swag
swale
swam
swamp
swan
swank
swap
sward
swarm
swash
swat
swatch
sway
swear
sweat
Swede
sweep
sweet
swell
swept
swerve
swift
swig
swim
swine
swing
swipe
swipes
swirl
swish
Swiss
switch
swoon
swoop
swore
sworn
____
____

SW /sw/ Initial—two syllables

swallow
swallows
swami
swampland
swampy
swan dive
swanky
swap shop
sweater
sweat gland
sweat pants
sweat shirt
sweat suit
Sweden
Swedish
sweeper
sweeping
sweepstakes
sweetbread
sweet corn
sweeten
sweetheart
sweet pea
sweet tooth
swelling
swelter
swifter
swim fins
swim mask
swimmer

swimming
swimsuit
swindle
swindled
swinger
swinging
Swiss cheese
switchback
switchboard
switchbox
swivel
swollen
____
____
____

SW /sw/ Initial—three syllables

swallowtail
swastika
sweet and sour
sweetening
sweltering
swift-footed
swimming hole
swimming pool
swine fever
swinging bridge
swinging door
Switzerland

RST /rst/ Final—one syllables

burst
cursed
first
forced
hurst
Hurst
nursed
pierced
thirst
worst
____
____

RST /rst/ Final—two syllables

airburst
cloudburst
coerced
dispersed
divorced
endorsed
enforced
imbursed
immersed
outburst
rehearsed
reversed
sunburst
unversed
____

RTS /rts/ Final—one syllable

arts
blurts
carts
charts
courts
darts
flirts
forts
hearts
parts
ports
quarts
shirts
shorts
skirts
sorts
sports
spurts
squirts
warts
____

RTS /rts/ Final—two syllables

airports
alerts
concerts
departs
deserts
desserts
distorts
experts
exports
imports
inserts
inverts

passports
reports
resorts
reverts
seaports
supports
transports

SER /sɚ/ Medial—three syllables

glossary
grocery
nursery
sponsorship
Switzerland
ulcerate

SER /sɚ/ Medial—four syllables

accessory
nursery man
nursery school
rhinoceros

SER /sɚ/ Final—two syllables

bracer
chaser
closer
creaser
crosser
dicer
dresser
grocer
guesser
kisser
lacer
leaser
lesser
nicer
pacer
piercer
placer
presser
racer
saucer
slicer
splicer
tracer
ulcer

SER /sɚ/ Final—three syllables

aggressor
assessor
compressor
conducer
embosser
enticer
eraser
horse racer
officer
oppressor
possessor
producer
professor
progressor
reducer
successor
transgressor

SER /sɚ/ Final—four syllables

dog sled racer
interlacer
predecessor
reproducer

NSER /nsɚ/ Final—two syllables

answer
cancer
Cancer
censor
chancer
dancer
denser
fencer
glancer
lancer
prancer
spencer
Spencer
sponsor
tensor

NSER /nsɚ/ Final—three syllables

advancer
announcer
condenser
dispenser
enhancer
entrancer
extensor
romancer

STER /stɚ/ Medial—three syllables

asterisk
castor oil
history
mastering
masterpiece
mastery
oyster crab
westerly
yesterday

STER /stɚ/ Medial—four syllables

master-at-arms
masterfully
prehistory
preposterous
sister-in-law
southeasterly
upholstery

STER /stɚ/ Final—two syllables

aster
blister
booster
Buster
caster
Chester
cluster
coaster
Custer
duster
Easter
faster
fluster
foster
Foster
hamster
holster
lobster
luster
master
mister
monster
muster
oyster
pastor
pester
plaster
poster
roadster
roaster
rooster
roster
sister
spinster
tester
thruster
toaster
twister
Webster
youngster

STER /stɚ/ Final—three syllables

adjuster
ancestor
bandmaster
canister
disaster
forecaster
gangbuster
Grand Master
half-sister
minister
postmaster
register
resister
scoutmaster
semester
shipmaster
sinister
Sylvester
taskmaster
toastmaster
upholster
Worcester

STER /stɚ/ Final—four syllables

administer
flabbergaster
Gila monster
prime minister
quartermaster
roller coaster

SKR /skr/ Initial—one syllable

scram
scrap
scrape
scratch
scrawl
scream
screech
screen
screw
scribe
scrimp
script
scroll
Scrooge
scrub
scrunch

SKR /skr/ Initial—two syllables

scraggly
scramble
scrambled
scrapbook
scraper
scrapper
scratchy
scrawny
screening
screenplay
screentest
screwball
scribble
scribbled
scrimmage
scripture
scrub nurse
scrumptious
scruple

SKR /skr/ Initial—three syllables

screen writer
screwdriver
scrupulous
scrutinize
scrutiny

SKR /skr/ Medial—two syllables

ascribe
ascribed
corkscrew
describe
described
discreet
escrow
ice cream
inscribe
muskrat
postscript
prescribe
prescribed
silkscreen
subscribe
subscribed
subscript
transcribe
transcribed
____
____

SKR /skr/ Medial—three syllables

description
descriptive
ice-cream man
ice-cream truck
inscription
manuscript
prescription
skyscraper
subscription
____
____
____

SKS /sks/ Final—one syllable

asks
basks
casks
desks
disks
flasks
husks
masks
risks
tasks
tusks
____

SKW /skw/ Initial—one syllable

squab
squad
squall
square
squash
squat
squaw
squawk
squeak
squeal
squeeze
squelch
squib
squid
squint
squire
squirm
squirt
squish
____
____

SKW /skw/ Initial—two syllables

squabble
squabbling
squad car
squadron
squalid
squally
squalor
squander
square dance
square deal
square feet
square foot
square inch
squarely
square knot
square meal
square mile
square off
square root
squarest
square yard
squashy
squatted
squatter

squatting
squatty
squeaky
squeamish
squeegee
squeezer
squeezing
squelcher
squiggle
squirmy
squirrel
squirt gun
squishy
____
____

SKW /skw/ Initial—three syllables

square away
square inches
square meters
square rigger
square shooter
squashiest
squeezable
____
____

SPL /spl/ Initial—one syllable

splash
splat
splay
spleen
splice
spliced
splint
split
splits
splotch
splurge
____

SPL /spl/ Initial—two syllables

splashdown
splash guard
splatter
splendid
splendor
splicer
splicing
splinter
split shift
splitting
splutter
____

SPL /spl/ Initial—three syllables

splintery
split entrance
split entry
split level
split second
____
____
____
____

SPR /spr/ Initial—one syllable

sprain
sprang
sprawl
spray
spread
spree
sprig
spring
sprint
sprite
sprout
spruce
sprung
spry
____

SPR /spr/ Initial—two syllables

spraddle
sprayer
spray gun
spreader
spreadsheet
springboard
Springfield
springing
springtime

sprinkle	sprinkling	________
sprinkler	sprocket	________

SPR /spr/ Medial—two syllables

bedspread	hot springs	Rock Springs
hair spray	Hot Springs	________
handspring	offspring	________

SPR /spr/ Medial—three syllables

Brussels sprouts	shopping spree	Union Springs
ocean spray	Silver Spring	________

STR /str/ Initial—one syllable

straight	strength	stroke
strain	stress	strokes
strained	stressed	stroll
strait	stretch	strolled
strand	stretched	strong
strange	strict	strove
strap	stride	struck
strapped	strike	strum
straw	string	strung
stray	strip	strut
strayed	stripe	________
streak	stripped	________
stream	strive	________
street	strobe	________

STR /str/ Initial—two syllables

straggle	stretching	stringy
stranger	stretch-out	stripping
strapping	stretchy	striving
streaking	stricken	strobe lamp
streamer	strident	stroller
streamline	strike out	strolling
streetcar	strike zone	strongbox
strengthen	string beans	stronghold
stressing	stringent	strongly
stretcher	stringing	structure

strudel	strutting	________
struggle	strychnine	________
strumming	________	________

STR /str/ Initial—three syllables

straightforward	strawberry	structural
strait jacket	strenuous	________
strategy	string quartet	________
stratosphere	stroboscope	________

STR /str/ Initial—four syllables

streptococcus	stringed instruments	________
streptomycin	________	________

STR /str/ Medial—two syllables

abstract	distress	ostrich
airstrip	downstream	pastry
astray	frustrate	restrain
astride	gold stream	restrict
backstroke	high-strung	rostrum
bloodstream	instruct	seamstress
bowstring	minstrel	shoestring
breaststroke	mistreat	side street
constrict	mistress	sidestroke
construct	monstrous	upstream
destroy	nostril	vestry
distract	obstruct	________

STR /str/ Medial—three syllables

Astrodome	destructive	orchestra
astronaut	distraction	reconstruct
Australia	distribute	restraining
Austria	doll stroller	restricting
chemistry	Gaza Strip	restriction
comic strip	illustrate	Sunset Strip
construction	industry	tapestry
demonstrate	instruction	________
destroyer	instructor	________
destruction	instrument	________

STR /str/ Medial—four syllables

apostrophe
astrology
astronomer
astronomy
baby stroller
band instruments
candy striper
catastrophe
catastrophic
demonstration
distribution
illustration
industrial
industrious
instrumental
orchestra pit
pedestrian
reconstruction
string orchestra
____
____

STR /str/ Medial—five syllables

administration
astronomical
boa constrictor
instrumentalist
____
____

STS /sts/ Final—one syllable

beasts
blasts
boasts
casts
dusts
feasts
fists
frosts
ghosts
guests
gusts
hoists
hosts
lasts
lists
mists
nests
pastes
pests
posts
priests
quests
rests
roasts
roosts
tastes
tests
thrusts
toasts
twists
vests
wastes
wrists
yeasts
____
____

STS /sts/ Final—two syllables

adjusts
arrests
artists
assists
Baptists
broadcasts
chemists
conquests
consists
contests
contrasts
defrosts
dentists
detests
digests
druggists
enlists
exhausts
exists
florists
forecasts
forests
gate posts
harvests
insists
invests
locusts
mainmasts
Marxists
miscasts
newscasts
outposts
post-tests

pre-tests
protests
requests
resists
sandblasts
sand casts
stylists
toothpastes
tourists
typists

LTS /lts/ Final—one syllable

belts
bolts
colts
faults
jolts
kilts
malts
melts
molts
pelts
quilts
salts
silts
stilts
tilts
vaults
welts
wilts

LTS /lts/ Final—two syllables

adults
consults
insults
pole vaults
revolts
seat belts

MPS /mps/ Final—one syllable

amps
blimps
bumps
champs
chumps
clamps
clumps
cramps
crimps
dumps
glimpse
imps
jumps
lamps
limps
lumps
mumps
primps
pumps
ramps
romps
shrimps
skimps
slumps
stamps
stumps
thumps
tramps
trumps

SH

Pronounced: /ʃ/

Spelled: sh, ce, ch, ci, psh, s, sch, sci, se, si, ss, ssi, su, ti

SH /ʃ/ Initial—one syllable

chaise
chef
Cher
chic
shack
shad
shade
shaft
shag
shake
shale
shall
shalt
sham
shame
Shane
shank
shan't
shape
share
shared
shares
shark
sharp
shave
shaw
shawl
shay
she
sheaf
shear
shears
sheath
sheaves
shed
she'd
sheen
sheep
sheer
sheered
sheet
sheik
shelf
shell
she'll
shelve
she's
shield
shift
shim
shin
shine
shined
ship
shipped
shirk
shirt
shoal
shoat
shock
shocked
shod
shoe
shone
shook
shoot
shop
shopped
shore
shorn
short
shot
should
shout
shove
show
showed
shown
shucks
shun
shunt
shush
shut
shy
sure
____
____
____
____
____
____
____
____

SH /ʃ/ Initial—two syllables

chagrin
chalet
chamois
chapeau
charade
Charlene
Charlotte
chartreuse
chateau
chauffer
chenille
Cheri
Cheryl
chevron
Chevy
Cheyenne
chiffon
chignon
Chinook
shabby
shackle
shaded
shade tree
shading
shadow
shadowed
shady
shaggy
shag rug
shaker
Shakespeare
shaking
shaky
shallow
shallows
shamble
shamefaced
shameful
shameless
shammy
shampoo
shamrock
Shanghai
Shannon
shanty
shape-up
shaping
sharing
Sharon
sharpen
sharper
sharp-set
shatter
shattered
shaving
Shawnees
shearing
Sheba
shedding
sheepdog
sheepish
sheepskin
sheeting
sheetrock
Sheffield
Sheldon
shellac
Shelley
shellfish
shellproof
shelter
sheltered
shepherd
sherbet
Sherese
sheriff
Sherlock
Sherman
Sherry
Sherwood
Sheryl
Shetland
shilling
shimmer
shimmy
shinbone
shindig
shiner
shingles
shin guard
shining
shiny
shipboard
shipload
shipmate
shipment
shipping
shipwreck
shipyard
shirker
Shirley
shirtwaist
shiver
shocking
shock wave
shoddy
shoebrush
shoehorn
shoelace
shoeshine
shoeshop
shoestring
shoji
shopper

shopping
shopworn
shoreline
Shoreview
shoreward
shortage
shortbread
shortcake
shortcut
shorten
shorthand
shorthorn
shortly
shortstop
short-term
short wave
shorty
shotput
shoulder
shovel
showboat
showcase
showdown
shower
showered
showing
showman
showroom
showy
shudder
shuffle
shutdown
shut-in
shutoff
shutout
shutter
shuttle
Shylock
shyly
shyster
sugar

SH /ʃ/ Initial—three syllables

chandelier
chaperone
charlotte russe
Charlottesville
Charlottetown
Chicago
chivalry
shadowbox
shadowy
shampooing
shantytown
sharpener
sharpening
sharp-witted
shatterproof
shaving brush
shaving cream
shaving soap
sheepherder
sheet metal
sheet music
shelled pecans
shelled walnuts
Sheridan
shipbuilder
shipmaster
ship-to-shore
shivering
shoemaker
shooting star
shopkeeper
shopping bag
shopping cart
shopping mall
shore patrol
shortening
short-handed
short order
short-sighted
short story
shot-putter
shoulder bag
shuffleboard
shutterbug
shuttle bus
sugarbush
sugar cane
sugar-coat
sugar-cured
sugarhouse
sugar loaf
sugar pine
sugar plum
sugary

SH /ʃ/ Initial—four syllables

shaving lather
Shenandoah
Sherwood Forest
Shetland Islands
Shetland pony
shopping center
sugarberry
sugar daddy
sugaring off
sugar maple
____
____

SH /ʃ/ Medial—two syllables

action
anxious
ashamed
ashes
ashore
auction
backsheesh
bashful
bishop
bloodshot
bushes
bushy
cashbook
cashier
cashmere
caution
cautious
clamshell
cocksure
conscience
conscious
courtship
crankshaft
cushion
dashboard
dashing
diction
dish cloth
dishes
dishful
fashion
fiction
fishes
fishing
flashback
flash bulb
flash card
flashcube
flash flood
flashing
flashlight
flushing
fractions
freshman
friction
function
gashes
glacier
gracious
gusher
handshake
hardship
horseshoe
inshore
insure
kosher
lasher
lotion
luscious
machine
makeshift
mansion
masher
mention
midship
mission
moonshine
motion
musher
mushing
Nashville
nation
nightshade
nightshirt
notion
nutshell
ocean
offshoot
offshore
option
outshine
outshoot
pawnshop
pension
pressure
pushcart
pushing
push-ups
quotient
ration
ricksha
roughshod
rusher
rushes
rushing
sanction

seashore
section
shipshape
shoeshine
shoeshop
smashing
snapshot
snowshoe
social
soft-shell
special
stanchion
station
steamship
suction
sunshine
tension
thrasher
thresher
tissue
traction
unsure
usher
washboard
washbowl
washcloth
washday
washer
washing
washout
washstand
washtub
Welshman
windshield
wishbone
wishes
wishful
woodshed
workshop
worship
____
____

SH /ʃ/ Medial—three syllables

absorption
addition
admission
adoption
affection
ambition
assumption
attention
attraction
audition
Ayesha
beanshooter
beautician
beauty shop
blood pressure
Britisher
British Isles
bus station
carnation
clinician
cockleshell
collection
commission
compassion
completion
complexion
compulsion
condition
conduction
confession
conjunction
connection
constriction
construction
contraption
convention
conviction
correction
creation
crustacean
deception
description
destruction
detection
devotion
dictation
dimension
direction
distinction
distraction
donation
elation
emotion
eruption
essential
exception
exertion
extinction
extraction
eyelashes
financial
fire station
fisherman
fishermen
fishery
fishing hole
fishing pole
fishing rod
formation

foundation
frustration
furnishing
gas station
goldfish bowl
high pressure
horseshoer
impression
infection
infraction
initial
initialed
injection
inscription
inspection
instruction
insurance
intention
kingfisher
lavishness
location
low pressure
luxury
migration
musician
narration
national
New Hampshire
nonchalant
nourishes
nourishment
nutrition
nutritious
objection
official
omission
oppression
oration
ovation

parachute
partition
pay station
penmanship
pensioner
perfection
permission
physician
pincushion
plantation
polishing
position
possession
potential
prescription
pressuring
prevention
procession
production
profession
progression
promotion
protection
publisher
punishment
quotation
ramshackle
reaction
reception
reduction
reflection
regression
rejection
relation
restriction
ricochet
salt shaker
salvation
secretion

selection
sensation
solution
space station
spear fishing
starvation
subscription
sufficient
suspicion
technician
temptation
toothbrushes
tortoise shell
tradition
train station
transaction
transcription
transition
translation
trash masher
unshaken
unshaven
vacation
vibration
vivacious
vocation
washable
Washington
way station
wishing well
____
____
____
____
____
____
____
____
____

SH /ʃ/ Medial—four syllables

acceptation
accomplishment
adding machine
admiration
adoration
affirmation
aggravation
amputation
application
artificial
aspiration
aviation
beneficial
cash register
celebration
combination
commendation
compensation
competition
complication
composition
comprehension
concentration
condensation
confidential
congregation
conservation
constitution
consultation
contribution
conversation
corporation
cultivation
declaration
dedication
definition
delegation
demonstration
derivation
designation
desperation
destination
dictionary
dietician
disposition
domination
education
elevation
establishment
estimation
exclamation
exhalation
expectation
explanation
exploration
exportation
generation
genuflection
graduation
habitation
hesitation
illustration
imitation
inauspicious
inclination
indication
inflammation
information
inhalation
initialize
insatiable
inspiration
institution
insulation
intermission
introduction
intuition
invitation
irritation
isolation
lifeguard station
limitation
locomotion
malformation
malnutrition
maturation
mediation
meditation
moderation
navigation
negotiate
nomination
obligation
observation
occupation
operation
opposition
orthodontia
persecution
perspiration
police station
politician
population
preparation
presentation
preservation
proclamation
proficiency
publication
radiation
rationalize
recitation
recognition
recollection

reconstruction
registration
regulation
relaxation
repetition
reproduction
reputation
reservation
resignation
resolution
respiration
restoration
retardation
revolution
sanitation
satisfaction
separation
situation
social worker
speech clinician
station wagon
stationary
stimulation
substitution
superstition
termination
toleration
transportation
vaccination
variation
vegetation
ventilation
weather station
____
____
____
____
____
____

SH /ʃ/ Medial—five syllables

abbreviation
acceleration
accommodation
administration
amplification
approximation
articulation
asphyxiation
association
certification
classification
colonization
communication
congratulations
consideration
continuation
cooperation
coordination
deceleration
determination
discrimination
dissatisfaction
elaboration
elimination
evaporation
exaggeration
examination
humiliation
imagination
incineration
initiation
interpretation
investigation
manipulation
mathematician
modification
multiplication
nationality
organization
participation
preoccupation
procrastination
pronunciation
recommendation
refrigeration
representation
sophistication
____
____
____
____
____
____
____

SH /ʃ/ Medial—six syllables

decolonization
disarticulation
disorganization
misinterpretation
mispronunciation
misrepresentation
postexamination
precommunication
rehabilitation
uncoordination
____
____

SH /ʃ/ Final—one syllable

ash
bash
blush
brash
brush
bush
cache
cash
clash
crash
crush
dash
dish
fish
flash
flesh
flush
fresh
gash
gnash
gosh
gush
hash
hush
Josh
Kush
lash
leash
lush
mash
mesh
mush
Nash
plush
push
rash
rush
sash
slash
slosh
slush
smash
splash
squash
squish
swash
swish
thrash
thresh
thrush
Tish
trash
Trish
wash
Welsh
wish
____

SH /ʃ/ Final—two syllables

abash
afresh
anguish
backlash
backwash
banish
blackfish
blackish
blandish
blemish
bluefish
blueish
British
bulrush
burnish
car wash
catfish
cherish
childish
clothes brush
codfish
crawfish
Danish
dervish
elfish
English
enmesh
eyelash
eyewash
famish
finish
Finnish
flatfish
flourish
foolish
furbish
furnish
galosh
garish
garnish
goldfish
gooseflesh
goulash
grayish
greenish
hairbrush
hogwash
inrush
Irish
kibosh
lavish

modish
mouthwash
mustache
nail brush
nourish
paintbrush
parish
perish
pinkish
polish
Polish
potash
publish
punish
radish
reddish
refresh
relish
rosebush
rubbish
sagebrush
Scottish
scrub brush
selfish
sheepish
shellfish
shoebrush
skirmish
skittish
sluggish
snobbish
Spanish
Standish
starfish
stylish
sunfish
Swedish
tarnish
ticklish
toothbrush
unlash
unleash
vanquish
varnish
Wabash
whiplash
whitefish
whitewash
whitish
wood thrush
Yiddish
____
____
____

SH /ʃ/ Final—three syllables

accomplish
admonish
astonish
babyish
demolish
diminish
distinguish
embellish
establish
extinguish
horseradish
licorice
McIntosh
Old English
outlandish
relinquish
replenish
Scotch-Irish
steeplebush
succotash
underbrush
unselfish
yellowish
____

SH /ʃ/ Final—four syllables

bayberry bush
cranberry bush
mulberry bush
raspberry bush
satellite dish
strawberry bush
undernourish
____
____

SHL /ʃl/ Final—two syllables

bushel
crucial
facial
glacial
marshal
partial
racial
social
spatial
special
____
____

SHL /ʃl/ Final—three syllables

commercial
essential
financial
fire marshal
impartial
initial
judicial
official
potential
provincial
torrential
____

SHL /ʃl/ Final—four syllables

antisocial
artificial
beneficial
consequential
differential
influential
nonessential
preferential
prejudicial
presidential
residential
____

SHR /ʃr/ Initial—one syllable

shrank
shred
shrew
shrewd
shrews
shriek
shrift
shrike
shrill
shrimp
shrine
shrines
shrink
shrive
shroud
shrove
shrub
shrug
shrugged
shrugs
shrunk
____
____
____

SHR /ʃr/ Initial—two syllables

shredded
Shreveport
shrewdly
shrewdness
shrewish
shrillest
shrimp boat
shrimper
Shriners
shrinkage
shrinking
shrivel
shriveled
shriven
shrubby
shrugging
shrunken
____
____
____
____

SHR /ʃr/ Initial—three syllables

shriveling
shrubbery
____
____
____
____

SHR /ʃr/ Medial—two syllables

enshrine
mushroom
preshred
preshrink
preshrunk
unshred
washrag
washroom
____

SHER /ʃɚ/ Medial—three syllables

fisherman	fishery	____________
fishermen	pressuring	____________

SHER /ʃɚ/ Final—two syllables

crusher	masher	thrasher
glacier	plusher	thresher
gusher	pressure	usher
kosher	rusher	washer
lasher	squasher	____________

SHER /ʃɚ/ Final—three syllables

blood pressure	kingfisher	publisher
Britisher	low-pressure	trash masher
high-pressure	New Hampshire	____________

RSH /rʃ/ Medial—two syllables

airship	marshal	portion
earshot	martial	warship
Marsha	partial	worship

RSH /rʃ/ Medial—three syllables

censorship	martial arts	partnership
commercial	martial law	pastorship
contortion	membership	proportion
distortion	overshade	scholarship
fire marshal	overshine	sponsorship
foreshadow	overshoes	undershirt
leadership	overshoot	undershot
Marshal Sea	overshot	undershrub
marshmallow	ownership	watershed

RSH /rʃ/ Medial—four syllables

antique airship	overshadow	treasurership
chancellorship	thundershower	undersheriff
Marshall Islands	torsionally	____________

RSH /rʃ/ Final—one syllable

harsh	kirsch	marsh

T

Pronounced: /t/
Spelled: t, ed, ght, th, tt, tw

T /t/ Initial—one syllable

tab
Tab
tabs
tack
tact
Tad
Taft
tag
tagged
tail
tailed
tails
take
tale
talk
talked
tall
tame
tamed
tan
tang
tank
tanned
tap
tape
taped
tapes
tapped
taps
tar
tart
task
taste
taught
taunt
taut
tax
tea
teach
teak
teal
team
tear
tears
tease
Ted
tee
teen
teeth
teethe
tell
ten
tend
tense
tent
tenth
term
tern
test
thyme
tick
ticked
tide
tie
tiff
tight
tights
till
tilt
Tim
time
timed
tin
tip
tipped
tips
tire
Tish
to
toad
toast
Todd
toe
toil
toll
Tom
tomb
ton
tone
toned

tongue
too
took
tool
tooth
top
tops
torch
tore
toss
tossed
tot
touch
tough
tour
tow
towed
town
toy
tub
tube
tuck
tucked
tucks
tug
tugged
tune
tuned
tunes
turf
Turk
turn
turned
tusk
two
type
typed
____
____

T /t/ Initial—two syllables

tabby
table
tabled
tablet
taboo
tackle
tacky
taco
tactful
tadpole
taffy
tagging
tailback
tail coat
tail end
tailor
tailored
tailpiece
tailpipe
tailspin
Taiwan
takedown
taken
takeoff
takeout
taking
talcum
talent
tallow
tally
tambour
tamer
tamest
taming
Tammy
tamper
tandem
tangent
tangle
tango
tank car
tanker
tankful
tankship
tank truck
tanner
tanning
tantrum
tap dance
tape deck
taper
taping
tapping
tardy
target
tariff
tarnish
tartan
tarter
Tarzan
task force
tassel
taste buds
tasted
tasteful
tasting
tasty
tattered
tattle
tattler
tattoo
Taurus

taxi
tax rate
tax stamp
Taylor
tea bag
teacher
teaching
teacup
teahouse
tea-leaf
teammate
teamster
Teamsters
teamwork
teapot
tearful
tearing
tea shop
teaspoon
technique
Teddy
Teena
teenage
teeny
teepee
teeter
teller
telling
temper
tempest
temple
tempo
tenant
tender
tendon
tennis
tension
tepid
Terence
termite
terrace
terry
Terry
Texas
textbook
texture
Thomas
Tibet
ticket
tiger
tightrope
tightwad
timber
timecard
timely
time-out
Tina
tingle
tinsel
tiny
tiptoe
tired
tissue
tizzy
toadstool
toaster
Toby
today
toddle
toddler
toilet
token
tollbooth
toll bridge
toll call
toll road
Tommy
tom-tom
tonic
tonight
tonsil
toolbox
toolhouse
toothbrush
toothpaste
toothpick
topaz
topic
topline
topnotch
topping
topple
topsoil
torrent
tortoise
torture
toss-up
total
totem
tour guide
tourist
towel
tower
towline
town clerk
town hall
townhouse
township
T-shirt
Tuesday
tugboat
tulip
tumbler
tumor
tuna
tundra
tunic

tunnel
turban
turkey
turnip
turnoff
turnpike
turqouise
turret
turtle
Tuscan
tussle
tutor
two bits
two-fold
two-piece
two-some
two-way
tycoon
Tyler
typhoon
typist
____
____
____

T /t/ Initial—three syllables

tablecloth
tablespoon
tabulate
Tahiti
Tahitian
takeover
talented
talent scout
talent show
talkative
tallyho
tallysheet
tamale
tamarind
tambourine
tameable
tamper-proof
tangerine
tangible
tantalize
tantamount
tape player
tapestry
tarpaulin
tarter sauce
tattletale
taxable
taxicab
taxiway
taxpayer
teaberry
teachable
teacher's aide
tea garden
teakettle
tea party
teaspoonful
technical
teddy bear
teenager
Tel Aviv
telecast
telegram
telegraph
telephone
telescope
Teletype
televise
tempera
temptation
tenderloin
tennis ball
tennis court
tennis shoes
Tennyson
tentacle
tentative
terminal
terrier
terrific
testament
testify
test pilot
tetherball
Theresa
tidal wave
Timothy
Titanic
Tobias
toboggan
together
Tomasa
tomato
tomorrow
tornado
tortilla
tournament
tuition
turpentine
turtledove
two-cycle
two-sided
two-wheeler
tympanist
typewriter
typical
____

T /t/ Initial—four syllables

tabernacle
table tennis
tachometer
talcum powder
tanning center
tape recorder
tape recording
tapioca
tax deduction
taxidermy
taxonomy
teeter-totter
telephone book
telephone booth
telephone pole
television
temperature
territory
testimony
Texas City
Texas Rangers
Texas longhorn
timidity
topography
typographic

T /t/ Initial—five syllables

technicality
tuberculosis
typographical

T /t/ Medial—two syllables

atom
attend
attic
baited
baton
batted
batter
batting
battle
beater
beauty
better
Betty
biting
bitten
bitter
blotter
boating
booted
booting
boot-up
booty
brighter
Britain
British
butane
butter
button
cater
chatted
chatter
cheated
cheater
cheetah
cited
city
clatter
clutter
coated
cottage
cotton
crater
critter
cutter
cutting
data
dating
daughter
detail
deter
detour
ditty
duty
eaten
eating
Eaton
eighteen
eighty
Eton
Etta
fatal
fatten
fatter
fighter
fitted
fitting

fittings
flatten
flatter
flitted
floated
floater
floating
flutter
footage
freighter
fritter
getting
glitter
grater
greater
greeted
greetings
gritted
guitar
gutters
Haiti
hatter
heated
heater
heighten
high tide
high time
hitter
hooted
hotel
hotter
jetties
jetting
jetty
jitter
jitters
jotted
kitten
kitty

knitted
knitting
knotted
later
Latin
latter
lattice
letter
lettuce
lighter
liter
litter
loiter
looted
lotto
low tide
matted
matter
meeting
metal
meter
mighty
mitten
motel
motor
motto
mutter
mutton
naughty
neater
netted
netting
nighttime
nineteen
ninety
Nita
notate
noted
notice

nutty
otter
Otto
outtalk
patent
patted
patter
pattern
Patti
Patty
petal
Peter
pewter
photos
pitied
pitter
pity
platter
plotted
plotter
potter
pouting
pretty
putter
putty
quitter
quota
quoted
quoter
rated
rating
rattle
Rita
rooted
rotate
rotor
rotten
routed
satin

Saturn
scatter
scouting
seated
setter
setting
shatter
shooting
shutter
sighted
sitter
sitting
sit-up
skater
skating
sleeting
smatter
smitten
spatter

splatter
splitting
spotted
spotter
sputter
squatter
stated
stutter
suited
sweater
sweating
sweeten
sweeter
sweetie
tighter
title
tooted
total
totem

Toto
tutor
utter
vital
voted
voter
waiter
water
wattage
wetting
whiter
witty
writer
write-up
written
yachting
____
____
____

T /t/ Medial—three syllables

acquitted
admitted
Aletta
Anita
anteater
atom bomb
attitude
auditor
autobahn
baritone
Baton Rouge
battalion
Bay City
beautiful
beauty shop
Benita
bike safety
botany

boutonniere
bus safety
butterfly
butterscotch
buttonhole
catering
chain letter
Charlottetown
Chinatown
city hall
city lot
computed
computer
cottage cheese
creator
data base
data disk
delighted

demoted
denoted
devoted
dictator
diluted
disputed
editor
elated
entitle
equator
excited
fairy tale
farsighted
Fayetteville
fire safety
flotilla
flutter kick
forgotten

fresh-water
gas meter
Gettysburg
globe trotter
Globe Trotters
gratify
heated pool
heating pad
hospital
hot water
ice water
indebted
invited
inviting
janitor
jitterbug
Juanita
Jupiter
latitude
lettering
limited
litterbug
littering
Little League
located
locater
monitor
narrator
nearsighted
newsletter
noticing

notify
omitted
outwitted
permitted
photograph
photo lab
potato
predator
promoter
putting green
quick-witted
quieter
rattlesnake
recital
regretted
reheated
related
remittance
repeated
rotary
rotation
safety belt
saltwater
saluted
saluting
Saturday
senator
shortsighted
shot-putter
skywriting
sonata

spectator
spotting scope
stuttering
talkative
theater
tidewater
tomato
totem pole
transistor
translator
typesetter
typewriter
typewritten
unbeaten
united
United
uniting
unity
unsuited
uprooted
visitor
vitamin
voting booth
waterbed
water bug
white water
woodcutter
____
____
____
____

T /t/ Medial—four syllables

agitator
alligator
alma mater
altimeter
aviator
baby rattle

baby-sitter
beauty salon
boating safety
calculator
centimeter
climbing safety

commentator
competitor
cultivator
decorator
diameter
dormitory

driving safety
duplicator
educator
elevator
escalator
excavator
flying safety
generator
incubator
kilometer
legislator
liberator
litter barrel
moderator
navigator
nominator
numerator
operator
parking meter
peanut butter
percolator
perimeter
potato chips
radiator
riding safety
safety glasses
safety helmet
speedometer
thermometer
underwriter
United States
vegetables
ventilator
video tape
violator
vitamin C
walking safety
water safety
____
____
____
____

T /t/ Medial—five syllables

anatomical
denominator
deteriorate
hippopotamus
hot water bottle
hot water heater
potato salad
refrigerator
Sagittarius
saltwater taffy
____
____

T /t/ Final—one syllable

at
ate
bait
bat
beat
beet
bet
bit
bite
blight
bloat
blot
boat
boot
bought
bout
brat
Brett
bright
brought
brute
but
byte
cat
caught
chat
cheat
Chet
chit
chute
cleat
clot
clout
coat
coot
cot
crate
cut
cute
date
dot
doubt
drought
Dwight
eat
eight
fat
fate
feat
feet
fight

fit
flat
fleet
flight
flit
float
flout
flute
foot
fought
frat
fraught
freight
fret
fright
fruit
gait
gate
get
gloat
gnat
goat
got
gout
grate
great
greet
grit
gut
hat
heat
height
hit
hoot
hot
hut
it
jet
jot

jut
jute
Kate
Kit
kite
knight
knit
knot
kraut
late
let
light
lit
loot
lot
lute
mat
Mat
mate
meat
meet
met
might
mite
moat
mute
mutt
naught
neat
net
newt
night
not
note
nut
oat
ought
out
pat

Pat
peat
pet
Pete
pit
plat
plate
pleat
plight
plot
pout
Pratt
put
putt
quit
quite
quote
rat
rate
Rhet
right
rite
root
rot
rote
rout
route
rut
sat
scat
scoot
Scott
scout
seat
set
sheet
shoat
shot
shout

shut
sight
sit
skate
skeet
skit
slat
slate
sleet
slight
slit
slot
smit
smite
snoot
snout
soot
sought
spat
spit
spite
splat
split
spot
spout
sprite
sprout
squat
state
stout
straight
strait
street
strut
suit
suite
swat
sweat
sweet
taught
taut
that
thought
throat
tight
toot
tot
tote
trait
treat
trite
trot
trout
tut
tweet
vat
vet
vote
wait
watt
weight
wet
what
wheat
Whit
white
wit
writ
write
wrote
wrought
yacht
yet
____
____

T /t/ Final—two syllables

about
acute
afloat
air freight
Annette
athlete
await
basket
bike route
bonnet
Boy Scout
bracelet
Bridget
budget
burned-out
cadet
camp-out
cassette
Charlotte
checkmate
civet
classmate
clean-cut
closet
Collette
combat
commute
compete
complete
compute
conceit
concrete
corvette
create
DeWitt
dead weight

debate
deceit
defeat
deflate
delete
deplete
devote
devout
discreet
diskette
dispute
donate
doormat
doughnut
downright
dragnet
droplet
dropout
duet
dugout
Dutch treat
edit
elite
enroute
equate
estate
exit
faucet
fire hat
fish bait
flashlight
footnote
forget
forgot
format
fresh fruit
gambit
gazette
Gillett

granite
grapefruit
grass hut
green light
habit
helmet
helpmate
high hat
hip boot
houseboat
ice-skate
inflate
instate
irate
jacket
jackpot
Jeannette
King Tut
knockout
kumquat
lifeboat
locate
locket
lookout
lowfat
Main Street
mandate
market
merit
migrate
minute
misquote
moonlight
Nanette
narrate
negate
nugget
offset
outshoot

outvote
parrot
peanut
playmate
pocket
poet
pollute
profit
promote
prorate
quartet
quiet
quintet
rabbit
racket
racquet
rebate
receipt
red light
regret
relate
remote
repeat
reset
restate
rivet
robot
rocket
rotate
rowboat
sailboat
salute
shipmate
showboat
snowboot
speedboat
spreadsheet
square knot
stoplight

sunlight
sunset
tablet
tailgate
throughout
Tibet
toilet
tomcat
top hat
typeset
unfit
unit
unite
uproot
upset
vacate
wallet
walnut
watch out
webbed feet
whole-wheat
without
Yvette
____
____
____
____

T /t/ Final—three syllables

absolute
acclimate
accurate
acrobat
adequate
advocate
aeronaut
agitate
alphabet
antidote
apricot
arrowroot
astronaut
attribute
bassinet
billy goat
bluebonnet
cabinet
calculate
Camelot
celebrate
chariot
chocolate
circulate
clarinet
clothes basket
coconut
compensate
complicate
cookie sheet
copyright
coronet
county seat
cowboy boot
decorate
dehydrate
delegate
delicate
democrat
desolate
destitute
deviate
diplomat
dissipate
dynamite
educate
elevate
execute
featherweight
fishing net
gadabout
gold nugget
granny knot
halibut
Harriet
heavyweight
hesitate
hibernate
hockey skate
imitate
implicate
incomplete
institute
irritate
isolate
laundromat
legislate
Margaret
May basket
moderate
motivate
motorboat
navigate
nominate
nonprofit
obligate
obstinate
omelet
one-way street
operate
overboot
overcoat
overeat
overrate

overshoot
overstate
overwrite
paperweight
parachute
parakeet
parking lot
patriot
persecute
pilot boat
populate
prosecute
radiate
rainbow trout
recreate
regulate
reinstate
renovate
reunite
riverboat
roller skate
sauerkraut
scuttlebutt
separate
silver plate
simulate
situate
solar heat
Soviet
speculate
stimulate
stock market
substitute
terminate
thereabout
thermostat
tourniquet
underset
undershot
vaccinate
vegetate
ventilate
violate
violet
wastebasket
watertight
whereabout
____
____
____
____

T /t/ Final—four syllables

accelerate
accentuate
accumulate
anticipate
approximate
aristocrat
asphyxiate
associate
certificate
cooperate
coordinate
decelerate
Easter basket
forget-me-not
immaculate
incriminate
interrogate
invalidate
officiate
originate
refrigerate
regenerate
shopping basket
supermarket
unfortunate
____
____

FT /ft/ Medial—two syllables

after
chieftain
Clifton
driftwood
fifteen
fifteenth
fifty
half time
left field
left hand
lifter
lift-off
lift truck
lofty
nifty
rafter
ruffed grouse
sifter
softball
soft drink
softness
software
softwood
thriftless
thrift store
thrifty
____

FT /ft/ Medial—three syllables

afterglow	afterwards	soft-shell crab
afterlife	afterworld	thereafter
aftermath	after-years	thriftier
aftermost	hereafter	thriftiest
afternoon	leftovers	thriftily
aftertaste	shoplifter	________
afterthought	soft-hearted	________

FT /ft/ Final—one syllable

aft	laughed	soft
cleft	left	swift
craft	lift	Taft
croft	loft	theft
daft	oft	thrift
deft	raft	tuft
draft	rift	waft
drift	roofed	weft
gift	ruffed	________
goofed	shaft	________
graft	shift	________
heft	shrift	________
huffed	sift	________

FT /ft/ Final—two syllables

adrift	hayloft	spacecraft
aircraft	ingraft	spendthrift
airlift	life raft	uncuffed
aloft	makeshift	uplift
crankshaft	night shift	witchcraft
day shift	ski lift	woodcraft
gearshift	skin graft	________
handcraft	snowdrift	________

FT /ft/ Final—three syllables

birthday gift	leisure craft	water craft
Christmas gift	overdraft	________
handicraft	pleasure craft	________
leather craft	rubber raft	________

KT /kt/ Medial—two syllables

active
cactus
Choctaw
doctor
doctrine
factor
Hector
lecturn
necktie
octane
octave
pectin
practice
spectant
tractor
vector
victim
victor
Victor
____
____

KT /kt/ Medial—three syllables

activate
actively
affected
affective
attracted
attractive
bisected
character
conducting
conductor
connecting
connector
deducted
destructive
detective
dictaphone
dictation
dictator
director
doctoral
effective
elective
elector
electron
erector
exacting
exactly
factitious
factory
hectagon
impacted
inactive
infected
inflicting
instructor
neglected
nocturnal
objected
objective
obstructing
octagon
October
octopus
pact-maker
perspective
practical
prospective
prospector
reactor
selective
spectator
transacting
____
____

KT /kt/ Medial—four syllables

activity
bacteria
benefactor
deductible
destructible
directory
objectable
predictable
respectable
retractable
Victoria
____

KT /kt/ Final—one syllable

act
backed
biked
blocked
booked
checked
cooked
cracked
docked

ducked
duct
fact
faked
hiked
joked
kicked
knocked
leaked
liked
locked
looked
packed
pact
peaked
picked
poked
raked
reeked
rocked
sacked
sect
shocked
sneaked
soaked
spooked
squeaked
stacked
staked
stocked
strict
tacked
tact
talked
ticked
tracked
tract
tricked
trucked
tucked
walked
wrecked
____
____
____

KT /kt/ Final—two syllables

abduct
abstract
affect
afflict
aspect
attacked
attract
barebacked
bisect
collect
compact
conduct
conflict
connect
constrict
construct
contact
contract
convict
correct
deduct
defect
deflect
deject
depict
detect
detract
direct
dissect
distract
district
effect
eject
elect
enact
erect
evict
evoked
exact
expect
extract
impact
induct
infect
inflict
inject
insect
inspect
instruct
intact
neglect
object
obstruct
perfect
predict
prefect
product
project
prospect
protect
protract
react
reflect
reject
respect
restrict

retract
select
subject
subtract
suspect
transact

KT /kt/ Final—three syllables

architect
cataract
derelict
dialect
disconnect
disinfect
incorrect
indirect
intellect
interject
intersect
misdirect
overact
recollect
reelect
self-respect
subcontract
viaduct

TL /tl/ Medial—two syllables

atlas
butler
lightly
outlaw
outlet
outline
outlook
potlatch
potluck
settler

TL /tl/ Medial—three syllables

anciently
Atlanta
Atlantic
irately
outlining
outlying
perfectly
politely
quietly
sedately

TL /tl/ Final—three syllables

belittle
capital
entitle
immortal
parental
pedestal
rose beetle
segmental
skeletal
subtitle

TL /tl/ Final—four syllables

accidental
congenital
continental
elemental
fundamental
horizontal
incidental
monumental
noncommittal
oriental
sentimental
thermos bottle
tittle tattle

LT /lt/ Medial—two syllables

alter
alto
Colton
cultist
delta
falter
faultless
filter
guilty
halter
hilltop
Hilton
melted
molten
poultry
quilting
salted
shelter
smelter
voltage
Walter
welter
yuletide
____
____
____
____

LT /lt/ Medial—three syllables

alternate
altitude
Central Time
cultism
cultivate
dial tone
faultfinding
loyalty
malted milk
multiple
multiply
multitude
novelty
penalty
resulting
revolted
royalty
saltshaker
specialty
voltmeter
welterweight
____
____
____

LT /lt/ Medial—four syllables

altimeter
altogether
cultivator
difficulty
multiplier
seat belt safety
____
____
____

LT /lt/ Final—one syllable

belt
bolt
built
colt
dealt
dwelt
fault
felt
guilt
halt
hilt
jilt
jolt
kilt
knelt
lilt
malt
melt
molt
pelt
quilt
salt
shalt
silt
smelt
spilt
stilt
tilt
vault
volt
Walt
welt
wilt
Wilt
____
____

LT /lt/ Final—two syllables

adult	default	result
asphalt	exalt	revolt
bank vault	exult	rock salt
black belt	fan belt	seat belt
blue belt	farm belt	tumult
cobalt	insult	white belt
consult	pole vault	________
Corn Belt	Renault	________

LT /lt/ Final—three syllables

difficult	patchwork quilt	thunderbolt
garlic salt	Roosevelt	________
leather belt	somersault	________

NT /nt/ Medial—two syllables

ante	entrance	painter
antler	entry	painting
banter	fainted	pantry
cantor	frantic	plaintiff
center	frontal	plaintive
centered	gentle	planter
central	granted	planting
chanting	grantor	pointer
contempt	hinted	pointing
contend	hunter	pontiff
content	hunting	printed
contest	huntress	printer
context	into	printing
contort	junta	punted
contour	mantle	quaintly
country	mental	rental
county	mentor	rented
dainty	minted	saintly
dental	Monty	Santa
dented	nineteen	scented
dentist	ninety	shanty
Denton	onto	slanted
enter	painted	splinter

squinted
squinter
syntax
tantrum
tinted
Trenton
vantage
vented
vintage
wanted
wanton
winter
____
____
____

NT /nt/ Medial—three syllables

advantage
Antarctic
Atlantic
attentive
carpenter
centerpiece
Centerville
Central Park
Central Time
consented
container
contented
contention
contentment
contestant
continent
continue
counterfeit
enchanted
encounter
enterprise
entertain
eventful
fantasy
gigantic
imprinted
incentive
indented
interact
intercede
intercept
intercom
interest
interface
interfere
interfold
intersect
interval
interview
invented
inventor
Kentucky
Kon Tiki
misprinted
parental
presenting
re-enter
repentant
repented
repenting
resented
resentful
resentment
romantic
Santa Claus
Santa Cruz
Santa Fe
self-centered
seventeen
seventy
storm center
tentative
tormentor
transplanting
wintergreen
wintertime
____
____
____

NT /nt/ Medial—four syllables

accidental
adventurer
antagonist
antagonize
antecedent
cantilever
commentary
contaminate
contemplating
continental
contingency
continual
continuous
continuum
conventional
departmental
differential
disadvantage
egocentric
governmental
horizontal

instrumental
integrity
interesting
intermission
intersection
intimidate
monumental
oriental
ornamental
pedimental
pigmentation
presentation
radiant heat
radiantly
regimental
representant
rudimental
sacramental
sentimental
supplemental
trans-Atlantic
transcendental
uneventful
unprevented
unrepentant
Valentine's Day
ventriloquist
yellow bunting
____
____

NT /nt/ Medial—five syllables

antibiotic
contaminated
contemporary
differentiate
disinterested
documentary
elementary
experiential
intermediate
international
involuntary
orientation
parliamentary
Protestantism
representation
supplementary
temperamental
testamentary
____
____
____

NT /nt/ Final—one syllable

ant
aunt
bent
blunt
brunt
bunt
can't
cent
chant
count
dent
don't
faint
feint
flint
front
gaunt
gent
grant
Grant
grunt
haunt
hint
hunt
jaunt
lent
lint
meant
mint
mount
paint
pant
pent
pint
plant
point
print
punt
quaint
quint
rant
rent
runt
saint
scant
scent
sent
shunt
slant
spent
sprint
squint
stunt
taunt

tent
tint
vent
want
went
won't
____
____
____

NT /nt/ Final—two syllables

absent
accent
account
affront
agent
ailment
amount
anoint
appoint
ascent
aslant
basement
Belmont
blueprint
brilliant
buoyant
cement
client
cogent
cold front
comment
consent
constant
content
descent
discount
distant
eggplant
enchant
entente
event
extent
ferment
foment
For Rent
frequent
gallant
garment
hydrant
imprint
indent
infant
instant
intent
invent
judgment
merchant
moment
movement
newsprint
oil paint
ointment
pageant
parchment
parent
patent
patient
pavement
payment
peasant
pennant
percent
pheasant
pigment
pinpoint
placement
pleasant
poignant
potent
preprint
present
prevent
prudent
quadrant
quotient
rampant
recent
recount
remnant
resent
rodent
sea front
segment
sergeant
serpent
servant
shipment
silent
spearmint
stagnant
standpoint
statement
strident
stringent
student
talent
tenant
torrent
transient
transplant
treatment
urgent

vacant	________________	________________
valiant	________________	________________
Vermont	________________	________________
vibrant	________________	________________

NT /nt/ Final—three syllables

abundant
accident
accountant
adjacent
adornment
advancement
affluent
allotment
amazement
amendment
amusement
announcement
apartment
apparent
appointment
arrangement
atonement
commencement
compartment
competent
compliment
component
consonant
contentment
continent
convenient
decedent
dependent
descendant
detergent
different
diligent
dissonant
document
dominant
efficient
elephant
elopement
emigrant
encroachment
enjoyment
enrollment
filament
ignorant
immigrant
implement
improvement
impudent
incident
indignant
inherent
innocent
insolvent
installment
instrument
investment
lenient
lieutenant
ligament
malignant
management
measurement
monument
nourishment
nutrient
occupant
operant
opponent
orient
ornament
palpitant
parliament
peppermint
permanent
persistent
petulant
precedent
president
prominent
Protestant
punishment
radiant
recurrent
refreshment
regiment
relevant
reluctant
represent
requirement
resentment
resident
resistant
respondent
restaurant
retirement
reverent
ruminant
sediment
sentiment

subjacent
subsequent
succulent
sufficient
supplement
sycophant
tenement
testament
tolerant
tournament
variant
vigilant
violent
wonderment
____
____
____
____

NT /nt/ Final—four syllables

accomplishment
adolescent
advertisement
apportionment
astonishment
determinant
entertainment
environment
equivalent
establishment
expedient
experiment
extravagant
independent
indifferent
ingredient
intelligent
intolerant
iridescent
magnificent
noncombatant
obedient
participant
precipitant
predicament
predominant
preponderant
presentiment
reinforcement
significant
single parent
subservient
superjacent
temperament
understatement
vice-president
____
____
____

NT /nt/ Final—five syllables

insignificant
interdependent
superintendent
____
____
____
____
____
____

PT /pt/ Final—one syllable

chapped
chipped
chopped
clapped
clipped
crept
dipped
dripped
dropped
flapped
flipped
flopped
griped
gripped
heaped
hoped
hopped
kept
lapped
leaped
mapped
mopped
napped
nipped
peeped
piped
plopped
popped
propped
rapped
reaped
ripped
roped

scooped
scoped
scraped
scrapped
script
seeped
shipped
shopped
sipped
skipped
slept
slipped
snapped
snipped
stepped
stopped
strapped
swapped
swooped
taped
tapped
tipped
topped
trapped
tripped
typed
wept
wiped
wrapped
yipped
zapped
zipped

PT /pt/ Final—two syllables

abrupt
accept
adapt
adept
adopt
bankrupt
concept
corrupt
disrupt
Egypt
erupt
escaped
except
galloped
gossiped
postscript
precept
subscript
unwrapped

PT /pt/ Final—three syllables

intercept
non-adept

TS /ts/ Medial—two syllables

batsman
Betsy
Datsun
gutsy
itself
jet set
jetsam
Matson
Mezzo
Nazi
outsell
outset
outside
outsing
outsit
outsize
outsold
outsole
Patsy
pit saw
pizza
pretzel
quartzlike
quetzal
ritzy
schizo
schizoid
schnitzel
Scotsman
Scottsville
sitz bath
Watson
yachtsman

TS /ts/ Medial—three syllables

Fitzgerald	outsider	ritziest
gutsiness	pit sample	________________
outselling	ritzier	________________

TS /ts/ Medial—four syllables

outsettlement	pizzicato	________________
pizzeria	schizophrenic	________________

TS /ts/ Final—one syllable

ants	gates	nuts
aunts	gents	oats
baits	gnats	pants
bats	goats	pats
bites	grates	pets
bits	greets	pits
blitz	grits	plates
blots	guts	pleats
boats	hoots	pots
boots	huts	putts
cats	jets	quits
cheats	kites	quotes
chutes	knits	rates
cleats	knots	rats
crates	let's	rights
cuts	lights	roots
dates	loots	rots
debts	lots	routes
eats	lutes	routs
fates	mates	ruts
fights	mats	scouts
fits	meats	Scouts
Fitz	meets	seats
flats	mites	sets
fleets	mitts	sheets
flits	mutes	shoots
floats	nets	shorts
flutes	nights	sights
fruits	notes	sites

sits
skates
skits
slates
slats
slits
slots
spits
splits
sports
spots
spouts
states
threats
tights
toots
totes
vats
votes
waits
wants
weights
wits
writes
yachts
____
____

TS /ts/ Final—two syllables

acquits
admits
ballots
biscuits
bonnets
brackets
buckets
cadets
carrots
cold cuts
comets
commits
commutes
cornets
cutlets
debates
defeats
denotes
dictates
diets
digits
doughnuts
duets
eaglets
edits
emits
equates
faucets
footlights
footnotes
forfeits
garnets
giants
Giants
giblets
Girl Scouts
goblets
hatchets
ice boats
ice skates
ignites
inlets
insights
invites
jackets
jackpots
kumquats
lifeboats
limits
locates
lockets
lookouts
magnets
mallets
markets
mascots
merits
midgets
minutes
muskets
muskrats
narrates
nuggets
omits
orbits
outfits
outwits
pamphlets
parrots
peanuts
pellets
permits
pheasants
pilots
pirates
pivots
planets
playmates
pockets
poets
polecats
portraits
primates
profits

promotes
pullets
pulpits
puppets
quintets
rabbits
rackets
raincoats
rebates
receipts
recites
recruits
red-hots
regrets
repeats
retreats
ringlets
riots
rivets

robots
rockets
roommates
rotates
rowboats
sailboats
salutes
secrets
senates
skillets
slingshots
snapshots
sockets
speedboats
spirits
spotlights
steamboats
tablets
targets

termites
thickets
tickets
tidbits
tomcats
tugboats
two-bits
unites
units
visits
wallets
whaleboats
whole notes
____
____
____
____
____
____

TS /ts/ Final—three syllables

copyrights
dominates
elevates
estimates
irrigates
irritates
isolates
kilowatts
minuets
motorboats
nominates
ocelots
omelets

opposites
overcoats
parachutes
parakeets
parasites
patriots
penetrates
powerboats
prohibits
radiates
regulates
roller skates
satellites

separates
shelled walnuts
silhouettes
skyrockets
statuettes
tolerates
violets
____
____
____
____
____
____

TS /ts/ Final—four syllables

initiates
marionettes
Massachusetts

originates
participates
____

____
____
____

ST /st/ Initial—one syllable

stack
stacked
staff
stag
stage
staged
stain
stair
stairs
stake
staked
stale
stalk
stall
stalled
stamp
stamped
stand
star
starch
stare
stared
start
state
states
stave
stay
steak
steam
steed
steel
steep
steer
stem
stemmed
step
stepped
stern
stew
stick
stiff
still
stilt
sting
stink
stir
stirred
stitch
stock
stocks
stoke
stole
stomp
stone
stood
stool
stoop
stop
stopped
store
stored
stork
storm
stout
stove
stow
stub
stubbed
stud
stuff
stump
stun
stung
stunk
stunned
stunt
sty
style
____
____
____

ST /st/ Initial—two syllables

stable
stagecoach
stagger
staircase
stallage
stallion
stammer
stampede
standard
Stanford
Stanley
stanza
staple
starboard
starfish
starling
statement
statesman
static
station
statue
steadfast
steady
steamboat
steamer
steamship
steeple

steerage
steel wool
sterling
Steven
steward
Stewart
sticky
stifle
stinger
stingray
stirrup
stock car
stocker
Stockholm
stocking
stockroom
stocky
stockyard
stolen
stomach
Stone Age
stoneware
stonework
stoplight
stop-off
stoppage
stopper
stopping
stopwatch
storage
storehouse
storeroom
stories
stormy
story
stovepipe
stowage
stubble
stubborn
stubby
stuck-up
student
studied
study
stuffing
stuffy
stumble
stunning
sturdy
sturgeon
stutter
stylish
stylist
stylize
stylus
stymied
____
____
____
____

ST /st/ Initial—three syllables

stadium
stalactite
stalagmite
stateswoman
statistics
steam engine
steam shovel
stepbrother
stepfather
stepladder
stepmother
stepping stone
stereo
sterilize
stethoscope
stimulate
stimulus
stock exchange
stock market
stomach ache
stonecutter
stopover
storm cellar
storm center
storm warning
storm window
storybook
stowaway
studio
studious
study group
study hall
stumbling block
stupendous
stuttering
____
____
____
____

ST /st/ Initial—four syllables

stationary
stationery
station master
station wagon
____
____

ST /st/ Medial—two syllables

abstain
bandstand
beefsteak
breastbone
bus stop
cast iron
castoff
Chester
chestnut
chopsticks
coastal
Coast Guard
coastline
constant
costume
crystal
Crystal
custom
destine
distal
distance
distant
distaste
distend
distill
distinct
distort
disturb
drugstore
drumstick
dustcloth
Easter
eastern
eastward
Einstein
estate
Estelle
Ester

footstep
footstool
frostbite
frosting
ghastly
ghost town
grandstand
grindstone
hailstone
hailstorm
hasty
haystack
head start
headstone
homestead
hostage
hostel
hostess
hostile
housetop
Houston
iced tea
install
instance
instant
instead
instep
instinct
justice
keystone
lasting
limestone
lipstick
livestock
milestone
mistake
mister
mistook

misty
mostly
mustang
nasty
North Star
pastel
pastels
pastime
pastor
pester
piston
postage
postal
postcard
posted
posting
postman
postmark
postpaid
postpone
postscript
question
restless
rhinestone
rustic
rusty
Rusty
sandstorm
shoe store
shortstop
smokestack
substance
sustain
sweepstakes
tasty
test tube
toadstool
tombstone

tungsten
turnstile
two-step
vista
waistband
western
West Point
westward
withstand
withstood
wristband
yardstick
____
____
____

ST /st/ Medial—three syllables

accustom
adjustment
armistice
artistic
asbestos
assistance
assistant
astonish
bus station
bystander
candlestick
castanets
castaway
consistent
constitute
contestant
crop duster
custody
customer
destiny
destitute
devastate
distasteful
distemper
distiller
distinction
distinguish
establish
estimate
existence
fantastic
festival
fiesta
gas station
gymnastics
high-stepping
historic
hockey stick
honesty
injustice
installment
instantly
institute
intestine
investment
justify
Lone Star State
long distance
majestic
majesty
mastodon
mistaken
northwestern
Northwestern
obstacle
outstanding
pasteurize
pedestal
persistent
photostat
pogo stick
postage stamp
postmaster
postmistress
post office
predestine
Protestant
questioner
question mark
questionnaire
resistance
sarcastic
shooting star
siesta
southeastern
space station
substandard
substantial
substation
substitute
summer stock
superstar
sustenance
testament
testify
thermostat
tossed salad
tostada
train station
understand
understood
vestibule
youth hostel
____
____
____

ST /st/ Medial—four syllables

consistency
constituent
constitution
Costa Rica
custodian
customary
establishment
grocery store
historian
hysterical
institution
interesting
investigate
misunderstand
misunderstood
optimistic
pessimistic
posterior
questionable
readjustment
realistic
relay station
solar system
superstition
T.V. station
testimony
unaccustomed
understanding
United States

ST /st/ Medial—five syllables

constituency
investigative
postmeridian
predestination
unquestionable

ST /st/ Final—one syllable

baste
beast
best
blast
blest
boast
boost
bussed
bust
cast
chest
coast
cost
crest
crossed
crust
dressed
dust
east
faced
fast
feast
fist
frost
fussed
ghost
guest
gust
haste
hoist
host
iced
jest
just
last
least
lest
list
lost
mast
messed
midst
missed
mist
moist
most
must
nest
passed
past
paste
pest
placed
post
pressed
priest
quest
raced
rest
roast
roost
rust
taste

test
thrust
toast
twist
vast
versed
vest
voiced
waist
waste
west
wist
wrest
wrist
yeast
zest
____
____

ST /st/ Final—two syllables

abreast
adjust
against
almost
amidst
arrest
artist
assist
August
Baptist
bed rest
biggest
breakfast
broadcast
chemist
choicest
combust
compost
conquest
consist
contest
contrast
cutest
cyclist
deepest
defrost
dentist
detest
digest
driest
druggist
earnest
eldest
embossed
enlist
ernest
exhaust
exist
Far East
farthest
flautist
florist
forecast
forest
French toast
furthest
gatepost
greatest
gymnast
half-mast
harvest
honest
inquest
insist
invest
Key West
largest
locust
longest
loosest
loudest
low-cost
lyrist
Midwest
milepost
modest
nearest
neatest
newest
newscast
nicest
Northeast
Northwest
oldest
outpost
poorest
post-test
pre-test
pronounced
protest
request
resist
richest
ripest
robust
safest
sandblast
sand-cast
sawdust
sheerest
shrillest
signpost
sleekest

slickest
slowest
slyest
smallest
smartest
smoothest
Southeast
Southwest
steadfast
strongest
stylist
subsist
suggest
tempest
thinnest
toothpaste
tourist
trimmest
truest
typist
unjust
unrest
upmost
utmost
widest
youngest
____
____
____
____

ST /st/ Final—three syllables

activist
amethyst
analyst
atheist
bassoonist
classicist
daintiest
dramatist
fuzziest
happiest
hornet's nest
hungriest
idealist
immodest
interest
journalist
kindliest
littlest
loveliest
luckiest
Middle East
monarchist
narrowest
naughtiest
novelist
optimist
organist
overcast
parcel post
pessimist
pharmacist
physicist
pianist
prettiest
quietist
rebroadcast
roomiest
satirist
scientist
silliest
skinniest
smelliest
soggiest
soloist
specialist
stockiest
theorist
therapist
thriftiest
tidiest
trombonist
unbalanced
unnoticed
uppermost
vocalist
wealthiest
____
____
____
____

ST /st/ Final—four syllables

antagonist
apologist
autonomist
biologist
economist
enthusiast
geologist
iconoclast
naturalist
nonconformist
orthodontist
otologist
pathologist
philanthropist
psychiatrist

psychologist
rhinologist
unhappiest
urologist
ventriloquist
violinist
____
____
____

ST /st/ Final—five syllables

audiologist
audiometrist
cardiologist
entomologist
etymologist
ophthalmologist
ornithologist
____
____

TR /tr/ Initial—one syllable

trace
traced
track
tracked
tract
trade
trades
trail
trailed
trails
train
trained
trait
tram
tramp
tramped
trance
trap
trapped
trash
trawl
tray
tread
treat
treats
tree
trek
trench
trend
Trent
tress
tribe
trice
trick
tried
tries
trill
trim
trimmed
trip
tripe
tripped
Trish
trite
trod
troll
troop
troops
trot
troth
trough
trounce
trout
trow
Troy
truce
truck
trucked
trudge
true
trump
trumped
trunk
trunks
truss
trust
truth
truths
try
____
____
____

TR /tr/ Initial—two syllables

tracing
tracker
tracking
trackless
track meet
traction
tractor
Tracy
trademark

trade name
tradesman
trade wind
trading
traduce
traffic
tragic
trailer
trainee
trainer
training
trainman
traitor
tramcar
tramline
trammel
tramper
trample
trampler
trampling
tramway
tranquil
transact
transcend
transcribe
transcript
transept
transfer
transfix
transform
transfuse
transgress
transient
transit
translate
transmit
transmute
transom
transpire
transplant
transport
transpose
transverse
trapdoor
trapeze
trapper
trapping
trappings
trash can
travel
traveled
traverse
trawler
treadle
treadmill
treason
treasure
treating
treatment
treaty
treble
tree house
trekking
trellis
tremble
trembling
tremor
trenchant
trencher
Trenton
trespass
trestle
triad
trial
tribal
tribesman
tribesmen
tribune
tribute
trickle
trickster
tricky
trident
trifle
trifler
trifling
trigger
trillion
trimmer
trimming
trimmings
trinket
trio
triple
triplet
triplex
tripod
tripping
triumph
trivet
trodden
Trojan
trolley
trombone
trooper
troopship
trophy
tropic
trotter
trotting
trouble
troubled
troubling
troublous
trouncing
trousers
trousseau

trowel
truant
trucking
truckle
truckled
truck route
truck stop
Trudy
truffle
truly
Truman
trumpet
trundle
trustee
trustees
trustful
trusting
trusty
truthful
trying
tryout
____
____
____

TR /tr/ Initial—three syllables

traceable
trachea
trackable
tractable
trade union
trading post
tradition
traducement
traducer
tragedy
tragical
trailblazer
trailer camp
trailer court
trailer park
train station
trainable
training aid
training school
traitorous
trammeling
trampoline
tranquilest
tranquilize
transaction
transcendent
transcribing
transcription
transference
transferring
transfigured
transformer
transfusion
transgression
transgressor
transition
transitive
translation
translator
translucent
transmission
transmitter
transonic
transparent
transpolar
trapezoid
traveler
treacherous
treasure chest
treasure house
treasure hunt
treasure map
treasurer
treasury
tremendous
tremulous
trespassing
triangle
triathlon
tribunal
trickery
tricolor
tricycle
trilogy
Trinidad
trinity
triplicate
triumphal
triumphant
trivial
tropical
troubadour
troublesome
truculence
truculent
truism
trumpery
trumpeter
trundle bed
trustworthy
truthfulness
____
____
____
____
____
____

TR /tr/ Initial—four syllables

tracking station
traditional
tragedian
tragedienne
tragically
trajectory
tranquility
tranquilizer
trans-Andean
transatlantic
transcendental
transferable
transferential
transforamtion
transitional
transitory
transmigration
transmutation
transparency
transplantation
transportation
treasonable
trepidation
triangular
tribulation
tributary
triennial
triplicating
triumphal arch
____

TR /tr/ Initial—five syllables

tracheotomy
traditionally
transcendentalist
transcontinental
transfiguration
triangulation
trigonometry
triviality
____

TR /tr/ Medial—two syllables

actress
attract
betray
central
citrus
contract
control
country
detract
detrain
Detroit
doctrine
dog track
entrance
entry
extra
extract
extreme
field trip
firetrap
fire truck
horse trail
intrigue
matrix
matron
mattress
metric
neutral
neutron
nitrate
pantry
partridge
Patrick
patrol
patrolled
patron
pine tree
portrait
portray
poultry
protract
protrude
race track
retract
retreat
retrieve
round trip
sentry
ski trail
spectrum
subtract
sultry
tantrum
tightrope
untried
untrue
untruth
waitress
____
____
____
____
____

TR /tr/ Medial—three syllables

attraction
attractive
Australia
Beatrice
Central Park
concentrate
contraction
contradict
contrary
country club
countryside
detraction
detriment
electric
electron
extremely
infantry
inside track
intricate
introduce
maple tree
matriarch
metrical
metronome
nitrogen
nutrient
nutrition
nutritious
orchestra
outrageous
patriarch
Patricia
patriot
Patriots
patrolman
penetrate
petrify
poetry
postmistress
protractor
railroad track
rainbow trout
reentry
retraction
retrenchment
retrieval
retriever
retrieving
retrograde
retrogress
retrospect
ski patrol
spectroscope
state trooper
subcontract
subtraction
subtropics
untruthful
victrola
____
____
____
____
____
____
____

TR /tr/ Medial—four syllables

catastrophe
concentration
contribution
control tower
controversy
electrical
electrician
electronics
entrepreneur
extravagance
extravagant
geometry
illustrated
introduction
matriarchy
matriculate
matrimony
metric system
metropolis
no trespassing
paratrooper
patriotic
patrolwoman
pedestrian
petrified wood
petroleum
remote control
retribution
retroactive
retroflexion
retrogression
retroversion
St. Patrick's Day
subtropical
ultrasonic
unobtrusive
ventriloquist
____
____
____
____
____

TR /tr/ Medial—five syllables

electricity
metropolitan
pediatrician
____
____
____

RT /rt/ Medial—two syllables

artful
artist
barter
Bertram
Burton
Carter
carton
cartoon
cartridge
cartwheel
certain
charter
Cortez
courthouse
courtyard
curtain
Curtis
dirty
fertile
forty
fourteen
garter
Gertrude
hearty
martin
Martin
Marty
martyr
mortal
mortar
Myrtle
partake
parted
parting
partly
partner
partridge
part-time
party
pertain
portage
Portage
porter
Porter
porthole
Portland
portrait
portray
quarter
quartet
quart jar
quarto
shortage
shortcake
short-changed
short-cut
shorten
shorthand
shorthorn
shortly
shortstop
shortwave
Shorty
smarter
smartly
sorting
sport car
sporting
sportive
sportsman
sporty
squirting
started
starter
startle
thirteen
thirteenth
thirty
tortoise
turtle
vertex
warthog
wiretap
____

RT /rt/ Medial—three syllables

advertise
Alberta
aorta
apartment
artichoke
article
artifact
artisan
assortment
bartering
cartilage
certainty

certified
certify
chartering
compartment
courtesy
departed
department
deportment
fertilize
fortieth
fortify
garter snake
Gilberta
headquarters
heartbroken
heartily
immortal
importance
important
liberty
light-hearted
particle
partition
partnership
portable
property
quarterback
report card
reporter
reporting
Roberta
Roquefort cheese
short circuit
shortening
short-handed
short-sighted
short story
soft-hearted
sportsmanlike
sportsmanship
sportswoman
sportswriter
summertime
support group
support staff
thirtieth
tortilla
turtledove
vertebra
vertebral
vertical
vertigo
____
____
____
____
____
____
____
____

RT /rt/ Medial—four syllables

advertisement
articulate
artificial
certificate
certified check
certified mail
comfortable
convertible
departable
fertility
invertebrate
Liberty Bell
participate
participle
particular
porterhouse steak
portfolio
property tax
Puerto Rico
refertilize
reportedly
self-imparting
short division
short-handedness
short-sightedness
smart-alecky
unfortified
unimportant
unsportsmanlike
well-fortified
well-supported
____
____
____
____
____

RT /rt/ Medial—five syllables

false advertising
opportunity
past participle
pertinacity
quarterly report
uncomfortable
____
____
____

RT /rt/ Final—one syllable

art
Bart
Bert
blurt
cart
carte
chart
court
Curt
dart
dirt
flirt
fort
girt
heart
hurt
Kurt
mart
part
pert
port
quart
quirt
shirt
short
skirt
smart
snort
sort
sport
spurt
squirt
start
tart
thwart
wart
____
____
____
____
____
____

RT /rt/ Final—two syllables

advert
airport
Albert
alert
apart
assert
athwart
avert
comfort
concert
convert
Delbert
depart
deport
desert
dessert
distort
divert
dress shirt
effort
Elbert
escort
evert
exert
expert
export
extort
filbert
Gilbert
go-cart
Head Start
Herbert
Hubert
impart
import
inert
insert
invert
Lambert
outsmart
oxcart
passport
pushcart
report
resort
revert
Robert
seaport
Shreveport
sportshirt
stalwart
subvert
support
sweatshirt
sweetheart
transport
transvert
T-shirt
unhurt
yogurt
____
____
____
____
____
____

RT /rt/ Final—three syllables

a la carte	introvert	shopping cart
counterpart	liverwort	tennis court
davenport	martial art	trailer court
disconcert	miniskirt	undershirt
extrovert	preconcert	________
hula skirt	retrovert	________

TW /tw/ Initial—one syllable

twang	twice	twinge
tweak	twig	twinned
tweed	twigged	twirl
tweet	twill	twist
tweeze	twilled	twitch
twelfth	twin	________
twelve	twine	________
twerp	twined	________

TW /tw/ Initial—two syllables

twangle	twilight	twirler
twangy	twin bed	twister
tweedle	twinborn	twisting
tweedy	Twin Falls	twitch grass
tweezers	twinkle	twitter
twenty	twinkling	________
twiddle	twin sheet	________

TW /tw/ Initial—three syllables

twentieth	twilight sleep	twinflower
twenty-five	twinberry	twisted pine
twenty-one	Twin Cities	________
twenty yards	twin-engine	________

TY /tj/ Medial—two syllables

courtyard	light-year	________
front yard	________	________

TY /tj/ Medial—four syllables

credit union	meticulous	________

RCHT /rtʃt/ Final—one syllable

arched
marched
parched
perched
scorched
searched
starched
____
____

RKT /rkt/ Final—one syllable

arcked
barked
irked
jerked
marked
parked
sparked
worked
____

RKT /rkt/ Final—two syllables

embarked
postmarked
remarked
uncorked
unmarked
unworked
____
____
____

LTS /lts/ Final—one syllable

belts
bolts
colts
faults
jolts
kilts
malts
melts
molts
pelts
quilts
salts
silts
stilts
tilts
vaults
welts
wilts
____
____
____

LTS /lts/ Final—two syllables

adults
consults
insults
pole vaults
revolts
seat belts
____
____
____

RST /rst/ Final—one syllables

burst
cursed
first
forced
hurst
Hurst
nursed
pierced
thirst
worst
____
____

RST /rst/ Final—two syllables

airburst
cloudburst
coerced
dispersed
divorced
endorsed
enforced
imbursed
immersed

outburst	sunburst	______
rehearsed	unversed	______
reversed	______	______

RTS /rts/ Final—one syllable

arts	hearts	sports
blurts	parts	spurts
carts	ports	squirts
charts	quarts	warts
courts	shirts	______
darts	shorts	______
flirts	skirts	______
forts	sorts	______

RTS /rts/ Final—two syllables

airports	exports	seaports
alerts	imports	supports
concerts	inserts	transports
departs	inverts	______
deserts	passports	______
desserts	reports	______
distorts	resorts	______
experts	reverts	______

STR /str/ Initial—one syllable

straight	strength	stroke
strain	stress	strokes
strained	stressed	stroll
strait	stretch	strolled
strand	stretched	strong
strange	strict	strove
strap	stride	struck
strapped	strike	strum
straw	string	strung
stray	strip	strut
strayed	stripe	______
streak	stripped	______
stream	strive	______
street	strobe	______

STR /str/ Initial—two syllables

straggle
stranger
strapping
streaking
streamer
streamline
streetcar
strengthen
stressing
stretcher
stretching
stretch-out
stretchy
stricken
strident
strike out
strike zone
string beans
stringent
stringing
stringy
stripping
striving
strobe lamp
stroller
strolling
strongbox
stronghold
strongly
structure
strudel
struggle
strumming
strutting
strychnine

STR /str/ Initial—three syllables

straightforward
strait jacket
strategy
stratosphere
strawberry
strenuous
string quartet
stroboscope
structural

STR /str/ Initial—four syllables

streptococcus
streptomycin
stringed instruments

STR /str/ Medial—two syllables

abstract
airstrip
astray
astride
backstroke
bloodstream
bowstring
breaststroke
constrict
construct
destroy
distract
distress
downstream
frustrate
gold stream
high-strung
instruct
minstrel
mistreat
mistress
monstrous
nostril
obstruct
ostrich
pastry
restrain
restrict
rostrum
seamstress
shoestring
side street
sidestroke
upstream
vestry

STR /str/ Medial—three syllables

Astrodome
astronaut
Australia
Austria
chemistry
comic strip
construction
demonstrate
destroyer
destruction
destructive
distraction
distribute
doll stroller
Gaza Strip
illustrate
industry
instruction
instructor
instrument
orchestra
reconstruct
restraining
restricting
restriction
Sunset Strip
tapestry
____
____
____

STR /str/ Medial—four syllables

apostrophe
astrology
astronomer
astronomy
baby stroller
band instruments
candy striper
catastrophe
catastrophic
demonstration
distribution
illustration
industrial
industrious
instrumental
orchestra pit
pedestrian
reconstruction
string orchestra
____
____

STR /str/ Medial—five syllables

administration
astronomical
boa constrictor
instrumentalist
____
____

STS /sts/ Final—one syllable

beasts
blasts
boasts
casts
dusts
feasts
fists
frosts
ghosts
guests
gusts
hoists
hosts
lasts
lists
mists
nests
pastes
pests
posts
priests
quests
rests
roasts
roosts
tastes
tests
thrusts
toasts
twists
vests
wastes
wrists
yeasts
____
____
____
____
____

STS /sts/ Final—two syllables

adjusts
arrests
artists
assists
Baptists
broadcasts
chemists
conquests
consists
contests
contrasts
defrosts
dentists
detests
digests
druggists
enlists
exhausts
exists
florists
forecasts
forests
gate posts
harvests
insists
invests
locusts
mainmasts
Marxists
miscasts
newscasts
outposts
post-tests
pre-tests
protests
requests
resists
sandblasts
sand casts
stylists
toothpastes
tourists
typists
____
____
____
____
____

TER /tɚ/ Medial—three syllables

aftermath
afterward
alternate
artery
attorney
buttercup
butterfly
butterscotch
counterfeit
determine
enterprise
entertain
eternal
external
factory
interact
interblend
intercede
intercept
intercom
interest
interfere
interpret
intersect
interval
interview
lateral
lettergram
letterhead
lettering
loitering
lottery
motorboat
motorhome
nectarine
outer space
pottery
quarterback
quarterly
shutterbug
smattering
splintery
utterance
utterly
uttermost
veteran
water bed
waterbird
water bug
watercress
waterfall
waterfowl
waterfront
water hole
waterline
waterlogged
watermark
water plant
waterproof
water rat

watertight
waterway
waterwheel
waterworks
yesterday
____
____
____
____

TER /tɚ/ Medial—four syllables

alternative
directory
eternity
externalize
illiterate
interesting
intermission
intersection
literature
motorcycle
predetermine
quartermaster
quartersection
watercolor
watering place
water lily
watermelon
water polo
water skiing
____
____

TER /tɚ/ Medial—five syllables

disinterested
distributorship
intermediate
international
literarily
uninterrupted
unutterable
veterinary
water buffalo
____
____
____

TER /tɚ/ Final—two syllables

batter
beater
better
bitter
bloater
blotter
brighter
butter
canter
chatter
cheater
clatter
clutter
crater
critter
cutter
daughter
eater
fatter
fighter
flatter
floater
flutter
freighter
fritter
glitter
grater
greater
gutter
heater
hitter
hotter
later
latter
letter
lighter
liter
litter
loiter
matter
meter
motor
mutter
neater
otter
patter
pewter
platter
plotter
potter
putter
quitter
quoter
rotor
scatter
setter
shatter

shutter
sitter
skater
slaughter
smatter
spatter
splatter
spotter
sputter
squatter
stutter
sweater
tighter
traitor
tutor
twitter
utter
voter
waiter
water
whiter
writer

TER /tɚ/ Final—three syllables

anteater
auditor
beanshooter
chain letter
computer
creator
dictator
editor
equator
fire fighter
gas meter
globe trotter
high water
janitor
Jupiter
locater
monitor
narrator
newsletter
predator
promoter
saltwater
Senator
shot-putter
spectator
stonecutter
storm center
theater
tidewater
transistor
translator
typesetter
typewriter
visitor
wood cutter

TER /tɚ/ Final—four syllables

agitator
alligator
alma mater
altimeter
aviator
calculator
centimeter
commentator
competitor
cultivator
decorator
demonstrator
diameter
duplicator
educator
elevator
escalator
excavator
generator
incubator
kilometer
legislator
liberator
moderator
navigator
nominator
numerator
operator
parking meter
peanut butter
percolator
perimeter
radiator
thermometer

TER /tɚ/ Final—five syllables

accelerator
amphitheater
anemometer
denominator

STER /stɚ/ Medial—three syllables

asterisk
castor oil
history
mastering
masterpiece
mastery
oyster crab
westerly
yesterday

STER /stɚ/ Medial—four syllables

master-at-arms
masterfully
prehistory
preposterous
sister-in-law
southeasterly
upholstery

STER /stɚ/ Final—two syllables

aster
blister
booster
Buster
caster
Chester
cluster
coaster
Custer
duster
Easter
faster
fluster
foster
Foster
hamster
holster
lobster
luster
master
mister
monster
muster
oyster
pastor
pester
plaster
poster
roadster
roaster
rooster
roster
sister
spinster
tester
thruster
toaster
twister
Webster
youngster

STER /stɚ/ Final—three syllables

adjuster
ancestor
bandmaster
canister
disaster
forecaster
gangbuster
Grand Master
half-sister
minister
postmaster
register

resister	Sylvester	________
scoutmaster	taskmaster	________
semester	toastmaster	________
shipmaster	upholster	________
sinister	Worcester	________

STER /stɚ/ Final—four syllables

administer	prime minister	________
flabbergaster	quartermaster	________
Gila monster	roller coaster	________

TH

Pronounced: /ð/
Spelled: th, the

TH /ð/ Initial—one syllable

than	thence	thine
that	there	this
that's	there's	those
the	these	thou
thee	they	though
their	they'd	thus
their's	they'll	thy
them	they're	________
then	they've	________

TH /ð/ Initial—two syllables

The Hague	therein	thusly
themselves	thereof	thyself
thenceforth	thereon	________
thereby	thereto	________
therefore	therewith	________

TH /ð/ Initial—three syllables

that-away	thereafter	thereupon
thereabout	thereunder	________

TH /ð/ Medial—two syllables

although	clothing	heather
bather	dither	Heather
bathing	either	lather
bother	father	leather
breather	fathom	loathful
breathing	feather	loathing
brethren	gather	loathsome
brother	heathen	mother

neither
other
others
rather
rhythm
rhythmic
rhythms
seething
slither
smither
smoother
smoothest
smoothly
smoothness
smother
soothing
southern
teething
tether
thither
tithing
unscathed
weather
weathered
whether
whither
withdraw
withdrawn
withdrew
wither
withstand
worthy
zither
____
____
____

TH /ð/ Medial—three syllables

another
bathing cap
bathing suit
bellwether
bothersome
brotherhood
brotherly
fairweather
fatherhood
fatherland
fatherly
Father's Day
Father Time
featherbed
featherbone
featherbrain
featherhead
featherstitch
featherveined
featherweight
feathery
fine weather
gathering
godfather
godmother
grandfather
grandmother
half brother
hitherto
housemother
ingather
leathercraft
leatherette
leatherneck
leather work
motherhood
motherland
motherless
motherly
Mother's Day
Netherlands
nonetheless
otherwise
pinfeather
rhythm band
smithereens
southerly
southerner
southernmost
stepbrother
stepfather
stepmother
sunbathing
Sutherland
tetherball
together
unfathomed
ungathered
weatherboard
weather-bound
weathercock
Weatherford
weatherglass
weatherman
weather map
weatherproof
weatherstrip
weather-wise
weatherworn
____
____
____
____
____
____

TH /ð/ Medial—four syllables

altogether
brother-in-law
chicken feathers
eagle feather
father-in-law
Father's Day card
ingathering
leather jacket
leather worker
mother-in-law
Mother's Day card
Netherlander
outer clothing
patent leather
shaving lather
stormy weather
togetherness
weatherbeaten
weather radar
weather report
weather signal
weather station
weather woman
____

TH /ð/ Final—one syllable

bathe
blithe
breathe
clothe
lathe
loathe
scathe
scythe
seethe
sheathe
smooth
soothe
swathe
teethe
tithe
wreathe
writhe
____

TH /ð/ Final—two syllables

enwreathe
sun bathe
unclothe
unsheathe
unswathe
____

THD /ðd/ Final—one syllable

bathed
breathed
clothed
loathed
scathed
seethed
sheathed
smoothed
soothed
swathed
teethed
tithed
writhed
____
____

RTH /rð/ Medial—two syllables

farther
farthest
farthing
further
norther
northern
swarthy
worthy
____

RTH /rð/ Medial—three syllables

airworthy
blameworthy
farthermost
furthermore
northerly
Northern Cross
northern lights
Northerner
northernmost
noteworthy
seaworthy
swarthier

thankworthy	worthiest	
trustworthy	worthily	
unworthy	worthiness	
worthier	Worthington	

RTH /rð/ Medial—four syllables

nevertheless		
unseaworthy		
unworthiness		

THZ /ðz/ Final—one syllable

bathes	smoothes	wreathes
breathes	soothes	writhes
loathes	teethes	
seethes	tithes	

TH

Pronounced: /θ/
Spelled: th

TH /θ/ Initial—one syllable

Thad
thane
thank
thanked
thanks
thatch
thatched
thaw
thawed
Thebes
theft
theme
thick
Thier
thigh
thin
thing
things
think
thinned
third
thirst
thong
thongs
Thor
thorn
thorned
thorns
Thorpe
thought
thoughts
thud
thug
thumb
thumbs
thump
thumped
____
____

TH /θ/ Initial—two syllables

thankful
thankless
thank-you
Thatcher
Thea
Theda
Thelma
theme song
thermal
thesis
theta
thicken
thicket
thickness
thickset
thick-skinned
thighbone
thimble
thinker
thinking
thinner
thinnest
thinning
thin-skinned
third base
third class
Third World
thirteen
thirty
thistle
thither
thorax
Thoreau
Thornton
thorny
thorough
thoughtful
thoughtless
thought-out
thousand
thumbnail
thumbscrew
thumbtack
thumping
thunder

thundered
Thursday
Thurston
thymus
thyroid
______
______
______
______

TH /θ/ Initial—three syllables

Thackeray
thankfulness
thanksgiver
thanksgiving
thank-you card
thank-you note
theater
theistic
thematic
Theodore
theorem
theorize
theory
therapist
therapy
thermostat
thesaurus
Thespian
thickener
thickening
thimbleful
thinkable
thinking cap
third baseman
third party
thirty-eight
thirty-five
thirty-four
thirty-nine
thirty-one
thirty-seven
thirty-six
thirty-three
thirty-two
thistledown
thoroughbred
thoroughfare
thoroughly
thoroughness
Thousand Oaks
thunderbird
thunderbolt
thunderclap
thundercloud
thunderhead
thundering
thunderous
thunderstorm
thunderstruck
thundery
Thuringer
______
______
______

TH /θ/ Initial—four syllables

Thanksgiving Day
theatrical
Theodora
theology
theoretic
therapeutic
thermometer
thermostatic
threateningly
thundershower
______
______

TH /θ/ Initial—five syllables

theologian
theosophical
thermodynamic
______
______
______

TH /θ/ Medial—two syllables

Athens
athlete
author
Bethel
bathhouse
bathmat
bath oil
bath salts
bathtub
Bathurst
Bethune
breathless

buckthorn
Cathay
diphthong
Ethan
Ethel
ether
ethics
ethnic
ethos
ethyl
faithful
fifth grade
frothy
Gothic
Hawthorne
Kathleen
Kathy
lethal
Luther
Mathis
Matthew
methane
method
methyl
misthink
mothball
mothy
mouthful
mouth guard
mouthless
mouthpiece
mouthwash
naphtha
Nathan
nothing
outthink
pathway
pithy
playthings
python
rethink
Reuther
rosethorns
Rothchild
Ruth Ann
ruthful
Ruthie
ruthless
sixth grade
Smithfield
something
South Bend
South Bridge
Southdown
southeast
southland
southpaw
Southport
South Seas
southward
southwest
toothache
toothbrush
toothful
toothless
toothpaste
toothpick
toothsome
truthful
truthless
withdraw
withdrew
withheld
withhold
within
without
withstand
youthful
zither
____
____
____
____
____
____
____
____

TH /θ/ Medial—three syllables

aesthetic
Agatha
amethyst
anything
apathy
atheist
Athena
athletic
authentic
authorize
authorized
authorship
batholith
bath towel
bath water
bathyscaphe
bathysphere
Bethany
Bethesda
Bethlehem
biathlon
breath-taking
cathedral
coauthor

decathlon
Dorothy
empathy
ethical
everything
faithfully
faithfulness
faithlessness
Hathaway
Ithaca
Jonathan
Katherine
Klamath Falls
lethargic
lethargy
lithograph
Lutheran
Mammoth Cave
marathon
math homework
methodic
Methodist
methylene
moth-eaten
mythical
Nathaniel
nothingness
Othello
paint thinner
pathetic
pathfinder
pentathlon
prosthesis
Rathskeller
ruthlessly
ruthlessness
sagathy
southeaster
southeastward
stethoscope
sympathize
sympathized
sympathy
thirty-third
Timothy
tooth decay
tooth fairy
tooth powder
triathlon
two-thirty
wherewithal
youth football
youthfully
youthfulness
youth hockey
youth hostel
youth soccer
____
____
____
____
____
____
____
____
____

TH /θ/ Medial—four syllables

anathema
anesthetic
anesthetist
antipathy
apathetic
arithmetic
atheism
athletic club
authority
bathometer
bathymetry
calisthenics
Catholic Church
diathermy
Dorothea
ethereal
ethnology
group therapy
hypothesis
hypothesize
hypothetic
isothermal
lithographer
lithographic
mathematics
mythologist
mythology
pathologist
pathology
play therapy
South Africa
South China Sea
South Dakota
South Korea
South Pacific
South Vietnam
sympathetic
sympathizer
sympathizing
sympathy card
____
____
____
____
____

TH /θ/ Medial—five syllables

amphitheater	Elizabethan	South America
anesthesia	Ethiopia	South Carolina
authenticity	hydrotherapy	________________
Catholicism	psychotherapy	________________

TH /θ/ Final—one syllable

bath	heath	sloth
Beth	Keith	smith
Blythe	kith	Smith
booth	lath	south
both	length	swath
breath	math	teeth
broth	moth	tooth
cloth	mouth	troth
couth	myth	truth
death	oath	warmth
depth	path	with
doth	pith	wrath
drouth	quoth	wreath
faith	Roth	youth
Faith	Ruth	________________
froth	Seth	________________
growth	sheath	________________
hath	sleuth	________________

TH /θ/ Final—two syllables

Ardith	Dartmouth	forthwith
Babe Ruth	Deep South	goldsmith
bear with	dishcloth	Griffith
beneath	dog tooth	half-truth
bequeath	Duluth	headcloth
betroth	dustcloth	hot bath
bike path	Edith	ingrowth
birdbath	eyetooth	Judith
blacksmith	flight path	Kenneth
broadcloth	floorcloth	locksmith
by-path	forsooth	Macbeth
cheesecloth	Fort Smith	mammoth

oilcloth
outgrowth
phone booth
Plymouth
Portsmouth
Sabbath
sailcloth
sand cloth
steam bath
sun bath
sweet tooth
tollbooth
uncouth
untruth
upgrowth
zenith

TH /θ/ Final—three syllables

aftermath
arrowsmith
baby's-breath
baby teeth
baby tooth
bridal path
bubble bath
chicken broth
coppersmith
cottonmouth
eightieth
fiftieth
flannelmouth
fortieth
ironsmith
Meredith
monolith
Nazareth
neolith
ninetieth
overgrowth
silversmith
sixtieth
tablecloth
thirtieth
tigermoth
Turkish bath
twentieth
undergrowth
underneath
voting booth
whirlpool bath
wisdom teeth
wisdom tooth

TH /θ/ Final—four syllables

Elizabeth
seventieth
telephone booth

DTH /dθ/ Final—one syllable

breadth
width

DTH /dθ/ Final—two syllables

bandwidth
hairbreadth
hundredth
thousandth

DTH /dθ/ Final—three syllables

one hundredth
two thousandth

LTH /lθ/ Medial—two syllables

filthy	stealthy	________
healthful	Waltham	________
healthy	wealthy	________

LTH /lθ/ Medial—three syllables

filthiest	unhealthy	________
stealthiness	wealthier	________
unhealthful	wealthiest	________

LTH /lθ/ Final—one syllable

filth	stealth	wealth
health	tilth	________

NTH /nθ/ Medial—two syllables

anthem	enthused	panther
anther	menthol	unthink
enthuse	monthly	________

NTH /nθ/ Medial—three syllables

Anthony	synthesize	unthoughtful
Cynthia	synthetic	________
Samantha	unthankful	________
synthesis	unthinking	________

NTH /nθ/ Medial—four syllables

anthology	enthusiast	pyracantha
Corinthian	mentholated	________
Corinthians	parenthesis	________

NTH /nθ/ Final—one syllable

month	plinth	________
ninth	tenth	________

NTH /nθ/ Final—two syllables

billionth	fifteenth	seventh
Corinth	fourteenth	sixteenth
dozenth	millionth	thirteenth
eighteenth	nineteenth	________

NTH /nθ/ Final—three syllables

amaranth
eleventh
hyacinth
labyrinth
seventeenth

NGTH /ŋθ/ Medial—two syllables

lengthen
lengthways
lengthwise
lengthy
strengthen

NGTH /ŋθ/ Final—one syllable

length
strength

NGTH /ŋθ/ Final—two syllables

full-length
half-length
wave-length
whole-length

THR /θr/ Initial—one syllable

thrall
thrash
thread
threads
threat
three
thresh
threw
thrice
thrift
thrill
thrilled
thrills
thrive
thrived
throat
throb
throbbed
throne
throned
throng
through
throve
throw
thrown
thrum
thrummed
thrush
thrust

THR /θr/ Initial—two syllables

thralldom
thrasher
thrashing
threadbare
threaded
threader
threading
threadlike
thread mark
thready
threaten
threefold
threepence
three-ply
threescore
threesome
threesquare
thresher
threshold
thriftless
thrift shop
thrift store
thrifty
thriller
thrilling
thriver
thriving
throaty
throbbing
thrombus

throttle
throttling
throughout
through street
throwback
thrower
throw in
throwing
throw rug
thrumming
thrusting
thruway

THR /θr/ Initial—three syllables

threatening
three-bagger
three-base hit
three-decker
three-quarters
three-wheeler
thresher shark
thriftier
thriftiest
thriftily
throatier
throatiest
thrombosis
throwaway

THR /θr/ Initial—four syllables

threateningly
three-legged race
three-ring circus
threshing machine
throat microphone

THR /θr/ Medial—two syllables

anthrax
bathrobe
bathroom
cutthroat
drive-through
enthrall
enthrone
free throw
Guthrie
heartthrob
Jethro
look-through
outthrew
outthrow
spendthrift
unthread
unthrone
walk-through
Winthrop
wood thrush

THR /θr/ Medial—three syllables

anthracite
anthropoid
arthritic
arthritis
brown thrasher
flamethrower
follow-through
hermit thrush
overthrow
Plymouth Rock
unthreaded

THR /θr/ Medial—four syllables

erythrocyte
javelin throw
misanthropic
philanthropist

RTH /rθ/ Medial—two syllables

Arthur	earthquake	North Shore
Bertha	earthward	North Slope
birthday	earthworm	North Star
birthmark	earthy	northward
birthplace	forethought	northwest
birthrate	forthright	Swarthmore
birthright	forthwith	Swarthout
Carthage	fourth grade	unearthed
Eartha	hearthstone	worthless
earthborn	Martha	worthwhile
earthbound	Northcutt	________
earthen	northeast	________
earthling	northland	________
earthly	North Pole	________
earthnut	Northport	________

RTH /rθ/ Medial—three syllables

afterthought	MacArthur	overthrow
arthritic	northeastern	Parthenon
arthritis	northeastward	Port Arthur
birthday card	Northampton	unearthing
earthenware	northwestern	unearthly
earth science	Northwestern	________
earthshaking	orthodox	________
forthcoming	orthoscope	________

RTH /rθ/ Medial—four syllables

birthday party	North Dakota	orthopedic
earth satellite	orthodontics	orthopedics
Happy Birthday	orthodontist	unearthliness
Martha's Vineyard	orthogenic	________
merthiolate	orthographic	________
North Africa	orthography	________

RTH /rθ/ Medial—five syllables

North America	orthochromatic	orthogenetic
North American	orthodontia	orthographical
North Carolina	orthogenesis	________

RTH /rθ/ Final—one syllable

berth	fourth	worth
birth	girth	________________
dearth	hearth	________________
earth	mirth	________________
firth	north	________________
forth	swarth	________________

RTH /rθ/ Final—two syllables

childbirth	rebirth	________________
Ellsworth	thenceforth	________________
Emsworth	unearth	________________
Fort Worth	Wadsworth	________________
henceforth	Wentworth	________________
Kenworth	Woolworth	________________

V

Pronounced: /v/
Spelled: v, vv, f, ph

V /v/ Initial—one syllable

vague
Vail
vain
Val
vale
valve
vamp
van
Van
Vance
vane
vase
vast
vat
Vaughn
vault
veal
veer
veil
vein
vend
vent
verb
verge
Vern
verse
versed
verve
vest
vet
vex
Vi
Vic
vice
vie
vile
vim
Vince
vine
vise
vogue
voice
voiced
void
voile
volt
vote
vouch
vow
vowed
____
____
____
____

V /v/ Initial—two syllables

vacant
vacate
vaccine
vacuum
vagrant
vagus
valance
valet
valiant
valid
valise
valley
valor
value
valued
vamoose
vampire
Vanda
Van Dyke
Van Gogh
vanguard
vanish
van line
vanquish
vapor
varied
varmint
varnish
vary
vassal

vaudeville
Veda
Velma
velour
velum
velvet
vendor
vendue
veneer
vengeance
Venice
venom
venous
ventage
venture
venue
Venus
Vera
verbal
verbose
verdant
Verde
Verdi
verdict
Verlene
vermeil
vermin
Vermont
Vernon
version
versus
vessel
Vesta
vestal
vestige
vestry
veto
via
vial
viand
vibrate
vicar
Vichy
vicious
Vicky
victim
Victor
Vida
vigil
vigor
Viking
villa
village
villain
Vincent
vineyard
vintage
viper
Virgil
Virgo
virtue
virus
visa
visage
vision
visit
visor
vista
vital
viva
vivid
vocal
voiceless
volley
volume
vortex
voucher
vowel
voyage
Vulgate
vulture
vying

V /v/ Initial—three syllables

vacancy
vacation
vaccinate
vacillate
vagabond
vagrancy
Valeda
valentine
Valerie
validate
Valley Forge
valueless
valuer
Van Buren
Vancouver
vanilla
vanity
vaporize
variance
variant
varicose
various
varsity
vascular
Vatican
vegetate
vehement

vehicle
velation
vendetta
venerate
venetian
venison
venomous
ventilate
ventricle
veracious
Vera Cruz
veranda
verbatim
verbiage
verify
verity
Vero Beach
Verona
versatile
versify
vertebra
vertebrate
vertical
vertigo
vesical
vestryman
veteran
viaduct
vibration
vicarage
vice versa
vichyssoise
victory
video
Vienna
Vietnam
vigilant
vilify
villager
vindicate
vindictive
vinegar
viola
Viola
violate
violent
violet
Violet
violin
Virginia
virulent
viscera
visible
visited
visiting
visitor
visual
vitally
vitamin
vivacious
Vivian
vocalize
vocation
volatile
volcanic
volcano
volition
volleyball
voluble
volunteer
voyager
Voyager
vulcanize
____
____
____
____
____

V /v/ Initial—four syllables

vaccination
vacillating
vacuity
Valencia
Valentine's Day
validity
valuable
vaporizer
Varanasi
variable
variation
variegated
variety
vasomotor
vegetable
vegetation
vehemently
velocity
venerable
ventilation
veracity
verbalizing
veritable
vermiculate
vernacular
Veronica
Vesuvius
vicarious
vice-president
vicinity
vicissitude
Victoria
Victorian

victorious
video game
video tape
Vietnamese
vindictively
violinist
virologist
virtuoso
viscosity
visionary
visitation
voluminous
voluntary
vulnerable
____

V /v/ Initial—five syllables

vaporization
vasodilator
vegetarian
verification
verisimilar
veterinary
vicariously
video cassette
vindicatory
visceromotor
vital statistics
vitrification
vocabulary
vocationally
vociferously
volatility
____
____

V /v/ Initial—six syllables

valedictorian
variability
vasodilatation
veterinarian
video recorder
vulnerability
____
____
____

V /v/ Medial—two syllables

advance
advent
adverb
adverse
advice
advise
advised
anvil
Ava
avail
avenge
averse
avert
avid
avoid
avow
beaver
bevel
bevy
bivalve
bovine
bravo
canvas
cavern
cavort
Chavez
chevron
Chevy
civet
civic
civil
cleaver
Cleveland
clever
cloven
clover
Clovis
convent
converge
converse
convert
convex
convey
convict
convince
convoy
convulse
cover
covered
covet
covey
cravat
craven
crevice
David
Davis
Davy

Denver
device
devil
devise
devoid
devolve
devote
devour
devout
diva
divan
diver
diverge
divert
divide
divine
divorce
divot
dovecote
dovetail
drive-in
drivel
driver
driveway
eavesdrop
envied
envoy
envy
Eva
evade
even
evening
event
ever
every
evict
evil
evoke
evolve

favor
fever
flavor
gavel
given
giver
giving
govern
grapevine
gravel
gravy
Grover
haven
haven't
having
havoc
heaven
heavy
Hoover
hovel
hover
invent
inverse
invert
invest
invite
invoice
invoke
involve
Ivan
ivy
java
Java
Kiva
lava
lavish
leaving
level
lever

Levi
levy
lively
liver
livid
living
louver
lover
loving
movement
mover
movers
moving
naval
navy
never
novel
novice
oval
over
pivot
prevail
prevent
private
proverb
provide
provoke
quaver
quiver
ravel
raven
ravine
reveal
revenge
reverse
revert
revise
revive
revolt

revolve
rival
river
rivet
rover
Rover
savage
saver
saving
savvy
seven
seventh
sever
severe
shaving
shiver
shrivel
sliver
Stephen
Stevie
swivel
travel
waiver
waver
weaver
weaving
weever
weevil
woven
____
____
____
____

V /v/ Medial—three syllables

aboveboard
advantage
adventure
advertise
advisement
adviser
advocate
aggravate
all over
au revoir
avalanche
avarice
avenue
average
aversion
bedcover
bedevil
bereavement
beverage
Beverly
boulevard
bravado
bravery
brevity
caravan
carnival
carnivore
cavalcade
cavalier
cavalry
caviar
cavity
Cherryvale
Cherryville
chivalry
circumvent
civilian
civilize
clairvoyance
clavicle
connivance
convention
convergence
convergent
conversion
conveyance
conveyer
convolute
convulsion
convulsive
covenant
coverage
covering
covetous
crossover
daredevil
davenport
deliver
depriving
devastate
develop
deviate
deviled eggs
devilfish
devilish
devilment
devious
devotion
disavow
discover
disfavor
divergent
diversion
dividend
division
divisor
driveable
elevate

eleventh
endeavor
enliven
envelope
environ
envision
evangel
evasion
Evelyn
everglade
everyday
everyone
everything
everywhere
evident
excavate
favoring
favorite
favorless
Fayetteville
feverish
fevery
flavedo
flavorful
flavoring
flavorous
flavorsome
flavory
forever
forgiven
frivolous
Geneva
Genevieve
governance
governess
government
governor
hay fever
high-level

Hoover Dam
hovering
however
Hudsonville
improvement
improver
improving
improvise
improvised
innovate
intervene
introvert
invalid
inveigle
invention
inventive
inventor
invested
investment
ivory
Ivy League
ivy vine
Jacksonville
javelin
jovial
lavender
lavishly
layover
leftover
leftovers
leverage
levitate
lime flavor
livable
liverwurst
lovable
maneuver
maverick
medieval

misgiving
moreover
movable
navigate
nevermore
Nile River
novelty
November
obvious
Oliver
olivine
ovation
oven door
ovenware
overact
overalls
overawe
overblown
overboard
overcall
overcame
overcast
overcoat
overdo
overdone
overdoor
overdue
overflow
overgrow
overhand
overhaul
overhear
overheard
overjoy
overjoyed
overlap
overlay
overlook
overnight

overpass
override
overrun
overseas
oversee
oversight
overtake
overtime
overture
overweight
overwhelm
overwork
overwrite
palaver
Passover
pavilion
Peace River
persevere
pet haven
popover
poverty
prevalence
prevention
previous
privacy
privation
privilege
provender
providence
provider
providing
Provincetown
provincial
proving ground
provision
provoking
quavering
quivering
ravenous
receiver
recover
Red River
rendezvous
renovate
retriever
revenue
reverence
reverent
reverie
reversal
revision
revulsion
Rhine River
Rhone River
rivalry
rivulet
Roosevelt
saliva
Salt River
samovar
savings bond
savory
scavenger
screwdriver
seventy
several
skin diver
skin diving
souvenir
sovereign
soviet
Soviet
spring fever
stopover
subdivide
subversive
Sunnyvale
Thanksgiving
traveler
travelogue
travertine
trivial
truck driver
turnover
uncover
universe
Vancouver
vivacious
vividly
vividness
whatever
whenever
wherever
whichever
whoever
whomever
whyever
____
____

V /v/ Medial—four syllables

abbreviate
activator
advantageous
adversary
adversity
advertisement
advertising
advisable
alleviate
ambivalence
ambivalent
available

aviary
aviation
avionics
avocado
avocation
avoirdupois
Bavaria
Bavarian
beverages
Beverly Hills
Bolivia
Bolivian
captivity
carnivorous
charivari
controversial
controversy
conventional
conversation
convertible
convivial
convocation
covered wagon
cultivation
cultivator
delivery
derivation
derivative
devaluate
development
deviation
devitalize
disadvantage
discovery
diversify
diversity
divinity
divisible
driving safety
elevation
enviable
environment
equivalent
equivocate
evacuate
evaluate
evangelic
evangelist
evaporate
eventual
everlasting
everybody
evidently
evolution
favorable
impoverish
inadvertent
innovation
interwoven
intravenous
inventory
invertebrate
investigate
invidious
invigorate
invincible
invisible
invitation
irreverence
jovially
longevity
mint flavoring
misadventure
nativity
nevertheless
oblivion
Olivia
orange flavor
overbearing
overpower
poison ivy
positively
prevaricate
receivership
recovery
redeliver
renovation
revelation
reversible
revolution
scuba diver
scuba diving
severity
sovereignty
taxi driver
television
unavailing
universal
unsavory
vivisection
whatsoever
whensoever
Yukon River
____
____
____
____
____
____
____
____
____
____
____
____
____
____

V /v/ Medial—five syllables

anniversary	inevitably	revolutionize
apple turnover	invariable	Soviet Russia
benevolently	involuntary	Soviet Union
civilization	irreverently	unequivocal
devaluation	observatory	university
governmentally	prevocational	________________
individual	recovery room	________________
inevitable	relativity	________________

V /v/ Medial—six syllables

availability	eventuality	special delivery
conversationally	involuntarily	unequivocally
developmentally	observationally	________________
environmentally	revolutionary	________________

V /v/ Final—one syllable

Bev	groove	save
brave	grove	shave
cave	halve	shove
chive	have	sieve
cleave	heave	sleeve
clove	hive	Steve
cove	I've	stove
crave	jive	strive
Dave	Jove	suave
dive	knave	they've
dove	lave	thrive
drive	leave	trove
drove	live	waive
Ev	love	wave
eve	mauve	weave
Eve	move	we've
five	nave	wove
gave	of	you've
give	pave	________________
glove	prove	________________
grave	rave	________________
grieve	rove	________________

V /v/ Final—two syllables

above
achieve
alive
approve
archive
arrive
beehive
behave
behoove
believe
bereave
captive
cold wave
concave
conceive
conclave
connive
contrive
cursive
deceive
deprave
deprive
derive

disk drive
disprove
enclave
endive
festive
forgave
forgive
foxglove
ground wave
heat wave
high dive
improve
mangrove
missive
motive
naive
native
nose-dive
olive
Olive
outlive
passive
relieve

relive
remove
reprieve
reprove
retrieve
revive
shock wave
short wave
sky wave
skydive
sound wave
survive
votive
____
____
____
____
____
____
____
____
____
____

V /v/ Final—three syllables

adaptive
Christmas Eve
convulsive
curative
decisive
destructive
devisive
effective
effusive
elusive
expensive
formative
fugitive

Genevieve
impressive
Mammoth Cave
microwave
misbehave
negative
New Year's Eve
nutritive
obsessive
offensive
positive
primitive
relative

sensitive
talkative
tentative
tidal wave
transitive
____
____
____
____
____
____
____
____

LV /lv/ Medial—two syllables

Alva	salvaged	velvet
Alvin	salvo	________________
Calvin	shelving	________________
Cleveland	silver	________________
culvert	solvent	________________
salvage	solving	________________

LV /lv/ Medial—three syllables

Alvina	quicksilver	solvable
dissolving	resolving	Sylvia
evolvement	revolving	velveteen
galvanic	salvation	velvety
galvanize	silver fox	wolverine
insolvent	silver-plate	________________
involvement	silversmith	________________
involving	silverware	________________
pulverize	silvery	________________

LV /lv/ Final—one syllable

delve	solve	________________
salve	twelve	________________
shelve	valve	________________

LV /lv/ Final—two syllables

absolve	evolve	________________
bivalve	involve	________________
devolve	resolve	________________
dissolve	revolve	________________

LVD /lvd/ Final—one syllable

delved	________________	________________
shelved	________________	________________
solved	________________	________________

LVD /lvd/ Final—two syllables

absolved	involved	unsolved
dissolved	resolved	________________
evolved	revolved	________________

LVZ /lvz/ Final—one syllable

delves	shelves	wolves
elves	solves	
selves	valves	

LVZ /lvz/ Final—two syllables

dissolves	resolves	
evolves	revolves	
involves	themselves	
ourselves	yourselves	

RV /rv/ Medial—two syllables

carver	Kerrville	serving
carving	larva	starving
carvings	marvel	survey
corvette	Marvin	survive
dervish	Mervin	swerving
fervid	nervous	
fervor	perverse	
Harvard	scurvey	
harvest	servant	
Harvey	server	
Irving	service	

RV /rv/ Medial—three syllables

Centerville	preserver	surveyor
conserver	preserving	survival
conserving	reserving	surviving
deserver	reservoir	survivor
deserving	self-service	survivors
enervate	serviceman	unnerving
fervently	servicemen	Waterville
marveling	services	wood carving
marvelous	servicing	
Minerva	servitude	
observance	starvation	
observant	supervise	
observer	survey crew	
observing	surveying	

RV /rv/ Medial—four syllables

conservation	observation	soapstone carvings
conservative	perseverence	subservient
conservator	preservation	survey party
effervescent	reservation	survival kit
enervated	reservations	survivorship
enervation	serviceable	topsy-turvy
intervention	service station	______
life preserver	servicewoman	______
nervous system	servicewomen	______

RV /rv/ Final—one syllable

carve	serve	verve
curve	starve	______
nerve	swerve	______

RV /rv/ Final—two syllables

conserve	observe	self-serve
deserve	preserve	______
hors d'oeuvre	reserve	______

RVD /rvd/ Final—one syllable

carved	starved	______
curved	swerved	______
served	______	______

RVD /rvd/ Final—two syllables

deserved	reserved	______
observed	unnerved	______
preserved	______	______

RVZ /rvz/ Final—one syllable

carves	scarves	turves
dwarves	serves	wharves
nerves	starves	______

RVZ /rvz/ Final—two syllables

conserves	observes	______
deserves	preserves	______

VER /vɚ/ Medial—three syllables

advertise
average
beverage
Beverly
bravery
conversion
coverage
covering
diversion
evergreen
favorite
flavoring
Hoover Dam
ivory
leverage
liverwurst
overalls
overboard
overcast
overcoat

overcome
overdo
overdraft
overdue
overflow
overgrow
overhand
overhaul
overhead
overhear
overjoy
overlap
overlook
overnight
overpass
overrun
overseas
overshoe
oversight
overtake

overtime
overture
overweight
overwhelm
overwork
overwrite
poverty
reverence
reverent
several
Silver Age
silverware
silvery
slavery
subversive
thievery
wolverine

VER /vɚ/ Medial—four syllables

Beverly Hills
controversy
conversation
covered wagon
delivery
discovery

diversity
favorable
invertebrate
nevertheless
overpower
receivership

recovery
universal

VER /vɚ/ Final—two syllables

beaver
cleaver
clever
clover
cover
Denver
diver
driver

ever
favor
fever
flavor
giver
Grover
Hoover
hover

lever
liver
louver
lover
mover
never
over
plover

quaver	sever	________
quiver	shiver	________
river	sliver	________
rover	waiver	________
Rover	waver	________
savor	weaver	________

VER /vɚ/ Final—three syllables

deliver	recover	whoever
discover	retriever	whomever
endeavor	Rhone River	whyever
forever	screwdriver	________
hay fever	skin diver	________
however	stopover	________
leftover	turn over	________
maneuver	uncover	________
moreover	Vancouver	________
Passover	whatever	________
preserver	whenever	________
quicksilver	wherever	________
receiver	whichever	________

VER /vɚ/ Final—four syllables

life preserver	whatsoever	________
redeliver	whensoever	________
scuba diver	whosoever	________

VY /vj/ Medial—two syllables

graveyard	________	________
________	________	________

VY /vj/ Medial—three syllables

behavior	________	________
________	________	________

VZ /vz/ Medial—two syllables

dove's nest	________	________
eavesdrop	________	________
thieves' den	________	________

VZ /vz/ Final—one syllable

beeves
calves
caves
chives
cloves
coves
craves
dives
doves
drives
eaves
fives
gives
gloves
graves
grieves
grooves
groves
halves
hives
hooves
jives
knaves
knives
leaves
lives
loaves
loves
moves
paves
peeves
proves
raves
roves
salves
saves
shaves
shoves
sieves
sleeves
thrives
waves
weaves
wives
____
____
____
____
____
____
____

Pronounced: /w/
Spelled: w, o, u, hu, ju

W /w/ Initial—one syllable

once
one
wad
wade
Wade
waft
wag
wage
wagged
waif
wail
waist
wait
waive
wake
walk
walked
wall
Walt
waltz
wan
wand
want
ward
Ward
ware
warm
warn
warned
was
wash
washed
wasp
waste
watch
watched
wave
waved
waves
wax
way
Wayne
we
we'd
we'll
we're
we've
weak
wealth
wean
wear
weave
web
wed
wee
weeds
week
weep
weigh
weight
weights
weird
well
Welsh
were
west
wet
wick
wide
wife
wig
wild
will
Will
willed
wilt
Wilt
win
wince
wind
wing
winged
wings
wink
wipe
wire
wise
wish
wisp
wit

witch
with
woe
wok
woke
wolf
won
won't
woo
wood
woods
wool
word
words
wore
work
worked
world
worm
worn
worse
worth
would
wound
wow
____
____

W /w/ Initial—two syllables

Juanna
Juarez
one-time
one-track
oneself
Ouija
Wabash
wabble
wabbly
Waco
waddle
wading
wafer
waffle
wager
wagging
waggle
wagon
waistline
waited
waiter
waiting
waitress
waken
wake-up
Waldo
Waldon
walker
Walker
walk-in
walking
walkout
walk-through
Wallace
wallet
Wallis
wallop
Wall Street
Wally
walnut
walrus
Walter
Wanda
wander
wanly
wanting
warbler
wardrobe
warehouse
warmed-up
warm-ups
Warner
warning
warrant
Warren
Warsaw
washbowl
washcloth
washed-out
washed-up
washer
washing
washrag
washroom
wasteful
wasteland
wasting
watchdog
watch guard
watchman
watch out
watchword
water
wattage
wattled
waving
wavy
waxing
wayside
wayside
weakness
wealthy
weaning
wearing

weary
weasel
weather
weathered
weaver
webbing
Webster
wedding
wedlock
Wednesday
weedy
weekday
weekend
weekly
weeping
weepy
weevil
Weighbridge
weigh-in
weighted
welcome
Welden
welfare
well-done
well-groomed
well-known
well-off
Wendy
West Point
Westport
wetter
wettest
wicker
wide-screen
widespread
widow
wiener
wiggle
wiggly
wigwam
Wilbur
Wilda
wild boar
wildcat
wildfire
wildlife
Wild West
Wilhelm
Willard
willful
William
Willie
willies
willing
Willis
willow
Wilma
Wilson
Wilton
wind-bells
windbreak
windburn
winded
winding
windlass
windmill
window
windpipe
windproof
windshield
windsock
windstorm
wingspread
winter
wireless
wiring
wisdom
wishbone
wishful
wishing
witchcraft
withdraw
withdrawn
withdrew
withers
within
without
witness
witty
wizard
wizened
wobble
wolf cub
wolf pack
woman
women
wonder
woodchuck
wood duck
wooden
Woodrow
woodshed
wordbook
wording
wordless
wordy
workbench
workbook
worker
working
work load
workout
workroom
workshop
world's fair
worn-out
worried

worry ______ ______
worship ______ ______
worthy ______ ______
wounded ______ ______

W /w/ Initial—three syllables

Juanita
onceover
one-bagger
one-base hit
one-sided
wading pool
wage earner
wagoner
Wagoner
Waikiki
walking stick
walkover
wallaby
wallpaper
wanderer
wandering
wanderlust
warm-blooded
Washington
water bed
water bird
water bug
watercraft
waterfall
waterfront
water hole
watering
water line
water logged
Waterloo
watermark
waterpaints
water plane
waterproof
water ski
water snake
waterspout
waxed paper
way station
wearisome
weather-bound
Weatherford
weatherman
weather map
weathervane
wedding cake
wedding day
wedding march
wedding ring
weight lifting
well-mannered
well-to-do
West Berlin
Westchester
westerly
West Indies
Westminster
wide-angle
widower
wilderness
wiliness
Williamsburg
Williamstown
willingness
willpower
windbreaker
windjammer
window box
window shade
window sill
window-shop
Winnipeg
wintergreen
wintertime
wire cutter
wirephoto
wire service
Wisconsin
wisdom teeth
wisdom tooth
witch hazel
witness-box
witness stand
wolverine
Woman's Club
wonderful
wood-carver
wood carving
woodcutter
wooden shoes
woodpecker
word-of-mouth
workable
working class
World Series
worrisome
Wyoming
______
______

W /w/ Initial—four syllables

walking safety	weatherbeaten	Winnebago
washing machine	weather bureau	wishy-washy
water closet	weather radar	withholding tax
watercolors	weather report	wonderfully
water faucet	weather signal	wooden nickel
water jacket	weather station	woolgathering
water lily	West Germany	word processor
watermelon	West Virginia	______________
water polo	will-o'-the-wisp	______________
water safety	wind instrument	______________
water skiing	window-shopping	______________

W /w/ Medial—two syllables

always	eyewink	kiwi
await	freeway	landward
awake	gangway	leeward
award	gateway	leeway
aware	goodwill	lifework
away	green wax	lightweight
awoke	greenwood	midway
beadwork	ground wave	midweek
beeswax	guesswork	Midwest
bewail	halfway	mouthwash
beware	hallway	network
bewitch	handwork	new wave
blue wax	hardware	northwest
Bowen	haywire	one-way
bow-wow	heat wave	outward
bulwark	highway	Owen
byway	homework	pathway
causeway	housework	peewee
cobweb	iceway	pow-wow
cold wave	inward	raceway
DeWitt	jaguar	railway
driveway	jaywalk	rainwear
Edward	jetway	red wax
Edwin	Jewish	reward
eyewash	Key West	rewind

reword
rework
rewound
ringworm
roadway
roadwork
rosewood
roundworm
San Juan
sand wasp
sandwich
sandworm
sandwort
schoolwork
seatwork
seawall
seaward
seaway
seaweed
Sea World
shoe wax
short wave
sidewalk
sideways
ski wax
sky wave
skyway
small world
someone
someway
sound wave
southwest
throughway
two-way
unworn
watchword
waxwing
waxwork
wayward
well-worn
werewolf
wherewith
woodwork
Woolworth
worldwide
____
____
____

W /w/ Medial—three syllables

awaken
backwater
bewaring
candlewax
candlewick
castaway
Chihuahua
Chippewa
chuck wagon
Civil War
dental wax
dumbwaiter
edelweiss
expressway
eyewinker
eyewitness
fishing worms
fizz water
forty-watt
Halloween
handiwork
hardware store
Hawaii
Hawaiian
hideaway
high water
Hollywood
inwardly
ironware
ironwood
ironwork
ironworks
kilowatt
long-winded
microwave
Midwestern
midwinter
Milky Way
New Windsor
nonworker
northwestern
Number One
office work
one-way drive
one-way street
outwardly
pea weevil
pocket watch
rainwater
rewarded
rewiring
sandalwood
sandwiches
sandwich man
seaworthy
southwestern
spider web
straight-away
tidal wave
unaware
unwilling
walkaway
wash and wear

water wave	well-wisher	wishing well
waterway	welterweight	wishing well
water wings	wherewithal	woodworking
waterworks	whippoorwill	________
weather-wise	wide-awake	________

W /w/ Medial—four syllables

covered wagon	southwesterly	weeping willow
pussy willow	station wagon	welcome wagon
rewardable	water wagon	________

DW /dw/ Initial—one syllable

Duane	dwell	Dwight
dwarf	dwelled	________
Dwayne	dwelt	________

DW /dw/ Initial—two syllables

dwarfish	dwindle	________
dwelling	dwindling	________

GW /gw/ Initial—one syllable

Guam	Guelph	Gwin
guan	Guinn	Gwyn
guar	Gwen	________

GW /gw/ Initial—two syllables

guaco	guanine	Gwenda
guana	guano	________
guanay	guava	________

GW /gw/ Initial—three syllables

guacharo	Guayama	Guinevere
guanaco	guayule	Gwendolyn
Guarani	Guenevere	________

GW /gw/ Initial—four syllables

guacamole	Guadalupe	________
Guadalcanal	Guantanamo	________
Guadalquivir	Guatemala	________

GW /gw/ Initial—five syllables

guacamole dip
Guadalajara
Guadalupe Palm
Guantanamo Bay

GW /gw/ Medial—two syllables

agua
aguar
anguine
anguish
anguished
dogwood
hogwash
jaguar
language
languet
languid
languish
lingua
lingual
linguist
penguin
pinguid
ragweed
sanguine
ungual
unguent
unguis
wigwag
wigwam

GW /gw/ Medial—three syllables

alguazil
alguien
bilingual
distinguish
extinguish
iguana
inguinal
La Guaira
language arts
language cards
languages
languishing
languishment
linguiform
linguistics
sign language
tagua nut
teguexin
unguical

GW /gw/ Medial—four syllables

Aguadilla
Agua Fria
extinguisher
La Guardia
language patterns
language workbook
sanguineous
unguentary

KW /kw/ Initial—one syllable

choir
quack
quacked
quad
quaff
quaffed
quag
quail
quaint
quake
quaked
qualm
quark
quart
quartz
quash
quashed
quay
queen
quell
quelled
quench
quenched
quest
quick
quid
quill

quilt
quince
quints
quip
quipped
quirk
quirt
quit
quite
quiz

KW /kw/ Initial—two syllables

quadrant
quadrate
quadrille
quadroon
quagga
quagmire
quaintly
Quaker
quaking
qualmish
quantize
quantum
quarrel
quarreled
quarry
quartan
quarter
quartet
quartile
quarto
quartzite
quasi
quatrain
quaver
queasy
Quebec
Queen Anne
quencher
queried
query
quester
question
questioned
quibble
quickbread
quicken
quickened
quickie
quickly
quicksand
quickstep
quiet
quilted
quilting
Quincy
quinine
quinsy
quintain
quintet
quisling
quitclaim
quitter
quiver
quizzer
quonset
quorum
quota
quotient

KW /kw/ Initial—three syllables

quadrangle
quadratic
quadriceps
quadrifid
quadrillion
quadruped
quadruple
quadruplet
Quakertown
qualified
qualify
qualities
quality
quandary
quantity
quarantine
quarrelsome
quarterback
quarterdeck
quarterhorse
quartering
quarter note
quavering
question mark
questionnaire
quicksilver
quick-tempered
quick-witted
quiescent
quietly

quintessence
quintuple
quintuplet
quixotic
quizzical
quotable
quotation

KW /kw/ Initial—four syllables

quadrangular
quadrennial
quadriplegic
quadruplicate
qualifier
qualitative
quantifier
quantitative
quartermaster
questionable
quinine water
quinquennial
quotation mark

KW /kw/ Initial—five syllables

quadrilateral
qualification
quantitatively

KW /kw/ Medial—two syllables

acquaint
acquire
acquired
acquit
aqua
awkward
backward
backwash
backwoods
banquet
bequeath
bequeathed
bequest
bookworm
brick wall
cakewalk
catwalk
chickweed
equal
equalled
equate
equip
equipped
frequence
frequent
inquest
inquire
inquired
knockwurst
likewise
liquid
loquat
lukewarm
milkweed
misquote
request
require
required
sequel
sequence
sequenced
sequin
shock wave
tranquil
unquote
walkway

KW /kw/ Medial—three syllables

acquaintance
acquainted
acquiesce
acquiesced
acquiring
acquittal
acquittance
acquitted
antiquate
aqualung
aquanaut
aquaplane

aquatic
aquatint
aqueduct
aqueous
aquiline
chuck wagon
chuckwalla
consequence
consequent
disquiet
equaling
equalize
equalized
equated
equating
equation
equator
equerry
equinox
equipage
equipment
equipping
equity
frequency
headquarters
hindquarter
inequal
infrequent
inquirer
inquiring
inquiry
liquefy
liquidate
liquified
loquacious
misquoted
misquoting
requirement
requiring
requisite
requital
requiter
sequential
sequoia
subsequent
tranquilize
tranquilly
unequal
unequaled
unquestioned
____
____
____
____
____
____
____
____
____
____
____
____
____

KW /kw/ Medial—four syllables

acquiescence
acquiescent
acquisition
acquisitive
antiquary
antiquated
antiquation
antiquity
aquamarine
aquarium
Aquarius
consequential
disqualified
disqualify
disquietude
disquisition
equality
equalizer
equalizing
equidistant
equitable
equitation
equivalence
equivalent
equivocal
equivocate
infrequented
inquisition
inquisitive
inquisitor
liquefaction
liquefying
liquidating
liquidation
liquidity
loquacity
post headquarters
requisition
tranquility
tranquilizer
unfrequented
unqualified
unquenchable
ventriloquist
____
____
____
____

KW /kw/ Medial—five syllables

antiquarian
disqualifying
equanimity
equatorial
equiangular
equilateral
equilibrium
equivalency
equivocation
unequivocal
unquestionable

RW /rw/ Medial—two syllables

airways
careworn
carwash
carwax
Corwin
doorway
Erwin
fairway
farewell
fireweed
firewood
fireworks
forward
Irwin
Norway
Sherwood
shoreward
therewith

RW /rw/ Medial—three syllables

afterword
afterworld
netherward
silverware
spiderweb
straightforward
thenceforward
underwaist
underwear
underweight
underwent
underwood
underworld
water wings
waterways
waterworks
wonder-world

RW /rw/ Medial—four syllables

underwater

SW /sw/ Initial—one syllable

suave
suede
suite
swab
swag
swale
swam
swamp
swan
swank
swap
sward
swarm
swash
swat
swatch
sway
swear
sweat
Swede
sweep
sweet
swell
swept
swerve
swift
swig
swim
swine
swing
swipe
swipes
swirl

swish
Swiss
switch
swoon
swoop
swore
sworn

SW /sw/ Initial—two syllables

swallow
swallows
swami
swampland
swampy
swan dive
swanky
swap shop
sweat gland
sweat pants
sweat shirt
sweat suit
sweater
Sweden
Swedish
sweeper
sweeping
sweepstakes
sweet corn
sweet pea
sweet tooth
sweetbread
sweeten
sweetheart
swelling
swelter
swifter
swim fins
swim mask
swimmer
swimming
swimsuit
swindle
swindled
swinger
swinging
Swiss cheese
switchback
switchboard
switchbox
swivel
swollen

SW /sw/ Initial—three syllables

swallowtail
swastika
sweet and sour
sweetening
sweltering
swift-footed
swimming hole
swimming pool
swine fever
swinging bridge
swinging door
Switzerland

SKW /skw/ Initial—one syllable

squab
squad
squall
square
squash
squat
squaw
squawk
squeak
squeal
squeeze
squelch
squib
squid
squint
squire
squirm
squirt
squish

SKW /skw/ Initial—two syllables

squabble
squabbling
squad car
squadron
squalid
squally
squalor
squander
square dance
square deal
square feet
square foot
square inch
square knot
square meal
square mile
square off
square root
square yard
squarely
squarest
squashy
squatted
squatter
squatting
squatty
squeaky
squeamish
squeegee
squeezer
squeezing
squelcher
squiggle
squirmy
squirrel
squirt gun
squishy
____
____
____
____
____

SKW /skw/ Initial—three syllables

square away
square inches
square meters
square rigger
square shooter
squashiest
squeezable
____
____

TW /tw/ Initial—one syllable

twang
tweak
tweed
tweet
tweeze
twelfth
twelve
twerp
twice
twig
twigged
twill
twilled
twin
twine
twined
twinge
twinned
twirl
twist
twitch
____
____
____

TW /tw/ Initial—two syllables

twangle
twangy
tweedle
tweedy
tweezers
twenty
twiddle
twilight
Twin Falls
twin bed
twin sheet
twinborn
twinkle
twinkling
twirler
twister
twisting
twitch grass
twitter
____
____

TW /tw/ Initial—three syllables

twentieth	Twin Cities	____________
twenty yards	twin-engine	____________
twenty-five	twinberry	____________
twenty-one	twinflower	____________
twilight sleep	twisted pine	____________

WH

Pronounced: /hw/, /ʍ/, /w/
Spelled: wh

WH /wh/ Initial—one syllable

whack
whale
wharf
what
what's
wheat
wheel
wheeled
wheeze
whelk
whelm
whelp
when
whence
where
where'd
whew
whey
which
whiff
while
whir
whine
whirl
whish
whisk
whist
Whit
white
why

WH /wh/ Initial—two syllables

whacking
whaleboat
whalebone
whaler
whammy
whapper
whate'er
whatnot
wheat cakes
wheaten
wheat germ
wheedle
wheelchair
wheeling
Wheeling
wheezing
wheezy
whereas
whereby
wherefore
wherein
whereof
whereon
wherry
whether
whetstone
whicker
whiffet
whimper
whimsy
whining
whinny
whiplash
whippet
whipping
Whipple
whirlpool
whirlwind
whirring
whiskbroom
whiskers
whisper
whistle
whistled
whistler
whistling
white belt
white bread
whitecap
whitefish
white goods

Whitehorse
White House
whiten
white sale
white sauce
White Sea
white shark
whitewash
whither
Whitney
whittle
whittling
whiz-bang
whizzing

WH /wh/ Initial—three syllables

whatever
wheelbarrow
whenever
whereabouts
whereupon
wherever
wherewithal
whichever
whiffletree
whimpering
whimsical
whippoorwill
whirlabout
whirligig
whirlpool bath
whispering
Whitaker
Whitechapel
white water
Whitewater

WH /wh/ Initial—four syllables

whatsoever
wheelbarrow race
whensoever
whichsoever
whippersnapper

WH /wh/ Medial—two syllables

buckwheat
cartwheel
erstwhile
meanwhile
nowhere
pinwheel
somewhere
whim-wham
whole wheat
worthwhile

WH /wh/ Medial—three syllables

anywhere
color wheel
everywhere
Ferris wheel
four-wheeler
free-wheeler
overwhelm
steering wheel
three-wheeler
two-wheeler
wagon wheel
whole wheat bread

Y

Pronounced: /j/
Spelled: eu, y, g, i, j, u, ll

Y /j/ Initial—one syllable

Jung
use
used
yacht
yak
Yale
yam
yang
yank
yanks
yap
yard
yarn
yaw
yawl
yawn
ye
yea
year
yearn
yeast
yell
yelled
yelp
yen
yes
yet
yew
yield
yip
yipe
yoke
yolk
yon
yore
York
you
you'd
you'll
you're
young
Young
your
yours
youth
yowl
Yule
yum
yurt
____
____

Y /j/ Initial—two syllables

Eubanks
euchre
Euclid
Eugene
Eula
Eunice
Europe
Ewan
ewe lamb
Ewell
Ewing
Johann
U-boat
U-bolt
ukase
Ukraine
union
unique
unit
unite
Ural
U.S.
usage
used cars
useful
useless
user
using
usurp
Utah
U-turn
yacht club
yachting

yachtsman
Yahoo
Yalta
yammer
Yancy
Yangtze
Yankee
Yankees
yardage
yardarm
yardbird
yard goods
yard grass
yardman
yard sale
yardstick
yarrow
yearbook
yearling
yearlong
yearly
yearning
year-round
yeasty
yelling
yellow
yelper
yeoman
yes ma'am
yes man
yeti
Yetta
Yiddish
yielding
yield sign
yippee
yodel
yodeler
Yoga
yogi
yogurt
yokel
yonder
Yonkers
Yorkshire
you-all
younger
youngest
youngster
Youngstown
yourself
youthful
yo-yo
Yuba
yucca
Yukon
yule log
yuletide
Yuma
yummy
____
____
____

Y /j/ Initial—three syllables

eugenic
eulogize
eulogy
Eurasia
eureka
Eureka
eurythmics
eustachian
eutaxy
Johannes
Uganda
Ulysses
unicorn
uniform
union card
Uniondale
unionize
Union Springs
union suit
unison
united
unity
universe
Uranus
Uriah
Uruguay
U.S.A.
usable
U.S. Mail
usual
usury
utensil
Utica
utilize
uvula
yachtswoman
Yankified
yardmaster
year-end sale
yellow-dog
yellowbird
yellow rose
Yellowstone
yeomanly
yeshiva
yesterday
Yolanda
Yom Kippur

youth football
youthfully
youthfulness
youth hockey
youth hostel
youth soccer
Yucatan
____
____

Y /j/ Initial—four syllables

European
ubiquitous
ukelele
unanimous
unicycle
Union City
united front
United States
universal
uranium
urology
U.S.S.R.
usurious
utilities
utility
utopia
year-end clearance
yellow daisy
yellow fever
yellow jacket
Yellowstone Park
Yosemite
youth basketball
Yukon River
____
____
____

Y /j/ Initial—five syllables

university
U.S. Post Office
utilization
Yugoslavia
Yugoslavian
____

Y /j/ Medial—two syllables

Bayonne
bayou
buoyant
cow yard
Doyan
kayak
lawyer
loyal
Maya
Mayan
new year
New Year's
New York
oyes
oyez
Paiute
reuse
reused
royal
Royals
savior
sawyer
Sawyer
Toya
yo-yo
____
____

Y /j/ Medial—three syllables

buoyancy
coyote
Hawaiian
kayaking
La Toya
loyalty
Malayan
New Year's Day
New Year's Eve
no U-turn
papaya
reunion
reunite
royalist
Royal Oak
royalties
royalty
thirty yards
Tocayo
Tom Sawyer
tortilla
____
____
____

Y /j/ Medial—four syllables

Bayou Vista	New York City	teriyaki
employer	New York Harbor	twenty-yard line
Happy New Year	papaya tree	________
Himalaya	Royal Highness	________
lawyer's office	sukiyaki	________

BY /bj/ Medial—three syllables

ambulance	tabulate	________
ambulate	tubular	________

BY /bj/ Medial—four syllables

contributor	tabulator	________
distributor	tribulation	________
tabulated	tributary	________

DY /dj/ Medial—two syllables

woodyard	________	________
________	________	________

DY /dj/ Medial—three syllables

Scotland Yard	________	________
trade union	________	________

GY /gj/ Medial—two syllables

egg yolk	figured	________
figure	figures	________

GY /gj/ Medial—three syllables

figure eight	figure skate	transfigured
figure-ground	figuring	________
figurehead	regular	________
figure out	regulate	________

GY /gj/ Medial—four syllables

father figure	regulating	________
figure skating	regulation	________
regularly	triangular	________
regulated	________	________

KY /kj/ Medial—two syllables

backyard	dockyard	__________
brickyard	stockyard	__________

KY /kj/ Medial—three syllables

calculate	ocular	speculate
calculus	oculist	succulent
Hercules	porcupine	Tokyo
molecule	secular	__________

KY /kj/ Medial—four syllables

accusation	gesticulate	spectacular
articulate	lenticular	speculation
calculated	molecular	vermicular
calculator	particular	vermiculate
curriculum	ridiculous	__________
executor	security	__________

LY /lj/ Medial—two syllables

all year	Dahlia	stallion
billiards	failure	trillion
billion	Julia	valiant
bouillon	Julian	value
bullion	million	valued
coal yard	millionth	William
collier	school yard	zillion
Collier	school year	__________

LY /lj/ Medial—three syllables

alienate	Centralia	regalia
Amelia	Cornelia	valiancy
Australia	cotillion	valiantly
Australian	familial	valuate
azalea	familiar	valueless
battalion	four billion	valuing
billiard ball	magnolia	Vermillion
billionaire	medallion	Williamsburg
bouillon cube	millionaire	__________
Camellia	rebellion	__________

LY /lj/ Medial—four syllables

billiard table
chameleon
familiarize
Julius Caesar
salutation
valuable
valuation
valuator

MY /mj/ Medial—two syllables

farmyard

MY /mj/ Medial—three syllables

amulet
communist
emulate
simulate
stimulant
stimulate
stimulus

MY /mj/ Medial—four syllables

Bohemian
stimulation

NY /nj/ Medial—two syllables

banyan
barnyard
bunion
Bunyan
canyon
Daniel
genial
genius
junior
Junior
Kenya
Kenyon
lanyard
minion
Muñoz
onion
Runnion
senior
señor
Spaniard
spaniel
Tanya
unused
vineyard

NY /nj/ Medial—three syllables

ammonia
annual
banyan tree
begonia
Black Canyon
congenial
convenience
convenient
dominion
geniuses
golden years
Grand Canyon
ingenious
lunula
lunular
manuscript
minuet
monument
Paul Bunyan
señora
sinuate
Virginia
zinnia

NY /nj/ Medial—four syllables

annual wage
annually
biannual
Boulder Canyon
centennial
cocker spaniel
continual
Dominion Day
filet mignon
gardenia
genuinely
January
manufacture
monumental
señorita
triannual
unusual
Virginia Beach
West Virginia

PY /pj/ Medial—two syllables

leap year
shipyard

PY /pj/ Medial—three syllables

deputize
deputy
impudence
impudent
populace
popular
populate
populous
stipulate

PY /pj/ Medial—four syllables

manipulate
popularize
popularly
popular song
popular vote
population
stipulation
unpopular

RY /rj/ Medial—three syllables

lumberyard
lunar year
solar year
yesteryear

RY /rj/ Medial—four syllables

labor union

TY /tj/ Medial—two syllables

courtyard
front yard
light-year

TY /tj/ Medial—four syllables

credit union
meticulous

VY /vj/ Medial—two syllables

graveyard	________________	________________

VY /vj/ Medial—three syllables

behavior	________________	________________

YER /jɚ/ Medial—three syllables

figure eight	figurine	________________
figurehead	________________	________________

YER /jɚ/ Final—two syllables

failure	junior	savior
figure	lawyer	senior

YER /jɚ/ Final—three syllables

behavior	familiar	refigure
employer	peculiar	Tom Sawyer

YER /jɚ/ Final—four syllables

misbehavior	trial lawyer	________________
power failure	unfamiliar	________________

Y-blend in first syllable /j/ —one syllable

butte	few	Hughes
Butte	fjord	mew
cube	fuel	mule
cue	fume	muse
cued	fumes	mused
cure	fuse	pew
cured	hew	pure
cute	hue	skew
dew	huge	view
feud	Hugh	________________

Y-blend in first syllable /j/ —two syllables

Beaufort	bugle	Cuba
beauty	bugler	cubic
Beulah	bureau	cubit
Buford	butane	cue ball

cuing
Cupid
cure-all
Curie
cutest
cutie
Dewey
feudal
furor
fusion
futile
future
Hubert
hubris
Hughie
Hugo
human
humane
humid
humor
humus
mule deer
Munich
mural
music
muted
pewter
puny
pupa
pupil
puree
purely
purer
purest
skewer
skewing
viewer
view point
viewy
____
____
____
____
____
____

Y-blend in first syllable /j/ —three syllables

beauteous
beautician
beautified
beautiful
beautify
beauty shop
beauty sleep
Buchanan
bureaucrat
cubical
cubic foot
cubic inch
cubic mile
cubic yard
cucumber
cumulate
cumulus
cupola
curative
curio
curious
cuticle
cutie pie
fugitive
funeral
fuselage
fusillade
Hueytown
Hugoton
humanist
humanize
human kind
humanly
human rights
humidor
humoresque
humorist
humorous
Munich Pact
muralist
Muriel
museum
musical
music box
music hall
musician
music stand
muted horn
mutual
punier
puniest
purified
purify
Puritan
purity
viewable
view finder
____
____
____
____
____
____
____
____
____

Y-blend in first syllable /j/ —four syllables

beauty salon
bureaucracy
bureaucratic
cubic measure
cumulative
curiously
humanity
human nature
humidify
humidity
humiliate
humility
municipal
munificent
musical chairs
mutual fund
____
____

Y-blend in second syllable /j/ —two syllables

abuse
accuse
accused
acute
adieu
amuse
amused
Bayview
Bridge View
Clearview
commute
compute
confuse
confused
confute
Danube
debut
defuse
depute
effuse
emu
excuse
excused
Fairview
Grandview
immune
impure
impute
infuse
Lakeview
menu
preview
profuse
rebuke
rebuked
refuge
refuse
refused
refute
rescue
rescued
review
reviewed
reviews
secure
secured
Shoreview
sun-cured
transfuse
transmute
tribune
tribute
vacuum
vacuumed
volume
volumed
volumes
Zebu
____
____
____
____
____

Y-blend in second syllable /j/ —three syllables

accusing
acuate
amputate
amputee
amusement
amusing
annual
Bermuda
communal
commuter
commuting
computer
Confucius
confusion
debutant
document
excusing
genuine
imputed
infusion
manual

Manuel	refugee	securing
peculiar	refusing	slide viewer
previewing	refuted	transfusion
profusely	refuting	tribunal
profusion	rescuing	Van Buren
profusive	reviewing	________
rebuking	Samuel	________

Y-blend in second syllable /j/ —four syllables

accumulate	community	refutative
acuity	genuinely	security
acupuncture	impunity	________
amusement park	impurity	________
communicate	refutation	________

Y-blend in third syllable /j/ —three syllables

attribute	Harborview	overview
barbeque	interfuse	ridicule
Blue Danube	interview	Riverview
continue	malamute	scenic view
continued	manicure	vestibule
contribute	miniscule	________
curlicue	Mountain View	________
execute	Oceanview	________

Y-blend in third syllable /j/ Medial—four syllables

barbecue chips	contribution	intramural
barbecue grill	distributed	intramurals
barbecue sauce	distributing	manicurist
barbecued steak	distribution	therapeutic
continual	evacuate	________
continuing	evacuee	________
continuous	evaluate	________

NKY /nkj/ Medial—two syllables

junkyard	thank you	________

NKY /nkj/ Medial—three syllables

thank-you card	thank-you note	________

Z

Pronounced: /z/
Spelled: z, zz, s, ss, ssc, x

Z /z/ Initial—one syllable

czar
Zach
zag
zagged
Zane
zap
zapped
zax
zeal
Zeb
Zed
zee
Zek
Zeke
Zen
zest
Zeus
zinc
zing
zip
zipped
zone
zoned
zoo
zoom
zoomed
zooms
zounds
____
____
____
____
____
____
____
____

Z /z/ Initial—two syllables

xebec
zagging
zany
zapping
Zardax
zealot
zealous
zebra
zebu
Zelda
zenith
zephyr
zero
zeroed
zeros
zestful
zeta
zigzag
zillion
Zion
zip code
zipper
zipping
zippy
zircon
zither
Zoe
zombie
zonal
zone time
zoning
zooming
zoom lens
zoospore
zoot suit
Zorro
Zouave
Zulu
Zurich
zygote
____
____
____
____
____
____
____
____

Z /z/ Initial—three syllables

czarevitch
czarevna
czarina
czarism
xylophone
Zachary
Zambezi
Zambia
Zanzibar
zebra fish
zeppelin
zero hour
zeroing
zestfully
zigzagging
zinc oxide
zinnia
zirconate
zodiac
zonation
zucchini
Zululand
Zuyder Zee
zymosis
____
____
____

Z /z/ Initial—four syllables

Zacharias
Zamboanga
zeroing-in
zinciferous
zirconium
zoning permit
zoographer
zoography
zoologist
zoology
zootomy
Zoroaster
zygomatic
zymology
____

Z /z/ Medial—two syllables

asthma
Aztec
bazaar
beeswax
benzene
blazer
blizzard
Boise
brazen
brazier
Brazil
breezy
bruiser
business
busy
buzzard
buzzer
buzzing
Caesar
causeway
cheesecake
cheesecloth
cheesy
chisel
chosen
cleanser
closes
closet
clothesline
clothespin
clumsy
cosmic
cosmos
cousin
cozy
crazy
cruiser
daisy
Daisy
dazzle
desert
deserve
design
desire
dessert
diesel
disease
dismal
dissolve
dizzy
doesn't
dozen
dozing
drizzle
drizzly
easel
easement
easy
enzyme
Ezra

fizzle
flimsy
frazzle
freezer
freezing
frenzy
frizzle
frowzy
frozen
fuzzy
gazelle
gazette
gazing
geyser
gizzard
grizzly
guzzle
has-been
hasn't
hazard
hazel
Hazel
hazy
houses
housing
husband
isn't
jasmine
Kaiser
Kansas
laser
lazy
Lisbon
Liza
lizard
loser
lousy
mazy
measles
miser
Moses
Moslem
music
Muslim
muslin
muzzle
nasal
newsprint
newsreel
newsstand
noisy
nosebleed
nosegay
nosy
nozzle
observe
oozing
Ozzie
pansy
pheasant
Pisa
plaza
pleasant
poison
posy
presence
present
preserve
presume
prison
puzzle
quasar
quizzer
raisin
raising
razor
reason
resent
reserve
reside
resign
resist
resolve
resort
resound
result
resume
risen
rises
rising
Rosa
rosin
rosy
scissors
season
sizzle
sleazy
sneezing
spasm
squeezer
stanza
Susan
Susie
Suzanne
teaser
teasing
thousand
Thursday
tizzy
treason
trouser
Tuesday
tweezers
tweezing
user
visit
visor

wasn't	wisecrack	________________
weasel	wiser	________________
Wednesday	wizard	________________

Z /z/ Medial—three syllables

accusal	Gaza Strip	raspberry
accuser	gazebo	razorback
advisor	horizon	refusal
Alonzo	horned lizard	reprisal
amazing	imprison	requisite
Amazon	inasmuch	resemble
amusing	incisor	reservoir
artisan	Louisa	resident
azalea	magazine	residue
bonanza	mezzanine	résumé
bulldozer	misery	resurrect
busily	Missouri	Roosevelt
composer	museum	rosary
cosmetic	musical	sousaphone
deep freezer	music box	Susanna
deposit	music hall	teasingly
desertion	musician	trail blazer
disaster	newspaper	trapezoid
divisor	New Zealand	usable
easier	observing	visited
easiest	opposite	visiting
easily	physician	visitor
emblazon	position	________________
exquisite	president	________________
freezing point	prisoner	________________
fusible	quizzical	________________

Z /z/ Medial—four syllables

advertising	divisible	horizontal
advisable	Eisenhower	imprisonment
appetizer	Elizabeth	influenza
atomizer	fertilizer	inquisitive
desirable	fertilizing	invisible
diesel engine	gymnasium	Kalamazoo

miserable
miserably
Montezuma
observation
observership
poison ivy
preservable
preservation
reservation
resolution
seismologist
stabilizer
supervisor
vaporizer
____
____
____
____

Z /z/ Medial—five syllables

cosmopolitan
desirableness
dramatization
Elizabethan
lapis lazuli
Louisiana
mechanization
observatory
organization
Presbyterian
____
____

Z /z/ Final—one syllable

as
awes
bees
blaze
blows
blues
bows
boys
braise
breeze
browse
bruise
buys
buzz
cause
cheese
choose
chose
clause
close
clothes
clues
craze
crews
cries
crows
cruise
cues
days
daze
does
doze
draws
dries
dues
ease
eyes
fez
fizz
fleas
flows
freeze
fries
froze
fuse
fuzz
gauze
gaze
glaze
glows
goes
graze
grows
guise
has
Hayes
haze
he's
hose
Hughes
is
jays
jazz
joys
Kaz
keys
knees
laws
lies
Liz
lose
maize
mews
news
noise

nose
ones
ooze
owes
Oz
pause
paws
peas
phase
phrase
pies
plays
please
poise
pose
praise
prize
prose
quiz
raise
rays
raze

razz
rise
rose
Rose
rouse
rows
says
seas
sees
seize
she's
shoes
size
skies
skis
sneeze
snooze
spies
squeeze
stews
tease
these

those
threes
ties
toes
toys
trays
trees
tries
twos
use
views
was
ways
weighs
wheeze
whizz
whose
wise
____
____
____
____

Z /z/ Final—two syllables

ablaze
accuse
advise
agaze
always
amaze
amuse
applause
appraise
Aries
arise
arose
arouse
arrows
babies

baptize
bases
because
blue cheese
blue eyes
blue jays
blue skies
bulldoze
Burmese
bylaws
byways
carouse
chastise
Chavez
Chinese

comas
commas
compose
comprise
confuse
cookies
Cortez
cream cheese
crochets
deep freeze
defies
defrays
degrees
denies
despise

disclose
disease
disguise
dispose
dress shoes
echoes
enclose
enthuse
essays
excuse
expose
fire hose
first prize
French fries
glasses
grand prize
highrise
highways
house keys
Indies
judges

ladies
Lopez
Louise
missus
misuse
Mrs.
oppose
pieces
pillows
Pisces
play shoes
primrose
propose
red rose
refuse
repose
revise
sea breeze
series
sideways
sixes

snowshoes
South Seas
stories
Suez
sunrays
sunrise
suppose
surprise
sweetpeas
Swiss cheese
tacos
third prize
track shoes
transfuse
trapeze
Valdez
whereas
____
____
____
____

Z /z/ Final—three syllables

advertise
Alcatraz
ballet shoes
bananas
baseball shoes
beautifies
besieges
challenges
cheddar cheese
compromise
corduroys
criticize
dominos
downhill skis
dramatize
Eloise

empathize
emphasize
exercise
expressways
fantasize
garden hose
harmonize
immunize
iodize
Japanese
magnetize
marshmallows
mayonnaise
mechanize
memorize
merchandise

modernize
motorize
multiplies
nasalize
nurseries
organize
overseas
paralyze
potatoes
publicize
realize
recognize
Santa Claus
Santa Cruz
second prize
standardize

stereos	tennis shoes	water skis
sunglasses	theorize	World Series
supervise	tomatoes	wrestling shoes
sympathize	tragedies	yellow rose
synthesize	unionize	__________
systemize	Vera Cruz	__________

Z /z/ Final—four syllables

alphabetize	familiarize	refineries
analyses	generalize	secretaries
antagonize	initialize	societies
apologize	internalize	__________
basketball shoes	loganberries	__________
cross-country skis	musical chairs	__________

BZ /bz/ Final—one syllable

babes	garbs	rubs
bibs	gobs	sobs
cabs	grubs	stubs
clubs	hobs	subs
cobs	hubs	swabs
crabs	jibes	tabs
cribs	jobs	throbs
cubes	knobs	tribes
cubs	labs	tubes
dabs	lobes	tubs
debs	mobs	webs
dubs	nabs	__________
fibs	probes	__________
fobs	ribs	__________
gabs	robes	__________

BZ /bz/ Final—two syllables

bathrobes	doorknobs	ice cubes
bathtubs	earlobes	sand crabs
bear cubs	flashcubes	sea crabs
book clubs	girls' clubs	spareribs
boys' clubs	golf clubs	wolf cubs
cobwebs	health clubs	__________

ZD /zd/ Final—one syllable

braised	hosed	sized
brazed	paused	sneezed
breezed	phased	teased
caused	phrased	wheezed
closed	pleased	________
dazed	posed	________
eased	praised	________
gazed	raised	________
grazed	seized	________

DZ /dz/ Final—one syllable

adds	leads	sides
aids	lids	sleds
beads	loads	slides
bids	modes	spades
codes	needs	speeds
creeds	nodes	suds
crowds	nods	tides
dads	odds	toads
deeds	odes	trades
fades	pads	wades
fads	pleads	wads
feeds	pods	weds
floods	raids	weeds
gods	reads	woods
goods	reds	________
grades	rides	________
guides	rids	________
heads	roads	________
hides	seeds	________
kids	shades	________
lads	sheds	________

LDZ /ldz/ Final—one syllable

builds	molds	yields
fields	scalds	________
folds	scolds	________
holds	worlds	________

GZ /gz/ Medial—two syllables

exact
exalt
exam
exempt

exert
exhaust
exhort
exile

exist
exult
zigzag
____

GZ /gz/ Medial—three syllables

eczema
exacting
exaction
exactly
examine
example

exemption
exertion
exertive
exhaustion
exhaustive
exhaustless

exhibit
existence
existent
exotic
exultant
____

GZ /gz/ Medial—four syllables

exactitude
exaggerate
examinant
examinate
examinee
exasperate
executant
executive
executrix
exemplary

exemplify
exemptible
exhaustible
exhibitive
exhibitor
exhilarant
exhilarate
exhortation
existential
exonerate

exorbitance
exorbitant
exordium
exuberance
exuberant
exuberate
exultancy
exultation
____
____

GZ /gz/ Medial—five syllables

exaggeration
exaggerative
exaggerator
examinable
examination
exasperation

executory
exercitation
exhibitory
exhilaration
exhilarative
exoneration

exonerator
exorbitancy
exotically
exuberancy
____
____

GZ /gz/ Final—one syllable

bags
begs
bogs
bugs

cogs
digs
dogs
eggs

gags
hogs
hugs
jigs

jogs
kegs
lags
legs
logs
lugs
mugs
nags
pegs
pigs
rags
rigs
rogues
rugs
sags
tags
togs
tugs
wags
wigs
____
____
____
____

LZ /lz/ Medial—two syllables

bailsman
fool's cap
fool's gold
salesman
school zone
____
____
____
____

LZ /lz/ Final—one syllable

aisles
bails
bales
balls
bells
Bill's
bills
boils
bowls
calls
Charles
chills
coils
deals
dills
dolls
drills
eels
fails
falls
feels
files
fills
foals
foils
fools
fouls
frills
gales
gals
gills
goals
grills
growls
gulls
hails
halls
heels
hills
holes
hulls
jails
kneels
males
meals
miles
mills
moles
nails
oils
pails
peals
piles
pills
poles
polls
pools
pulls
quails
quills
rails
reels
roles
rolls
rules
sails
sales
scales
scowls
seals
sells
shrills

sills
skills
skulls
smells
smiles
snails
snarls
soils
soles
souls
spells
spills
spoils
spools
squalls
squeals
stalls
stools
strolls
styles
tails
tales
tells
thrills
tiles
toils
tolls
tools
walls
wells
whales
wheels
wills
wools
yells
____
____
____
____

LZ /lz/ Final—two syllables

angels
annals
ant hills
barrels
baseballs
battles
bluebells
bottles
bundles
bushels
camels
candles
capsules
carols
cattails
cradles
cymbals
dawdles
details
dwellers
eggshells
equals
females
fiddles
finals
footballs
formals
fossils
fuels
gruels
handles
hymnals
jewels
kindles
ladles
middles
needles
nettles
noodles
paddles
petals
poodles
portholes
pretzels
prevails
profiles
propels
pupils
quarrels
quetzals
rascals
rattles
rebels
recalls
refills
rentals
reptiles
retails
reveals
riddles
rivals
roll calls
saddles
sandals
sawmills
scandals
seagulls
seashells
settles
signals
Sioux Falls
skittles

snowballs
softballs
tadpoles
tattles
tittles
toadstools
toddles
toenails
tonsils
towels
windmills
____

LZ /lz/ Final—three syllables

aerials
animals
annuals
axials
basketballs
bass viols
Blue Angels
bookmobiles
burials
buttonholes
cannonballs
cardinals
Cardinals
carnivals
carousels
casseroles
cathedrals
coveralls
enamels
fairy tales
festivals
fingernails
generals
principals
projectiles
rehearsals
rituals
spectacles
syllables
utensils
volleyballs
____
____

LVZ /lvz/ Final—one syllable

delves
elves
selves
shelves
solves
valves
wolves
____
____

LVZ /lvz/ Final—two syllables

dissolves
evolves
involves
ourselves
resolves
revolves
themselves
yourselves
____

MZ /mz/ Medial—two syllables

doomsday
groomsman
helmsman
Jamestown
thumbs down
thumbs up
time zone
____
____

MZ /mz/ Final—one syllable

beams
bums
calms
charms
chimes
clams
climbs
comes
crams
creams
crimes
crumbs
deems
dimes
dims

domes
dooms
drams
dreams
drums
flames
foams
fumes
games
gems
gums
gyms
hams
hems
homes
hums
James
jams
Jim's
lambs
limbs
limes
looms
palms
Pam's
psalms
rams
reams
Reims
rhymes
rims
roams
rooms
Sam's
seems
shames
stems
sums
tames
teams
Thames
themes
thumbs
times
trams
trims
____
____

MZ /mz/ Final—two syllables

Adams
assumes
bedrooms
daydreams
exams
schoolrooms
windchimes
____
____

NZ /nz/ Medial—two syllables

benzene
Bronze Age
clansman
frenzy
Kansas
Wednesday
____
____
____

NZ /nz/ Final—one syllable

bans
Benz
bins
bones
bronze
buns
canes
cans
chains
chins
cleans
clowns
coins
cones
crowns
Dan's
deans
dines
drains
fans
fines
fins
gains
grains
groans
jeans
lanes
lawns
leans
lines
loans
manes
mines

moans
moons
Nan's
nines
nouns
pains
pans
pens
phones
pines
pins
plains
planes
plans
prunes
puns
queens
rains
shines
shins
signs
skins
sons
spans
spins
spoons
stains
stones
swans
tans
teens
tens
thins
tins
tones
tons
trains
tunes
twins
vans
vines
wanes
wins
zones
____
____
____
____

NZ /nz/ Final—two syllables

balloons
batons
blue jeans
buttons
cake pans
cartoons
chickens
complains
detains
Great Plains
hailstones
heavens
kitchens
lions
machines
Marines
mountains
napkins
nations
notions
oceans
opens
outshines
pecans
pie pans
pigeons
platoons
puffins
ravens
remains
retains
ribbons
robins
sevens
sidelines
soybeans
swim fins
trombones
wagons
____
____
____

NDZ /ndz/ Final—one syllable

bends
binds
ends
finds
glands
grinds
hands
kinds
lands
lends
mends
minds
ponds
rends
rinds

sands
sends
sounds
spends
stands
tends
winds

NGZ /ŋz/ Final—one syllable

bangs
brings
fangs
gangs
gongs
hangs
kings
pangs
pings
rings
sings
songs
stings
swings
things
tongs
wings
wrongs

NGZ /ŋzz/ Final—two syllables

cravings
drawings
paintings
pavings
savings

RZ /rz/ Final—one syllable

airs
bars
bears
blares
blurs
bores
burrs
cares
cars
chairs
cheers
choirs
chores
clears
cores
dares
doors
ears
errs
fairs
fares
fears
fires
firs
flares
floors
fours
furs
gears
glares
hares
hears
heirs
hers
hires
hours
jars
jeers
lures
mares
mars
Mars
nears
oars
ours
pairs
pears
peers
piers
pores
pours
purrs
rears
roars
scares
scars
scores

scours
shares
shears
shirrs
shores
sirs
slurs
smears
snares
snores
soars
sores
sours
spares
spars
spears
spurs
squares
stairs
stares
stars
steers
stirs
tears
theirs
tires
tours
wares
wars
wears
wires
years
yours
____
____
____

RZ /rz/ Final—two syllables

admires
affairs
allures
altars
anchors
angers
answers
antlers
appears
arbors
aspires
Azores
backfires
badgers
barbers
batters
bazaars
beavers
beggars
bidders
binders
bleachers
blisters
boilers
bookstores
borders
boulders
boxers
breakers
brokers
builders
burners
buzzers
callers
campers
campfires
captors
captures
carvers
cashiers
casters
catchers
cedars
checkers
colors
compares
crackers
declares
devours
diners
dinners
dippers
divers
doctors
dollars
downstairs
drawers
dressers
drivers
drummers
empires
errors
explores
farmers
fenders
fielders
figures
fillers
filters
fingers
fixtures
Flanders
flatcars
flickers
fliers

flippers
flounders
flowers
founders
fractures
glaciers
guitars
ignores
indoors
lathers
matures
members
minors
molars
movers
odors
outdoors
pillars
pliers
poplars
posters
powders
powers
quarters
rangers
razors
readers
refers
rivers
rockers
rollers
rompers
roosters
rulers
rumors
scissors
seashores
showers
sisters
slippers
slivers
sneakers
sparklers
speakers
squad cars
tankers
tweezers
umpires
upstairs
vampires
velours
vespers
wafers
____
____
____
____
____
____
____
____
____
____

RZ /rz/ Final—three syllables

adventures
amateurs
ancestors
announcers
anteaters
beginners
bystanders
calendars
campaigners
candy bars
carpenters
carriers
diapers
dinosaurs
disappears
discovers
engineers
erasers
fasteners
firecrackers
foreigners
horse lovers
leftovers
loudspeakers
managers
polar bears
professors
propellers
receivers
recorders
recovers
registers
remainders
reporters
sandpipers
screwdrivers
state troopers
studded tires
teenagers
unawares
volunteers
____
____
____
____
____
____
____

RDZ /rdz/ Final—one syllable

bards	gourds	yards
beards	guards	________
birds	hoards	________
boards	lords	________
cards	towards	________
chords	wards	________
cords	words	________

RDZ /rdz/ Final—two syllables

backyards	lifeguards	Spaniards
blackbirds	lizards	surfboards
bluebirds	orchards	timecards
buzzards	postcards	vineyards
clipboards	punch cards	wizards
cupboards	rear guards	________
discards	rewards	________
flashcards	score cards	________
kick boards	shepherds	________
leewards	skateboards	________
leopards	songbirds	________

RLZ /rlz/ Final—one syllable

Charles	pearls	whorls
curls	purls	________
Earl's	snarls	________
girls	swirls	________
gnarls	twirls	________
hurls	whirls	________

RVZ /rvz/ Final—one syllable

carves	serves	________
dwarves	starves	________
nerves	turves	________
scarves	wharves	________

RVZ /rvz/ Final—two syllables

conserves	observes	________
deserves	preserves	________

THZ /ðz/ Final—one syllable

bathes
breathes
loathes
seethes
smoothes
soothes
teethes
tithes
truths
wreathes
writhes

VZ /vz/ Medial—two syllables

dove's nest
eavesdrop
thieves' den

VZ /vz/ Final—one syllable

beeves
calves
caves
chives
cloves
coves
craves
dives
doves
drives
eaves
fives
gives
gloves
graves
grieves
grooves
groves
halves
hives
hooves
jives
knaves
knives
leaves
lives
loaves
loves
moves
paves
peeves
proves
raves
roves
salves
saves
shaves
shoves
sieves
sleeves
thrives
waves
weaves
wives

ZER /zɚ/ Medial—three syllables

misery
observing
reservoir

ZER /zɚ/ Medial—four syllables

miserable
miserably
observation
preservation
reservation

ZER /zɚ/ Final—two syllables

blazer	geyser	riser
bruiser	hawser	squeezer
buzzer	laser	user
Caesar	loser	visor
cleanser	miser	Windsor
cruiser	quizzer	________
freezer	razor	________

ZER /zɚ/ Final—three syllables

accuser	deep freezer	________
adviser	divisor	________
bulldozer	incisor	________
composer	trailblazer	________

ZER /zɚ/ Final—four syllables

appetizer	polarizer	________
atomizer	stabilizer	________
fertilizer	vaporizer	________

ZL /zl/ Final—two syllables

chisel	frizzle	nuzzle
damsel	fusil	puzzle
dazzle	grizzle	schnozzle
diesel	guzzle	sizzle
drizzle	Hazel	weasel
easel	muzzle	________
fizzle	nasal	________
frazzle	nozzle	________

ZL /zl/ Final—three syllables

appraisal	embezzle	________
arousal	refusal	________
disposal	witch hazel	________

ZH

Pronounced: /ʒ/
Spelled: si, g, s, z, zi

ZH /ʒ/ Initial—one syllable

Jacques ________________ ________________

ZH /ʒ/ Initial—two syllables

jabot ________________ ________________
Jacquerie ________________ ________________
Joinville ________________ ________________

ZH /ʒ/ Initial—three syllables

Jacques Bonhomme
Javary
Joinvile
Jolivet
____
____

ZH /ʒ/ Medial—two syllables

Asia
azure
bijou
bourgeois
brazier
closure
crosier
crozier
fusion
glazier
Hoosier
leisure
lesion
measure
Persia
Persian
pleasure
regime
seizure
treasure
version
vision
____
____

ZH /ʒ/ Medial—three syllables

abrasion
adhesion
allusion
ambrosia
amnesia
aphasia
artesian
aspersion
aversion
casual
Caucasian
cohesion
collision
collusion
composure
conclusion
confusion
contusion
conversion
corrosion
decision
delusion
derision
diffusion

disposure
diversion
division
elision
elusion
emersion
enclosure
envision
erasion
erosion
evasion
exclusion
excursion
explosion
exposure
fantasia
incision
inclosure
inclusion
intrusion
invasion
inversion
leisurely
measurement
measuring
obtrusion
occasion
Parisian
persuasion
precision
profusion
protrusion
provision
reclusion
remeasure
revision
seclusion
subversion
transfusion
treasurer
treasury
usual
usury
visual
____
____
____
____

ZH /ʒ/ Medial—four syllables

accusation
Asiatic
casually
disillusion
measurable
measuring cup
measuring tape
pleasurable
Polynesia
subdivision
supervision
television
unusual
usually
usurious
visualize
____
____

ZH /ʒ/ Final—one syllable

beige
loge
luge
rouge
____
____

ZH /ʒ/ Final—two syllables

barrage
collage
corsage
garage
massage
menage
mirage
prestige
____

ZH /ʒ/ Final—three syllables

Baton Rouge
bon voyage
camouflage
concierge
decoupage
entourage
fuselage
sabotage
____
____
____
____

ZHER /ʒɚ/ Medial—three syllables

azurite	measurement	treasury
glaziery	measuring	________
leisurely	treasurer	________

ZHER /ʒɚ/ Medial—four syllables

measuring cup	pleasurable	________
measuring tape	Treasure Island	________

ZHER /ʒɚ/ Final—two syllables

closure	pleasure	________
leisure	treasure	________
measure	________	________

ZHER /ʒɚ/ Final—three syllables

composure	exposure	________
displeasure	foreclosure	________
enclosure	remeasure	________

SOUNDS SO SWEET
Reproducibles for Building Articulation Skills
by Linda Shackelford, M.A., CCC-SLP, and Laurie Hanuscin, M.A., CCC-SLP

Encourage home carryover with your young clients with more than 60 reproducible articulation drills. Each section is easy to understand, especially for parents. Reproduce a specific activity, add a target sound, number of trials, and send home to encourage parental involvement. Use each lesson to isolate specific syllable, word, phrase, and sentence level.

Catalog No. 7699-Y $29

SOUNDS LIKE FUN!
Reproducible Articulation Stories and Games
by Anne M. Bilgo, M.S., SLP, and Susan Kleinhans, B.A.

Target the correct production of initial /k/, /l/, /h/, /g/, /s/, /z/, /f/, /v/, /th/, and /sh/ sounds. You'll have a collection of 10 amusing sound-weighted stories and many related, reproducible activities. While each story focuses on a different sound, all feature simple phonemic structures, sentences, and story lines for easy recall. Promote carryover by providing parents with questions for eliciting the targeted sound in the home environment.

Catalog No. 7784-Y $29.95

CARRYOVER ACTIVITIES FOR THE /er/ SOUND
Working with ER/IR/OR/UR
by Barbara Martin, M.S., CCC-SLP

These easy-to-use, reproducible activities and worksheets are designed exclusively for your clients who can correctly pronounce vowelized /r/ sounds—*her, sir*—in all word positions, but can't carry over these sounds into conversation. Students will have fun with memory exercises, sequencing activities, vocabulary development, and more.

Catalog No. 7670-Y $29

YOU SOLVE IT
Carryover Articulation Stories for /s/ and /r/
by Kathleen Rose Taylor, M.S.

Target the phonemes /s/ and /r/ with 16 reproducible cliffhanger mysteries and problem-solving stories. Each sound-weighted story has been left open-ended for your students to solve in their own way. You'll have guided discussions at the end of each story for comprehension, thinking, and analysis by students. Bridge the gap between structured drill and spontaneous conversation with ease!

Catalog No. 7741-Y $23

3830 E. Bellevue/P.O. Box 42050
Tucson, Arizona 85733
(602) 323-7500